SEMINAR

The Story
of the
American Press Institute

by
Don E. Carter
and
Malcolm F. Mallette

Published by the American Press Institute
11690 Sunrise Valley Drive
Reston, Virginia 22091

Copyright© 1992 by Don E. Carter and Malcolm F. Mallette

International Standard Book Number: 0-9633143-0-0

Library of Congress Catalog Card Number: 92-71647

Printed in the United States of America

Contents

Introduction
Preface
Acknowledgments

	Prologue	1
1.	The Experiment Begins	7
2.	Seed From a Classroom	15
3.	The Founder	20
4.	A Home at Columbia	26
5.	The Journalism Dean	41
6.	A Large, Quiet Man	46
7.	116th Street and Broadway	52
8.	The Table of Sharing	60
9.	Mentor in Buffalo	77
10.	The Master of Anecdote	85
11.	A Dream Job for Monty	94
12.	Mr. Inside, Mr. Outside	105
13.	How the Word Spread	117
14.	Going Global	128
15.	The Quest for Solvency	142
16.	Tension and Divorce	148
17.	Big Ben	161
18.	Selling the Mousetrap	168
19.	Devotion and Discussion	180
20.	Hard Work and High Jinks	195
21.	The Staff Grows	210
22.	The Big Apple Sours	221
23.	Chairman Ottaway	230
24.	A Decision to Move	238
25.	Farewell, Columbia	251
26.	Broadway to Boondocks	259
27.	Adding On	268
28.	Monty's Legacy	280
29.	More Training, More Choices	295
30.	New Directions	308

Appendix A
Appendix B
Index

To the newspaper men and women

who have attended the

American Press Institute

and the seminar discussion leaders

who have shared with them

their experience and knowledge

Introduction

By James H. Ottaway

O f all the organizations with which I have been associated, the American Press Institute is Number One.

In the early 1950s, when we were publishing the Endicott (New York) Daily Bulletin, we heard about the American Press Institute and its seminars at Columbia University in New York City. In those days, API seminar members stayed in Columbia's John Jay Hall in dormitory style. Gene Brown, who had joined our organization in 1944, and I attended the third of API's newly introduced Management and Costs seminars, in May 1951.

In 1957, my wife Ruth and I attended a Publishers and Editors Seminar together. It was the first time that a woman had attended that kind of seminar, and initially it caused quite a stir. By then, seminar members stayed in a rickety university-owned hotel on the edge of campus, the King's Crown. After Ruth and I spent a few days in that hotel, where you could hardly open your door without running into the bed, she was enthusiastically accepted.

Ruth and I attended that seminar, which focused on the news operation, because we thought that perhaps we were looking at the bottom line more than we were the quality of our newspapers (by then we owned several). It was an exciting, worthwhile experience.

API then was still quite new, and J. Montgomery (Monty) Curtis, the executive director, was having difficulty getting enough newspaper men and women to attend seminars. So we arranged for him to come to a New York State Publishers Association meeting in Cooperstown. There Monty made his pitch for API and, Monty being Monty, he attracted new members.

Starting in 1958, I served 25 years on the API Advisory Board at Columbia and the subsequent Board of Directors at Reston, 10 of them as chairman of the latter. I saw many changes, much growth—and several crises.

The first crisis during my board service occurred in 1970, when it became obvious that API had to move from the Journalism Building at Columbia because of limited space there. After looking at several locations, we settled on Reston, Virginia. A Sheraton hotel was about to be built in Reston, and we found four nearby acres at $80,000 an acre on Sunrise Valley Drive. We contracted with the Sheraton to accommodate our seminar members and were among the hotel's first customers.

Then how to get the money to leave Columbia and strike out on our own? Turner Catledge, executive editor of the New York Times, had been a key figure on the API Advisory Board for years. But he had retired to New Orleans. The problem of raising funds was much on my mind—I had become board chairman in 1968—while Ruth and I were visiting my mother in California. We decided to return to New York by way of New Orleans and sound out Catledge. I visited the Catledge home, a replica of their New York City apartment, and talked to Catledge about taking the chairmanship of the campaign. His wife Abbie was present. Turner said he would let us know.

That evening, the four of us were having dinner at the Ponchartrain Hotel. After a few drinks, he suddenly turned to me and said: "I accept." His wife looked surprised. All of us associated with API were delighted.

So we organized a campaign team to raise the necessary money. One trip that I'll never forget was with Turner Catledge in 1973. In the Ottaway Newspapers plane, I flew to Tuscaloosa, Alabama, to meet Catledge, who came up from New Orleans. Next morning, we had an 8 o'clock appointment at the Tuscaloosa News. Catledge had reached Tuscaloosa late the night before, and we hadn't had an opportunity to get our act together.

I said to him: "Turner, what are we going to say when we meet Buford Boone?" He replied: "I'll be the evangelist shaking the cymbal, and you hold the tin cup."

That was our script. For a week, seeking money for API, we toured several Southern states. Everywhere, Catledge had many newspaper friends. We filled the tin cup and more.

Once API was operating successfully in Reston, I retired as chairman in 1978. Joe Pulitzer, publisher of the St. Louis Post-Dispatch, left the board the same year. He was the all-time leader in terms of board service with 28 years.

The great satisfaction of my 25 years with API was taking part in its growth as the pioneer and number-one newspaper training center and its tremendous contribution to improving the quality of newspapers in the United States and Canada.

I want to pay special tribute to Walter Everett, who was API executive director, 1967-75. Walter guided us through the difficult transition from Columbia University to Reston. Also, to Mal Mallette, who as director of development, helped us raise the money. Earlier, he had headed API, 1975-79. And Monty Curtis, who had left API's staff in 1967 after 20 years of service, still supported API with his ideas and vigor as a board member.

I'd also like to pay tribute to the other board members with whom I served and who devoted countless hours to help API succeed.

They include Frank Batten, Don Graham, Eugene Pulliam, John Troan, Robert N. Brown, Tim Hays, Rollie Melton, Jim Sauter, Bob Chandler, Ed Lindsay, Pat O'Callaghan, Punch Sulzberger, Peter Macdonald, Bill Taylor, Joe Pulitzer, Al Neuharth, Newby Noyes, Scotty Reston and John Motz.

The story of the American Press Institute is an exciting, important chapter in the history of newspapers. It merits being told in permanent form. My fellow board members often discussed the need for a book such as this. Many newspapers or newspaper groups have commissioned histories of their own organizations. They include Ottaway Newspapers, which celebrated its 50th anniversary in 1986.

After my time with API, the Board of Directors endorsed the idea of a definitive history and promised financial support. One board member who pushed especially hard for a history to be written was Don E. Carter, who had been exceptionally close to API as a seminar member and frequent discussion leader. Appropriately, with Mal Mallette, he formed the editor-writer team.

This book is more than a bare-bones recital of how API came into being just after World War II. It is also the story of certain talented and dedicated individuals and should be of interest to anyone who has ever read a newspaper and wondered about the people who produce them.

Preface

The first thought that a history of the American Press Institute should be written took root about 1974, when API left Columbia University in New York City after 28 years there and moved to its own building in Reston, Virginia.

The move brought new realization of the struggles involved in the founding and growth of the institute and the important role it was playing in improving newspaper quality. All this deserved being recorded in cohesive form.

From time to time, the need for a history was mentioned by members of the board of directors and the executive staff. When Malcolm F. Mallette was reassigned from director to director of development in 1979, the board encouraged him to begin gathering materials for a history to be written in the unspecified future. Accordingly, he took several preliminary steps.

For one, he spent a day tape-recording an interview with Turner Catledge, the retired executive editor of the New York Times, who had played a key role in nurturing the infant API and possessed a rich lode of anecdotes. For another, Mallette asked several persons who had been close to API—as Advisory Board members, staff members and discussion leaders—to set down their recollections.

One of those persons was J. Montgomery (Monty) Curtis, who had served 20 years on the API staff, 16 as director or executive director. In 1979, at age 72, Curtis was a vice president of Knight-Ridder Newspapers and still fiercely proud of API. He wrote not just a memo for the history file but a long manuscript that he clearly hoped would be published as his personal memoir.

The timing for a mini-history was appropriate. An addition to the five-year-old API building was under construction, and plans were being made for a gala dedication. Publishing the Curtis memoir would be a nice touch, especially because he was about to retire and thus would leave the API Board of Directors.

So the memoir—15,000 words, 54 pages and titled "API: A

Personal Remembrance"—was distributed in connection with the building-addition dedication. That led the board to put aside plans for a full-blown history of the institute.

When Curtis died in Miami Beach in 1982, his will named as executor Don E. Carter, who had worked in Knight-Ridder's Miami headquarters with Curtis as vice president/news. Carter had succeeded his friend Curtis on the API board. But Carter would shortly also retire and move to Sea Island, Georgia, where he could not legally serve as executor.

Curtis' secretary, Trudi Murmann, had kept meticulous files on Curtis' voluminous correspondence and speeches. Carter was interested in those files. When nobody else asked for them, Murmann shipped the 14 crates to Carter.

Carter proposed to Mallette that they jointly write a biography of Curtis. Mallette urged broadening the idea to a history of API, in which Curtis would surely be a leading figure. In February 1988, the Board of Directors approved the writing of an API history and assured publication.

Carter and Mallette agreed to a division of work: Carter would cull from the 14 crates those documents pertinent to a history and serve as editor. Mallette, who had retired from API in 1987 and still lived in Reston, would undertake additional research and write the manuscript. That's the way this book was done, with editor in Sea Island and writer in Reston coordinating by mail and telephone.

The history of an organization is often written for a major anniversary. API could have delayed this project until 1996, its 50th year. But that would have risked the loss of vital resources, the persons who remembered API's early years.

Then, too, documents have a way of fading or being discarded. Indeed, some key documents for this history were brittle and barely legible. We were fortunate to have as a central resource the papers of Monty Curtis. Those papers have now been given a permanent home in the library of West Virginia University, where Curtis graduated in 1928.

For editor and writer, producing this book was a labor of love, which is not to say it was not often hard work. As career newspapermen, we had written and edited millions of words, but rarely in stories of more than 5,000 words. This narrative runs more than 100,000 words. The task has given us new admiration for historians.

Don E. Carter   Malcolm F. Mallette
Sea Island, Georgia   Reston, Virginia

December 1991

Acknowledgments

This book could not have been written without the help of dozens of friends of the American Press Institute. Former seminar members and discussion leaders responded generously when asked to describe their experience with API. Many, but not all, of those helpers are mentioned in the book.

Dr. and Mrs. Harry C. Law of Cattaraugus, New York, made available dozens of letters from J. Montgomery Curtis, who had been their boarder in Buffalo. Joe Mehr sent copies of pertinent stories from the library of the Providence Journal. Barry Brown supplied background on his father, API founder Sevellon Brown. John L. Taylor gave helpful background on his father Floyd Taylor, API's first director. Vincent S. Jones, an early discussion leader, combed his files for information on API's early years.

Fred Knubel and Nancy A. Carmody graciously responded to several requests to the Columbia University Office of Public Information. Charles Saunders of Richmond Newspapers forwarded stories on Douglas Southall Freeman. Freeman's daughter, Mrs. Leslie Cheek Jr., reviewed in manuscript the chapter on her father.

Yvonne Egertson guided searches of the American Newspaper Publishers Association library. Helen Curtis Pohlman, the sister of J. Montgomery Curtis, virtually wrote a family history in replying to inquiries about her brother. Trudi Murmann, secretary to Curtis for many years, sent several key letters and her own recollections. Mrs. Richard T. Baker recalled days when her late husband was a Columbia journalism professor.

John H. McMillan graciously read the entire manuscript and offered invaluable suggestions. Several other persons read selected portions of the manuscript and commented helpfully. They included: John E. Leard, Frank Quine, Don Lippincott and Woody Wardlow, who also ferreted out typographical errors in the page proofs. Edmund C. Arnold's gracious advice guided the design of the book.

At API, where the manuscript was written, William L. Winter made efficient facilities available. With assists from Robert Secundy, Clarice Hillstrom not only explained the mysteries of a word-processing system but also computer-generated the page layouts. Carol Ann Riordan created the picture pages, and John Finneman shepherded printing arrangements. John S. Goodreds served patiently as liaison to fellow members of the API Board of Directors.

No one assisted more than Walter Everett. He wrote several memos that provided both detail and insights not available elsewhere. In painstaking fashion, he also replied to telephone calls and a score of letters. Reviewing the manuscript, he called attention to omissions, vagueness, and misunderstandings. And he graciously refrained from comment when he read his own profile in manuscript.

To all the helpers, named or not named, we offer our deep appreciation.

Prologue

On October 25, 1980, 140 guests gathered under a green-striped tent staked into the asphalt parking area of the American Press Institute in Reston, Virginia. The fluttering canvas protected them from pelting rain but not from gusty winds that convulsed the tent and made the speaker, awaiting her turn on the program, consider heading for the shelter of the handsome two-story building 30 feet behind her.

But the tent held, thanks to members of the American Press Institute staff who clutched the wobbling support poles until the ceremony ended. Then the guests filed quickly into the building for a reception, catered dinner and newspaper talk.

The occasion was the dedication of the new wing of the American Press Institute, or API as it is known to newspaper men and women. The wing enlarged the building by half and provided facilities so that the American Press Institute, a non-profit center for the mid-career training of newspaper men and women from the United States and Canada, could hold two seminars simultaneously.

On that Saturday, 26 members of a Circulation Managers Seminar, who came from 22 states and three provinces of Canada, were enjoying the weekend respite from their arduous nine-day program. Most of the members were in Washington, D.C., 18 miles to the east. But a few joined the guests, partly to see the newspaper dignitaries and enjoy the dinner.

Already on hand were a few of the 31 teachers of journalism who would take part in API's first Journalism Educators Seminar starting the next day. When that seminar convened, API for the first time would be holding two seminars concurrently to meet the demand for training that erupted as newspapers fought to keep circulation abreast of population growth.

Only six years earlier, in 1974, 300 guests from across the U.S. and Canada had gathered under a similar tent, also under threatening clouds, to dedicate the original API building. Almost all had played a role in the transplanting of API from New York City to its own new home in the planned community of Reston.

They were a proud mixture of newspaper people—from the executive suite to the newsroom to the delivery route. Many had found their careers broadened by API seminars. Many had contributed building funds from the corporate coffers or their own pockets.

The 1974 dedication marked the end of a frenzied four years during which API searched for a new homesite and funds to build that home. The institute had received what someone called a friendly eviction notice from Columbia University in New York City, where it had operated for 28 years in quarters in the Journalism Building.

That building also housed Columbia's prestigious Graduate School of Journalism. For a while, that school and API were closely linked, though not financially.

At Columbia, the American Press Institute slowly blossomed. But by the late 1960s Columbia University itself was in trouble. It lacked building space and capital funds. Distinguished Nobel Laureates sometimes had little more office space than a clerk.

One year, Columbia operated at a loss of $16 million. Austerity brought the next year's deficit down only to $15 million. Reluctantly, Columbia began divesting itself of a number of institutes that had been formed there in halcyon days. API knew that sooner or later Columbia would reclaim API's space.

In the 28 years at Columbia, API worked its way through problems large and small and a crisis or two. They included an ongoing struggle for funds, the unexpected death of its first director, and a dark interval when the Internal Revenue Service initially denied an application for the tax exemption that was vital to establishing API as a not-for-profit educational organization in the Commonwealth of Virginia.

Along the way, API pioneered mid-career training for newspapers. Mid-career, or in-service, training was non-existent in the newspaper field at the end of World War II. Turner Catledge of the New York Times used to say that mid-career training of that era consisted of editors shooting the breeze at the Waldorf-Astoria Hotel bar during an editors convention. Mid-career training is now widespread, but API was the first to provide it and has touched the most newspaper people.

Through its seminars, API played a major role in guiding the newspaper industry through a period of accelerating growth, change and challenge. By October 1980, after 35 years of existence, API had conducted 460 seminars.

Some 13,200 newspaper men and women had attended those

seminars, coming from 1,046 daily and 214 weekly newspapers in 50 states, the District of Columbia, nine provinces of Canada, Puerto Rico, Guam and occasionally from abroad.

So that gusty dedication Saturday in 1980, as the buffeted tent threatened to collapse but held, was symbolic of API's existence. The speaker, Katharine Graham, chairman of the board of the Washington Post Company, knew her subject. The Washington Post alone had sent 60 staff members to API seminars.

When she rose to speak, one eye on her text, the other on the convulsive tent, Mrs. Graham said, "The fact that we have gathered in the Virginia countryside for another dedication—just six years to the day after the formal opening of the new API meeting place here—clearly recognizes the way American and Canadian newspapers have increasingly turned to API for assistance in putting out better publications...Over the past three and one-half decades no single organization has done more to elevate the standards of our profession."

Six years earlier, Eugene Patterson, president and editor of the St. Petersburg Times and Evening Independent, had been the principal speaker at the dedication of the original API building.

"We're gathered here," Patterson said, "...to warm a house that stands as a remarkable symbol of our profession's commitment to do better than we have done with what we've got and to do more...

"American and Canadian newspaper owners simply determined that they wanted to put out better newspapers, and with the API as their joint vehicle they've done it...Through the unique formula of cross-criticism, Socratic argument and teaching by peers, the institute has extended the reach of all of us."

After the 1974 dedication, guests trooped inside a striking, functional building paid for by contributions totaling $2.6 million from newspapers, newspaper groups, and newspaper-related foundations and associations.

In 1980, contributions for the building addition totaled $1.93 million. Both times, the newspapers of the U.S. and Canada had come through handsomely.

Those on the speaker's platform in 1980 could relate many a story about the tortuous trail API had beaten. They included:

• James H. Ottaway, chairman of the API Board of Directors, 1968-1978, the years in which API decided to leave its Columbia University home, found a suitable location, raised funds and constructed its own building. All this not knowing at the outset if the newspaper industry would respond with contributions.

• J. Montgomery Curtis, an API associate director, 1947-1951, and then its director and executive director, 1951-1966. Curtis had become known as "Mr. API."

• Walter Everett, who served on the API staff, 1949-1975, his 26 years the greatest length of service by any person. Everett was API executive director, 1967-1975, the years of meticulous preparation for the move to Reston and the move itself.

• Howard H (Tim) Hays, the board chairman who had succeeded Ottaway and pushed for enlarging the building to accommodate a flood of seminar nominations.

• Arthur Ochs (Punch) Sulzberger, publisher of the New York Times, whose newspaper had been a prime supporter of API from the sprouting of the idea.

Those and other dignitaries, and many of the guests, represented the growing success of API. For example, when API departed in 1974 from Columbia University, it had held 321 seminars in 28 years, and reached a record of 19 seminars a year. Membership averaged 557 in the last three years at Columbia. By 1985, API was holding 31 seminars a year, and membership surpassed 1,000 in 1981-82.

But in the beginning was the idea. And the idea caused a fortuitous confluence of several leading newspaper traditions and the people who helped forge those traditions.

The idea was spawned by Sevellon Brown, editor and publisher of the Providence Journal and Evening Bulletin, newspapers of nationally recognized quality. He enlisted the help of Columbia University, its Graduate School of Journalism and its dean, Carl W. Ackerman.

At Brown's urging, 38 newspapers or newspaper organizations, including his own, contributed to a fund to get the experimental API started. For it was an experiment; the founding contributors provided only enough money for an initial two years of operation. If the experiment had not taken root by then, it was to be abandoned.

Sevellon Brown's idea was inspired by a lecture on editorial writing by Douglas Southall Freeman, editor of the Richmond News Leader and Pulitzer-Prize-winning author of American biographies.

The confluence of journalistic leaders continued with the appointment of Floyd Taylor as API's first director. Taylor's newspaper background came in part from the New York Herald Tribune, a great newspaper that, lamentably, was to fail.

The confluence widened more with the arrival of J. Montgomery Curtis, whose newspaper philosophy had been molded by his legendary managing editor at the Buffalo Evening News, Alfred H. Kirchhofer. In 35 years of newspaper-related work, 20 of them at API, Curtis never wavered from the Kirchhofer influence.

In 1949, Walter Everett joined the API staff, bringing with him more of the Providence Journal influence.

Then in 1951, Ben Reese, 35 years with the St. Louis Post-Dispatch, 13 as managing editor, came aboard as resident co-chairman of the Advisory Board. Reese brought the constructive influence of the Post-Dispatch, which had won four Pulitzer Prizes during his years there.

Too, there was the Advisory Board, chosen from newspapers that supported the API cause. They added uplifting influence.

This book is in part the story of the coming together of those journalists together with a few others—and their philosophies on newspapering.

More than that, though, it is the story of the struggle of an idea, the mixture of skepticism and support, the tensions between a journalism school and a mid-career training institute in the same university building, the struggle to make ends meet, the changing ambience at Columbia, the departure from Columbia, the watershed transformation to a Virginia corporation, the labor of moving to a new home, and the opportunities that home provided.

1

The Experiment Begins

On the Monday morning of September 26, 1946, 26 newspaper editors from across the United States left their spartan quarters in a Columbia University dormitory in upper Manhattan. They breakfasted amid the clatter of metal trays in the student cafeteria 13 floors below. Then they walked diagonally across the campus quadrangle that had once been a baseball diamond where a student named Lou Gehrig hit legendary home runs.

They entered the Journalism Building at 116th Street and Broadway, built with a bequest from Joseph Pulitzer, the immigrant newspaper publisher, and filed into a large, high-ceilinged room on the ground floor.

There they took assigned seats around a huge, polished walnut table with an open center. Then, with curiosity and a touch of journalistic skepticism, they turned their attention to the four men at the table's head.

The first seminar of the American Press Institute was about to begin. With it, so too, would begin the first program to provide mid-career training of the newspaper men and women of the United States and Canada—indeed much of the world.

Nearly a half-century later, when mid-career training is commonplace in the newspaper business and most other human enterprises, background is necessary to understand the skepticism of 1946. In that year, the American Press Institute—API—was very much an uncertain pioneer.

Its founders represented only 38 daily newspapers, and they had built in a provision for failure. If API did not prove itself in two years, if newspapers across the two countries did not respond by sending staff members to API seminars, then the institute would be dissolved.

That uncertainty was palpable in 1946, a year after the end of World War II and 10 years after the idea for a mid-career training center had been conceived by one of the men at the head of the seminar table, Sevellon Brown, editor and publisher of the Providence Journal and Evening Bulletin.

The 10-year delay tested the patience of Sevellon Brown, ever a mover and shaker. The delay resulted from not only a global conflict but also the considerable insularity of daily newspapers of that time with widespread resistance to change.

Ironically, newsrooms were the stronghold of this stubborn isolation even though they prided themselves on reporting change.

The American Newspaper Publishers Association, the trade association for the United States and Canada, had been established in 1886 and held annual conventions. But its activities related mainly to the business side of newspapers.

State press associations also concentrated on the business side and lobbying state legislatures, where anti-press proposals sometimes spawned.

The American Society of Newspaper Editors came along in 1923. By 1946 it had 445 members, most of whom attended an annual convention held in Washington or New York. Discussions on politics and government, not newspapering techniques, dominated those programs, although ASNE periodically addressed ethical issues of journalism.

Turner Catledge, later executive editor of the New York Times, recalled that editors would often sit at the bar of the ASNE convention hotel and hash over the workaday problems of putting out a newspaper. But there the matter was usually dropped. Managing editors of newspapers that subscribed to the Associated Press wire service had begun meeting annually in 1933. But they focused on gripes about the AP. Not until 1947 did that focus begin to broaden.

In contrast, other newspaper departments were doing better at pooling knowledge. Specialists in advertising, circulation and printing had their own organizations and exchanged ideas. For the newsroom, though, almost no institutions, certainly none of a structured nature, existed to offer opportunities for personal growth in the craft or profession of journalism.

Separate schools of journalism had existed since 1908, when the University of Missouri opened its journalism school. Columbia's School of Journalism welcomed its first class in 1912. By 1946, 73 schools or departments of journalism existed in the U.S. with some 14,000 students.

Higher education had concerned itself primarily with beginners. In a few years, journalism schools would sprout like mushrooms as graduates began invading newsrooms in surging numbers. Before World War II, the typical American newsroom held only a sprinkling of staff members with a college degree. Sevellon Brown himself had no formal education beyond high school.

Journalism schools occupied themselves with the rudiments of reporting, writing and editing, together with providing a liberal arts education. Once on the job, though, beginners encountered a progression of problems as they moved through the ranks. For the reporter promoted to city editor (in those days, city editors were always men) usually would find himself woefully unprepared to supervise the work of others. He was totally ignorant of management and had no place to turn for help.

Individual newspaper staffs lacked knowledge of the experience of other staffs. Innovative ideas within a newsroom often were shot down by a growled explanation: "We've always done it this way." That explanation would be heard countless times in API seminars, where group ridicule usually caused the explainer to have second thoughts. Thus API opened windows to the winds of change.

Perhaps it was newspaper competition of the 1940s, especially in the larger cities, that caused newsrooms to resist ideas generated elsewhere. When Turner Catledge was assistant managing editor of the New York Times, he later recalled, his managing editor, Edwin L. James, would never attend meetings of the American Society of Newspaper Editors.

"We were, I suppose," said Catledge, "like so many papers, perhaps more like ourselves than anybody else, because we on the Times were smug; we thought we could do it better than anybody else." The trade magazine, Editor & Publisher, wrote of the audiences at ASNE and AP editors' conventions: "Mostly they are lectured and 'speeched at' unto boredom. There is little discussion of techniques and what occurs is hampered by the size of the groups."

Other newspapers were not without their own degrees of smugness. Now, however, through the tenacity of Sevellon Brown and a core group that he enlisted, the 25 members of that first API seminar were launching a breakthrough.

The format of the program made a pooling of experience certain. Other editors had also sought to attend. But Brown and API's first director, Floyd Taylor, limited attendance to 25 to insure that everyone could speak out.

A member of that first seminar, Michael J. Ogden, then news editor of the Providence Evening Bulletin, recalled 40 years later that the first members were receptive. "There were those," he wrote, "who were uncertain whether entrenched editors, having reached a certain status, might not balk at this interruption, in effect re-educating them. Actually, this was not the feeling of the editors; the reservation may have been more in the minds of some publishers."

These were newspapermen of considerable standing. Ten were managing editors, eight assistant managing editors and seven news editors. Some had traveled far; four were from California, another from Salt Lake City. Several of the largest and best newspapers in the country were represented, including the New York Times, Los Angeles Times, Washington Evening Star, Philadelphia Evening Bulletin, Detroit News, Cleveland Press and Atlanta Journal. (See Appendix A for the complete membership.)

A few mid-size papers were included, among them the Mobile Register, Trenton Times, and Waterbury Republican and American. In years to come, staff members from smaller newspapers, even down to circulations of 10,000 and below, would comprise about half the total yearly memberships, and many seminars were designed especially for smaller newspapers.

Those very first seminarians included men accustomed to creature comforts. By all accounts, though, they indulged in only good-natured grousing at being housed in John Jay Hall, the dormitory, and having to clump down a corridor to communal toilets and showers. When New York City elevator operators went on strike during the seminar, the editors climbed the stairs with minimal grumbling, though with considerable puffing.

The time had come, these members apparently recognized, for smugness to end. For newspapers, this recognition was a needed step if they were to flourish in the postwar years because the war's end unleashed unprecedented commercial and technological production in the information business.

Saturating television was less than a decade away. Within the decade, photocomposition of type would be invented in France and would quickly replace around the world the cumbersome hot-metal system and the Linotype of Ottmar Mergenthaler, first used at the New York Tribune in 1886.

The offset printing method would be refined for use on high-speed web presses, and converting to offset from the traditional letterpress would open new horizons for color printing. Computers powered by vacuum tubes would be miniaturized by transistors and would become central to writing, type composition, and news transmission.

And, with the conversion to peacetime, society itself was also changing at a bewildering pace. The baby boomers, those born in the fertile period between 1946 and 1964, entered a world where TV and film clawed at the dominance of the printed word and new rivals like direct mail fought for part of the advertisers' dollars. Within two decades of that first API seminar, newspapers would be scrapping desperately to defend their household penetration and advertising share of market.

The share of advertising market for U.S. dailies would plunge over 45 years from 34 to 25 percent. In Canada, where figures dating before 1976 were not available, the advertising share for dailies fell in 15 years from 29.5 to 22.5 percent, despite strong circulation gains.

In the United States, the population soared in early postwar years. But, even after dailies became dedicated to sharing techniques and resultingly improved in quality, their household penetration plummeted, from about a high of 1.3 copies per household to about 0.7 by 1990.

In 1946, 1,749 English-language daily newspapers were published in the United States, with a total daily circulation of 48,384,188. Sunday circulation hit a record high 39,860,036. Canada, where blue laws prohibited Sunday issues, published 90 dailies with a total circulation of 2.9 million.

In New York City alone, including the Eagle and the Citizen in Brooklyn, there were 13 English-language dailies. Others included were the Journal-American, Mirror, News, Post, Times, World-Telegram, Herald Tribune, and Sun. The News, the largest U.S. daily, had a circulation of 2,354,444 on weekdays and 4,599,524 on Sunday.

The 76 U.S. newspaper chains owned only 21 percent or 368 of the dailies. Forty-five years later, in contrast, there would be 135 chains, owning 1,228 or 76 percent of the surviving 1611 dailies. Of the 108 Canadian dailies by then, 95 were owned by chains, mainly Southam and Thomson.

Canadian dailies peaked at 110 in 1986, helped by the introduction of Sunday issues after blue laws were relaxed. Too, several successful tabloids replaced failed broadsheet papers.

Those statistics illuminate the problems that in 1946 lay over the horizon. At the time, the primary wartime problems confronting newspapers, newsprint and manpower, were easing. During the war, newspaper staffs had been curtailed. Many papers made do with skeleton staffs and local reporting suffered. The columns were largely filled with wire news, especially from the battlefronts.

And—an augury of the future—newspapers had been heavily staffed by women. Most editors in 1946 were rebuilding their staffs with returning servicemen, shifting the emphasis from international and national news to local coverage.

Although few dailies foresaw the sweeping economic and techno-logical changes ahead, they knew they faced competition from radio. It had fostered interest in news and provided a non-print choice. No longer could newspapers deliver the news first; radio had taken that role. So newspapers had to move beyond the basic reporting of who, what, when and where to begin explaining the significance of events.

After another early API seminar (only six were held each year for the first seven years), Max K. Gilstrap wrote in the Christian Science Monitor: "Newsmen have known for a long time that their papers have fallen short of serving the public as they should, despite their commendable work. With little competition, editors have clung to horse-and-buggy techniques."

To the four men at the head of the API seminar table at that first seminar in September 1946, it was clear that newspapers must upgrade staff capabilities. Standing with Sevellon Brown, who provided the idea, were three other key figures in the experiment.

Carl W. Ackerman, dean of the School of Journalism, in concert with Brown, had persuaded the Columbia trustees to approve formation of the institute and provide quarters and supporting facilities. Grove Patterson, editor-in-chief of the Toledo (Ohio) Blade, had contributed to the founding fund and was named first chairman of the Advisory Board. Floyd Taylor, a seasoned newspaperman and professor at the journalism school, had been chosen by Brown and Ackerman as the first director of API.

In keynoting remarks, Brown said, "We are here to pioneer for American journalism—indeed, I hope for world journalism—in an experiment in professional education on a high level...If this institute is to succeed, it must be the living symbol of a newborn determina-tion of publishers, editors and reporters of newspapers to strive unceasingly to improve themselves that they may fulfill their obliga-tions with increasing effectiveness in this critical period of human history...

"The experiment is very much in your hands, gentlemen. You will mold the character of these seminars by your discussions, by trial and error..."

With the launching amenities over, the 25 editors went to work. Floyd Taylor, the director, and his lone assistant, Associate Director Claude A. Jagger, who was on leave from the Associated Press, had worked feverishly to prepare this first program. They scheduled 21 topics and 48 speakers in three weeks. The workload typified the hundreds of seminars to follow. Program topics included both newspapering techniques and social and political problems.

Among the non-newspaper speakers (in later seminars they

would be called discussion leaders) were George Gallup and Elmo Roper, authorities on public opinion polls; Paul G. Hoffman, president of Studebaker Corporation, and James B. Carey, secretary-treasurer of the Congress of Industrial Organizations. The newspaper-based speakers ranged from reporters to librarians to production managers to Robert Gunning, a specialist on clarity in writing.

Behind the scenes, the worry about the response by newspapers—would they send members?—would soon be joined by a succession of other worries. A scarcity of operating funds would furrow API staff brows for years. Should seminar subject matter be expanded to cover all phases of newspaper operation, not just reporting and editing the news? And a cold war over turf would develop, as the institute, financed totally by newspaper funds, feared that it would be assimilated by the Graduate School of Journalism.

But such worries were behind the scenes. In the seminar room, members were caught up in a blizzard of ideas and shared experience. Thrown together for days (two weeks shortly evolved as the usual seminar length), the members worked hard and often played hard in the pleasure dome of New York City. A saying developed that API seminars proved that humans could exist for two weeks without sleep. Members who had never attended college came to regard Columbia as their alma mater and proudly displayed their certificates of attendance as they would a diploma.

Back home, and perhaps caught up on sleep, returning members briefed colleagues on what they had learned at API. The pebble-in-the-pond principle was at work. Seminars often inspired members to new dedication. Seminar-acquired skills opened new career doors. Those ticketed for promotion were often sent to API to prepare for the transition.

The career progress of widely known newspaper men and women can be traced by their changing job titles as they attended first one seminar and then, a few weeks or even months later, another. It became commonplace for budding stars to attend three or four seminars; indeed two persons attended seven.

No women attended an API domestic seminar until the Librarians Seminar in the third year. API delayed inviting women until appropriate housing could be found—John Jay Hall was all-male. Edith Barber of the New York Sun, president of the New York Newspaper Women's Club, called it "segregation."

"No newspaper conference will be complete without women," she declared.

At national or regional meetings, API alumni began to gather and recall API seminar experiences. To squeeze in a reunion at one annual convention, the API alumni hoisted Bloody Marys at 7:00

a.m., then breakfasted together and staged a program spoofing API.

Regionally, in both the U.S. and Canada, the seminar idea pioneered by API was copied in miniature, all to the good of newspapers.

The records show that it all began on that Monday morning in September 1946. The reality, however, goes back to a day in 1936 when Sevellon Brown visited a classroom at the Columbia School of Journalism.

2

Seed From a Classroom

The history of API has been marked by a handful of great newspapermen who brought their high principles, drive and magnetic personalities to the scene at just the right time. That was true at the beginning.

Douglas Southall Freeman, who was editor of the Richmond News Leader for 34 years and won Pulitzer Prizes for his biographies of Robert E. Lee and George Washington, was teaching a Columbia University course in editorial writing when Sevellon Brown visited the class during the spring of 1935-36.

His son, Sevellon Brown III, nicknamed Jeff, one of Brown's three children, was among the 65 journalism students that day, and Brown decided to look in on one of his son's classes. The senior Brown, at the time managing editor of the Providence Journal, was probably in New York in his role as a member of the School of Journalism's advisory board.

If Brown had happened upon a lesser teacher than Freeman he might not have had the idea that led to the forming of API.

Between 1934 and 1942, Freeman at times pursued three careers at once: a full-time editor at Richmond, a professor at Columbia and virtually a full-time biographer. His workload was prodigious. As a military historian, he lectured at the Army War College. He began a radio news broadcast in 1925—he was a pioneer in the field—and continued over the years.

On a clock behind Freeman's office desk at the News Leader hung a cardboard sign that read:

"Time alone is irreplacable; waste it not."

He never had the sign-painter's spelling error corrected. His intellectual power, physical vigor and time management were legendary.

Freeman arose at 3:15 a.m. and drove daily to the News Leader, an afternoon newspaper, by 4:40 a.m. On the way, he saluted the famous equestrian statue of Lee on Richmond's Monument Avenue. At his office, he checked the Associated Press news report and wrote two columns of editorials by 8 a.m.

Next, Freeman met for several minutes with reporters. Freeman knew virtually everything that was going on in town, and the challenge to reporters was to voice a "tidbit" that was new to him.

Then Freeman walked through the newsroom, across a boardwalk on a low building-connector roof to the studios of the newspaper-owned radio station WRNL. So precise was his time management that he frequently entered the studio for his morning 15-minute newscast just as the announcer was saying, "And here is Dr. Freeman." The title came from the doctorate in history he had earned at Johns Hopkins University after graduating from Richmond College, now the University of Richmond.

Broadcast over, Freeman made up the editorial page (he was an honorary member of the typographical union from the days when he composed his editorials on a hot-metal linecasting machine) and handled editorial chores until 11 a.m. He then took a 15-minute nap on his office couch.

Brief naps were a key to his remarkable capacity for work. "All you need to do," he once said, "is lose consciousness." After the nap, he accepted visitors and handled correspondence until his second newscast, at noon. Freeman lunched at home with his wife, took another 15-minute nap, and worked on his biographies until 6 p.m.

He allotted himself 14 hours of literary work at home each week. The eldest of his three children, Mary Tyler (Mrs. Leslie Cheek Jr.), said that twice while she was growing up the family moved to a larger house to give her father sufficient room for his home office and hundreds of books.

After dinner, Freeman spent time with his family. He went to bed at 8:30 if he didn't have an evening speaking engagement. He delivered as many as 100 speeches a year.

Freeman worked 20 years on his four-volume biography of Robert E. Lee, which won the Pulitzer Prize in 1934. How did he do it all, especially the writing of history, even with his precise time management?

He once said, "Outside writing by a newspaperman is primarily a matter of foregoing other things...If he wants the leisure that unhurried composition and painstaking revision demand, he must pay the price. I think this must be true of all those who desire to write but earn their living in some other way."

At Columbia, where journalism education became a graduate school in 1935, Freeman was a prize recruit of Dean Carl Ackerman. Freeman consented to Ackerman's blandishments despite the logistical problems of commuting weekly from Richmond because his two daughters and son were at college age. He needed extra income. Columbia paid him $7,500 a year.

One night a week, he boarded a Pullman car at Union Station in Richmond, rode overnight to Penn Station in New York City, and took the subway to 116th Street.

Freeman lectured for two hours in the morning, sent students on research and writing assignments, and discussed their resulting editorials, written under deadline pressure, in mid-afternoon. At 8:30 p.m. he entrained for Richmond, taking the editorials for grading by a colleague in Richmond. By going direct from the Richmond station to the News Leader he would be at his newspaper work at the usual pre-dawn hour.

Freeman was determined to use his phenomenal energy efficiently. While taking his doctoral degree at Johns Hopkins, he decided that his habitual seven hours of sleep were excessive. So each night he carefully set his alarm clock two minutes earlier. In 30 days he had adjusted to six hours of sleep.

In the 1954 bicentennial history of Columbia University, Richard T. Baker wrote of Freeman: "In the melodious diphthongs of Virginia his lectures frequently held the students spellbound for hours on end and ranged over subjects as far apart as military strategy in the Spanish Civil War and the newspaperman's religious practices. He knew everything that was alive in the news, and he knew it in its historical perspective. This, coupled with his own example of disciplined habits of research and communicative writing, made him one of the giants in the School of Journalism's hall of fame."

John Leard, who became executive editor of the News Leader and Richmond Times-Dispatch, recalled that Freeman lectured in deep tones, blended specifics with humor and referred to himself as "this old tramp newspaperman." He spoke in complete sentences— "in paragraphs," said Leard—and rarely used notes. His theme: "What we need is more facts and less bull."

In Sevellon Brown, the visiting managing editor, Freeman found a kindred spirit. Brown possessed many of the Freeman qualities, certainly the intellectual power, drive and commitment to factual reporting. When Brown died in 1956, his pivotal visit to the Freeman class two decades earlier was described in these words in an editorial tribute in the Providence Journal: "Mr. Brown's intense interest was engaged by the theories and ideas, as well as by the practical instruction of the experienced Virginian."

Richard T. Baker wrote in the Columbia history that Brown was "so stimulated by the ideas he heard and so fascinated by the informal way the ideas were debated and brought to life for the students by their own questioning and arguing that he turned to Dean Ackerman and said, 'This kind of thing ought to be made available to everybody in the newspaper business.' "

Brown already was an advocate of education for working journalists. He frequently invited public figures to brief editorial writers in his newspaper's imposing, book-lined library. In "The Providence Journal—150 Years," Charles H. Spilman and Garrett D. Byrnes wrote that important visitors to Providence seemed to welcome invitations to the editorial conference.

"A general, the wife of the current president of the United States, an official of the United Nations, a state official or prominent businessman, someone just returned from a diplomatic post in a difficult corner of the world. What they had to say never was repeated outside that room—that was the understanding—but their knowledge and wisdom were extended to the editorial writers, who would thus be able better to comment on affairs for the Journal's readers."

Fairly soon after Brown heard Freeman lecture, the Providence editor told colleagues, he had begun to ask himself, "Would not this kind of instruction be more valuable if men who are actually writing editorials could benefit from it as well as the youngsters who have not even tried their wings in the business?"

Although the last years of the Depression and the subsequent war blocked action, Brown described his idea to other editors around the country and sought their reaction.

There was much to think about. A training center would require not only initial funds but also a staff and a home. For a home, it seems likely that Brown had Columbia University in mind from the start. New York City was the communications center of the U.S. It was headquarters to the three wire services, the Associated Press, United Press and International News Service. New York City's newspapers sold millions of copies.

It was a transportation hub, even if remote from the western states. Grand Central and Penn stations bustled. The subway system was efficient. Visiting New York City with its Broadway theaters and other attractions would be a pleasurable prospect for the journalists Brown sought to attract.

As his plans for API took more definite shape, Brown's career advanced. In 1938 he became editor of the Providence Journal newspapers and in 1942 he was additionally named publisher. He had the clout to marshal support from his own newspapers.

"One afternoon in 1945," Garrett and Byrnes later wrote in their book, "Sevellon Brown summoned to the editorial library a group of news executives and reporters. Among them was Walter B. Everett, then city editor of the Evening Bulletin, who later would play a prominent part in the scheme that the Journal editor laid before the gathering.

"He had been contemplating something, he (Brown) said, that he thought might contribute to the advancement of journalism in the country. How would it be, he asked, if an institute were set up, possibly at some university, to which working newspaper men and women could come for mutual discussion under the leadership of experts, of the problems of their profession?

"The group was enthusiastic, especially the reporters. They told him that every time they went out of town to cover some event that drew reporters from a wide area of the country they fell into such discussions and always derived benefit from knocking brains with their peers. If they learned nothing else, said one man, they found that what they had believed to be their own unique problems were really almost universal in the business."

Apparently, Brown's thinking and his focus on Columbia was more advanced than he revealed to his Providence staff. In 1940, John Leard, then a journalism student, was meeting with Dean Carl W. Ackerman when the dean received a phone call. Ackerman told Leard the call had been from the American Federation of Labor offering financial support for a nascent plan for mid-career training of journalists. Leard recalled that Ackerman made it clear to the caller that funds would come only from newspapers.

Brown had joined the Providence newspapers in 1920. On the 25th anniversary of his arrival, the directors of the Providence Journal Company donated to Brown $10,000 to help establish a newspaper training center.

The motion came from Brown himself. The resolution stipulated that in cooperation with newspapers and press associations an American Press Institute be established "within Columbia University in New York City...for the better training of working newspaper men and women in the techniques of reportorial and editorial practices and for seminar studies in subjects currently related to the news..."

In seeking donations, one should never pass an empty collection plate; people are more likely to give when they see that others have already contributed. Sevellon Brown had his seed money. It was time to pass the collection plate in the newspaper business.

3

The Founder

A PI's founder, Sevellon Brown, spent most of his half-century career on the oldest major daily newspaper of general circulation in continuous publication in the United States, the Providence Journal. The Hartford Courant predated the Providence Journal, but was issued as a weekly. The New York Journal of Commerce began daily publication six months before the daily Journal came into existence, but it was a specialized publication, not a general interest daily.

Sevellon Brown was 33 years old in 1920 when he was summoned by the Journal from its Washington bureau to become managing editor. He remained with the newspapers of the Providence Journal—the morning Journal, the afternoon Evening Bulletin and the Sunday Journal—until he retired in 1954, two years before his death. In those 34 years, Brown guided the Journal from modest status to a rank among the nation's best newspapers.

Time magazine once described the Journal as "the conscience of New England." It won Pulitzer Prizes in 1973 and 1974, and long has been known regionally as "the Bible of New England." Because of its in-house training and high standards, the nation's largest newspapers often have looked to Providence when recruiting.

Eight years after Brown retired, the excellence that he had instilled in the Providence newspapers was illustrated by an episode at API. A discussion leader, preparing for a presentation on news content, had examined the breadth of coverage of newspapers represented in a seminar. He disregarded the top stories—those each paper automatically published on the front page—and compiled a list of important secondary stories on a chosen day. He selected 21 such stories.

At the seminar the discussion leader told the 29 members the results. One represented newspaper had printed only five of the secondary stories. Most other papers had published 10 or so. Only one paper in the seminar had carried all 21 stories—the Providence Journal.

Mike Ogden, the Providence executive editor, was one of the seminar members. That night he telephoned his managing editor in Providence and asked, "Did you have an extraordinarily big paper last Tuesday?" No, he was told, just a paper of normal size, and why did he ask? "Tell you about it later," Ogden said cryptically, "the long-distance wires are burning out of here." Of course the callers were other seminar members telling their papers how they had fared in the discussion leader's test of news coverage and judgment.

Sevellon Brown's father, Sevellon Alden Brown, began his career as a schoolteacher in Cayuga Village in upstate New York. William Seward, a friend who became a U.S. senator and secretary of state for President Lincoln, persuaded him to join the Department of State in Washington as an administrative officer.

His son, Sevellon Ledyard Brown, was born November 23, 1886. Because his father died when he was only 14, Sevellon, the son, never finished high school. A lack of money apparently caused him to drop out.

Brown's shortened formal education could account for his later devotion to ongoing training of newspaper men and women. Though his formal education was cut short, he became a highly educated man. Three colleges recognized him with honorary doctorates. "Newspapers," he once said, "were my college."

The record is silent on Brown's first jobs. He eventually struck out for Milwaukee to sell classified advertising for the Milwaukee Journal. He soon moved to Chicago and a wire-service job. It may have been with the United Press, which was established in its modern form in 1907. When Brown moved again it was back to Washington as a United Press reporter at the age of 21 or 22.

In the winter of 1911-12, he left reporting to serve as chief of foreign intelligence for the State Department. In Washington, then and now, government often dangled better salaries before journalists. Presumably that was the case with Brown. After his government stint, he signed on first with the New York Morning Sun and then the New York Herald. During World War I he went into the Army and eventually became a captain in the Ordnance Corps.

At war's end, Brown returned to Washington in 1919 as correspondent for the Providence Journal. In 1911 he had married Elizabeth Bonney Barry, daughter of David S. Barry, the Journal's Washington correspondent. When Barry retired from newspapering to become sergeant-at-arms of the Senate he had recommended his son-in-law as successor.

Stephen O. Metcalf, president of the Journal Company, already knew about Brown. They had met when Metcalf visited Barry's home years earlier. Metcalf obviously liked what he saw because he called Brown to Providence as managing editor in 1920.

Brown was a rather short man, friendly but formal, with eyes that became piercing when directing a question. He wore conservative business suits, and his office furnishings were equally austere. When he was angry, his voice rose several notches, his eyes widened and glared. Staff members regarded him with respect and awe.

The Journal's obituary editorial said that Brown never played at what some call "the newspaper game or indulged himself with the romanticism of newspapering." When Brown University awarded him an honorary doctor of laws degree in 1952, the citation dwelt upon "his sensitiveness to the obligations that go with the right to freedom of expression."

A memo to a staff member from SB, as he was known in-house, aroused concern. A summons to his office engendered acute anxiety. As he aged, he developed a sense of humor, especially with veteran staffers. Slowly he was perceived as having a bark worse than bite. But not at first.

In 1954, on his last day before retirement, Brown walked through every room on each of the four floors of the Journal Building on Fountain Street and shook the hand of every man and woman who was working under his direction. "He was unsmiling—it wasn't easy for him," Spilman and Byrnes wrote, "but he wanted to take his leave of each person, individually."

Brown was brought to Providence from Washington because of turmoil created by his flamboyant predecessor, John R. Rathom, the editor-general manager of the Journal. Rathom was a native of Australia with a mysterious past. In 1906 as an unemployed reporter he had somehow talked his way into being hired as managing editor. He became editor in 1912.

Byrnes and Spilman wrote of Rathom: "He was to create more excitement and raise more hell than any other man ever connected with the paper. He got himself and the Journal into hot water, really hot water, several times and enjoyed every minute of it...His tendency toward extravagant tales that strayed beyond the facts was to get him into trouble."

During World War I, Rathom, through connections with British Intelligence, published several sensational stories, some true, some British propaganda. There were also other departures from sound journalism.

Rathom is important to this narrative because the Journal needed a new editor who by instinct or mentoring elsewhere possessed the highest standards and ability to innovate. Whatever their source, Brown possessed both. He was installed as managing editor, technically under Rathom's purview. But Brown was running the news side of the papers by the time Rathom died in 1923.

Brown, who became editor in 1938 and editor and publisher in 1942, displayed in Providence a penchant for action.

Most reporters and desk editors then worked six days a week for the Evening Bulletin and three or four nights for the Journal. Almost everybody worked Saturday nights, putting out the Sunday Journal. It was a staggering workload.

Brown established separate staffs for the morning and afternoon newspapers. That quickly fostered intense competition, which must have been to Brown's liking for he wanted coverage on everything that moved. He ordered a reorganization of the state news staff, stipulating that in tiny Rhode Island one outlying news office or another should be no more than 20 minutes from any breaking story in the state. Stories from those bureaus flowed into Providence by train, trolley, car, bus and telephone.

The state news offices became a training ground for new hires. Everyone started at a state office, often in Fall River, just across the border in Massachusetts.

Years later, the initial on-the-job training in the bureaus was followed by formalized training courses in Providence. The defect of that program, Spilman and Byrnes wrote, "was that it began after the news men or women had been employed for six months or more during which they frequently had been tossed in alone among the sharks." It was also true that at a bureau a new reporter tended to adopt the reportorial habits of the bureau manager, good and bad.

Here again, a connection can be seen with the American Press Institute, whose seminars not only aided those already chewed by sharks but also often taught those preparing for promotion how to fend off the sharks they would soon encounter.

In the early 1920s, the ranks of newspaper columnists were expanding. Scores of columnists were trying to syndicate their opinions out of Washington. Some, Spilman and Byrnes wrote, were informed, some were not. Brown didn't like any of them. He called them "trained seals" and "exhibitionists."

He set out to develop his own group of columnists from within his staff. Editorial writers and reporters who had something to say beyond their daily assignment were encouraged to say it.

Brown was a scrapper with strong likes and dislikes. He hated wrongdoing, public or private. Brown and his aggressive deputies led the Providence papers deep into investigative reporting long before the term was coined. In 1947, when the Pawtucket city council enacted a blanket abatement of city taxes on real estate and personal property and refused to disclose the list of those receiving abatements, the Journal went to court.

Brown brought suit because he believed abatement records were public records and the newspaper had an obligation to present the records to the public for examination.

In a U.S. District Court hearing, the judge asked Brown if the Journal's board of directors had authorized the suit. Brown replied: "They did not. I, myself, authorized it. If I were with a newspaper as editor and the ownership or the board of directors would not let me bring a suit of this sort, I would leave that newspaper. I would not consider it an honorable paper."

Pawtucket took decisions favorable to the Journal all the way to the Supreme Court. On December 5, 1951, the Pawtucket appeal was denied. The Journal had won.

In its obituary tribute, Brown colleagues wrote that he was an exacting taskmaster. "His wrath was ferocious at sloppy, inaccurate or stupid work; he was intolerant of unintelligent reporting, such as failure to ask the right questions. 'It is not enough,' he once said, 'that a reporter report exactly what he sees or hears. Unless he understands what he sees or hears, his report will be meaningless or misleading.' "

Brown demanded a thorough report every day of all important local, national and world news. He made the Journal a newspaper of record. It printed texts of important speeches and the minutiae of court and town records. He broadened Washington coverage, developed local columnists, started a cultural news section and expanded business coverage.

On matters of taste, his standards were more rigid for the Journal than for its younger sister paper, the Evening Bulletin. He once upbraided the Journal managing editor for publishing a Marilyn Monroe picture that Brown thought too sexy.

Defending himself, the managing editor cited the actress' immense popularity and the fact that the Bulletin had earlier published a similar picture. Brown is reported to have replied scathingly: "You can run Miss Monroe's ass in the Evening Bulletin, but don't do this (jabbing at the offending picture) in the Journal."

Walter Everett recalled Brown as a great editor and publisher— fair, appreciative of good work, always ready to back reporters, and sometimes surprisingly tolerant. Once, an inebriated reporter provoked an argument with Brown at a party for Journal employees in a Providence hotel. Brown made a conciliatory response that only infuriated the reporter. He swung a fist at Brown, knocking his glasses to the floor.

Other guests shoved the reporter into a broom closet and bolted the door. The party resumed. Forgotten, the reporter remained in the closet until morning, when a startled maid opened the door. He had a colossal hangover and could hardly move after sleeping upright. But he pulled himself together and reported for work on the night shift.

Everyone expected the reporter to be fired. But day after day nothing happened. Eventually, the staff figured out the message: Under Sevellon Brown's code you could be summarily fired for any serious dereliction that hurt the newspaper, but you could swing at the publisher and be forgiven.

A few weeks before his death in 1956, Brown was asked: "What are the really basic elements in the successful publication of free, independent, responsible and successful newspapers?"

He replied: "The only basic reason for the existence of a newspaper is to report the news—accurately, responsibly, interestingly and as completely as you can.

"The only valid purpose for reporting the news is to have it read— not glanced at or ignored, but read. (And I consider advertising to be an important form of news.)

"If you do this job with skill and persistence in a literate area you will get circulation. How much circulation depends upon your ability and the area population.

"If this area has a retail trading center and enough buying power, advertising will grow with circulation. Again, how much advertising depends upon your ability and the capacity of your area.

"But as you do all of these things—and they involve illuminating the news with comment, leading the community, entertainment content, business management, mechanical productions, administration, sales, research, investments, property management, promotion and public relations—never forget that the first essential is reporting the news. Without that you can have no permanent and worthwhile success."

Brown was a giant of his time. Despite all his accomplishments and honors, he told a group of journalism students at the University of Missouri that the opportunity to initiate the American Press Institute "was the deepest gratification of all my work as a newspaperman."

Years after the 1945 meeting in Providence, when Brown sought reaction to his idea that would result in API, Walter Everett thought back to his years on Sevellon Brown's newspapers. "I was impressed by how logical it was," Everett said, "for him to have created the Institute, and by the extent to which his newspaper ideals found expression in the new organization."

At API, others with similar high ideals would soon add their influence to that of Sevellon Brown.

4

A Home at Columbia

With seed money of $10,000 from the Providence Journal and endorsement of his idea by its reporters and editors, Sevellon Brown intensified his campaign.

Brown had written on August 23, 1945, to his longtime friend, Carl W. Ackerman, dean of the Graduate School of Journalism at Columbia University, and proposed that an American Press Institute be established at Columbia. Brown was confident he could go forward with his brainchild and had even settled on its name.

On the same day, September 13, that the Providence Journal authorized the $10,000 contribution Brown again wrote Ackerman. He said that the resolution by the Providence Journal board, which mentioned only reportorial and editorial practices and issues in the news, was probably too restrictive, noting, for example, that news-papers would benefit from knowing more about FM radio.

But at the outset he thought the institute should be devoted to news and editorial subjects. "For in this undertaking," Brown wrote, "my heart is in the newsroom."

"Newsmen," Brown wrote, "cannot all their lives give out and not have the stimulation and refreshment of such opportunities as the Institute could offer them recurrently.

"Education FOR journalism is essential, yet not enough by itself...There is a crying need for education and training IN journal-ism throughout (a newspaperman's) professional career, at least for every above-average newspaperman."

It was natural for Brown to turn to Ackerman and Columbia. Both his sons graduated from the Graduate School of Journalism—Sevellon III (Jeff) in 1936 after first attending Amherst, and Barry in 1941 after earning an undergraduate degree at Princeton. Then, too, there was the elder Brown's membership on the school's board of advisors.

On January 7, 1946, Ackerman brought Brown's plan before the journalism faculty. He enclosed in his letter to the faculty a copy of Brown's August letter to him and a copy of his own letter to the acting president of Columbia University, Frank D. Fackenthal, in which he supported Brown's proposal.

Ackerman referred to Brown's August 23 letter as a proposal "in the form of an inquiry." Despite this reference, it is likely that the two men had conferred repeatedly on Brown's idea, perhaps going back to its genesis in 1936.

The chronology suggests that Ackerman and Brown were prepared to move quickly once adequate funds had been pledged by newspapers. The interval between Brown's August 23 letter and Ackerman's January 7 letter was apparently used for fund-raising, including the vital seed money from the Providence Journal.

It was a critical time for all colleges and universities. They faced the postwar influx of students, a great percentage of them veterans. Fackenthal, the acting president, could have understandably shelved the Brown proposal on the basis that he faced more pressing demands.

But he did not. Fackenthal had served at Columbia since his graduation from Columbia College in 1906. He had been appointed provost in 1937 and was asked in September 1945 to serve as acting president upon the retirement of Nicholas Murray Butler, president since 1902.

Brown's proposal for an institute at Columbia "appealed to me as practical and worthwhile," Ackerman wrote his faculty, "but I knew we could not consider any additions to our program of education or change in Journalism Building until sufficient funds were available."

Ackerman's use of "we" in connection with fund-raising could mean that he was actively involved in the solicitations. But there is no other indication of that. More likely, the dean saw his role as staying informed as Brown pinned down pledges. It made more sense for a publisher/editor rather than a journalism dean to seek funds for the training of working newspapermen.

Ackerman attached a copy of Brown's prospectus. It envisioned six seminars a year and a self-supporting institute at the end of two years of operation "from fees graded to the size of newspapers...We may ask the larger newspapers to pay from $500 to $1,000 per man for training; smaller, not more than $200 and possibly as little as $100 per man selected."

An initial fund-raising goal of $120,000 had been set (apparently by Ackerman and Brown), he wrote, but pledges had already exceeded $180,000. (This was the only time a figure of that size was recorded anywhere, so perhaps some pledges were not paid.)

Ackerman noted, "It is also significant that this is the first time since Joseph Pulitzer endowed our school that we have received financial support from the newspaper industry...We have sufficient funds to undertake expansion of the school's services to journalism."

The words "school's services to journalism" are significant because of the tensions and questions of control that would develop within three years between the institute—totally financed in operations by newspapers—and the school.

Ackerman recommended "the most practical" location for the institute as "the entire ground floor" of the Journalism Building. A preliminary estimate put the cost of remodeling at $60,000 to $75,000.

His letter to Fackenthal, the dean told his faculty, "embodies the experience Mr. Brown and I have had in our conferences and correspondence with editors and publishers."

Thus, despite the absence of other evidence, Ackerman was again describing himself as playing a central role in the birth of API.

Ackerman disclosed more about the intended relationship between the journalism school and API—or at least his version of it. "From an administrative standpoint, the Institute will be under a board of directors. It will be linked by the presence of the Dean as a board member. The director of the Institute will be a member of the faculty of Journalism. Members of the Faculty who may be selected for services to the Institute may also be elected to the board of the Institute."

Ackerman planned to formally submit the proposal to his faculty on January 15, 1946, just a week after he had told them of the plan.

Ackerman's letter to Fackenthal on January 7 included an estimate of annual expenses for the American Press Institute:

Director	$10,000
Director's expense	2,000
Administrative office	7,000
Two secretaries	4,000
Office expenses	5,000
Printing and promotion	5,000
Dean's Expenses	3,000
Conference leaders	
140 days at $50 per day	7,000
Travel and Expenses	
of Seminar leaders	7,000
	$50,000

Fackenthal replied the next day. A handwritten notation on the reply stated that a copy had been sent to Sevellon Brown two days later, probably by Ackerman.

The acting president said he had found Ackerman's letter "most interesting. When the Faculty makes its recommendations I will try to have early consideration and approval given, in order that you may proceed with surety.

"There is one point that bothers me, and that is the matter of space. It seems to be almost impossible that another place can be found for the bookstore at this time, and I think you should plan on other quarters."

The bookstore, bordering Broadway, took up the west end of the first floor of the seven-story Journalism Building. The east end of the ground floor was then devoted largely to the so-called city room of the school—a huge lecture room filled with scarred desks bearing battered typewriters. Dean Ackerman and Associate Dean Herbert Brucker occupied offices fronting on a large lobby. Other activities were also housed in the building, including offices for the Pulitzer Prizes.

In 1946, the School of Journalism enrolled only 65 students. So it was feasible for Ackerman to propose surrendering the ground-floor space to API. As matters eventually worked out, the bookstore remained in place, with the rest of the ground floor going to API. Ackerman and Brucker moved to new offices upstairs. When it met, the journalism faculty unanimously approved the institute, and Columbia trustees agreed February 4. Minutes of the trustees meeting contain statements about the early administrative organization of the institute:

"The Director of the Institute will be nominated by the Trustees for a two-year period by the Dean of Journalism with the advice and approval of the Board of Directors of the Institute (later named the Advisory Board) also appointed by the Trustees. The Director will have a seat on the Faculty of Journalism and will have the title of Associate Dean.

"In order to provide administratively for the inclusion of the Institute as part of the School of Journalism, the Dean of the Faculty recommends the appointment of an Associate Dean...(who) under the general direction of the Dean of the faculty would serve as director of the Press Institute."

That word "administratively" opened the way to varying interpretations. In Ackerman's view, the word could mean full control. In API's view, it could mean administrative detail but not policy.

Arthur Hays Sulzberger, publisher of the New York Times, was a Columbia trustee. Surely, Sulzberger's approving vote was assured in advance. After all, the New York Times was a contributor to the founding fund, and that contribution predated the trustees' meeting.

The trustees also approved the appointment of Floyd Taylor as director and associate dean.

Blessed by Columbia, Brown quickly took his next step. On February 14-15, 1946, he convened at the Hotel Waldorf-Astoria representatives of the publishers who had donated funds for an American Press Institute.

They were 22 in number, including Brown himself. They were joined by Ackerman, and Taylor, who had been doubling as a Columbia journalism professor and New York Herald Tribune editorial writer. He had been jointly selected by Brown and Ackerman as API's first director and approved by Columbia's trustees. The other newspapermen who attended were:

George E. Minot, managing editor, Boston Herald

Edwin B. Wilson, editor, Brooklyn Eagle

A. H. Kirchhofer, managing editor, Buffalo Evening News

E. Z. Dimitman, executive editor, Chicago Sun

William B. Ruggles, editor, Dallas News

W. S. Gilmore, editor, Detroit News

Robert U. Brown, editor, Editor & Publisher

Lloyd Gregory, managing editor, Houston Post

John H. Carter, editor, Lancaster (Pennsylvania) Newspapers

Turner Catledge, assistant managing editor, New York Times

Allen W. Smith, managing editor, Passaic (New Jersey) Herald News

Dwight S. Perrin, managing editor, Philadelphia Evening Bulletin

Ben Reese, managing editor, St. Louis Post-Dispatch

Louis B. Seltzer, Cleveland Press (representing Scripps-Howard newspapers)

Grove Patterson, editor, Toledo Blade

Fred W. Burgher, managing editor, Trenton (New Jersey) Times

W. H. Grimes, editor, Wall Street Journal

Alexander F. Jones, managing editor, Washington Post

Eugene Meyer, editor, Washington Post

William W. Vosburgh, editor, Waterbury (Connecticut) Republican

M. H. Williams, executive editor, Worcester (Massachusetts) Telegram and Evening Gazette

Turner Catledge of the New York Times first heard of the planned meeting at the Waldorf-Astoria when his managing editor, Edwin L. James, asked him to see Times' publisher Arthur Hays Sulzberger. Sulzberger instructed him to represent the Times. At the Waldorf-Astoria, Catledge found the discussion was led by Brown, Ackerman and Floyd Taylor.

"It was already set," Catledge recalled years later, "that he (Taylor) was to be the director, the first director of API. I was immediately impressed by him."

Catledge also recalled that Ackerman obviously was interested in having API "almost as an adjunct if not even a part of the school of journalism at Columbia."

Had Sevellon Brown thought out how API would be structured and how it would work? As Catledge remembered it, most of those matters were to be left to Taylor.

Brown stressed the importance of a fund beyond the amount already assured. Catledge thought Brown had an endowment in mind. Indeed there was a failed attempt the next year to raise an endowment. A second attempt decades later, after API had moved to Virginia, raised more than $1 million.

Catledge recalled that Brown "also had some grandiose ideas about what we could all do. We could have these meetings covered from the inside. We could have our seminars, we could have reports made on them, write papers on them, all that sort of thing...He was just spawning ideas..."

The Waldorf-Astoria meeting lasted two days. On the first night Brown held a news conference and announced the establishment of the American Press Institute. Its purpose, he said, would be:

> *"To contribute to the improvement of American newspapers by giving opportunity to experienced newspapermen of all categories to study and discuss at Columbia University the techniques of their work and the social, economic and political problems of the day."*

That statement of purpose, written by George W. Potter, chief editorial writer of the Providence Journal, was set forth on an imposing plaque of wood with metal letters. The plaque was mounted for years on a wall of the API conference room at Columbia.

Brown disclosed other details. The institute had been founded by a group of 27 American daily newspapers and Editor & Publisher magazine, the trade publication. They had contributed $142,000— enough for two years of operation. Seminar members would be selected by Floyd Taylor, the director, assisted by a board of editorial advisers to be appointed by Columbia trustees.

Six seminars a year would be held for a two-year experimental period. Each would be attended by 25 newspapermen of similar interests. The seminars would last approximately a month. Seminars would be held for editorial writers, managing editors and news editors, general reporters, city editors, city hall reporters and other groups.

The plan called for publishers to pay the costs of those attending the seminars, including tuition, lodging and board. Seminar members would reside together and eat in the same dining room.

For the experimental two years, it was planned to have 120 men from small newspapers enrolled at an average of $400 each and 30 at $1,000 each from larger newspapers. Under this plan, 10 large newspapers would be given the opportunity to pay $3,000 each into the institute and be able to select three of their own men to attend the seminars. Brown's fee system was to be significantly revised.

The only members of the standing faculty would be Ackerman, Taylor and an assistant. The institute would be run on a pay-as-you-go basis with the $142,000 held as a reserve.

Brown listed the following as original sponsors of the institute:

Boston Herald
Brooklyn Eagle
Buffalo Evening News
Chicago Sun
Dallas Morning News
Detroit News
Editor & Publisher
Evening Star, Washington, D.C.
Gannett Publishing Company of
    Augusta, Maine
Herald News of Passaic, New
    Jersey
Houston Post
Lancaster (Pennsylvania) News-
    papers
Los Angeles Times
New York Times
Daily Oklahoman
Oklahoma City Times
Philadelphia Evening Bulletin
Oregon Journal of Portland
Providence Journal-Bulletin
San Francisco Chronicle
Scripps-Howard Newspapers
St. Louis Post-Dispatch
Tacoma (Washington) News
    Tribune
Toledo Blade
Trenton Times Newspapers
Wall Street Journal
Washington Post
Waterbury (Connecticut) Re-
    publican and American
Worcester (Massachusetts)
    Telegram and Evening
    Gazette.

Brown did not announce the membership of the Advisory Committee. That action apparently was taken the next day when attendees also visited the Journalism Building. The Advisory Committee, later renamed the Advisory Board, comprised:

To serve one year: Catledge, Gilmore and Patterson.
To serve two years: Sevellon Brown, Carter and Kirchhofer.
To serve three years: Gregory, Jones and Williams.

In reporting on the meeting to acting president Fackenthal, Ackerman recommended the nominees (Columbia trustees routinely approved all API recommendations) and said, "These are good men, representing large and small newspapers."

Ackerman's letter offered other information:

"The editors recommended that I make an effort to raise the capital fund to at least $200,000, if possible, after we have paid all of our bills for structural changes in Journalism Building and for our costs up to September 1946.

"The editors decided to recommend a flat fee of $180 per man per week, to include the cost of the Institute, housing and meals. For two-week seminars, the cost would be $360, for four weeks $720.

"The editors decided that it would be desirable and necessary to have an understanding with the University with regard to recommendations for the expenditure of capital funds and for the use of fees for the annual operating costs of the Institute...The reason for attempting to add to the capital at this time is in order to insure the operation of the Institute in lean years when newspapers may not be able to pay $180 per week per man."

Ackerman added that several editors expressed appreciation to Fackenthal "for your good sportsmanship by attending the Thursday night dinner when they were still keenly interested in their own problems and were really not in the mood that they should have been to take up with you the many questions of the relationship of the Institute to the University. On Friday they were much more aware of this, and I think all of them wished that you could have been present the second day.

"There is not the slightest doubt about the virility of the newspaper support which we have, and there is certainly not the slightest doubt but that Mr. Taylor and I have a terrific job on our hands."

Fackenthal replied, "The proposals all seem to be in order, especially if what goes on under the proposals is subject to guidance by you and Professor Taylor."

In regard to the relationship between API and the university, Fackenthal responded, "I suggest that you talk with (the secretary of the university) in the near future to plan some statement of preroga-tives, so that some years hence we do not get into difficulties with a group of this kind from outside the University. If we start work along a good line, with the people who are keenly interested, I am sure we can defend against difficulties later, when others come in."

Discussion of the institute-university relationship might have headed off battle lines that were drawn later. Nevertheless, the editors had worked fruitfully at the Waldorf-Astoria, turning Sevel-lon Brown's dream into the basic form of the American Press

Institute.

The institute's first director, Taylor, went right to work. Only three weeks elapsed before he put his plan for the institute into a memo to all persons involved to that point. He marked it "confidential" until certain recommendations could be ratified by Columbia trustees.

Taylor's memo said: "The name American Press Institute is appropriate and should not be changed." First-year seminars should be limited to six, with a probability of expansion later, so that the administrative staff could establish high standards. The seminars in the first year would be as announced by Brown with the one for managing editors and news editors first.

Seminars should last two to four weeks, two weeks when the material could be presented quickly (as in the case of picture editors) and four weeks when thorough and prolonged discussion is essential (as in the case of editorial writers).

The fee should be $180 per week to cover tuition, room and board. That fee was deemed sufficient for sound operation and "so that the Dean of the Graduate School of Journalism and the Director of the Institute" will have leeway in choosing living quarters, providing for meals, and providing substantial honorariums to discussion leaders who will conduct seminars and experts who will discuss their specialties."

Taylor's memo said that the $180-per-week fee would be the same for all members. This revised original plans under which 10 large papers would have been asked to pay $3,000 a year for a guarantee of three seminar members.

Additional capital funds should be sought (some additional money was in sight at the time of the meeting) until available capital reached $200,000, Taylor wrote. Such capital would make future expansion possible without additional solicitation at the time. At the meeting, several persons emphasized that many papers had not been given opportunity to contribute; such an opportunity should be offered "to prevent spreading of the erroneous idea that the original sponsors wanted to make the Institute a closed corporation."

In fact, 38 newspaper organizations and their executives were listed for 10 years in the API bulletin as founders. An extra 10 newspapers had quickly added their contributions to those of the 28 originally announced by Brown.

As printed in the early API bulletins, the founders of the Institute were:

Frank S. Baker, publisher, Tacoma News Tribune

Paul Bellamy, editor, Cleveland Plain Dealer

George C. Biggers, executive vice president and general manager, Atlanta Journal

Paul Block Jr., publisher, Toledo Blade

George F. Booth, editor and publisher, Worcester Telegram and Evening Gazette

James Wright Brown, president, Editor & Publisher, New York City

Sevellon Brown, editor and publisher, Providence Journal

Edward H. Butler, editor and publisher, Buffalo Evening News

Norman Chandler, president, Los Angeles Times

R. B. Chandler, publisher, Mobile (Alabama) Register

Robert Choate, publisher, Boston Herald

W. H. Cowles Jr., publisher, Spokesman-Review, Spokane, Washington

James M. Cox, publisher, Dayton Daily News

Edward M. Dealey, president, Dallas Morning News

Dow H. Drukker Jr., publisher, Herald-News, Passaic, New Jersey

E. W. Fairchild, president, Fairchild Publications, New York City

Marshall Field, publisher, Chicago Sun

Guy P. Gannett, publisher, Gannett Publishing Company, Augusta, Maine

E. K. Gaylord, president and publisher, Daily Oklahoman and Oklahoma City Times

W. P. Hobby, publisher, Houston Post

K. C. Hogate, president, Dow Jones & Company, New York City

P. L. Jackson, publisher, Oregon Journal, Portland

James Kerney Jr., editor and vice president, Trenton Times Newspapers

Robert McLean, president, Evening Bulletin, Philadelphia

D. H. Mahoney, vice president and general manager, Miami Daily News

Eugene Meyer, publisher, Washington Post

Edgar Morris, general manager, Daily News-Sun, Springfield, Ohio

Frank B. Noyes, president, Evening Star, Washington, D.C.

William J. Pape, president and publisher, Waterbury Republican and Waterbury American, Connecticut

Joseph Pulitzer, publisher, St. Louis Post-Dispatch

Ogden Reid, editor, New York Herald Tribune

Frank D. Schroth, publisher, Brooklyn Eagle

W. E. Scripps, president, Detroit News

Paul C. Smith, editor, San Francisco Chronicle

Merritt C. Speidel, president, Speidel Newspapers

J. Hale Steinman, president, Lancaster (Pennsylvania) Newspapers

Arthur Hays Sulzberger, publisher, New York Times

Scripps-Howard Newspapers (no individual's name listed)

An undated memo in the API files listed these newspapers as the founding contributors:

$10,000 each: Providence Journal-Bulletin; Buffalo Evening News; Times-Mirror Co., Los Angeles; Washington Post; Evening Star, Washington, D.C.; St. Louis Post-Dispatch; New York Herald Tribune; Detroit News; New York Times; Scripps-Howard Newspapers, New York.

$5,000 each: Cleveland Plain Dealer; Toledo Blade; Worcester Telegram-Gazette; Boston Herald-Traveler; Philadelphia Bulletin.

$2,000: Oklahoma Publishing Co., Oklahoma City.

$1,500: Fairchild Publications, New York.

$1,000 each: Tacoma News-Tribune; Atlanta Journal; Dayton Daily News; Dallas Morning News; Passaic Herald-News; Chicago Sun-Times; Gannett Publishing, Maine; Houston Post; Dow Jones & Company, New York; Oregon Journal, Portland; Trenton Times Newspapers; Miami Daily News; Waterbury Republican and American; Brooklyn Eagle; San Francisco Chronicle; Speidel Newspapers, Reno, Nevada; Lancaster Newspapers, Pa.

$500 each: Editor & Publisher, New York; Mobile Press Register; Daily News and Sun, Springfield, Ohio.

$200: Spokesman-Review, Spokane, Washington.

The generosity of these contributions can be judged today by the fact that it took almost seven 1990 U.S. dollars to equal the purchasing power of one 1946 dollar.

The institute, Taylor's memo continued, should insist upon prompt and constant attendance at seminars and should report to their publishers the failure of any men attending seminars to make the most of their opportunities. The bulletin of the institute should stress that attendance at seminars must not be considered a junket and "wives of those attending should be left at home and that constant attention to the business at hand will be expected."

Seminar members would be selected on nomination of publishers, regardless of whether the publishers were financial sponsors, with the director making the choice when more than 25 men were nominated. Newspapers should be permitted to send men in training, if desired, to any seminar—that is, an assistant city editor could attend a city editors seminar, especially if the assistant was in line for promotion to city editor.

Taylor concluded by saying that the decisions he outlined had been through formal resolutions for some policies: the fees, the Advisory Committee and the Founders Committee. In other matters decisions came from general agreement after discussion, with no need for a vote.

At Columbia, the word "year" referred to the two-semester academic year, September through June. In mid-summer, university activity was sharply reduced. With food service still available and little pressure on university housing, summer would seem an ideal time for API to hold seminars. But in those years, newspaper people concentrated their vacations in summer, and the API staff feared that nominations to seminars would evaporate.

Then, too, the staff needed time to recycle, to prepare for another round of seminars, and to take vacations. So it was logical to structure the seminar schedule parallel to the academic schedule. When the special seminars for foreign journalists began in 1948—one such seminar a year—API did operate those programs in the summer.

To schedule API programs parallel with the academic year meant that the first-ever API seminar would be held early in the fall semester of academic year 1946-47. That gave Taylor just six months to prepare.

No one had experience in putting together seminar programs. Everything had to start from scratch. Newspapers had to be invited to make nominations. From the resulting nominees list, seminar members had to be selected. Seminar topics had to be determined and appropriate experts found. Housing and food service had to be arranged, and an accounting system had to be set up within the Columbia financial framework.

Most of the ground floor of the Journalism Building required remodeling. A seminar table capable of seating 25 members had to be designed and constructed. Provision was needed for seminar members to transcribe on typewriters the handwritten notes they were expected to scribble during seminar sessions.

And at the time the staff to accomplish all that consisted of only Director Taylor. Moreover, he continued his part-time editorial writing at the Herald Tribune.

With the graduation of the class of 1946, most of the campus entered summer somnolence. But not the infant API, which through the spring meant Taylor, with assists from Brown and Ackerman.

Help was on the way. On June 6, Ackerman announced the appointment of Claude A. Jagger as associate director of API. Jagger, business news editor of the Associated Press and a former assistant general manager of the wire service, had been granted an 11-month leave by AP, effective July 1.

A stocky man with sparse light-brown hair, Jagger smoked a pipe and sometimes wore a thin mustache. He had attended Dartmouth College for three years, then finished his degree at the Columbia School of Journalism. In 1936 he had been president of the

Columbia University Journalism Alumni Association.

An unassuming, quiet man, Jagger, then 44, had been with the AP 19 years, having joined the wire service in New York City as a reporter. He had worked earlier on the Rochester (New York) Herald, the Worcester Telegram and the Providence Bulletin.

Jagger's trial by fire had come on October 29, 1929, the day of the great stock-market crash. On that black day, which plunged the country into the Depression, tickers fell hours behind actual trading.

Acting as financial editor, Jagger quickly recognized that the AP's regular Wall Street staff could not stay apace of the collapse. He called in reinforcements from the New York City staff and stationed staffers in all the big banks and brokerage offices throughout the financial district.

Jagger himself wrote the main story on that most terrible day in Wall Street history. Before the day finished, he had written 8,000 words to describe how billions of dollars of securities values had been lost amid the wild scenes on the exchange floor and the panic among investors.

Clearly, he was a competent man who could produce under pressure. He made a good partner for the pressure-laden Taylor. Through his AP work, Jagger was acquainted with scores of newspapermen across the country. Taylor, too, was widely acquainted in newspapering. Together, their contacts were immensely valuable in forging the early seminar programs.

But after API's first frenetic year, Jagger resigned to become president of the Hawaiian Economic Foundation, dedicated to the development of Hawaii. Perhaps he was attracted by a higher salary. Perhaps, having witnessed the struggles of the infant API, he saw bleak prospects there, though in resigning he said API faced a bright future—"It is no longer an idea or an experiment," he said. He was invaluable in API's startup year.

Editor & Publisher chronicled the countdown toward the first seminar. Its generous coverage was critically important in getting the word out to newspapers that might nominate seminar members. On June 15, E & P published a list of topics to be discussed at each of the six first-year seminars. Four seminars would be three weeks in length. Picture editors would be two weeks (afterward, those members said they needed more time), and editorial writers would meet for four weeks.

Taylor, probably in consultation with Brown and Ackerman, was setting up other requirements. Seminar nominees were required to have five years of experience on daily newspapers and their nomination must come from publishers or other principal executives, of their papers. The experience stipulation was a safeguard against a seminar of neophytes with no wisdom to share. It was selectively waived.

Nominations were to be made with the understanding that the fee would be paid a month in advance of the seminar.

In the last week of August, Taylor announced selection of the 25 members of the first seminar, held for managing editors and news editors, starting September 30. Editor & Publisher carried a short biography and picture of each member.

Except for the policy of limiting membership to 25 persons, the seminar would have been larger. Taylor wrote letters of regret to those who were turned away and also to their nominators.

Thus began an unpleasant task for API staff members over the years—explaining that their nominations had arrived too late for consideration. In those cases, the nominee was promised membership in the next similar seminar. Usually, nominations were accepted according to date received, but there were exceptions as API strove to serve a growing constituency. On the other hand, occasions came when nominations were grievously few, and staff members scrambled to fill empty seats at the oval table.

Meanwhile, the other startup work proceeded. On June 26, Ackerman wrote Fackenthal to request that the capital fund of API be mortgaged in the amount of $8834.79 for items, apparently furniture including the conference table, ordered from Macey-Fowler, 385 Madison Avenue, New York City.

This was one of the few precise financial records still available more than four decades later. Many of the still available figures on contributions, etc., don't add up to the dollar. But Monty Curtis often emphasized that API reimbursed Columbia for all remodeling materials and labor.

The university's building and grounds department supplied remodeling crews. They erected a partition in the former lecture hall/city room that created an API conference room of 30 by 60 feet and a smaller so-called writing room with a desk and typewriter for each seminar member.

There was also a locker room for members, which was converted years later into an office for the director. Taylor and Jagger occupied the offices previously held by Dean Ackerman and Associate Dean Brucker. Between the Taylor and Jagger offices, a third office was used by two secretaries. A smaller conference room was arranged near the bookstore. Much later, when the executive staff had grown to five persons, that conference room became the jam-packed central office for their secretaries.

Taylor and Jagger must have breathed more easily when the specially ordered furniture arrived—the seminar table in particular.

In its usual arrangement, the table comprised six sections of polished walnut. There were two long, straight sections and four curved sections, two of which completed the oval at each end. In this configuration, it measured 16 feet by 31 feet.

There were also two short flower tables, designed to double as segments of the larger table. Later, when seminar membership was increased from the original limit of 25 to 28 (and stretched now and then to as many as 32) the flower tables were added to the straight sides to provide additional room for members.

But the short sections were usually placed in the hollow center created by the other six sections and held bouquets of fresh flowers. Now and then the longer straight sections were moved aside and a table formed in a circle that would accommodate only 17 or 18 persons. This was done when a few early seminars drew memberships as few as 12, when members would have been scattered at a larger table.

Of course other details needed attention: chairs, name signs, carafes, menus and a myriad of others. Wooden chairs, used for the first few seminars, were later replaced by comfortable padded chairs. Sitting at least six hours a day on unpadded chairs caused seminar member backsides to complain.

Chromium-plated individual water carafes were added later, as were handsome name signs for members—both name and paper represented. Later, too, gold-colored drapes would be hung on the north end of the conference room, shielding the two windows that looked out on Columbia's busy Campus Walk, an extension of 116th Street.

The record is almost blank on the day-to-day activity that preceded the opening of the first seminar on September 30, 1946. Somehow, Taylor and Jagger and two secretaries, Mary Jane Blanton and Margaret Hanrahan, muscled and willed it all together.

Clearly, it must have been quite a summer.

5

The Journalism Dean

I t was Sevellon Brown's idea that led to the founding of the American Press Institute. But without the assistance of his friend, Carl W. Ackerman, dean of Columbia's Graduate School of Journalism, the founding of API would either have been delayed or have taken a different form at another location.

Brown needed a home where his idea could take root. Columbia was the logical place. But Brown also needed someone inside Columbia to push his proposal. Ackerman was that person.

Over the years, Ackerman's major role was elbowed into the background by API loyalists who depicted him as wanting to wrest control from the API Advisory Board and executive staff in order to make the institute an integral part of the Graduate School of Journalism.

Ackerman may well have had such aspirations, but they cannot be documented almost a half-century later. An abundance of statements from the API side suggest that Ackerman and his successor, Edward W. Barrett, cast covetous eyes on API with its base of newspaper support. But no evidence could be found to describe overt acts by Ackerman or Barrett.

Walter Everett recalled, though, that when he and Monty Curtis were API associate directors under Floyd Taylor they "sensed to the point of knowing that Ackerman tried to force on Taylor the dean's ideas of how the institute should be run. But Floyd kept his troubles to himself, and we never heard specifics...Also in the picture was strong-willed Sevellon Brown, who was often on the phone to Floyd."

Columbia trustees created API as an affiliate of the journalism school, but questions always existed of how close that affiliation was intended to be. After its first year, API prepared a promotional publication which said that the president and trustees of Columbia had approved the founding of API "as an affiliate, for administrative purposes, of the Graduate School of Journalism."

Those words, "for administrative purposes," were probably written by Taylor or certainly approved by him, and could reflect early discontent with orders coming downstairs from the dean's office. At the time, Taylor had been newly appointed by Ackerman, and the upward chain of command was Taylor to Ackerman to the university president. There was of course the API Advisory Board, and the university was usually amenable to its recommendations.

For several years, API seminar members saw Ackerman in a visible role. He was host at the opening dinner—at the Faculty Club in the early years—for each seminar group. For a time he took part in the opening and closing work sessions of each seminar. Gradually, he discontinued that participation, perhaps because of the pressure of his many other journalism-related projects.

In any case, the API staff was strongly protective and quick to rally against real or perceived threats. Tensions subsided only after Elie W. Abel succeeded Ed Barrett as dean in 1968, and more cordial relations were established.

But by Abel's time the steadily growing API was cramped in its Journalism Building quarters and beginning to think about finding additional space, on the Columbia campus or elsewhere.

Through many of API's 28 years at Columbia, two plaques hung on the wall of the seminar conference room. Behind the discussion leader, on the north wall, hung the statement of purpose of API. On the west wall, over a multi-shelved cabinet in which seminar members placed their own newspapers, hung the second plaque, which gave equal space to Brown as founder of API and Taylor as its first director.

No mention was made of Ackerman, probably because the Brown and Taylor plaques were not unveiled until after relations between API and the journalism school had become severely strained.

Each year, API's bulletin listed the schedule of seminars and described the nominating procedures and living and working arrangements. The early bulletins noted that Brown had conceived the idea and "proposed that Columbia University organize an Institute to conduct seminars for experienced newspapermen. Mr. Brown and Carl W. Ackerman, Dean of the Graduate School of Journalism, discussed the proposal with several of America's leading publishers, who gave it strong endorsement..."

In the 1960-1961 bulletin, however, Ackerman's name disappeared from the two-paragraph section on the founding of API. The section said that Brown discussed his idea with "Columbia University officers and with publishers and editors around the country." After several more issues, Ackerman's name was restored.

Ackerman was Columbia's journalism dean for 25 years, from 1931 to 1956, when he reluctantly retired at age 66 because of the university age limit for administrators. Sardonically, he pointed out that Dwight D. Eisenhower, who like Ackerman was born in 1890, was successfully running for president of the U.S. Ackerman denounced the waste of manpower and brainpower in "discarding educators and others over age 65."

When Ackerman died on October 9, 1970, at age 80, the New York Times carried an obituary of two-and-a-half columns. The Times called him the "foremost journalism educator in the nation" and credited him with transforming the Graduate School of Journalism "from a literary ivory tower to a practical training ground for newsmen." It also said he "co-founded the American Press Institute..."

The co-founding statement could well have been taken from Ackerman's biography in "Who's Who in America," and thus based on his own assertion. It's an overstatement to say Ackerman was a co-founder of API, but his key role cannot be minimized.

Ackerman was another of the major journalistic figures who provided impetus to API, a pioneering force for improving the news and editorial quality of newspapers.

Carl William Ackerman was born in Richmond, Indiana, and studied at the University of Chicago before graduating from Earlham College in Richmond in 1911. He was one of 12 members of the first Columbia School of Journalism class in 1913. Talcott Williams, the journalism school's first director, told Columbia President Nicholas Murray Butler that Ackerman was a "young man worth keeping your eye on."

Ackerman reported from Albany and Washington for United Press, then spent two years in Berlin, filing dispatches on World War I. When the U.S. entered the war, Ackerman became a correspondent for the New York Tribune and the Saturday Evening Post. He reported from Spain, Mexico, France and Switzerland and wrote four books during that period.

In July 1918, a brief wire story reported the execution of Russian Czar Nicholas and his family in Ekaterinburg, Siberia. Carr Van Anda, managing editor of the New York Times, asked Ackerman to get the full story. Ackerman crossed the Pacific by ship to Japan, proceeded to Vladivostok and then traveled 5,000 miles by train across Siberia.

In Ekaterinburg, Ackerman and the American consul general hired a troika—three horses hitched to a sleigh. Bundled in furs against numbing cold of 40 degrees below zero, they rode many miles to a monastery.

There they found a monk who had recorded the last days of the czar and his family. Ackerman examined the house and basement where the czar and his family had been executed by pistol shots.

Ackerman had to wait several weeks until a freight-refugee train left on the two-week journey to Vladivostok, where he cabled his story. Six months after he left New York, his exclusive story on the last days of the Romanoffs was printed on page one of the New York Times. Ackerman later gleefully told that the long cable had cost the Times $4,000.

When Ackerman returned from overseas, he founded the foreign news service for the Philadelphia Public Ledger and manned its London bureau for a time. In 1921, he entered public relations in a firm that bore his name and handled accounts for leading corporations, including Eastman Kodak. (In 1930, he published the last of his five books, a biography of George Eastman.)

Ackerman was public relations director for General Motors in 1931 when Columbia president Nicholas Murray Butler offered him the post of journalism dean. Ackerman's acceptance set off a furor. Many journalism alumni saw him as a public relations man and not a journalist despite his eight early years as a reporter.

Those protests did not faze Ackerman. He overhauled the journalism curriculum to require three years of general undergraduate study as a prerequisite to two years of concentrated journalism study.

"By requiring three years of college work of all students admitted to the School of Journalism," Ackerman wrote, "our student body will be provided with a broader cultural foundation." He also reorganized the journalism program along the lines of a newspaper office, with an eight-hour working day.

The two-year journalism curriculum prevailed from 1932 to 1935, when Ackerman pushed through a proposal to make journalism graduate study only, with courses compressed into a single year. Formalized lectures were largely abandoned, and students were assigned to report and write one or two stories every day. Thus was born the Graduate School of Journalism.

Ackerman became known as the "itinerant dean" because of his travels. Always espousing the value of journalism schools, he went around the world twice. In 1943, with encouragement from his Class of 1913 friend, Hollington K. Tong, then Chinese vice-minister of information, and with U.S. Department of State backing, he sent a four-man faculty team to found a journalism school in Chungking. In 1947, API's second year, Ackerman spent four months in South

America surveying journalism schools and recommending startup programs.

His absences, like the one in 1947, may have given API opportunity to loosen Ackerman's initial efforts at ruling with a tight grip.

At Columbia, Ackerman led a full-time faculty, but they were outnumbered by adjuncts, working newspaper men and women who taught part-time. He stressed the practical nature of instruction; after all, the students already had undergraduate degrees. He once said he had always wanted to move the journalism school to midtown New York, where it would be situated amid the working world of journalism and not so remote as a 15-minute subway ride away.

Ackerman was prim and reserved, no hail fellow, well met. Some saw him as cold and calculating. The spouse of one journalism faculty member recalled him as being "austere, cold, enterprising." He dressed conservatively and carefully. Suave and assured, he smiled frequently, but seldom warmly. He was an excellent fund-raiser.

Journalism students saw little of their dean. Each year, he welcomed the incoming class on opening day. Thereafter, he appeared infrequently except at major school functions. But on at least one occasion, he discarded his starchiness. An editor who had attended Columbia recalled that he was necking with a co-ed on a seldom-used stairway of the journalism building when Ackerman happened upon them.

"You'd better watch it," Ackerman told the alarmed journalism student. "You never know who might find you next time."

If not loved for his personality, Ackerman was widely admired by associates for his courage. A great promoter of his school, probably through lessons learned in his public relations years, Ackerman nonetheless drew his lines carefully when raising money. Shortly before his retirement, Ackerman proclaimed that the biggest problem facing journalism schools was whether to accept government or private foundation aid.

"I think the issue," he said, "is will they remain schools for newspapers or become schools for propaganda? If they accept government money or foundation money for specific purposes they can no longer remain free newspaper schools."

Who would not applaud such a principle, or the manner in which Ackerman worked on an almost global front to improve the quality of journalism training?

To API staff members, however, he was often a hair shirt. And within five years of API's founding, Ackerman's vision of his role in the institute influenced how others would enter the scene and play their own roles.

6

A Large, Quiet Man

F loyd Taylor, the first director of the American Press Institute, was an enthusiastic gardener. On the morning of August 24, 1951, he was working in the garden at of his home in Plandome, Long Island, when he went into the garage. His wife Marian found him there, dead of a massive coronary thrombosis. He was 49 years old.

The next day, the New York Herald Tribune described Taylor in an editorial written by Walter Millis:

"A large, quiet man, not without a twinkle in his eye, he never stooped to make an effect nor wrote a line in which he did not believe."

When API prepared a plaque to honor Taylor and its founder, Sevellon Brown, the words from the Herald Tribune editorial were used to describe the man who had guided the institute through its first five years.

Taylor gave API its essential form which still endures—the informal seminar as the educational tool of choice.

Floyd Taylor was a big, friendly bear of a man whose modesty belied his accomplishments and knowledge. From the days when he played guard and fullback at Riverside High School in California he stood six feet, two inches and weighed at least 215 pounds.

Floyd D. Rogers lived in a press hostel with Taylor in Chungking, China, during World War II, when Taylor was teaching journalism to the Chinese. Rogers recalled Taylor as a "very warm personality, lovely disposition, warm and relaxed, as unselfish a man as you could find."

Taylor exuded a "great feeling of competence," remembered Marjorie Baker, widow of Richard T. Baker, a Columbia journalism professor and briefly acting dean. "You just felt that Floyd was in control, but not in an arrogant way."

Walter Everett was a seminar member and then a guest discussion leader when he became acquainted with Taylor. Then as an associate director of API he worked with Taylor from 1949 until the latter's death in 1951.

"Floyd was a gentle, kindly, modest man," Everett recalled, "but he was a newspaperman and scholar of unusual ability, integrity, and vision."

In 1949, Howard H (Tim) Hays, who would become API's board chairman in 1978, attended an API Publishers and Editors Seminar. Hays was from the Riverside Daily Press and Daily Enterprise in Taylor's home town of Riverside.

He later recalled, "I was awed by Floyd himself. I couldn't imagine anybody better in the role—a consummate professional, but one with plenty of time to listen and explain. I needed all the journalism education I could get at that stage, and my three weeks with him opened my eyes."

Unlike the fastidious Brown and Carl Ackerman, Taylor wore suits of nondescript color and style, usually rumpled. His necktie was often askew.

When moderating seminars, Taylor set the pattern of informal but purposeful discussion that became the API hallmark. He was expert in encouraging participation by reticent seminar members and in keeping discussion leaders on track and on schedule.

Amid the pressures of API's early years Taylor always seemed relaxed and amiable. But his workload was enormous. He continued his part-time editorial writing for the Herald Tribune after he had been appointed API's director. That was understandable, considering that API began as a two-year experiment and could have folded after that trial period. He dropped his Herald Tribune duties in 1949.

On December 21, 1949, Taylor wrote Arthur Hays Sulzberger, publisher of the New York Times, to ask if the Times would give a dinner for 12 Japanese journalists—eleven men and one woman, who would be attending a January 1950 special seminar at API. The Times was frequently host to seminar groups for cocktails, dinner and discussion with editors and other executives.

In a postscript, Taylor wrote: "You may have heard that I have resigned from my Herald Tribune job. This job has been a little embarrassing to me in connection with my Institute work. But the most pressing reason for my resignation was I found myself putting in too many sixteen-hour days. I don't mind a twelve-hour day particularly, but longer ones seem a trifle on the strenuous side."

Nevertheless, Taylor was not one to share his woes. During his five years as director, he was frequently called to Ackerman's office and returned an hour or so later obviously downcast. But he never discussed his problems with the two associate directors, Everett and J. Montgomery Curtis.

Taylor's letters give evidence of graciousness. A letter to Vincent S. Jones offers an example. Jones, executive editor of the Utica (New York) Observer-Dispatch, was one of the early and frequent guest experts, who came to be known as discussion leaders. At the outset, API gave its discussion leaders an honorarium of $100. In fact that was the basic honorarium for decades, long after inflation had drastically diminished its buying power.

In August 1947, Taylor wrote Jones and asked him to be a discussion leader on the subject of news content at a seminar for managing editors and news editors, a program similar to the first-ever seminar in 1946. Preparations for a seminar started several weeks in advance. Taylor closed by writing:

"Our project seems to be going well...However, I am troubled by mounting expenses, as other people seem to be. Would you be indignant if we offered you $75 and expenses instead of $100 and expenses? I know this is unreasonable, but I do need to be penurious."

There was nothing stuffy about Taylor. Writing Vin Jones in November 1946, Taylor requested a biographical note of a couple of hundred words, to be used in introducing Jones as a speaker at the first City Editors Seminar. Taylor added: "If you can include a salty anecdote (or something else to relieve the monotony of birth date, employment record and so forth) it will help."

Taylor, Everett recalled, regarded newspaper men and women as very important people and wanted to accord them VIP treatment at API seminars. He took great care in planning and commissioning the huge conference table, the cabinet for seminar members' newspapers, the other furniture and the drapes that later covered the north wall of the conference room.

At the conference table, Taylor arranged for each member to have an executive-type blotter, a handsome name sign, an individual water carafe, sharpened pencils and note pad. Fresh from cluttered, gritty newsrooms, seminar members joked about how the conference room looked like the United Nations. But they loved it.

The first few API bulletins said: "The meals will be equivalent in quality to those served in a good restaurant." And for many years they were, until Columbia began struggling to hold down expenses in the late 1960s.

Taylor checked every menu in advance, a procedure that became API tradition. Dinners were four-course meals served in API's wood-paneled private dining room on the mezzanine floor of John Jay Hall, the newest of the residence halls, in which seminar members stayed for several years.

Taylor had great faith in the ability of newspaper people to teach each other. For that reason, he insisted that they be housed together during seminars and not bring family members to New York.

An early bulletin expressed his philosophy: "There is no attempt at indoctrination...There is no attempt to convince seminar members that any particular newspaper technique is ideal. Guest experts often express enthusiasm over one technique or another. But members of the seminars invariably present ideas of their own. They also explore the possible weaknesses of each technique under discussion. The result is that they return to their newspapers with clear pictures of the advantages and disadvantages of various techniques."

Taylor's parents moved to California from Oregon. His father became president of the Riverside City Council. His mother was an elementary-school teacher who died at age 102 in 1974. The family lived in the same block as the city library, which later bought the Taylor property for expansion. The library's proximity was a big influence on young Floyd, who was born in 1902.

A voracious reader, Taylor decided early that he wanted to be a newspaperman. He crossed the continent in 1919 to enroll at Columbia University, his son John recalled, because Columbia had an outstanding liberal arts program. He planned a five-year curriculum, three in liberal arts, then two in journalism.

At Columbia he told one and all that he was from California and quickly earned the nickname "Cal." After his fourth year, when he was editor of the Spectator, the student newspaper, Taylor left school because he had decided that the journalism courses weren't good enough.

Short of a degree because he had selected courses that interested him rather the required sequence, he went to work in 1923 for the New York Herald.

When the Tribune bought the Herald in 1924, Taylor was one of the few Herald staff members hired by the new Herald Tribune. Taylor was assistant night city editor when the Herald Tribune asked him, at age 27, to become sports editor. The sports department had a stable of good writers but lacked a competent editor.

Taylor, a sports fan, directed the sports department for two years. During that time he devised a way to make the widely read W. O. McGeehan turn in his column on time. Because of drinking bouts, McGeehan frequently missed deadlines. Taylor took McGeehan off the periodic payroll and paid him column by column, but only when McGeehan met his deadline.

In 1931, Taylor switched to the New York World-Telegram as a feature writer. He was later assistant city editor. At the World-Telly, owned by Scripps-Howard, Taylor once wrote a story that for some reason he didn't want printed under his byline. So he used the byline "Weston Barclay," taken from the fact that the newspaper was at West and Barclay streets.

Editor Roy Howard reportedly said it was a great story, and asked, "But who in hell is Weston Barclay?"

Taylor worked at the World-Telegram until 1943, when Columbia's Dean Ackerman received a letter from his Class of '13 classmate, Hollington K. Tong. Tong was an adviser to Generalissimo Chiang Kai-shek in a China that had been consumed by war since 1937.

Chiang wanted to call world attention to China's plight. One problem was the lack of trained journalists in China.

Tong asked his alma mater Columbia to assist. Working with the State Department, Ackerman recruited four U.S. working journalists to serve in China as guest experts in already existing agencies of information.

One of the initial four was Taylor, by then assistant city editor of the World-Telegram. Three other journalists were shortly added, on a related mission. They founded and operated the Graduate School of Journalism in Chungking and served variously for up to three years.

Taylor left China in 1944 to become an editorial writer at the Herald Tribune. Before leaving he was seated front row center in a picture of 41 smiling faculty, staff and students, several holding glasses and with the women concentrated around Taylor. It was a picture of wartime camaraderie and probably was taken at Taylor's going-away party.

A ribald poem based on Rudyard Kipling, which listed Taylor as its principal author, poked fun at the full faculty and many of the students. Part of the final verse read:

> *Ship me somewhere west of Suez,*
> *Where a man can drown his thirst;*
> *Where there may be ten commandments,*
> *But I'll break them, tenth to first!*
> *Where ten thousand bars are calling,*
> *O', it's there that I would be,*
> *Where the chorus girls are sprawling,*
> *Winking hungrily at me!*

Back in the U.S., Taylor turned to writing editorials, mainly on foreign affairs, for the Herald Tribune. Shortly he began doubling as an associate professor of journalism at Columbia, as a number of New York City newspapermen did. Concurrently with being named director of API in 1946, Taylor was promoted to full professor at the Graduate School of Journalism. But he apparently taught in the journalism school only rarely thereafter.

Taylor's stature domestically and internationally grew through API and the foreign seminars it began in 1948 at the request of the State Department, which wanted to introduce the concept of a free press to defeated Germany and Japan and elsewhere.

In 1951, Taylor co-presided over a group of editors from 15 countries in the API conference room. As guests of API and the American Society of Newspaper Editors, through financing by the Ford Foundation and the Carnegie Endowment for International Peace, they had conferred with American editors in Washington, Atlanta, Houston, San Francisco and Chicago.

The project was the brainchild of Lester Markel, Sunday editor of the New York Times, and it resulted in establishment of the International Press Institute, which still works to foster free and responsible journalism worldwide. Taylor was approached about becoming the first director of IPI. He chose to stay at API, not knowing that he had only months to live.

More than 600 newspaper men and women had attended API seminars by the time Taylor died in 1951. Editor & Publisher editorialized that "Mr. Taylor was not the creator of the Institute, but it will live as a memorial to this man who left an indelible mark on the men who participated through his untiring efforts in the cause of good journalism."

7

116th and Broadway

For nearly two decades, Columbia University was an idyllic site for the American Press Institute. The reasons were Columbia itself, with its superb resources, and the city—New York, New York, the Big Apple.

When API was founded in 1946 there existed a New York City that lives now only in memory. New York was the ultimate big-time—exciting, promising, and safe. Wide-eyed visitors, unthreatened, walked the streets for hours.

New York was the communications center of the country. The wire services, picture services, broadcasting systems, publishing houses and several of the greatest newspapers were based there. For ambitious journalists, New York was the place to be.

On Morningside Heights in upper Manhattan stood Columbia University, the nucleus of one of the greatest concentrations of educational resources and activity anywhere. Also located on Morningside Heights were four other institutions of higher learning: Barnard College, Teachers College, Union Theological Seminary, and the Jewish Theological Seminary of America.

Also on the Heights were the Juilliard School of Music, now moved downtown to Lincoln Center; the Interchurch Center; Riverside Church; and the Cathedral Church of St. John the Divine, the world's largest Gothic cathedral. Small wonder that Morningside Heights was called the Acropolis of America.

Perched on high ground above the Hudson River on the west and Harlem, below an escarpment, on the east, Columbia spread over 36 acres, between West 112th and West 123rd streets on the south and north, and between Broadway and Morningside Drive on the west and east.

Just across Broadway lay the affiliated Barnard College, a prestigious school for women. To the north stood Teachers College, famous for Horace Mann and other leaders of public education. Like Columbia, those institutions employed prestigious faculties, and their members were usually available for seminar assignments.

One of Sevellon Brown's goals was to provide a bridge between the academy and journalism. API's statement of purpose mentioned the study of the social, economic and political problems of the day. Where better for such study than Columbia?

Then, of course, there was Columbia's Graduate School of Journalism, regarded by many professionals as pre-eminent. Some of the most famous persons in journalism held degrees from Columbia. Seminar members were sometimes Columbia journalism graduates. For them, seminars were a homecoming.

On a pedestal in the Journalism Building lobby stood the Rodin bust of Joseph Pulitzer, whose bequest started the school. After 1951, API seminar members crossing the lobby could also read a bronze plaque presenting Pulitzer's most-often-quoted words:

> *"Our republic and its press will rise or fall together. An able, disinterested, public-spirited press with trained intelligence to know the right and courage to do it, can preserve that public virtue without which popular government is a sham and a mockery. A cynical, mercenary, demagogic press will produce in time a people as base as itself. The power to mould the future of the republic will be in the hands of the journalists of future generations."*

The offices of the Pulitzer Prizes, the most prestigious awards in journalism and the arts, were housed on the seventh floor of the Journalism Building. When the Pulitzer Prize recipients were announced each spring, word reached the API conference room immediately. Sometimes a newspaper represented in the seminar had won a Pulitzer, and a raucous celebration would erupt.

Getting to midtown New York for a seminar field trip or personal exploration was a simple task, accomplished by hailing the taxis that streamed down Broadway or by taking the subway.

Midtown New York was 15 minutes away on the IRT (for Inter-Borough Rapid Transit) subway, with its 116th Street station on Broadway a few steps from the Journalism Building.

Seminar members heading for midtown had a choice. They could stay on the Broadway local, which stopped at all stations, or cross the station platform at 96th Street and change to an express, which stopped only at 72nd Street before hurtling into the Times Square station at 42nd Street and Broadway.

When heading north to Columbia, though, there was also a choice of local or express, and the two subway lines sometimes confused seminar members. If they failed to transfer from the uptown express onto the Broadway local line at 96th Street they rode not to the desired stop at 116th and Broadway but to 125th Street in Harlem, many blocks from Columbia.

Confused or not, seminar members loved API's historic ambience. Columbia was the fifth oldest institution of higher learning in the United States. It was founded in 1754 as King's College by royal charter of King George II of England. Among its earliest students were John Jay, the first Chief Justice of the United States; Alexander Hamilton, the first secretary of the treasury; Gouverneur Morris, the author of the final draft of the U.S. Constitution; and Robert R. Livingston, a member of the five-man committee that drafted the Declaration of Independence.

In 1849, the college, renamed Columbia after the Revolutionary War, moved from its initial site in what is now lower Broadway to 49th Street and Madison Avenue. There it remained for 50 years. When Columbia finally moved in 1897 to Morningside Heights, the college retained ownership of its midtown property. That property was later leased to Rockefeller Center, and the rents became a large factor in university budgets.

The modern campus was built in 1897 on ground once occupied by Bloomingdale's Insane Asylum, a fact that wags pronounced appropriate whenever student high jinks reached a peak.

On Morningside Heights, the architectural firm of McKim, Mead & White designed a striking campus on which the 136-foot-high dome of the Roman classical Low Memorial Library rose over the landscape.

When student uprisings hit campuses nationwide during the Vietnam War, Low Library with its imposing dome, broad steps, and statue of Alma Mater became a national symbol of campus unrest as television cameramen swarmed to Columbia for background footage, whether the main action was at Columbia or not.

When API opened in 1946, Columbia and its affiliated institutions had a total enrollment of 28,108, largest in its 193-year history, as veterans swarmed back from World War II and took advantage of U.S. government benefits for GIs. Enrollment included 13,799 veterans. Of that total enrollment, however, only 2,423 students were attending the undergraduate school, Columbia College.

At the start of an API seminar, its members usually arrived on a Sunday by taxi or subway after first debarking at railway stations or airports. Few were the seminar members not impressed by their first glimpse of Columbia.

Then within hours they found themselves at the great oval table in the API conference room. As seminar members they were accorded the same privileges as full-time students, from the university medical facilities to use of the library and swimming pool. Not that many had time or need for such facilities. Nevertheless, it was all heady stuff.

But not perfect. Often, arriving members had been forewarned by previous seminar members about the housing, either at John Jay Hall, the newest of the Columbia dormitories, or, later, at the King's Crown Hotel. Warned or not, they were in for a jolt.

Appropriate housing for adult seminar members was a facility that Columbia could not provide. The API staff patiently fielded a stream of housing complaints from seminar members. Most of them, fortunately, were good natured.

From the opening 1946-47 through 1958-59, seminar members were assigned individual rooms on the 13th floor of John Jay Hall. Cubicle would be a better word to describe the accommodations. Each of the rooms reserved for API—25 in the beginning— contained a cot-like bed, a chair, a washbasin, a mirror, a table, and one window.

Down the hall were common showers and toilets. A pay telephone was in the same area. Members made their own beds.

Older seminar members in particular objected to the lack of private toilets, showers and telephone. The one elevator was crowded. Often there were long waits to get on. Worse, the elevator was out of service fairly frequently, meaning a 13-story climb.

No newspaperwomen attended API until the Librarians Seminar, a one-week program, December 6-10, 1948, when four were in the membership of 12. They were Clarissa Deming of the Waterbury Republican and American, Betty Louise Hale of the Brooklyn Eagle; Dorothy C. Gibson of the Afro-American Newspapers, Baltimore, and Kathryn E. Kelly of the Miami Herald.

They were housed in Johnson Hall, a dormitory for women at 411 West 116th Street, between Amsterdam and Morningside avenues. Women members were so few for many years that the annual API bulletin did not mention housing for women until the 1954-55 issue. This despite the 1946 outcry by several New York City newspaperwomen that API was "segregationist."

Thirteen women—there were no male members—attended the Women's Pages Seminar, June 6-17, 1949, the first of its kind. At that time, newspaperwomen were assigned to the women's news department. On some papers, it was called the society department.

So Johnson Hall was seldom called upon to house women

seminar members. In 1956-57, API's 11th year, the bulletin listed all 1,578 persons who had attended API's 67 seminars up to that time. Only 39 of the 1,578 were women, or more accurately, 38, because Rebecca Gross of the Lock Haven (Pennsylvania) Express attended twice—Publishers and Editors in 1949, and Management and Costs in 1952.

If seminar members disliked John Jay dormitory, Columbia students had their own complaint. It surfaced in a March 13, 1957, editorial in the Spectator, the student newspaper. It began:

"The American Press Institute has always been a mystery organization in our minds, in spite of the many signs that we've seen pinned to the walls, proclaiming its being. We wondered why this ghostly group was usurping John Jay Hall space that is sorely needed by Columbia College men."

The editorial quoted from the API bulletin the description about existing "solely for newspapers and is supported solely by them."

"Why was it necessary," the editorial continued, "for successful newspaper men—high-salaried publishers and editors—to inhabit 27 admittedly ascetic dormitory rooms (API had expanded from the earlier 25 rooms) for eight two-week periods out of the year when a long list of College freshmen would give one eye-tooth for a room in the dorms?"

The editorial noted that lack of dorm space forced many undergraduates to live in off-campus hotels and apartments in the area. It concluded:

"Yet Columbia College was founded in 1754 while the American Press Institute is now celebrating its tenth anniversary. We think this fact entitles us to a little more consideration than the 'Sorry, no rooms' that we've heard down at 125 Livingston (the housing office) for these four years."

Starting in 1959-60, men and women were housed in the Columbia-owned King's Crown Hotel at 420 West 116th Street, across from Johnson Hall east of Amsterdam Avenue. The bulletin announced that "seminar members will occupy rooms with private baths, telephones, and air-conditioning as needed..."

The King's Crown Hotel, used mainly by visitors to the university, had been plagued by a low-occupancy rate. That was not surprising considering the size of its rooms and sorry condition of its plumbing and heating and cooling. When the API bulletin mentioned "air-conditioning as needed" it should have said "when working."

The King's Crown wanted the API housing business. API had heard the John Jay complaints for years, including those from graduate students also housed on the 13th floor. The graduate students sometimes reported noisy parties held by seminar members.

The King's Crown had a resident manager. The thinking was that party noise could there be kept under control. Over the years, the API staff searched for other, modest-cost housing for seminar members close to Columbia. None could be found. The room rate at the King's Crown surely met the low-cost criteria. For years, the single-room rate was $16 a day. API absorbed that payment as part of the fee paid by seminar members.

When API's housing was switched to the King's Crown, Walter Everett remembered, the API staff touted the change to seminar members as a major improvement. The enthusiasm was short-lived. New problems replaced old ones. At John Jay Hall, especially in the early years, many seminar members regarded the return to dormitory life as a lark. At the King's Crown they compared the hotel unfavorably with others—any others—at which they had stayed.

The nine-story King's Crown was solid in its steel structure but little else. It was finally gutted in the 1970s. Its steel skeleton provided a framework for new apartments for married graduate students. Hearing of the reconstruction, seminar members who had stayed there commented that it had always seemed gutted to them.

Rooms at the King's Crown were shockingly small. Wayne Sargent of UPI once stayed in a room where the door wouldn't open all the way; it hit the bed. "You went in," Sargent recalled, "and then dragged your suitcase after you; or shoved it ahead." One wisecrack about the hotel: "The rooms are so small the mice are stunted."

The single rooms occupied by seminar members contained a narrow bed and a bureau, with barely space to walk between, and a small chair. When bureau drawers were opened, they touched the bed. Bathrooms were equally cramped. Faucets and commode tanks leaked more often than not. Bathtubs lacked drain stoppers.

In winter, the wind rattled the loosely-fitted windows, and icy air flowed over inadequate, clanking radiators. Members complained that they shivered in winter and sweltered in summer.

Walls were paper thin. Woe to members who tried to sleep while someone snored or roistered beyond the wall. Then there was the elevator, ancient, balky and slow. Members on the first three or four floors often chose the stairs.

Between 1959 and 1972-73 the King's Crown Hotel became a legend at hundreds of newspapers. In API's final year at Columbia, members were housed at Nicholas Murray Butler Hall, an apartment building at 400 West 119th Street. With the reconstruction of the King's Crown under way and API committed to move to Reston, the Butler Hall arrangement was stopgap but comfortable.

For nearly two decades, journalism included a proud fraternity of those who had survived two weeks at the King's Crown. At any newspaper meeting, mention of the King's Crown set off laughter and a stream of anecdotes. Through it all, the API staff doggedly forwarded complaints to the resident manager, usually to no avail.

Most of the time, seminar members combined their growls with good cheer. They belonged to the Order of the King's Crown. For the most part, they were willing to evaluate the total picture—the stimulating seminars, the camaraderie with other journalists, the hospitality such as dinners at the New York Times, lunch at the Associated Press or a reception at United Press International on the 37th floor of the New York Daily News building.

After all, most members spent little time in John Jay Hall or the King's Crown, although at times, as on a snowy evening, an incredible number of seminar members would shoehorn into a member's room for a bull session. For several years, there was a tiny bar on the King's Crown mezzanine. It thrived when seminars were in session.

Before dinner, cocktails were served in API's private dining room, paneled and elegant, on the mezzanine of John Jay Hall. Lunch also was served there. From the outset, anecdotes flowed from the evening cocktail hour.

At first, only martinis and Manhattans were served before dinner. Floyd Taylor, fussy about mixing his own dry martinis, specified formulas and brands. Drinks were passed on a large silver tray by a waitress in a black uniform and white apron with an excellent memory. As she approached each seminar member, she would rotate the tray so that his or her favorite drink was closest at hand.

This gracious routine changed later because seminar members wanted full bar service. A portable bar was set up in the dining room and fully stocked. It was manned by Columbia students who supposedly had attended bartender's school but who in some cases appeared to be learning on the job.

Mike Ogden of the Providence Journal attended a seminar at which the bartender was unusually slow. He would select a bottle, unscrew the top, pour out a measured ounce, screw the cap back, put the bottle in its place and slowly add mixer and ice.

Ogden, waiting in line, finally could not stand the delay.

"Son," he called out to the student bartender, "it really doesn't evaporate that fast."

Although seminar members usually pursued an intensive work schedule Monday through Friday, they still found time to absorb the atmosphere of Columbia University and Morningside Heights.

After breakfast in the student cafeteria, they usually read the student newspaper, which rarely lacked coverage of controversy. During the lunch break they often listened to one of the frequent student protests—protests came in all sizes—on the Low Library steps or College Walk, which was 116th Street between Broadway and Amsterdam. They browsed in the university bookstore, which had an entrance from the Journalism Building lobby, and bought Columbia sweatshirts and other mementos.

After the 30-minute cocktail period followed by dinner served at 6:30 p.m., the usual pattern for seminar members, especially those new to New York, was to make a foray or two to midtown. Finally, they began to explore Broadway, not the Broadway of midtown but the Broadway of Morningside Heights, between 110th and 116th streets.

It was an almost self-contained neighborhood, much as it is today. On the north it was anchored by the West End, a bar and grill and a favorite student hangout. On the south fringe was the Gold Rail, a dark pub.

In between were small shops, services and eating places. There was a shoeshine stand, a Chinese laundry, two branch banks, an open-front fruit market, a pharmacy, a drycleaner, a grill that specialized in blue-cheeseburgers, a barber and beauty shop, a second-hand book store and a family-owned chocolate shop widely regarded as one of the world's best.

In the middle of Broadway was a pedestrian mall. There, in good weather, the elderly would sun themselves. The IRT subway tunnel ran below the mall, and its sounds and smells came up through the grating.

At the West End or the Gold Rail or countless other watering holes, the newspaper talk continued, often far into the night. Away from deadlines, seminar members had time to reflect. They and their newspapers were challenged—at the polished oval table, in the scarred booths of the West End, or in a jammed dormitory or hotel room.

Sevellon Brown, the founder, wanted a forum for the exchange of ideas. On Morningside Heights, though probably not always in the manner envisioned, he had it.

8

The Table of Sharing

ach weekday for three weeks, the 26 members of API's first seminar—the one for Managing Editors and News Editors in 1946— gathered at the conference table from 9 a.m. to noon and from 2 to 5 p.m. Some sessions ran overtime. When not listening to one of the 38 guest experts at the formal sessions, they had discussed newspapering almost non-stop among themselves.

Now on Friday afternoon, October 18, 1946, after 14 1/2 working days, it was time to look back, time to restudy the trail they had blazed.

What had they learned? Were they returning home better able to improve their newspapers? If they had the three weeks (with Saturdays and Sundays free) to use over again, what would they do differently? Above all, was the infant API equal to the great hopes its founders had held for it? Or was the experiment doomed? Floyd Taylor and Claude Jagger, the associate director, wanted answers. Five more seminars lay ahead in that first year, 1946-47. A two-week seminar for Picture Editors would begin in just 10 days. How could they improve the format? How could they better brief the guest experts? Their questions were many.

Sevellon Brown had come in from Providence and Carl Ackerman down from upstairs. Robert U. Brown, editor of Editor & Publisher, had come, too, to continue his magazine's coverage of the infant API. The understanding was that Brown would not quote anyone by name without explicit permission, so that members could feel uninhibited.

James A. Pope, managing editor of the Louisville Courier-Journal, moderator for the final week, stayed over. That night, Sevellon Brown would hold a valedictory dinner, the last hurrah before members trudged home.

Later, in the magazine Journalism Quarterly, one seminar member, William S. Kirkpatrick, managing editor of the Atlanta Journal, wrote, "The critique session at the close of the first seminar resembled an old-fashioned religious experience meeting. Enthusiasm ran high."

Seminar members loosed not only a flurry of constructive criticisms but also their enthusiastic, unanimous approval of API. The verdict from the jury of seasoned editors, not given to unearned praise, was in.

The members said they would make long reports to their publishers. A majority said they would send further thoughts to API after reflecting on their experience. Nearly all members had taken extensive notes. One editor had typed notes of 65 pages, another had 57 pages.

Members agreed that they had profited as much by the associations with each other outside the seminar room as they had in the organized discussion. All reported that they were taking home many ideas for improving their newspapers. One editor had already sent home instructions for reporters to write briefer leads.

A few wondered if they could sell their publishers on the ideas gained. Others said their publishers had shown faith in sending them to the first API seminar and saw no problem in having new ideas accepted.

Two editors said the seminar was so successful that attempts would be made to emulate it elsewhere. Ackerman later closed the seminar with a warning against rapid duplication of the API idea around the country. He cited the growth of journalism schools with many small and inadequate institutions turning out "superficial products."

But the format would soon be copied in various sizes. As early as April 1948, a regional seminar modeled after API was conducted on two successive weekends at the University of Nebraska School of Journalism.

The idea had been planted by two returning API seminar members, Hugh A. Fogarty, city editor of the Omaha World-Herald, and H. Clay Tate, editor of the Bloomington (Illinois) Pantagraph.

On that Friday in 1946, the seminar members were weary. They discussed whether three weeks was too long. Two editors said the seminar should have been even longer. The members approved the three-week span by a three-to-two margin.

Opinion was divided on a suggestion that experts should hold forth in the mornings and the afternoons should be left open for further discussion of the day's topic among the members.

Taylor had asked for critical guidance, and he got it. Members agreed that some sessions had wandered from the assigned topic, and some guest experts had arrived unprepared. Too many sessions were crowded with two or three experts when one would have sufficed.

No seminar programs were printed—at least none was preserved in API files—on that first seminar. A printed program was a nicety for which Taylor and Jagger could not spare time while preparing the first seminars. Chances are that a mimeographed program was cranked out at the last minute, a session-by-session guide for seminar members.

The first printed program, apparently, was for the Picture Editors Seminar, the next in line, October 28-November 8. Although announced earlier under the title Picture Editors, the printed program, in recognition of the varied backgrounds of the members, called it the Seminar for Editors Responsible for Picture Production.

The City Editors Seminar, held next, had a general topic for each of the three weeks and a guest discussion leader for the second and third weeks. Later, the term "discussion leader" was used to describe the guest expert, and an API staff member moderated all sessions. But at the very beginning "discussion leader" was used to describe the moderator.

This arrangement reflected the time squeeze in which Taylor and Jagger found themselves. With a seminar in session, they sometimes desperately needed time to prepare future programs. So they hit upon the device of a guest discussion leader.

The first City Editors Seminar illustrated the weakness of having a guest discussion leader—that is, moderator—for portions of the program. Taylor moderated the first week, then frequently retreated to his office to handle other urgent matters. Fred Gaertner Jr., managing editor of the Detroit News, was discussion leader for the second week and William P. Steven for the third week. Steven was managing editor of the Minneapolis Tribune.

Gaertner and Steven brought additional newspaper skills to the assemblage. Not having been present at earlier sessions, they were hard pressed to avoid duplicating particulars discussed before they arrived.

Often, when a guest expert touched on an area covered earlier, a seminar member would sing out, "Hey, we covered that last week." So the use of a guest moderator, by whatever title, was scrapped as soon as staff workload permitted.

At the end of the first seminar, the discussion leaders (moderators) were criticized by seminar members not only for permitting the group to stray from the subject but also for failing to induce the few reticent members to speak up when they had something to contribute.

Taylor regarded member participation as essential. Guest speakers were told to expect frequent comments, even challenges. It took a nimble moderator to give both the guest experts and seminar members time to present their views.

These words on the matter of member input, probably written by Taylor, appeared in the 1946-47 API bulletin: "It may develop that on specific aspects of some of the problems discussed certain of the men attending seminars will have more knowledge than the experts who are brought in to talk and to answer questions. In such cases the men attending will be expected to share their knowledge for the benefit of fellow members of the seminar."

It was Taylor's conviction, which still controls, that API should not impose any views on members. After the first City Editors Seminar, a member described how the Taylor conviction on non-imposing worked:

"This is the way education ought to be. When I went to college, my professor told me what I ought to think and what I ought to do. I got the idea there was only one way that was right. This Press Institute method is better. You hear all sides, but nobody tells you what you ought to think. You make up your mind for yourself."

During the critique of the first seminar, for Managing Editors and News Editors, one editor suggested that after the first week, when members would be acquainted with one another, the discussion leader (read that as moderator) should be chosen from and by the members. That suggestion was voted down.

Opinion was divided on the relative value of abstract and concrete topics. One group wanted more discussion on the practical aspects of newspapering. The other group supported discussions on specialized topics like religious, educational and scientific news.

Members agreed that there should be a critical analysis of each newspaper represented. They also thought that they, as managing editors and news editors, could have benefitted by hearing from city editors and reporters on their impressions of managing editors.

Taylor and Jagger received more solid suggestions than they could quickly work into the format. But they also received high praise for what they had already accomplished. The quotes in Robert U. Brown's Editor & Publisher report included:

"The greatest thing in my experience—wish we could have a man here at every seminar."

"We learned from the experts, and we learned from ourselves. I want more of everything."

"Nothing comparable to it."

"It is going to be the greatest thing in American journalism."

Upon return to their newspapers, seminar members became

missionaries for API. Thus the membership of early years showed a strong tendency toward additional nominations by those same original newspaper participants. The 1949-50 bulletin noted that in the institute's first three years the following newspapers had sent five of more men to seminars:

San Francisco Chronicle
Miami Herald
Courier-Journal and Louisville
   Times
New York Times
Indianapolis Star
Dallas Morning News
Los Angeles Times
Evening Star (Washington)
Dayton Daily News and
   Dayton Journal-Herald
Daily Oklahoman and
   Oklahoma City Times
Cleveland Press

Worcester Telegram and
   Evening Gazette
Providence Journal and
   Evening Bulletin
Denver Post
Pittsburgh Post-Gazette
Oregon Journal
Chester (Pennsylvania) Times
Herald-News (Passaic, New
   Jersey)
Waterbury Republican and
   American
Evening Bulletin (Philadelphia)
Washington Post

Those 21 newspaper companies had sent more than 100 of the 384 newspaper men and women who attended the 18 seminars held in API's first three years. The seminar membership base needed broadening. Taylor used the 1949-50 bulletin as one broadening tool.

"While almost all of the papers listed above are large," the bulletin said, "the Institute is designed as much for newspapers printing a few thousand copies a day as it is for the great metropolitan papers. Some seminars are limited to men from small cities. Representatives of papers that cannot send more than one man to the Institute every few years are just as welcome as those from papers of high circulation.

"Men from papers not represented at the Institute in the past are just as eligible to attend its seminars as those from papers among the original sponsors. The same is true of men from papers not interested in making financial contributions. The Institute was founded to contribute to the improvement of all American newspapers."

In retrospect, those words were flawed in two respects. First, the repetition of "men" may have discouraged nominations of newspaper women, though that certainly was not the intention. Second, "American" may have been seen as less than a warm invitation to Canadian newspapers, again not the intention.

The first two Canadian seminar members came from the Globe

and Mail in Toronto, Duncan McNab Halliday at Picture Editors in 1946-47 and David A. Rhydwen at Librarians in 1948-49. After that, no more Canadians appeared until 1953-54, when four attended. Of the 1,578 members in the first 10 years, 29 were from Canadian papers.

An API survey in the late 1970s showed that over time some seven percent of all members were from Canada. That is roughly proportional to the ratio of newspapers and their staff members in the United States and Canada. Still, the fact that American Press Institute meant both the United States and Canada deserved better articulation during API's infancy.

A key figure in bringing Canadians to API was John E. Motz, publisher and editor of the Kitchener-Waterloo Record in Ontario. Motz attended the Publishers and Editors Seminar in 1954. He praised API to other publishers, and Canadian nominations began to flow. In 1959, API named the first Canadian to its Advisory Board. Motz was the man, and he served until his death in 1975, when he was succeeded by J. Patrick O'Callaghan, publisher of the Edmonton Journal.

Word of the infant API was slowly spread by means other than enthusiasm from seminar members returning home. A 1947 speech by James A. Pope of the Louisville Courier-Journal to a meeting of the American Association of Schools and Departments of Journalism, printed by Journalism Quarterly, was one example.

"The record of the press as a whole in training young people for the difficult and complex job of being good journalists is appalling," Pope declared. "Taking newspaper work as a profession (which it still isn't), the score is practically zero."

Only a few papers, he said, had any standards of employment or training. "A city editor will throw a piece of copy back at a reporter, or a slot man at a head writer, and that is the sum of it in hundreds of city rooms. Too often, the editor does not know just what he wants, or why. He cannot explain to the confused youngster what was wrong, what is right.

"A historic step to improve this situation has been made by the opening of the American Press Institute at Columbia University. There, if my experience as discussion leader at the Managing Editors Seminar was typical, editors who have fallen into provincial ruts will be shaken out of their lethargy and smugness. They will learn some of the things they were never taught as they came along the office route toward a key job. And they can in turn improve their newspapers by effectively polishing up the training you have begun."

Taylor and Jagger both took to the stump when their heavy workload permitted. Taylor, for example, made early speeches to meetings of the Pennsylvania Newspaper Publishers Association and the Georgia Press Institute.

While seminar members expanded their knowledge, the API staff modified seminar formats, procedures and subject matter. The process has never ended, even after almost 50 years. But, in his five years as API's first director, Taylor established a framework that largely endured.

The second seminar, the two-weeker for Picture Editors, illustrated the need for flexibility on membership size. The founders had stated that membership would be limited to 25. The successful opening seminar, however, brought a wave of last-minute nominations.

Taylor relaxed the limitation and admitted 27 members. They numbered 14 picture editors, one associate publisher, one general manager, four managing editors, three city editors and four heads of the photographic department.

There was no time—remember that the Picture Editors Seminar trailed the first program by only 10 days—to cut back on the number of guest experts, as the managing editors had suggested. More than 40 experts, invited well in advance, were brought in.

If scheduling 40 experts provided a problem in avoiding redundant discussion, members of the Picture Editors Seminar had no complaint on that score. Member complaints were mainly twofold. Aware that the Managing Editors and News Editors Seminar lasted three weeks, they wanted more time than the two weeks allotted them. And they despaired of ever doing away with cliche pictures like "Mayor Greets So-and-So" until managing editors began supporting innovation and creativity.

That was perhaps the first instance at API where philosophical conflicts on newspaper staffs became evident. Thousands would follow. In the off-the-record comfort of the conference room, members let their hair down. Solutions—or at least a better understanding of how a newspaper looks different from different positions—often resulted.

The Picture Editors Seminar also provided an early example of ingenuity. One member suggested how stilted city hall reception pictures could be avoided: Send two photographers; one would aim a dummy camera at the usual grouping and satisfy their egos, the other would snap an informal picture when the group relaxed.

API's third seminar, the three-week City Editors Seminar, December 2-20, 1946, was auspicious for several reasons. By then, Taylor and Jagger had introduced a few changes.

From the outset, API examined members of each seminar for possible future discussion leaders, those vital individuals who at first were called guest experts. No matter how thorough the planning for a seminar, success or failure rested largely with discussion leaders—their expertise, their preparation, and their manner of presentation.

Taylor and Jagger not only scrutinized seminar memberships for potential discussion leaders but they also asked seminar members to suggest persons from their own newspapers or anywhere else whom they thought could make a beneficial presentation.

Over the years, some of the most widely known persons in newspapering failed as discussion leaders, usually because they did not understand the intensive preparation needed and disregarded repeated advance warnings by API.

Big-name journalists sometimes mistakenly thought they could wing it—that is, carry the day on their name or experience. Seminar members sometimes asked why one or another famous journalist had not been invited. The answer often was that he (or she) had already been a discussion leader—and had fallen on his unprepared face.

Neil MacNeil, an assistant managing editor of the New York Times, attended the first seminar. He impressed Taylor and Jagger, and they brought him to the first City Editors Seminar as a guest expert—discussion leader. His topic: Press agents in relation to the city desk. He spoke, as the printed program described it, "on the efforts of press agents to influence the content of newspapers through city desks."

Fred Gaertner Jr., managing editor of the Detroit News, attended the first seminar. For the City Editors Seminar, he served as discussion leader for the second week—which is to say moderator—when the week's general topic was: "Responsibilities of city editors in handling specialized news."

Thus, with each seminar, API's ability to identify capable discussion leaders expanded. Sometimes misjudgments were made. Every API staff moderator had painful memories of members who displayed great potential during seminar discussion (or non-members who were highly recommended) only to fail miserably as discussion leaders.

An individual who spoke articulately as a seminar member was sometimes daunted under the burden placed on a discussion leader. And daunting resulted in bumbling.

The opening day of the City Editors Seminar in 1946 was historic in that it brought to API as a co-discussion leader J. Montgomery (Monty) Curtis. He was destined to serve 20 years at API, 16 of them as director or executive director—the same job with a modified title. For a generation of newspaper men and women, Curtis would become widely known as "Mister API."

One of the 26 seminar members was Walter Everett, city editor of the Providence Evening Bulletin, who would return to API three years later as an associate director, move up to managing director as deputy to Monty Curtis, succeed Curtis as executive director, guide API in its move from Columbia to its own building in Reston, Virginia, and serve API for 26 years, more than any other person.

On the opening morning of the City Editors Seminar, Ackerman and Taylor used the first hour to brief seminar members on procedures. Not until 1955 did a seminar printed program list a Sunday evening cocktail hour, dinner and briefing as part of the program. That innovation enabled a 9 a.m. start on Monday to begin discussing newspapering techniques.

In 1955 and after, the Sunday briefings were in API's private dining room at John Jay Hall. Before that, though, Sunday night dinners, apparently with little or no briefing, were held at the Faculty Club on Morningside Drive, a block from the main campus.

After the Ackerman-Taylor Monday briefing of the city editors, a five-hour session (with a lunch break) on organization and operation of a city desk began with Curtis, city editor of the Buffalo Evening News, and Charles H. Hamilton, city editor of the Richmond News Leader, as co-guest experts.

Their presence illustrated the manner in which Taylor and Jagger searched for guest experts. Using his Associated Press background, Jagger had received a recommendation of Curtis from Wes Gallagher, who had been AP's bureau chief in Buffalo from 1937 to 1939. Gallagher, back from war correspondent service in Africa and Europe, would later become AP's president.

In similar fashion, Hamilton had been recommended by Frank Fuller, AP's bureau chief in Richmond. Hamilton was later invited to join the API staff. After long consideration, he decided to stay in Richmond, where he later served 20 years as managing editor.

During his time of decision, he visited Columbia and found the newly arrived associate director of API, Curtis, living comfortably in a Columbia-owned apartment with three bathrooms.

"You'll find up here," Curtis told Hamilton with his usual joviality, "that prestige depends on how many bathrooms you have. One you're nothing; two maybe middle class. Happens I've got three—more than I need really." Perhaps it was the Curtis happiness that caused Hamilton in 1988, when he was in his mid-80s and consulting to Richmond Newspapers, to still wonder if he had made the right career choice.

The City Editors Seminar program was apparently the first to include what came to be known as clinic groups, a staple for almost all subsequent programs. For certain half-days, the membership was divided into four or more smaller groups, largely on circulation size or other similarities.

A chairman was appointed for each clinic group. At Columbia, each group gathered around its own table, two at opposite ends of the large conference room and two in the adjacent writing room, space filled mainly with typewriters at desks where members transcribed handwritten notes.

Under the procedure that evolved, members of each clinic group exchanged designated issues of their newspapers starting six weeks before the seminar. In advance, they critiqued other papers in the group, noting strengths and weaknesses. Their reports were made in clinic group meetings. Lively, sometimes heated discussion resulted.

In the clinic groups, any members who may have been reticent at the large conference table usually pitched eagerly into discussion at the smaller table. The format gave them little choice. From API, each member received clear and repeated instructions to come prepared to contribute in the clinic groups. Usually, no matter how busy putting out their own papers, members responded admirably.

But there were occasional exceptions. Then the wrath and scorn of peers struck the miscreants. Often, those who arrived ill-prepared toted clinic group papers to their rooms and burned the midnight oil to recoup their status in later group meetings.

At the close of the first City Editors Seminar, December 20, 1946, Taylor and Jagger must have had a harried Christmas. One month later, they were to begin API's longest seminar ever, a four-week Editorial Writers Seminar.

When the six first-year API seminars were announced in mid-1946, the synopsis for the Editorial Writers Seminar said: "In this seminar a week will be devoted to material on methods of editorial writing and three weeks to American foreign affairs, with emphasis on the relations of the United States and Russia." It listed several aspects of Russian relations such as Russia's stance in various regions, strategic considerations in relations with Russia, Russia and the American Communist Party, etc.

In the July 29, 1946, issue of the New York Journal-American, an editorial by E. F. Tompkins quoted part of the seminar synopsis and said:

"The apparent patter is 'party line' emphasis; the synopsis might be presented equally well by any of the Communist Party training schools...We doubt, therefore, if four weeks in a barracks at Columbia University under conditions of confinement resembling a concentration camp, with three weeks of 'instruction' on Soviet Russia, will give us anything new or enlightening."

Editor & Publisher magazine fired back in defense of API in its August 3, 1946 issue:

"The writer of that editorial did not know that the emphasis on Russia in that seminar was requested by the dozen important newspaper editors and managing editors who convened in New York several months ago to organize the Institute...It was further stipulated by the group that all seminars at Columbia should be discussion sessions and not instruction periods.

"Anyone who takes the time to look at the list of directors, advisory committee and founders of the American Press Institute can see for himself there is no possible danger of a 'party line' connection. That list of names reads like a 'Who's Who' of the top ranking American journalists, and there isn't one against whom the charge of 'Red' would stand up or who would tolerate such a connection in an enterprise such as the Institute to which they have given generously of their time and money.

"The American Press Institute was organized 'to contribute to the improvement of American newspapers by giving opportunity to experienced newspaper men and women of all categories to study and discuss at Columbia University the techniques of their work and the social, economic and political problems of the day.' It promises to do exactly that."

The flap was short-lived, and 26 editorial writers from across the U.S. enjoyed—and endured—the four-week seminar. One of the myriad speakers, Sir John Balfour, British minister to the United States, remarked upon the number of accents he had heard phrasing questions and said that at no other time had he had such an opportunity to talk to the whole United States as at the seminar.

George W. Potter, chief editorial writer of the Providence Journal, wrote: "...we had a Harvard Classics of modern events pumped into us endlessly.

"We lived in a monastic brotherhood, in small rooms close to one another. It seems to me that seldom has there been such a meeting of minds to concentrate upon the terrible and terrifying problems that confront the world today.

"Even in the 5-10-cent stud poker game we played nightly, the dealer, as he was laying down the cards, would say: 'I think Viner's theory of the use of the withholding tax in depression is not sound,' and that would set off a discussion as the cards were being played and as there was a raise you could hear between the poker terms the language of the discussion we had at the conference.

"...One of the best points of the seminar was the nightly meetings when the members explored one another's minds and found the sensitive differences that set one region off from the other.

"...And there was but one purpose. That is, that the information and knowledge gathered would be poured back into you, the reader, the person who pays a few pennies for this paper, that out of their tremendous effort you would be able to form a sounder judgment of affairs and make this mighty system of democracy work."

Another editorial writer who recorded some of his seminar experience was Leslie Moore of the Worcester Telegram and Gazette. In the Masthead, publication of the National Conference of Editorial Writers (like several other newspaper organizations, formed as a result of an API seminar), Moore wrote that Floyd Taylor was quick to acknowledge the experimental nature of API at that point (its fourth-ever seminar). Then Moore continued:

"Thank God it was experimental, too, else the 20 or so editorial writers who landed at Columbia that January, a bit skeptical but in good hope, would almost surely have been let off with a two-week deal. As it was, these guys came together—a small group but undoubtedly the largest assemblage of editorial writers as such in one spot in world history up to that moment—for four solid weeks of material that any journalism dean could easily have spread over a two-year curriculum, with plenty to spare for an evening class in continuing education.

"Most of us, indeed, had never come face to face with more than a half dozen other editorial writers before in our lives. Small wonder we were curious as we groped along the breakfast line after finding the dining hall that first cold morning."

The four-week Editorial Writers Seminar was followed by two three-week programs that wrapped up the 1946-47 maiden year. They were Reporters of Municipal Affairs, and General Reporters. Membership in the six seminars totaled 151, slightly more than 25 members per seminar.

Taylor had known all along that Jagger's 11-month leave of absence from the Associated Press would expire at the end of May and that he would have to recruit a replacement. But an announcement by the Hawaiian Economic Foundation, which Jagger joined as its first president, said that Jagger resigned from API on February 28, 1947. Nevertheless, Jagger apparently stayed on at API until May 1, when his resignation from both API and the AP was made known in New York. Jagger's successor would turn out to be Monty Curtis.

How soon Taylor, or Ackerman, Sevellon Brown or the Advisory Board planned to seek a replacement for Jagger could not be determined. One record says that the decision to hire Curtis was made August 4, 1947. But an announcement by Ackerman to the same effect did not come until a month later.

In either case, except for the two secretaries, Taylor apparently labored alone for several weeks through the summer of 1947.

API held only six domestic seminars a year for seven years, through 1952-53, although it began adding an annual foreign seminar in 1948-49 with a program for German publishers and editors under a grant from the Rockefeller Foundation. After that there was a seminar for Japanese newspapermen, representing another country defeated in World War II and trying to establish a free and effective press.

For domestic seminars, the annual total did not equal the first year's 151 members again until 1952-53, when 158 attended. After that year, API slowly increased the number of annual seminars.

In 1947-48, the second year and the first with Taylor and Curtis as the executive staff, the total slumped to 127, and the year after that to 106, the all-time low.

Strangely, the 1948-49 API bulletin announced enrollment limits for each of the year's seminars. The maximum for three seminars was 27, the number accommodated in the Picture Editors Seminar of 1946. But with API certainly wanting to build member totals these low maximums were set for three other seminars were: Pictures, 18; Librarians, 18; and Women's Pages 20.

The reason for these limitations cannot be ascertained 40 years later. Walter Everett, who joined the API staff in 1949, was mystified when the limitations were brought to his attention. In any event, the limitations totaled 137, and actual membership for the year was 106, the nadir.

Through the first two years, the two-man API executive staff was overwhelmed by a work load of seminars, introducing new ones, and making missionary speeches and trips designed to coax additional newspapers to use API's services.

Help came in January 1949 with the hiring of Jack B. Thompson, chief editorial writer of the Chester (Pennsylvania) Times, to plan and conduct the three-week seminar for Publishers and Editors of Small Dailies, January 10-28, 1949.

This was a new seminar, modeled after the two seminars for managing editors and news editors of large papers. Membership was limited to executives from papers of less than 30,000 circulation. Publishers were included in the title because on small papers publishers often had day-to-day newsroom responsibilities.

Thompson had attended the four-week Editorial Writers Seminar in January 1947. He accepted the API one-time moderating assignment by taking a leave of absence from the Chester Times.

Although API was announced as a two-year experiment, no one suggested on its second anniversary that it be dismantled. Taylor wrote an "Appraisal of API," a full-page piece that was carried in

Editor & Publisher on August 7, 1948. He wrote:

"...The outstanding fact in the Institute's favor is that so many newspapers have made use of ideas developed at its seminars...When strong and well edited newspapers in all sections of the United States find the Institute so useful, there no longer seems to be any reason to regard its programs as experiments.

"Perhaps the strongest evidence in this respect is the constant use made of the Institute by strong newspapers on the Pacific Coast, despite the cost and travel time involved in sending men to a city as far distant as New York.

"Since the average age of men who attend seminars is above 40 and the average newspaper experience is more than 20 years, almost every seminar member makes a material contribution to the round table talks that follow the opening remarks of discussion leaders.

"Anyone who attempted to assign credit to individuals for what has been accomplished in the seminars would find that he had hundreds of names to consider. Most of them would be names of newspaper men but the Institute also has had cooperation, on a generous scale, from other sources...University professors, for example, have commented in many instances that they greatly enjoyed appearing at seminars to lead discussions.

"The ideas of most obvious utility developed in seminars are those that can be put to immediate use. In some instances, publishers have declared that the value of single ideas obtained by men has been sufficient justification for sending them to Columbia, regardless of any other benefits received.

"There has been, in addition, another reaction which was a surprise to some of those who took part in the original planning of the seminar programs. This has been the inspiration created in the minds of scores of newspapermen by what they have heard during seminars.

"There has never been any deliberate intention to make seminars inspirational. Both in planning programs and in conducting them, the aim has been to relate all discussions as closely as possible to the day-to-day problems of publishing newspapers. The inspiration has been produced indirectly and as a byproduct of practical efforts.

"No institution, of course, is perfect. There have been weak points in each seminar—but fewer and fewer as time has gone on and as the Institute staff has gained more experience in planning and conducting seminars. Undoubtedly there always will be weak points of planning—one of the worst in the early days was in putting so much material in the program that seminar members could not absorb it all—but there is enough knowledge now of what makes a useful program so that there should not be many serious errors...

"One (argument) that has continued since the Institute started is on the length of seminars. The majority of seminar members, as well as most of the publishers who send them to the Institute, believe that three weeks is the best length for most seminars, but it will be advisable in the future to conduct an occasional seminar of a week or two for those who have a strong preference for extremely condensed sessions.

"The only serious weakness of the Institute is lack of an endowment. In the first two years, taken together, it was possible to avoid an operating loss. This was accomplished by charging a high fee ($180 a week a man), by using a small and heavily burdened staff to plan and conduct seminars, by refusing to spend money for ventures that seemed highly desirable (such as publication of some of the material developed at the Institute) and by free use of university facilities.

"If the Institute were generously endowed, the fees could be cut to a minimum, especially to make possible more participation by small dailies and weeklies. In addition, the staff could be increased by at least one man, making possible a sounder and more useful operation, and the best of the material developed in the seminars could be published for the benefit of all newspapers participating.

"The fruitful use that could be made of an endowment is apparent—so apparent that many supporters of the Institute believe it almost inevitable that one will be given eventually.

"The possibilities for the use of the Institute to contribute to the improvement of the American press is great. The importance of the press to the survival and improvement of America's democratic culture is obvious. Under these circumstances, the Institute's lack of an endowment offers a superb opportunity to prosperous men who believe in sound newspapers and recognize their essential function in a democratic society."

Taylor's appraisal was eloquent. An abortive effort to raise an endowment had indeed already been made, and in time the idea of publishing certain seminar materials would prove impractical and costly. Decades later an endowment would be generated, though probably not in the relative size that Taylor had in mind.

But soon to develop was the hard fact of a continuing dip in membership, to 127 in 1947-48 and to 106 in the third year, 1948-49.

Were there other reasons that seminar attendance would dwindle after the first year? Much later, Walter Everett thought the exceptional excitement of the inaugural year may have played a part. Certainly, the startup received broad and favorable coverage. But, he thought, there may also have been a mild backlash because seminar members returning to their papers tried to change too much too quickly.

Monty Curtis frequently told the story, perhaps hyperbolic, about an editor, just back from API, who strode into his newsroom and thundered, "By God, starting right now a lot of things around here are going to change."

I. William Hill of the Washington Evening Star told of a member of the first City Editors Seminar who compiled 31 specific changes he wanted to make and negotiated 13 of them with his publisher by telephone even before the seminar ended. Hill did not relate how the city editor bypassed his managing editor, but perhaps all changes had to be approved by the publisher.

The peril of homeward-bound seminar members wanting to autocratically impose changes became apparent to the API staff. Thus, after a while, the moderator always closed the seminar by counseling that change should be made at a measured pace, and always with full explanation of why change was desirable. Such counsel was important, for sometimes even the seminar members were reluctant to consider changes—and accepted certain new techniques only after hearing all views debated at API.

The most frustrated members were the few who went home to intransigent bosses who resisted all suggestions for change, no matter how logical or meritorious.

Sevellon Brown's vision for API was limited to news and editorial training. Nevertheless, only a profitable newspaper can remain free and vigorous. So starting in 1949-50, API's fourth year, Taylor and Curtis introduced non-news/editorial seminars, programs designed to increase newspaper revenues and hold costs in line.

They began with two seminars called Management and Costs, one for newspapers under 50,000 circulation, the other for over 50,000. The programs were aimed at publishers and general managers. Until a third executive staff member was added in 1954-55 and the number of annual seminars increased, API was able to hold the non-news/editorial seminars only by cutting back on the news-side programs.

That key decision that led to the gradual infusion of seminars for all newspaper departments and specialties. For example, a Newspaper Advertising Seminar, for newspapers under 75,000 circulation, was first held in 1951-52. Classified Advertising came along in 1953-54, and Circulation and Newspaper Promotion in 1954-55, with Mechanical Production in 1955-56. The latter program soon was renamed to New Methods of Newspaper Production. Other seminar titles were also adjusted when appropriate.

Meanwhile, suggestions for other kinds of seminars had been

made. In 1947, Dwight Bentel, a journalism professor, wrote Taylor to ask that API schedule a seminar for journalism educators. A number of other journalism educators supported the idea, although Frank Luther Mott, dean of the Missouri School of Journalism opposed it. Mott was quoted as saying:

"I am not at all sure that the American Press Institute would find a discussion of college journalism training valuable, or would make any special contribution to the cause; but if such a topic is placed on the agenda, the discussion ought to center around the accreditation program."

Taylor replied that he would consider the suggestion if enough support was shown by both journalism schools and newspapers. That support did not materialize until 1980 when API did begin holding a Journalism Educators Seminar, and then it was with the enrollment incentive of free tuition. A grant to API by the John Ben Snow Memorial Trust made this possible. The seminar became one of API's most successful.

API also received a request for a seminar for weekly newspaper editors. Taylor liked the idea, but when he sent out 310 questionnaires to leading weeklies to measure interest only 11 weeklies said they would definitely nominate a member to such a seminar. Fifteen others answered that they could not take part. There were no other replies.

Lack of financial resources or inability to meet deadlines with a staff member away were probably factors in the responses. Taylor expressed disappointment and said he hoped to schedule a weeklies seminar in a future year. Later, other occasional requests for a weeklies seminar were received. They finally began in 1976 when, at its Reston building, API could hold two seminars simultaneously.

The infusion of non-news seminars had scarcely begun when Taylor, the gracious, productive leader of API's first five years, was struck by his fatal heart attack in August 1951.

A new director had to be appointed. He would face problems of financial support, seminar membership that was growing slowly, and, perhaps most troubling of all, growing tensions between API and the Graduate School of Journalism.

9

Mentor in Buffalo

During his 20 years at API, J. Montgomery Curtis was its chief executive—director or executive director—for 16 years. Few men in the newspaper world were more widely known or celebrated than Monty Curtis. He was on a first-name basis with the titans of journalism. Anyone in newspapering had only to say "Monty" for all to recognize the reference to J. Montgomery Curtis.

Newspaper people are nothing if not informal. First-name salutations are the norm. Yet, when the semi-retired Curtis wrote Alfred H. Kirchhofer in 1981, he began:

"Dear Mr. Kirchhofer:"

Then Curtis said in part: "What API has done and is doing is a direct reflection of what you taught me.

"I have a 10-page guide sheet for examining newspapers and judging success and failure. It contains 98 questions in 17 sections. I have just re-read it, and every question reflects what I learned on the Buffalo Evening News. That is only one of your contributions to API."

A year earlier, Curtis, using the formal salutation, had written to Kirchhofer:

"I continue to do what I can to help newspapers become better at their jobs. It's the old story. Some do. Some don't. All the verities you taught me hold good every day."

Who was this Curtis mentor? Before retiring in 1966 at the age of 74, Alfred H. Kirchhofer had been the guiding force of the Buffalo Evening News, first as managing editor and then editor and executive vice president, for nearly four decades. Curtis worked for him for 15 years, resigning in 1947, but the two remained close.

Their closeness shows in several letters to different persons, including one in November 1980, to Henry Z. Urban, president and publisher of the Buffalo Evening News.

"At API for 20 years," Curtis wrote, " and down here (Miami) for 14, I must have heard the best newspaper thinking available anywhere in the world. And in matters of philosophy, principles, standards, and professional techniques I have heard nothing that I did not hear first from Mr. Kirchhofer."

To begin to understand Curtis, his newspaper philosophy and his personality, it is necessary first to look at Kirchhofer.

Kirchhofer's sway of Curtis never diminished. In retirement, Kirchhofer began researching a book on the Buffalo Evening News, a book he never completed because of his wife's illness, and asked Curtis for reminiscences. Curtis replied on March 26, 1969, with a letter and six-page memo that included these words:

"At API, where I associated with more than 5,000 newspapermen, we older ones sometimes recalled the Depression. There simply was not another place like the Buffalo Evening News for sound financial operation, professional excellence, integrity of purpose and humane treatment of employees."

Kirchhofer thanked Curtis by letter. Curtis promised to send further reminiscences, remarking:

"Your letter makes me glow. You know how I have always tried to earn your approval."

Through Curtis, Kirchhofer ranks high among the great newspapermen who influenced the course of API. Under his leadership, the Buffalo Evening News became one of the country's finest newspapers, superior in community service and breadth of coverage.

In 1980, in an ASNE Bulletin profile of Kirchhofer, the longtime editorial page editor of the Evening News, Millard C. Browne, wrote that if most legends are half-truths, the Kirchhofer legend was built on at least three-quarter truths and even whole truths slightly twisted out of context.

Kirchhofer anecdotes are myriad. One never left untold is that of the visitor's straightback chair in his newsroom office on the second floor of the Evening News building at Main and Seneca streets. Kirchhofer had the chair bolted to the floor so that it could not be hitched forward.

Kirchhofer was a fastidious man, said Curtis, who witnessed the bolting, "and he did not want a couple of the newsroom characters, who were anything but fastidious, to sit near him."

Then there were the Kirchhofer blue notes, half sheets of blue paper with "Office of the Editor" printed at left top. Kirchhofer fired them off by the dozens. His secretary of many years, Frances Hurley, recalled that they were "numerous, some critical, some educational, and many thank-you notes. Sympathy notes if a staff member had a death in the family or other problem.

"He read the Wall Street Journal, New York Times, Chicago Tribune, New York Herald and New York Daily News every night," Hurley said, "and if the (Buffalo Evening) News missed an important story, next morning blue notes flew asking why."

Kirchhofer's blue notes to his staff were crisp and to the point. Many contained a phrase or sentence that provided either a journalistic lesson or a call to higher professional purpose. Some Evening News staffers thought the blue-note barrage was "sort of chicken stuff," said Charles J. Young, for many years Evening News sports editor. "Really, it wasn't. It let everyone know the boss was reading every word of the paper. And it made everyone think about accuracy.

"The boss had a thing about middle initials. The city directory got a heavier workout there than in any other newsroom in the world. Some old-timers, covering church stuff, would write 'Jesus (NMI) Christ,' if they had to use that name."

Kirchhofer's primness was part of his legend. He believed that a newspaper should not offend any reader needlessly. His last style-book, dated September 1964 and signed with his usual "AHK," included these dictums:

"Avoid these words unless approved by someone in authority: adultery, abortion, call girl, ex-con, homosexual, lousy, love nest, orgy, pregnant, prostitute, rape, sexy, socialite, stink(y), strip tease."

His stylebook prohibited profanity ("Nobody swears in print, even in quotes, unless this is cleared with the proper editor"), and gruesome details ("Avoid mention of hideous creatures or gruesome circumstances. Tone down the bloodiness, the scare angles").

"Don't give cranks leeway in knocking respected institutions," he ruled. "Don't sob over criminals or accused persons—and don't build them up or glamorize them...The suffering of an animal or person should not be reported in a humorous manner...The News insists on good taste; anything that would offend readers is undesirable."

Rats and snakes were described as rodents and reptiles, and were never portrayed in pictures or cartoons. A Time magazine profile of Kirchhofer during the Eisenhower presidency quoted him as saying: "We don't use 'rat' on Page One unless it bit Eisenhower or he bit it."

"Times have changed since then," said sports editor Young. "But those were the rules when Monty and I were growing up at the News."

John N. Wheeler, onetime editor of the old Liberty magazine and later head of the Bell Syndicate, once said: "The three great managing editors I've known were Carr Van Anda of the New York Times, O.K. Bovard of the St. Louis Post-Dispatch and A.H. Kirchhofer of the Buffalo Evening News."

Carl E. Lindstrom, editor of the Hartford Times, had known Kirchhofer in professional associations for a quarter of a century. He called Kirchhofer "...a born newspaperman of incredible competence and frequent brilliance, absolutely devoted to the highest standards of newspaper work, a perfectionist who is intolerant of everything but the best writing and editing; the possessor of an uncanny instinct for the hidden error (or the missed point or angle) and a news and editorial writer of incredible speed and precision."

Elwood M. (Woody) Wardlow, a copy editor and copy desk chief under Kirchhofer, recalled the latter's work methods as editor. Each morning at precisely 8:30 a.m., AHK would enter the second-floor newsroom and go directly to his desk in an alcove in the southwest corner. Everyone counted on his timing, because there was a no-smoking rule in the newsroom. At 8:29, the news editor doused the smoking lamp.

Immediately upon Kirchhofer's arrival, the department heads lined up in the pecking order, eight or nine of them awaiting their turn with the boss. Usually, the news editor was first, followed by the city editor, sports editor, society editor, picture editor, feature editor, financial editor and, last, the editorial page editor, with whom Kirchhofer spent more time and discussed issues in the news.

"To the others," Wardlow said, "Kirchhofer gave marching orders in three or four minutes. He was always direct and succinct, and expected direct terse answers in return. His voice was surprisingly soft for a man who spoke with such authority. He rarely raised his voice; he didn't have to. First, he would outline what was wrong with the previous day's editions. Then he would outline what he expected that day from each department head."

Kirchhofer had another office, one flight up on the third floor. His secretary, Frances Hurley, had an adjacent office there. About 10:15 a.m., he would go to his third-floor office, where Hurley had placed his mail in meticulous piles by subject. Kirchhofer handled each piece of paper only once, replying by telephone, blue note or letter.

"The man had the ability to do two things mentally at the same time," Wardlow said. "He would ask you to give him an oral report on some complex thing, and while you were doing it he would type or read his mail, or even talk on the telephone. And he would never miss a word."

Kirchhofer's lieutenants conveyed orders, but rarely originated them. That caused problems later. When his successors expected the department heads to act as managers, said Wardlow, who became managing editor/administration, it turned out that most of them didn't know how.

"Mr. Kirchhofer was probably the most competent person I will ever know," said Wardlow. " He not only ran the newsroom, but also was the de facto publisher of the paper and also had unofficial oversight over the affiliated radio and television stations. And if he didn't actually run Buffalo, he came close enough that a lot of people thought he did."

Kirchhofer had a certain Teutonic appearance. His brown eyes offered a direct, penetrating gaze. He wore his thick, dark hair barely long enough to comb. He was a little over six feet tall, thin with a thin face. His carriage was erect, his dress immaculate, his eyeglasses rimless.

Despite his forceful, often abrupt manner with subordinates, he was shy in social situations. Nonetheless, he was deeply involved in civic activities, and his wife, the former Emma M. Schugardt, was regarded as an outstanding hostess.

Kirchhofer never held leisurely conversations with staff members. He spoke, they listened. Wes Gallagher, who joined the Associated Press in Buffalo in 1937 and became the AP's general manager 25 years later, called Kirchhofer one of the best editors in the country, perhaps "the hardest to work for" and one who "seldom gave anyone the time of day. Among Monty's jobs was the duty of soothing the egos that Kirchhofer had bruised badly. He was pretty good at it."

Away from the newsroom, Kirchhofer was unfailingly thoughtful, mannered and loyal. Charley Young told of a copy boy who was supporting his mother. When the copy boy needed surgery, Kirchhofer paid the bill. And, said Young, "he always had a tenner or fiver for some of his old-timers who got short between paydays."

"AHK was a true visionary," said Young. "He sensed that the old hard-drinking, hard-driving, rowdy reporters of that early time were a passing breed. But he valued their street smarts. They were the guys who drank with the mayor and police chief, called most people at city hall and police headquarters by first names, knew most of the brothels, bookies, numbers racket guys and pimps.

"He needed them to pour some of their reportorial skills into the new breed; generally better educated, more dedicated, more special-ized, and probably more career-oriented."

The Evening News published the news in a grayish format, mainly vertical columns that permitted the desired high story count. One of Monty Curtis' assignments for a while was to count the number of stories daily in the Evening News and the rival Times and Courier-Express and then report the totals to Kirchhofer. Invariably, the Evening News led by far.

Kirchhofer's insight about readers made the Buffalo Evening News one of the first to station full-time reporters in the suburbs and present their stories in makeover pages. Early, the paper gave full coverage to business, financial and industrial news. The newspaper was also among the first to have a science and health reporter. Curtis watched, participated and learned.

As a young assistant city editor, Curtis learned from Kirchhofer the importance of covering events that have direct impact on readers. When a flash flood swamped the East Side, Curtis managed to make page one of the final edition with a short story. He thought that took care of the flood.

On his way home, Kirchhofer stopped by the city desk.

"What," he asked Curtis, "are you doing with the flood story?"

"We made two paragraphs for the final edition."

"I mean for tomorrow."

"People will have forgotten about it by tomorrow."

"You have a night staff. Send a photographer and two reporters to the East Side. Take pictures of flooded basements. Have reporters interview housewives. Call the Public Works Commissioner and other officials and learn why the new storm sewers on the East Side could not handle this flood. They were built to take care of just such floods. Tomorrow I want at least eight or ten pictures showing the nuisance to householders, and several columns of type full of quotes."

Curtis thought the boss was wrong, but did as he was told.

Next day the morning Courier-Express had a routine story and one picture, the rival afternoon Times a rewrite of the morning story. In contrast, the Evening News was crammed with flood news. Housewives whose basements had been flooded were delighted by the Evening News coverage. Curtis told Kirchhofer that he had learned a lesson, that he hadn't thought the story would be worthwhile 18 hours or more after the flood.

Said Kirchhofer: "If you had ever had your own basement flooded, leaving a deposit of mud, making your house damp, ruining things in your basement, you would have known better the first time."

Kirchhofer deplored sloppiness, and insisted that staff members wear jackets and ties, even in the office. Curtis recalled a Monday morning when a reporter named Charlie Michie, after "a good weekend snorter," showed up in a dirty white suit. "He obviously had been sleeping in it and on floors," Curtis wrote to an editor friend.

Just as Michie arrived, so did a fire alarm, for a grain-elevator fire, one of the smokiest kind. Michie hurried to cover the fire. Soon he was back and at his typewriter, pounding out the story for the first edition—and still in that dirty suit.

At that moment Kirchhofer arrived, frowned at Michie and demanded: "What do you mean coming to work in a dirty suit like that?"

Quickly, Michie came back: "So, I come to work in a nice, clean white suit, and a son-of-a-bitch (Curtis) sends me to a grain-elevator fire."

Curtis never said a word, thus making points with his staff.

Alfred Henry Kirchhofer was born May 25, 1892, in Buffalo. Like Sevellon Brown of Providence, he never attended college. As a carrier, he delivered all the Buffalo papers of the early century, including the Buffalo Demokrat, a German-language daily. At Buffalo Central High School, he edited the school paper for two years.

After graduation, he worked briefly for the Bank of Buffalo. He was only age 18 when he became a copy boy at the Buffalo Commercial. Shortly, he was promoted to reporter. Then, for a two-dollar raise, he switched to the Buffalo Times and later reported for the Buffalo Courier.

In 1913, when he was 21, Kirchhofer and a partner started the Western New York Post in nearby Lancaster, New York. They soon sold out. Kirchhofer returned to the Times as a political reporter. In 1915, at age 23, he made his last job switch, joining the Buffalo Evening News.

After a local reporting stint, he covered the state legislature in Albany. In 1921—he was then 29—he opened the Evening News' Washington bureau. By March 1927, when he was summoned home to become managing editor, Kirchhofer was president of the National Press Club in Washington.

Kirchhofer regarded Buffalo as a small town at heart and sought to make the Evening News the newspaper of record in local coverage. His twin loyalties were to the owning Butler family and the newspaper. Though the Evening News was dull in appearance, the breadth and accuracy of coverage drove the flashier Buffalo Times out of business.

The Buffalo Evening News was one of API's founding newspapers. Its initial contribution of $10,000 equalled that of the other largest contributors. Kirchhofer served on the API Advisory Board in its first two years.

Late on the afternoon of March 31, 1966, he pinned a memo on the newsroom bulletin board, announcing that he would retire effective the next day. He stayed on for what he termed "special duties," but always in his third-floor office, one flight up. He never entered the newsroom again.

"I have loved every minute of this work," he wrote to the staff. "I love to work with words and phrases, and put them into the best juxtaposition; to dig for facts and array them for effective presentation."

He ended his farewell memo with these words: "The newspaper which intelligently and with integrity serves its constituency will continue to be an indispensable source of information and civic leadership. There is no substitute for news in the printed form. Words fly; written things remain."

A few sentences from Kirchhofer's presidential address to the American Society of Newspaper Editors (he was ASNE's president, 1937-38) reveal the fire that burned in him where newspapers were concerned:

"We have allowed critics of the press, who want to control our opinions and failing in that to lessen the force of our influence, to go unanswered. These critics want to mold our views to theirs; they want us to become propagandists for their causes.

"...It is the obligation of a free press to defend and interpret free institutions. History shows us that even the best of the politicians, job-seekers and office-holding bureaucracy tend to become self-serving. If they aren't thinking of re-election or reappointment, they are thinking of their place in the sun. It is the duty of the newspaper press to warn against such self-aggrandizement. To do this requires a high degree of competence, detachment and experience in our editors and reporters."

Kirchhofer made a lasting imprint on all who worked under him, and surely one of the strongest imprints was on Monty Curtis, who later would have the bully pulpit of the American Press Institute.

In 1977, Monty Curtis wrote from his Miami office to another Buffalo Evening News alumnus, Woody Wardlow, then managing editor at the newspaper:

"A picture of AHK hangs on my wall, so he is looking over my shoulder while I work. If I have the slightest tendency to stretch the truth, I glance at that stern visage and mend my ways."

10

The Master of Anecdote

J osiah Montgomery Curtis never lacked for an anecdote, usually about himself. He told them with relish and a radiant smile and concluded with a booming laugh, as though he were the listener and had just heard the story for the first time.

His first name rarely appeared in full, only the initial. But, as with everything else, he had a story about it. "I liked the name Josiah," he would say, "until I discovered in my Bible reading that Josiah was only a minor prophet."

After he resigned from the American Press Institute in 1967 to join Knight Newspapers as vice president/corporate relations, his interest in API never slackened. While serving on the API board for several years, his surveillance far surpassed his responsibility.

In 1981, after he had left the board, Curtis wrote to Rollan D. Melton of the Gannett Company, an API board member and treasurer: "Probably to the annoyance of the API staff, I stay in close touch. I have been away from it (API) for 15 years, but some factors remain rather constant. When I see the slightest indication of a departure from some of those, I howl."

Another time he wrote a newspaper friend and said of API: "I just can't seem to let go."

Curtis took almost proprietary pride in API's success under Walter Everett, his successor, and would say, "I've always said that all API lacked was good management." Listeners would laugh, but none with greater gusto than Curtis, the laughter flowing up from his thick chest.

"I was the cockiest reporter Wheeling ever saw," he once wrote. That referred to his first newspaper job, with the Wheeling (West Virginia) News Register, which he got at age 14. And listeners would laugh some more.

"I am such a smart aleck that I cannot restrain myself," he wrote in 1975 to James H. Ottaway Sr., then chairman of the API Board of Directors, "and that, sir, goes back to the days when at the age of six I stood on a soapbox in Elm Grove, West Virginia, and advocated causes, just any cause, I really didn't give a damn, to anyone who would listen."

His only sibling, sister Helen, two-and-a-half years his elder, confirmed that in this one recollection at least her brother did not exaggerate. "Mont (as he was known to his family) was well known for his ability to tell a good story and embellish the very simplest facts," she said. "He and I didn't always remember things the same."

Friends came to realize that when Curtis told those apparent exaggerations about himself he was really telling the truth—just wrapping it in humor. His close friend, Rolfe Neill, publisher of the Charlotte (North Carolina) Observer, said at a memorial service for Curtis in 1983, "If words were his work, humor was his play."

Curtis had his serious, even brooding moments, but if he had an audience, which he usually did, his humor poured out like water from an open spigot.

Although self-deprecating humor was his hallmark and despite his enormous contribution to API, Curtis was far from a model manager. He shot from the hip and often missed. He liked the big picture. Details bored him, unless he was scrutinizing a newspaper story for accuracy. Then no detail was too small. He was at his best when critiquing newspapers. Rolfe Neill said, "You'd never hire Monty to be your accountant."

Curtis once wrote about how he feared boredom. "I said, 'By God, I'm going to do something interesting.' And you know what? I've never been bored a day in my life."

As director of API, Curtis left most of the managerial detail to his deputy, Walter Everett, a master of detail and considered judgments. "I'm a promoter," Curtis would often say. And he was. From his first day at API in 1947 until his death on Thanksgiving Day in 1982 he promoted API. When Floyd Taylor hired him, Curtis' first letter to his new boss was a three-page compendium of ideas to promote the wobbly new institute.

Usually, only close friends recognized the many layers of the Curtis personality. Of course he had an oblique, self-deprecating anecdote about that, too. He would tell about the managing editor at his first paper in Wheeling, Elmer Cunningham. "I was glib and cocky then as now," he wrote to C.A. (Pete) McKnight, a retired editor of the Charlotte Observer. "Said Elmer: 'Mont, you can't fool me with your chatter. Beneath your shallow exterior lies a deep vein of superficiality.' "

Other friends—and they were legion—usually saw only the layers that Curtis chose to display. Bob Broeg, sports editor of the St. Louis Post-Dispatch, a seminar member and later several times a discussion leader, said Curtis reminded him a bit of Franklin Delano Roosevelt: "Impressive, charming, cheerful and so damned smart and also persuasive." All that was true.

Robert Danzig was an advertising executive for the Albany Times-Union when he met Curtis at an API Advertising Executives Seminar member in 1961 and saw him often afterward as the publisher at Albany and then as an executive of Hearst Newspapers. Danzig recalled: "Monty had a wide-open, flat-out, full-throttle love affair with newspapers. He infected you with that sentiment and, speaking for myself, the ember never dulled."

"True," said Curtis' closest friend on the Columbia University journalism faculty, John Hohenberg, long the administrator of the Pulitzer Prizes. "Curtis was tough, smart, shrewd, combative, pushy, hard-fisted and even insensitive at times, and he could swarm all over you if he thought you were half-hearted about some important project...

"If he was carried away by enthusiasm in some matter or other, he could make mistakes; however, he could also change course quickly whenever he became convinced he was wrong. And that, too, was a trait that endeared him to others..."

In the Miami Herald, Charles Whited described Curtis as "a curious blending of characteristics—folksy extrovert, fluid talker, deep thinker, a worrier about wet feet and drafts, swift and retentive reader, shrewd assessor of things and people."

Describing his first experience with API, Roger Tatarian, the retired editor of United Press International, illustrated the Curtis strength in unifying a seminar group. Just back in 1960 from 12 years overseas, Tatarian had just been named UPI's managing editor, in New York. He enrolled in an API seminar because he "wasn't up to speed."

"Everything I had heard about (Curtis)," Tatarian said, "made him sound about 10 feet tall and, by God, when I got there that is how tall his force of personality made him look. I have never seen anyone who was a more effective catalyst at making a cohesive group out of 20 or so disparate, and sometimes desperate, characters...Monty was a genius at sizing people up. He could spot a blowhard at 20 paces, but if he had to skewer one he did it deftly and privately."

"Monty could be quite firm and serious," said Edwin D. Hunter, who first attended API from Oklahoma City and became editor of the Houston Post. "But even with that (he would) have a twinkle in his eye." Hunter said Curtis smoothly warned members on what was expected of them by saying early on that API had been compelled to send only one participant home because of lack of attentiveness and failure to attend seminar sessions.

Curtis wasn't a slave driver, said Hunter, but it was always subtly clear that he had in mind the stake publishers had in the program. Publishers, of course, paid the bills. He also made it clear that editors and other executives back home expected a full report on seminar gleanings.

I. William Hill, retired managing editor of the Washington Evening Star, remembered the Curtis genius as "not in doing things so much as saying things that made you and me do them." He gave these examples of Curtis aphorisms:

• "You can tell a real newsman. Seeing Niagara Falls, he doesn't think of beauty, he wonders where all that water came from."
• "One way to judge a good obit is whether it makes the dead man seem alive."

Norman E. Isaacs remembered Curtis for his constant flow of suggestions. When Isaacs was executive editor of the Courier-Journal and Louisville Times, Curtis recommended that Isaacs have department heads (city editor, sports editor, etc.) list staff members on a value chart, top to bottom, and compare that ranking with the payroll ranking. Isaacs recalled that on the city staff, the top four on the value chart were low on the pay list, and the city editor's bottom three or four highest paid. That exercise, said Isaacs, was the beginning of "a major change in who-got-what."

Curtis was happiest when surrounded by newspaper men and women. He felt lost without a batch of newspapers to read. When talk turned to the responsibility of newspapers, he would switch quickly from humor to evangelistic seriousness. "This news business is a lonely business," he wrote. "We stand between those who wield power, be it government, labor, capital, church or bleeders for causes, and those upon whom they wield it. The power people loathe us for printing unfavorable truth. Their victims, whom we serve, give not a damn, misunderstand and return libel verdicts against us."

In his letters, Curtis was the master of the short sentence. In API seminars, he preached the clarity of short sentences and took deep pride in a widely quoted study, made for API by James H. Couey Jr. of the Birmingham News, that showed reader understanding diminishes as average sentence length increases.

Friends urged Curtis to write a book. He never did, though he made sporadic mentions of tossing notes into a folder against the time he would lash himself to the typewriter.

To a newspaper friend, he said, "Away back there in 1933 I was trying to write. I read somewhere that the thing to do was to compromise with your limitations. So, one morning I looked at myself in the mirror and said: 'Curtis, you cannot write. You really don't want to write. You just want to have written. Why don't you just try to be the best city editor in the country.' So I tried, and I have been a paper shuffler ever since...Who is to be remembered in this business? Paper shufflers? Never. The writers, absolutely. To whom do the readers respond? Paper shufflers? Never. They respond to the writers."

But Curtis could write, fast and well. His delightful letters proved that. For a while, he gave the idea of a book serious thought, even corresponding about technique with Columbia's Hohenberg, who had written several books. In a 1973 letter to Knight-Ridder executive Lee Hills he described his accumulation of material on newspaper accuracy and wrote that it "deserves a small, slim, rule-by-rule book after the fashion of 'The Elements of Style.'" The reference was to a widely admired book by William Strunk Jr. and E.B. White.

John Hohenberg urged Curtis to undertake a different theme. In a letter of August 24, 1982, just three months before Curtis' death, Hohenberg wrote:

"What is it (the book) about? It's about you. Who you are. What you did. What you thought. How everything turned out...It has to be about a strong and decisive personality. You...Who's going to read this? I'd say that everybody who has read and enjoyed the William Allen White autobiography or the Lincoln Steffens autobiography will like yours, and it will help a lot more young people today than either of the others."

Despite the encouragement by Hohenberg and many others, Curtis never started a book. Writing to William O. Beck of the Charlotte News, he said: "Some people say I should write a book. It is so much easier to just talk." Once again, Monty Curtis was being honest about himself.

Nevertheless, further evidence of Curtis' writing skill came from Trudi Murmann, for many years his secretary both at API and at Knight-Ridder. His readable letters, Murmann said, "seemed to come from him so effortlessly—either by dictation or drafted. He dictated 80 percent of his correspondence, and it was a pleasure to transcribe it."

For his written speeches, Curtis worked best at deadline. "It drove me crazy sometimes," Murmann recalled. Though Curtis would accept a speaking engagement, say three months in advance, nothing was done until three days before. He wanted his speeches to sound crisp and fresh, not canned.

Curtis worried about his health to the extent that he was something of a walking medical reference book. This could have resulted from twice being delirious during childhood measles and typhoid fever. Then too, in early adulthood he developed the arthritic left knee that limited him to non-combat duty in World War II. With his health in mind, he chopped wood, swam and hiked. At a health center in 1964 he was asked to take a deep breath and exhale into a lung-testing device. "I don't dare," said Curtis, who told the story often. "I have a 48-inch chest and it expands to 54. If I puff into this I'll break it."

"No you won't," the doctor said. So Curtis exhaled into the device—and broke it.

For Curtis, humor opened the door for his serious opinions, usually about newspapers, but ranging from politics to theology to classical music to professional sports. No matter the subject, Curtis had an opinion or an anecdote, called up from his voracious reading and prodigious memory. Years after they attended API, Curtis could still call most of the members by name.

In the late 1970s, Fred Dickey of the San Jose Mercury News and Curtis were watching a pro football game on TV and sparring over who was the most knowledgeable on sports. George Beebe of the Miami Herald was also in that motel room. He recalled that Dickey asked Curtis who played in the 1921 World Series.

Curtis replied that it was the New York Giants and the New York Yankees. The Giants won, four games to three. Then he recited the four starting pitchers for both teams and told who played in every position on the two teams. This was after Curtis had lain comatose for two months in a Wichita hospital, victim of a burst aneurysm. Friends had feared that his great memory might be affected.

Given his exceptional memory, his letters suggest that he sometimes modified his anecdotes to fit the occasion. For example, in 1971 he wrote Katie Righter, daughter of a former publisher of the Buffalo Evening News, to congratulate her on becoming engaged. "I was a hillbilly young reporter out of Appalachia," he wrote. "I wanted to work for a fine newspaper and I selected the BEN (Buffalo Evening News), applied for a job, and landed it, late in 1929."

However, in a 1979 letter to Tim Hays, then chairman of the API Board of Directors, Curtis wrote: "How did I get a job on the Buffalo Evening News? Only through a classified ad in old Furnald's Exchange, Springfield, Mass., later absorbed by E & P (Editor & Publisher). I knew nothing of the BEN. It was my luck to land on a great newspaper."

Curtis always had some nonsense going. That was typically true in the 1952 Managing and News Editors Seminar that Curtis moderated. One day it developed that Curtis had gone swimming during the luncheon break. "I'm a physical fitness nut," he told the members. "I want to develop my neck until it's so big I don't have to loosen my tie to slip it over my head." As a farewell gift, seminar members gave Curtis an axe, in recognition of his wood-chopping.

Curtis loved to collect unusual names, and friends sent him their findings. John S. Knight, editor of Knight-Ridder Newspapers, spotted this one in a news account and sent it to Curtis: W. Fauntleroy Pursley. Curtis filed a clipping from the Wall Street Journal about a brokerage firm named Hyer & Lower, Inc., filed it with the notation: "Don't believe it."

His favorite unusual name, he wrote, was Hilarius P. Windschitl, a fertilizer dealer from Horse Falls, North Dakota. Playfully, Curtis added that Windschitl perhaps belonged to the (fictitious) law firm of Dille, Dahley, Stahl and Doolittle.

He delighted in producing pleasant surprises for friends. Once, traveling abroad, he searched bazaars for miniature elephant figures to give to his old boss, Kirchhofer, who collected them. After a day of golf at which Paul Miller of Gannett was host, Curtis sent him a solid gold tee with his thank-you note.

And one day, chatting with the ticket agent at the 125th Street railway station, he learned that the man loved opera but had never seen a performance. By phone, Curtis persuaded the opera's public relations department to send the agent two complimentary tickets. He then arranged for a limousine and chauffeur for the agent on performance night.

Curtis loved talk. Rarely did he fail to dominate a conversation. Then it would not be for lack of trying. Again, he knew himself. He would proclaim: "I talk too much; I'm hereby taking a vow of silence." One time, he said, the vow held for all of 20 seconds.

But even if he were to be silent, an unlikely prospect, Curtis was a major figure in any group for his size alone. At age 15, he was six feet, five inches tall and weighed 205 pounds. He said that he grew too fast to be an athlete, a shame because he loved sports. At the University of West Virginia, he traveled with the football team—but as a clarinet and soprano saxophone player in the ROTC band.

As a mature adult, he was six feet, six inches, and 220 pounds. His frame was topped by a leonine head that once baffled newspaper friends in Texas seeking to find a ten-gallon hat large enough, an intended present in appreciation of a Curtis speech. He was quite handsome, with a firm jaw and a shock of brown hair, and seldom took a bad picture.

During World War II, Curtis worked for a while in the Pentagon in

Washington. Writing Charles H. Hamilton of the Richmond News Leader, Curtis recalled a day when he carried a message to a crusty old general. "He looked me up and down," Curtis wrote, "and said, 'Biggest damn messenger boy I ever saw.' "

"I never met Tom Wolfe (Thomas Wolfe, the novelist)," said John B. Lake, retired president of the St. Petersburg Times, "but Monty reminded me of what I imagined Tom Wolfe would be like." In fact, Tom Wolfe was one of Curtis' favorite authors.

This was the fellow who said he took a $5,000 annual pay cut when he left the Buffalo Evening News in 1947 to become an associate director at API, filling the shoes left vacant by the resigned Claude Jagger. In a letter Curtis later wrote that he saw in API an opportunity to help improve many newspapers. That was apparently true. But he once told an associate that he wanted to get away from the pressure of the city desk.

City editors everywhere work under pressure. That must have been especially true at the Buffalo Evening News, an afternoon paper with as many as seven editions and an editor, Kirchhofer, who insisted that today's news be in today's paper. In Buffalo, Curtis supervised four assistant city editors, two rewrite men and about 35 reporters. But, given the Monty Curtis personality, the greater lure of API was clearly the audience he would have in seminars—newspaper men and women from across the U.S. and Canada.

Floyd Taylor, API's first director, loved newspapers. Now in Curtis he had found an equal in that respect. Earl J. Johnson, the former editor of United Press International, wrote of Curtis: "He believes in newspapers the way Jeremiah believed in the destiny of Israel."

Columbia University would soon know that Curtis was around. When John Hohenberg, fresh from newspapering, joined the journalism faculty in 1950 he looked up Robert Harron, Columbia's director of public information, a former newspaper colleague.

Taking Hohenberg by the arm, Harron said, "I want you to meet a real powerhouse in our business. This guy is going to stir things up, I'll guarantee that." Who else but Monty Curtis?

Curtis was destined, after four years as an associate director, to become API's director after Floyd Taylor's fatal heart attack. As director, Curtis would stir things up in more ways than Harron may have had in mind.

From a historian's standpoint, Curtis was a treasure. His voluminous correspondence, his speeches—the ones he wrote out— and the memories of countless friends provide a record that is revealing, entertaining, and, on the principles of good newspapering, instructive.

At API, Curtis became an evangelist for improving newspapers.

His size, humor and dedication made him the target of every newspaper-related meeting chairman in the U.S. and Canada. On the platform, Curtis was rarely excelled.

When demands on him permitted, he prepared cogent messages on newspapering—on deadline as noted. When he had said yes more often than he should have—which was frequently—he could wing it, carpentering a speech from his bottomless bag of anecdotes and his unwavering convictions about newspapers and their responsibility.

On a hotel elevator in New York City one time, on the short ride up to the ballroom, he scribbled a few words on a wrinkled envelope. That was all he prepared to address several hundred members of a regional newspaper association. Other speakers might have trembled if faced with such an audience and just a wrinkled envelope to lean on. But Curtis responded to audiences like thespians who prefer the stage to film-making. His speech, spiked with anecdotes, earned ringing applause.

The endless supply of anecdotes sprouted from an early life that made for anecdotes. His career at API and afterward added to his store, right up to his death in 1982. Those who saw him last reported that he remained cheerful and never stopped talking newspapers.

11

A Dream Job for Monty

With one brief exception, Monty Curtis always wanted to be a newspaperman. That exception came when he was 13 years old and learned how much a workman made carrying bricks for his stepfather, who was building a new home for the family. Young Monty told his family that he wanted to be a hod carrier. A physical culturist, Curtis wrote later that at the time he relished the prospect of heavy labor.

His sister Helen, however, recalled that the main attraction was the high hourly wage. In either case, after that brief whimsy it was for him newspapers, only newspapers.

Curtis was born in Elm Grove, West Virginia, six miles from Wheeling, on November 11, 1905. His father, Allan Walker Curtis, a pioneer educator in that part of West Virginia, taught the eighth grade in the elementary school while also serving as principal.

Elm Grove had no high school then, and Allan Curtis wanted to give his students more than eight years of education. So he brought them back after the eighth grade and taught the equivalent of a freshman year: English, history, mathematics and Latin. After that, with his half-sister assisting him, he also taught the equivalent of a sophomore year.

Then a consolidated school opened in Sherrod, seven miles distant in neighboring Marshall County. Allan Curtis became its principal and moved his family to Sherrod. Helen recalled that to reach Sherrod from Elm Grove they went up Poor House Hill and followed the ridge southward.

Allan Curtis continued the double duty typical of those days and taught four subjects the first year in Sherrod. In Elm Grove his pay had been $80 a month, and he painted houses in summer to raise his income. At Sherrod his principal's pay climbed to $100 a month, together with a rent-free house the zenith in family income.

Monty Curtis' great grandfather was W.B. Curtis, a general in the Union army of the Civil War and later a state legislator. In the 1850s, he started a West Virginia normal school that became West Liberty State College. His son, J. M. Curtis, Monty's namesake and grandfather, joined his father's Union regiment at age 15 or 16.

Monty's mother, Zelda Epstein Curtis, an accomplished pianist, gave lessons that for a while provided the family's only income. She was one of seven children born to a physician father who had emigrated to the United States from Russia. Her mother had studied at the Leipzig Conservatory in Germany, where Zelda was born.

Monty Curtis' mother was the strongest influence in his life. By daughter Helen's account, she was stern, well organized and met strangers easily, a trait her son developed early.

Though Monty Curtis was proud of his half-Jewish heritage, he was reared a Presbyterian. He became an Episcopalian after his second marriage.

With his lineage of educators and musicians, Curtis loved learning and classical music. Early in his newspaper career he wanted to become a music critic. Fate took him in a different direction, but he never missed a chance to attend an opera or a symphony. He met Alma Heidee, his second wife whom he married in 1945, when both were Army officers during World War II and attended the same concert in Washington, D.C.

In Sherrod, where the Curtis family moved after the school consolidation, indoor plumbing was lacking. Water came from two iron pumps with long handles, one in the kitchen sink for a cistern, the other on the back porch and over a deep well, for drinking water.

For the first time, the family had a telephone, a party line operated by a hand crank. On snowy mornings a farmer named Talbot notified everyone through the party line that he would pick up the schoolchildren in his horse-drawn sled, filled with straw and blankets.

During the second of two winters in Sherrod, Monty Curtis suffered the first of injuries or serious illnesses that plagued him much of his life. On a bitterly cold night he came down from his unheated attic room to warm himself by the gas fireplace. His nightclothes caught fire.

His mother smothered the flames with a blanket, but Monty's backside was severely burned. Helen Curtis Pohlman, Monty's sister and only sibling, said almost eight decades later that those severe burns would have been treated today at a specialized burn center. Monty got only the local doctor's care.

Not wanting Monty, a first-grader, to miss school, his mother obtained a big wooden Arbuckle Coffee box at the country store across the road. She padded it so that Monty could lie face down and be comfortable. Each morning the school janitor would carry Monty to school and place him face down on the box. Monty spent several weeks of school on his stomach, prone atop the coffee box.

Despite Monty's burns, those were good years for him and his sister. The brief happiness and relative prosperity ended when the father took ill. A bed for him was placed in the living room. Helen remembered doctors from Wheeling consulting at her father's bedside. In June 1913, Allan Curtis died of a brain tumor. He was age 39.

Monty was seven years, 10 months of age; Helen 10 years and one month. Zelda Curtis, the mother, would survive her first husband until 1976, when she died at age 94.

The family was left without income. Zelda Curtis moved with her two children back to Elm Grove, where she rented two rooms and a bath on the second floor of a house. The mother obtained use of the living room for her piano and began giving lessons at 25 cents each. That income sustained the family. The mother soon moved the family to the rented first floor of a house a few blocks away and then to a rented house on Center Street.

This house had running water, though only cold. Illumination was by gaslights. Zelda's brother, George Epstein, a salesman for Abbots Drug Company, visited Wheeling regularly and came to Elm Grove for dinner and an evening of music. He sang while Zelda played the piano.

Sometimes, Monty and Helen sang duets at school or church functions. As Helen put it years later, "Our home always had music, books and love."

After three years of widowhood, Zelda Curtis remarried. Her groom was J. Oliver (Ollie) Butler, the Elm Grove town policeman. Later, he also carried mail in a nearby community. Helen was 13, Monty almost 11.

The expanded family needed more room and moved in with the new stepfather's parents, who had a spacious house not far away. Ollie's father was a carpenter. As a wedding gift, he supervised the building of a house for son Ollie and the new family.

The new structure, at 61 Center Street, became house number six for Monty and Helen. A coal furnace provided heat and electricity the lighting, though there was also a gas light in case the electricity failed. There were three large bedrooms, but only one bath.

The pre-adolescent Monty lingered in the bathroom when preparing to go out. Said the mother, irked, "If I ever build another house and it has only two rooms, they both are going to be bathrooms."

Later, Helen and Monty rode the streetcar to the new Triadelphia

High School. On the streetcar they saw coal miners, weary and homeward bound, covered with coal dust and still wearing their smelly carbide lamps.

Young Monty, beginning to think about career choices, reacted to the sight of the grimy miners. One summer he weeded onions on a truck farm. The experiences forged his resolve to find a career free of boredom. Years later, he wrote to a friend that by age 12 he was determined never to work in a coal mine or steel mill.

It's a wonder that Monty survived his childhood. Delirious first with measles as a young child, he was delirious again at age nine with typhoid. He probably caught that dreaded disease swimming in Eskew's swimming hole, close to where sewage emptied into the creek.

By sister Helen's account, Monty was a big child, active and destructive. He punched out the eyes of her china doll. He banged on her toy piano and loosened the keys. Once he pulled off the tablecloth when the table was set with dishes. While his mother was doing the laundry, he turned over a washtub filled with soapy water.

At Triadelphia High School, Monty entered journalism by writing the school letter that appeared in a Wheeling newspaper, the Intelligencer. Helen recalled that her brother sweat blood over that letter. Their mother would check it and turn it back to Monty until she thought it perfect. He had encountered his first tough editor. Those rewritten letters resulted in part-time work on the Intelligencer, at age 14.

The facts about Monty Curtis' high school years are elusive. His sister was attending first Marshall College in Huntington, then West Virginia University in Morgantown, and her recollections of Monty's activities are sketchy.

In a suggested introduction of himself prepared decades later, perhaps for a program chairman asking help, he wrote: "Was lucky in a mother who got him a job as a reporter on the Wheeling (W.Va.) News in 1919 to keep him off the streets and out of the pool room...Was luckier still in being allowed to work seven nights a week through high school."

Later, when he filled out a form for the Buffalo Evening News, he wrote: "Sept. 1919-Sept. 1923. Reporter, sports editor Wheeling Daily & Sunday News (working through high school.)" On another occasion he wrote facetiously of material deleted from his submitted biography by "Who's Who in America:"

• "Third-string middle linebacker for Triadelphia High School Tigers until clobbered by Butch Niemec, who later made All-American at Notre Dame.

- "(Won) first place (and this, so help me, is true) in the discus throw at the Ohio Valley Interscholastic track meet in May 1922. The Triadelphia team had no discus thrower. I was covering the damn thing for the Wheeling newspaper. The coach asked me to throw the discus. I took off my coat, cupped the damn thing in my right hand, took two steps across the ring (had I twirled I would have fallen on my face) and flung the discus 107 feet. I then retired at the top of my form."

After high school, Monty attended West Virginia University for a year, dropping out for lack of money. He worked 15 months on the Wheeling paper before going back to the university and earning a bachelor's degree while majoring in philosophy and editing the school newspaper, the Athenaeum.

Curtis treasured those difficult times. His recollections, though laced with a story-teller's talents, illustrated how those years forged his outlook on life. In one account, he called himself lucky to have worked on the Wheeling and Morgantown papers in the 1920s. "No union or child labor laws to tell us we could not work when we were 15...No bureaucrats to tell us we were poor, which we were but did not know it."

He described himself as "an ambitious kid (who) could volunteer for almost any assignment and get it" because the older men on the newspaper were overworked and underpaid. On the Wheeling Intelligencer he was "the newest of the cubs (a beginning reporter) at $12 a week, and not worth it."

Newsroom characters fascinated young Curtis. He divided them as "permanents," the ones with wives, children and mortgages, and "floaters," who quickly grew bored and "always hoped to find something interesting in the next city."

Once a chorus girl from a musical comedy troupe was stranded in Wheeling and worked briefly on the Intelligencer. She got her job on her figure, Curtis wrote. She left for other fields where "she didn't have to type, which she couldn't anyway."

Such was the stuff that later enabled Curtis to charm banquet audiences by flavoring his serious messages about newspapers with humorous anecdotes. But he was also learning to be a newspaper-man.

For three days in 1927 he reported from the crash scene of the dirigible Shenandoah and saw bodies strewn about. The airship crashed during a violent storm 60 miles from Wheeling. He interviewed President Warren G. Harding in Wheeling, using a box of Harding's favorite cigars to gain entry.

And he watched late-at-night poker games at the Intelligencer-

News building. One night one player, a maintenance man named McCrea, asked Curtis why he was so skinny. "I lied," Curtis wrote, "and told him that on my $15 a week I did not get enough to eat."

McCrea, by Curtis' account, pulled two dimes and a nickel out of the pot, shoved them at Curtis, and said: "This is for Mont's sandwiches. Twenty-five cents out of every pot for him."

"Well," Curtis wrote, in the West Virginia Fourth Estatesman, "it became a custom. And that is how I was able to go to West Virginia University as a freshman with $3,000 in the bank." Tales like this both challenge and delight a historian.

Curtis also wrote how the syndicated comic strips arrived in 30-day batches. As a high school freshman working part time at the newspaper he knew—and readers did not—what was going to happen.

In one popular strip, The Gumps, Curtis learned that a character named Mary Gold was going to die, even though a comic strip character had never died before. At Triadelphia High School, students speculated on the fate of Mary Gold.

Curtis took bets at 10-to-1 that she would die. For every nickel wagered, he won 50 cents. "Was it unethical," he wrote, "for me to collect money by betting on a sure thing? I never thought so. It was just a matter of superior knowledge."

Curtis graduated from West Virginia University in 1928 at the age of 22. The new graduate needed a job and headed south, apparently on a promise of work. He later wrote that he passed up one newspaper when the editor made no effort to get an important story in that afternoon's paper.

In one account he mentioned working briefly on the Savannah (Georgia) newspapers. His sister thought her brother had played piano for a while in a motion-picture theater; he had taken lessons from his mother.

In a 1972 letter to Creed Black, editor of the Philadelphia Inquirer, Curtis described working as a young reporter on the Pittsburgh Chronicle Telegraph, which later failed, and then moving to the Pittsburgh Gazette for a summer. Those jobs are mentioned nowhere else in available records.

At some point not long after college graduation, Curtis found newspaper work in Fairmont, West Virginia, 15 miles from Morgantown. There he met Amy Lee LaFollette and married her January 27, 1929. They were divorced in September 1940 after a separation of four-and-a-half years. By then, Monty worked on the Buffalo Evening News.

The Curtis career trail becomes fuzzy after his stay at Fairmont. Dates and stopovers vary substantially in his Who's Who in America account and in the biographical form he filled out at the Buffalo Evening News.

His sister Helen recalled that he was working at the Dominion-News in Morgantown when he underwent an appendectomy and was replaced. It was probably another kind of illness, because Curtis in a letter told of having appendicitis in Buffalo.

He had worked nights on the Morgantown paper while attending college—or, as he wrote in his suggested introduction for speech engagements—"while sleeping through West Virginia University, which made a mistake in graduating him and compounded it by giving him an honorary and unearned doctorate in 1966."

His sister recalled that her brother did well in subjects he liked; otherwise he studied just enough to get by. During summer breaks from college, he worked on the Wheeling Intelligencer.

With typical humorous self-deprecation, Curtis once wrote of his dancing skills: "When I trip a heavy fantastic, it is much like an ocean liner pushing the tug around. When I should have been learning the social graces, I was earning 25 bucks on Friday night playing (piano) in a combo at fraternity dances, and 50 bucks on Saturday nights (no Sunday paper in my university town then) at mining town brawls. The result is that I have much in common with both the elephant and the giraffe."

Curtis landed a job on the Buffalo Evening News in June 1929 and was assigned as a reporter to the financial news department. His first question to the financial editor, Hilton Hornaday, he later wrote, was: "What is a stock, and what is a bond?" Never one to pass up a good opening, Curtis added: "I never did graduate to debentures."

Curtis either developed homesickness for West Virginia or his first Buffalo winter wore him down. Filling out the Buffalo Evening News form, he wrote, "It got awfully cold that February (1930), so: 1930-Jan. 1931, city editor, Dominion-News (Morgantown)."

Of his return to Buffalo, he wrote waggishly: "It was also cold here in January, but the banks all busted in Morgantown and it was really a lot warmer up here."

In Buffalo, Amy and Monty Curtis rented a cottage on Wadsworth Street. When they separated, Monty became a boarder at the home of neighbors, Mr. and Mrs. Harry C. Law Sr. Everyone called her Dolly. Their one child, Harry Jr., became a physician. Curtis became a favorite of the Law family. The daughter-in-law, Rosemarie, saved the letters exchanged by Curtis and the Laws, many of them written when Curtis was in the Army. They tell of a loving relationship.

Separated from his wife, Curtis needed a family. He found it in the Laws. He attended their Unitarian church. His grand piano was installed in the parlor, and he sometimes played classical music by the hour. At one time, he knew by heart all of Beethoven's sonatas. Dolly Law bought an extra-long bed for her towering boarder. When Curtis acquired a black-and-white dog named Tippy at the dog pound, the Laws treated it like a beloved child.

Meanwhile, at the Buffalo Evening News Curtis was honing his skills. After three years as a reporter, he moved up to assistant city editor in 1934 and to city editor in 1937, at age 32.

Years later, writing a friend, he said the managing editor, Kirchhofer, "raised hell with me about two or three times a week and tried his best to make a good newspaperman out of me."

But there were other strong newsroom influences on Curtis, and he never forgot them. At the Evening News, for example, Curtis worked on the city desk across from an assistant city editor named Ed Lebherz. When Lebherz died in 1978, Curtis wrote to Woody Wardlow at the Evening News, saying that Lebherz had a "pleasant, calm, even serene attitude toward work...That was good for me because in those days of seven editions a day and all the pressures, I was inclined toward high tension and frequent outbursts. Ed calmed me down."

In that letter to Wardlow, Curtis reminisced about Buffalo colleagues: "...What a staff we had...The great generalist, Charlie Michie, who could cover anything...Jack Meddoff, our fastest writer...Don Bermingham who took us through the city affairs investigation without a libel or even a serious error. Lance Zavitz, a mercurial type who could be calmed down only by Ed (Lebherz), never by me. Steve Cain, the fastest and neatest rewrite man who ever lived..."

And so on. Then the poignant final sentence: "This letter is going on much too long, but I wanted to talk with someone about Ed Lebherz."

In any vocation, it is not unusual to hold sentimental affection for early colleagues. Curtis was age 73 when he wrote about Lebherz. But years before that, at the American Press Institute, Curtis would reminisce in similar fashion about Buffalo or Wheeling. Curtis, as his sister and Rosemarie Law recalled, loved children. With no children of his own, Curtis seemed to develop an extra measure of affection for fellow newspaper men and women.

In voluminous correspondence, letters that often ran several pages, Curtis usually offered a new reminiscence. A letter to Perry Morgan, editor of the Akron Beacon Journal, was typical. It concerned fillers, items of two or three lines used to fill out newspaper columns in the days of metal type. Today, computers make the columnar adjustments.

At the Evening News, Curtis wrote Morgan, an old-time staffer who knew local history was instructed to write local fillers. "He ranged from the only ginkgo tree in town to the four times Niagara Falls froze over. The composing room was delighted."

But Curtis had created a problem. Soon the author of the fillers was pounding on the city desk and saying: "Goddammit, you used only six of my fillers yesterday. Don't let those things go stale, Curtis."

Curtis related that the paper found grade-school classes making scrapbooks of local fillers. Then teachers complained that the BEN was not using enough fillers. A lot of people on the staff complained. The printers didn't like it. "The final blow to me came when the editor said: 'Curtis, can't you trim down those local stories enough to make room for Charlie's fillers?' "

Another time, Curtis recalled, one of his first Evening News assignments was to check names in a news release about a party being held by the Old Newsboys Association. Except for the first paragraph, it comprised names, names, names. "At least 125 were Polish names. The others were Italian, with a few Czechs, fewer Hungarians up in Riverside, and some Irishmen from the First Ward."

Curtis checked the names with Jimmy O'Keefe, a newspaper hawker who had an amazing knowledge about life in Buffalo. Curtis learned that almost all names in the news release were misspelled. "I learned the difference between czcny and zczhny. The Sobieskis gave me a little trouble, but I had a hell of a time with Krystafkiewicz. Anyway, I labored a long time over those names and turned them in about 5 o'clock."

The editor scanned the names, called Curtis to his desk and said: "In this town, you'll have to learn the difference between an O'Brien and an O'Brian. Those with an 'e' are Catholics. Those with an 'a' are Episcopalians."

At API, Curtis sometimes served as a discussion leader. His favorite subject was accuracy, and he would occasionally use his Buffalo experience to illustrate the need for absolute accuracy on the spelling of names—and everything else for that matter.

In Buffalo, Curtis developed a stiff left knee. His sister thought the problem traced to his brief fling at high school football. But it may have started when he fell while reporting a rare freezing-over of Niagara Falls. For a while, the knee joint locked, and Curtis hobbled about on crutches. He was treated by various doctors without success. One diagnosis was rheumatoid arthritis.

Finally, Curtis visited a Canadian doctor who broke the adhesions. Curtis discarded the crutches, but the knee remained intermittently troublesome. In 1948, while with API, he fell on ice, fractured the right kneecap in five places and was sidelined five weeks. Bad knees were his fate. He fought against them by lifting weights, walking and swimming.

When World War II began, Curtis thought he would be turned down by the draft board because of the faulty left knee. With that belief, he passed up an opportunity to join the Office of Censorship in Washington, saying that he could be of greater wartime service by remaining with the Evening News. On May 29, 1942, Selective Service Board 617 summoned Curtis for a physical examination.

At age 36, to his surprise, he was accepted for limited service and immediate duty. Curtis was assigned for a while to the recruiting office in Buffalo. But this was one case where the military recognized potential. Curtis was commissioned a second lieutenant on February 17, 1943, after completing the Army Administration Officer Candidate School in Grinnell, Iowa.

The new shavetail was assigned to Camp Holabird, Maryland. He lived off base, in Baltimore, driving each day in a rattly car to the camp, there to teach close-order drill and the cleaning of weapons. Then he was assigned to counter-intelligence at the War Department in Washington.

Charley Young, a Buffalo newspaper colleague, said Curtis served with the Office of Strategic Services, forerunner of the Central Intelligence Agency, and commanded from Washington a far-flung team with members in 25 to 30 spots around the world.

While in the Army, Curtis wrote frequently to Dolly Law in Buffalo. He told her that he could not inform her about his duties until Germany had been defeated. After the war, he wrote a newspaper friend that he had worked on the Manhattan Project—the development of the atom bomb.

Curtis rose to captain in April 1944 and to major in June 1945. After the war, he wrote to Mrs. Law at the time, he would not be able to speak of overseas adventure—for which he was repeatedly turned down, only how hot it was in Washington. "Well," he wrote, "...here is one who will never want to talk about it." And he rarely did.

In late 1945, Curtis was discharged and returned to his city editor's job at the Buffalo Evening News, moving from what were apparently pressure-laden military duties to the familiar pressures of putting out an afternoon newspaper. Curtis was apparently getting restless at the Evening News. On May 27, 1939, he had written a revealing letter from Buffalo to Mrs. Law when she was vacationing.

"This," he wrote, " was one of those nerve-frazzling, brain-cracking, soul-searing days when I come home wondering why I work as I do.

It's a familiar story to you, but it makes me very unhappy because I probably never will do anything about it except fume. And that is weak."

The Evening News at war's end offered little place for upward movement. Kirchhofer was in his heyday. He would continue as managing editor until 1956 and not retire as editor until 1966.

Still, Curtis may have been torn by the offer to join API. He was grateful for the excellent treatment by the Evening News. But he was probably yearning for a job more suited to his talents and personality.

Curtis reveled in his work at API. He knew that accepting certain tempting job offers to leave API would return him to a pressure-cooker. One flattering offer came in 1949, when he was still an associate director. It came from Lee Hills, executive editor of the Miami Herald. Impressed with what he had heard of Curtis and seen in a brief meeting, Hills offered Curtis a major post with the Herald, a job he later would identify only in general fashion.

In the late 1950s, Curtis wrote to Dolly and Louis Law from his home in Westchester County, New York: "Don't know whether Alma (his wife) told you we went to London in October. Ambassador (John Hay—Jock) Whitney, new owner of the New York Herald Tribune, wanted me to go to work as the boss man there. I said 'no,' although the income would have made me independently rich for the rest of my life. But I have a better job now. So why change?"

Curtis would not find his API years free of problems. What he did find was an almost perfect match of job and personality. In June 1967, when he had announced he would be leaving API after 20 years there, he wrote to a publisher in Iran who had attended one of API's foreign seminars. To recruit the seminar members, Curtis had traveled throughout the Middle East.

"My job at API has taken me to 56 different countries and to hundreds of hundreds of newspapers," he wrote. Not mentioned, but surely treasured by Curtis, were the hundreds of newspaper men and women who had come to him in API seminars.

Once Curtis wrote to a bedridden newspaper friend: "Some say 'Avoid Reminiscence.' I say to hell with them."

Far more than most other men, Monty Curtis had reason to reminisce.

12

Mr. Inside, Mr. Outside

During World War II, the U.S. Military Academy at West Point produced football teams that were undefeated for three seasons. Those Army teams were led by a bone-crunching fullback named Felix (Doc) Blanchard and an elusive halfback named Glenn Davis. Blanchard steamrollered through the middle of opposing lines. The versatile, quick-footed Davis bedeviled would-be tacklers with his open-field running.

In combination, they made each other more effective. Lauded by the nation's sportswriters, they became known as Mr. Inside (Blanchard) and Mr. Outside (Davis).

So when Walter Everett and Monty Curtis were pairing with such complementary cohesion at the American Press Institute in the 1950s and 1960s some described them as Mr. Inside and Mr. Outside, comparing them to the famous football players.

Curtis, the raconteur and promoter, was Mr. Outside—selling the idea of mid-career training to publishers and editors. Everett, the quiet, thorough administrator of impeccable judgment, was Mr. Inside, handling far more than his share of the detail requisite to successful seminars.

On the small API staff, obviously, the division of labor couldn't always be that clear-cut. But the strong pattern was there at API—Curtis to the outside, Everett to the inside.

Both liked the arrangement. Everett largely freed Curtis of details he disliked and also protected him from the impetuosity that mingled with his creativity.

Curtis never failed to say openly that in Everett he had exactly the right partner. Upon the death in 1951 of Floyd Taylor, API's first director, Curtis was senior to Everett in both age and, by two years, time with API. Curtis, therefore, was the logical candidate to succeed Taylor, and Columbia University shortly appointed him as director, on recommendation of the Advisory Board and the concurrence of journalism dean Carl Ackerman.

But Curtis valued Everett so highly that at first he proposed that they offer themselves as co-directors. Together, Curtis and Everett dropped the idea as impractical.

"Let me tell you about Walter," Curtis wrote to Tony Spina of the Detroit Free Press 24 years later. "I worked with him for 20 years. His judgment is superb... He saved me from many mistakes...He always likes to think things over and then give a calm opinion. He does not downgrade anything. He is just extremely careful."

It was a good summation that omitted one factor: the Everett tact. Time and again, Curtis would pour out ideas. Puffing on his pipe, Everett would listen quietly. He rarely failed to offer a good word about all the ideas. But then, usually in the form of a question, he would gently open the way for Curtis to shoot down his own ideas that were impractical.

"You're right, Walter," Curtis would say. "That's a damn fool idea. Forget it." There was never any sign that Curtis resented Everett's skillfully shunting his ideas into the wastebin.

That was Everett's way with not only Curtis but also with other colleagues. First, he would find a shred of merit in even the shakiest position and praise that shred. Then, meticulously, he would lay out his own analysis and depend on reason to prevail.

On rare occasions, reason did not prevail, as with one staff member who was not pulling his weight and repeatedly turned aside Everett's requests for a stronger effort. Everett reopened the issue several times and finally brought the laggard into a more acceptable position only by demonstrating exasperation.

Everett's diplomacy prevailed in a sticky episode during API's third seminar after the move to Reston, Virginia. That was in October 1974, and the seminar was for investigative reporters. Seminar members were housed and took meals at the nearby Sheraton Inn, which had opened only shortly before API completed its mid-summer move from Columbia University. Like a new ship, the Sheraton was on a shakedown cruise, and the API staff spent hours ironing out problems with the inn.

On the second or third evening of the seminar, the Sheraton manager called an API staff member in near panic. The seminar members had complained about the food quality, refused to eat dinner there and fanned out in then bucolic Reston to forage for food elsewhere. What was more, they told the Sheraton manager, they were not going to eat any more meals at the inn for the duration of the two-week seminar.

Though some seminar members have always had a knee-jerk tendency to criticize even first-rate meals, nothing close to this full-membership revolt had ever occurred. With almost two full weeks stretching ahead, what to do?

Everett was alerted. Next morning, he met with the food-strike ringleaders. He discerned that the other members had been stirred by only two or three core dissidents, one in particular. From a caterer, Everett ordered sandwiches, potato chips and softdrinks sent in for lunch at the API building. To the seminar members, he promised every effort to improve the Sheraton food, which apparently most members thought had been acceptable if not four-star all along.

Mollified, the chief dissident and the others returned to the Sheraton table.

In his years of co-managing with Curtis and also later when he was executive director, Everett snuffed out other fires with equal calm. As to teaming with Curtis, he later recalled that the Mr. Inside/ Mr. Outside relationship developed naturally; it wasn't planned or stated.

"Monty was superb as a public speaker, a one-on-one promoter, and a social conversationalist," Everett said. "He loved it. I, on the other hand, thoroughly enjoyed planning, organizing and even detail work such as fitting together a year's seminar schedule like a jigsaw puzzle. We shared all problems and decisions. Still, we gravitated toward our individual strengths. It was an entirely happy and harmonious relationship."

In 1965, 11 years after being named director, Curtis arranged to be designated executive director, so that he could elevate Everett from associate director to a new position, managing director. That was recognition of the deputy's role Everett had played all along.

Curtis-Everett formed the management team that phased in three associate directors and expanded the seminar programs in number and variety. When Curtis left API in 1967, there was no thought of any successor other than Everett. He remained in the top post until his retirement in 1975.

Everett's was the steady hand at the helm as API made the momentous decision to separate from Columbia and raise funds to construct its own building in Reston. No one else has matched Everett's 26 years with API in length of service.

In pressure situations, Everett maintained at least outward calm, and probably inner calm as well. He carried a heavy workload with seeming ease. Each morning, he would first take a moment to stoke his pipe with fragrant tobacco bought from a Madison Avenue shop.

He rotated several pipes.

Always dressed neatly and conservatively, he wore his suit jacket at his desk. Of average physical stature, he walked with a short stride and quick steps, always at a brisk clip. His pace was one of the few evidences of his busyness.

At Columbia, where air-conditioning was supplied by window units, he would cool his office to almost meat-locker frostiness. Colleagues meeting in Everett's office knew to wear their jackets. And still they shivered.

At his desk, piled high with letters and documents, Everett would reach into a stack and quickly pull out the sheet of paper he wanted. Colleagues, forever exploring in stacks on their own desks, were amazed by this faculty.

Moderating seminars, Everett's style departed greatly from that of Curtis. By his very nature, Curtis could not resist taking some of the spotlight from the discussion leader at the opposite end of the oval table. He tossed in anecdotes or opinions on the subject at hand.

In contrast, Everett was like the baseball umpire who makes all the right calls in undemonstrative fashion, moves the game along, but is almost invisible to players and fans alike.

Unlike Curtis, Walter Bentley Everett was no raconteur. But his pre-API life provided a wealth of anecdote potential. A quiet demeanor belied an adventuresome spirit and broad interests that ranged from stamp-collecting to the theater to professional football. For his biography in Who's Who in America, he boiled an exceptionally broad background down to six-and-a-half lines, four lines shorter than any other entry on the page and a meager indication of his accomplishments.

He did not mention, for example, that in 1975 he received the coveted Maria Moors Cabot Prize from Columbia University. Recipients of the annual award are selected from among journalists who have improved inter-American understanding in the Western Hemisphere. To select members for foreign seminars, Everett traveled extensively in Latin America and also encouraged many Latin American journalists to attend the regular API seminars.

Everett was born April 3, 1910, in Newark, New Jersey, the son of a lawyer father, Russell M. Everett, and Laura Bentley Everett. He grew up in nearby Summit and Bloomfield. Often he heard his father converse with an editor friend on the Newark News, then the dominant newspaper in northern New Jersey. Those talks aroused young Everett's interest in newspapers.

While attending Summit High School, he worked part-time on both the twice-a-week Summit Herald, which gave him no bylines, and the weekly Summit Press, where under the pen name Jack

Jacobus he previewed motion pictures at the local theater. That role brought him a handful of passes and additional popularity with schoolmates.

He then enrolled as a freshman at the University of Missouri with the aim of completing a five-year program that awarded double degrees—bachelor of arts and bachelor of journalism.

But that was not to be. At the end of his freshman year, Everett's father suffered a stroke. When a physician recommended a milder climate for the father, the family moved to a farm in Maryland. For a year, young Everett commuted to George Washington University in Washington, taking both day and night classes.

The father improved and wanted to return to Summit. So the family rented an apartment there. Son Walter, within commuting range, took night courses at Columbia University for a year. The father died at the end of the son's junior year, and Walter moved onto the Columbia campus for his final undergraduate year of journalism.

He was in the last Columbia journalism class before the dean began the change to a graduate school. The dean was Carl W. Ackerman. The paths that would lead to API were converging.

Everett received his bachelor-of-science degree in 1933. The Depression meant few newspaper jobs for the journalism graduates. Recognizing their poor prospects for employment, Everett and Samuel Lubell, a classmate who later gained national prominence as a political reporter and pollster, set out in a second-hand Ford on a free-lancing trip. Each carried about $100. They traveled for nine weeks in 22 states east of the Rocky Mountains.

Shrewdly, they had arranged for bread-and-butter money as correspondents for trade publications, which paid modestly but promptly. Everett's best free-lance account was Boot and Shoe Recorder. He became knowledgeable about footwear and reported on marketing trends from such places as Bismarck, North Dakota.

But the main Everett-Lubell objective was to write about the response to President Roosevelt's New Deal programs for economic recovery. They interviewed hundreds of people, especially farmers, whom they found bitter about agricultural controls, and their articles were printed in Current History, Scribner's magazine, Commentator, three or four newspapers, and Independent Woman, a serious women's magazine.

There were rejection slips as well, but by the time they returned to New York they were armed with enough bylines to enter the job competition.

Everett and Lubell went separate ways as newspaper reporters, but teamed again five years later for a second free-lance trip. This time, they traveled the South, Midwest and West, concentrating on relief and group health programs in industrial cities. To save on rooms and meals and also provide a mobile office, they towed a second-hand house trailer. They sold stories to the Saturday Evening Post, Collier's, the Reader's Digest, the Nation and the New York Times magazine, among others.

They profiled Gutson Borglum, who sculpted four Presidential heads on Mount Rushmore. They wrote of a bankrupt Indiana shoe factory that had been successfully taken over by the employees. They even wrote a light piece on a national convention of canary fanciers.

The acceptances were elating, but often came only after rejections or rewriting. Payment often did not reach them for months. With no fast-pay income from trade magazines, as they had five years earlier, expenses outran their income. By the time Everett and Lubell reached Miles City, Montana, they were down to their last few dollars.

The trailer's cupboard contained only a few cans of spaghetti. They existed on spaghetti for five days, until they reached Salt Lake City, where they sold the trailer and went their separate ways.

Lubell continued his free-lancing by hitchhiking, a common mode of travel in that Depression year of 1938. Everett spent several hours in the Salt Lake City public library, reading back issues of the three daily newspapers.

Because the Tribune was the largest and the one most like the Providence Journal, where he had worked between travels with Lubell, Everett walked into the Tribune newsroom and waited until the city editor, Ted Cannon, looked up from his assignment sheet. Everett said he wanted a job as a reporter. Cannon asked a few questions and then said: "We can use an extra reporter for a few days. Come in at noon tomorrow." The pay would be $45 a week.

Everett stayed a year, finding Utah with its Mormon culture an exciting new world for a reporter from the East. He covered federal court, the chamber of commerce and general assignment.

One regular chore was interviewing celebrities passing through Salt Lake City on the coast-to-coast Union Pacific trains. Tips came from press agents. During the train's 10-minute layover, Everett would dash aboard, locate the celebrity, ask enough questions for a story, and then scamper off to avoid being carried to the next station stop.

On one such assignment he met James A. Farley, then Postmaster General and a politician famous for remembering names. Fifteen years later, Everett unexpectedly met Farley in New York at a cocktail party for API seminar members. Farley greeted Everett by name and recalled the time and place of their sole previous meeting.

As a young reporter, Curtis had covered a major tragedy in the crash of the dirigible Shenandoah. In Utah, Everett covered the worst school bus accident in the nation's history. On December 1, 1938, in a blinding fog and snowstorm, a school bus laden with Jordan High School students pulled onto a grade crossing in the path of a speeding 51-car freight train, the "Flying Ute."

Twenty-three students and the driver were killed, 15 other students injured. With a dozen other reporters, Everett sought details of the accident that left fragments of bodies, clothing, textbooks and twisted metal scattered along 2,000 feet of track.

Later, hunting for obituary facts, Everett drove after dark to a remote country crossroads with four houses. "Each of the families had lost at least one child," Everett recalled. "The neighbors were all gathered in one of the kitchens, numb with grief."

Covering the tragedy was Everett's most vivid recollection of his Salt Lake City days. They ended when the Providence Journal unexpectedly invited him to return as assistant city editor, with an assurance that he would be promoted in six months.

Upon returning to New York after the first free-lance trip, the one just after his graduation from Columbia, Everett had found two jobs on the recommendation of Dean Ackerman. That, Everett said later, was to Ackerman's credit because of an episode when Everett was on the editorial board of his class yearbook.

A faculty committee headed by Ackerman announced the coveted Pulitzer Traveling Scholarship awards, grants for international travel. One award was given to a former student who a year earlier had been a faculty assistant grading the work of the current graduates-to-be.

Thinking that unfair, Everett wrote a yearbook editorial scathingly critical of Ackerman. He and classmates sent marked copies of the yearbook to the wire services and New York papers. All printed stories. That was the first adversarial relationship between Everett and Ackerman. It would be renewed some 16 years later when Everett joined API and engaged with Floyd Taylor and Curtis in a behind-the-scenes effort to make API independent of the Graduate School of Journalism and its dean.

Again, Ackerman showed no resentment. In fact, when Everett was promoted to API managing director and later to executive director, Ackerman sent a note saying he was glad for Everett and the journalism school. Everett last saw Ackerman when the dean emeritus was a feeble old man in a wheelchair, being pushed by a nurse on Broadway near the journalism building. He greeted Everett cordially, and they exchanged a few words.

Everett's first job after the initial free-lance tour, obtained on Ackerman's recommendation, was writing publicity for an obscure New York concert management agency, where he was assigned to promote a whistler. The whistler preferred classical recitals but also whistled with dance orchestras.

"This wasn't the greatest," Everett recalled, "but any employment was welcome in the Depression year of 1933."

A month later, Ackerman summoned Everett to his office, saying he had a real plum. Sevellon Brown, managing editor of the Providence Journal, was seeking a beginning reporter. Ackerman had recommended Everett. The job paid $25 a week.

Everett was elated. He looked up Providence on the map and took the next overnight boat from New York. At the Providence Journal, Everett was ushered in to meet Sevellon Brown. Brown assigned the new cub reporter to the Fall River, Massachusetts, office. Those who were successful in that forlorn, crime-ridden city of decaying cotton mills were assigned to other bureaus of the state-news staff and eventually to the city staff.

Earl Heathcote, the bureau manager, immediately sent Everett to cover a semi-professional soccer game. No matter that Everett had never watched an entire soccer game; such was life in the bureaus, where reporters covered a variety of stories. Noting Everett's thin jacket, poor protection against the cold of early December 1933, Heathcote stuffed a copy of the Sunday Journal between Everett's back and shirt.

After three years—and three bureaus—Everett was brought into the main office and worked as a reporter, copy editor and newscaster on the Journal's radio station. News was broadcast from the paper's newsroom. After a year of those mixed duties, Everett saw himself doing all right, but the road to promotion in Providence seemed long.

Meanwhile, his younger brother, William G. Everett, later president of Olin Ski Company, had gone to work in the circulation department of Greenwich Time, a newspaper in neighboring Connecticut. Greenwich Time needed a city editor and, on the brother's recommendation, offered the job to Walter Everett. He accepted. He left Greenwich after 18 months for his second free-lance excursion with Sam Lubell.

When Everett returned to the Providence Journal in 1939, it was as assistant city editor. A year later, he became city editor. After four years, he was appointed city editor on the larger sister newspaper, the Evening Bulletin.

During 12 years on the Providence papers, Everett had limited contact with Sevellon Brown, even when Everett was city editor. By then, Brown had been named editor and, soon after that, publisher. His office was on a different floor from that of the newsroom, and his orders came mostly through the managing editor or in memos.

Those were the years when city editors were supposed to crack the whip, and heaven help the reporter who strayed from perfection. Everett, though, either perceived the importance of more moderate ways or it was built into his personality.

Barry Brown, one of Sevellon Brown's two sons, was a reporter on Everett's staff before moving on to the paper's editorial page staff. He remembered Everett as organized and considerate, an editor who made the workplace pleasant and still got the job done.

John Strohmeyer, another reporter under Everett, became editor of the Bethlehem (Pennsylvania) Globe-Times and won a Pulitzer Prize there. He recalled Everett as "cool under fire, eminently fair, and admired for his news judgment...a highly respected craftsman."

Strohmeyer also recounted how Everett gave him and four other Columbia journalism students tryouts during Easter vacation in 1948. He saw Everett as a "compassionate leader who did not look down on this ragtag group of cub reporters."

Everett sent Strohmeyer to find out why a privately run diner managed to locate on city property in the middle of one of the busiest traffic squares in Providence. Strohmeyer traced deeds all the way back to Roger Williams, the founder of Providence. Tryout time ran out before Strohmeyer could pin down the story.

He told Everett something was fishy about that diner's sitting in the city square, and he would like to come back and finish the story after graduation. What Strohmeyer didn't realize was that the diner-in-the-square was an in-house ploy to test the staying power of beginners.

Everett hired Strohmeyer, and Strohmeyer handled dozens of investigative stories in Providence. He worked alongside such other future national leaders of journalism as Ben Bagdikian and John C. Quinn.

Bagdikian became a leading press critic and at retirement was dean of the graduate school of journalism at the University of California at Berkeley. Quinn was hired out of Providence College to take telephoned dictation. Everett quickly recognized Quinn's talent and moved him first to reporting and then to assistant city editor. Quinn moved on to become vice president/news for Gannett Company and later the editor of USA Today.

Everett attended the first API City Editors Seminar, in December 1946, and was brought back as a discussion leader. On his second turn as a discussion leader, Everett was asked by Floyd Taylor if someday he would be interested in joining the API staff. They discussed it briefly and only as a distant possibility.

So, a few months later, Everett was surprised to receive a telephone call at the Providence city desk from Edward Drew, the public relations director for Lever Brothers Company in Cambridge,

Massachusetts. Drew wanted to discuss the number-two position on his staff. Everett asked him how he happened to get his name. "From Floyd Taylor," Drew replied.

Everett was astonished that Taylor would encourage him to leave Providence. Drew said that he didn't know Taylor but had read a story about API in Editor & Publisher and thought API would be a good source for recruitment. Everett and Drew met twice in Boston. Lever Brothers was the third largest soap-products manufacturer and had a dynamic young president, Charles Luckman.

Everett's salary would be twice what he earned in Providence, with assured increases, an expense account, generous fringe benefits, a private office overlooking the Charles River and a full-time secretary. Everett took the job, but never asked Taylor about the recommendation, assuming that Drew's phone call to Taylor had caught the latter in a preoccupied moment.

Sevellon Brown, Everett said, was unhappy about his departure and would have been furious if he had known about Taylor's role.

At Lever Brothers, Everett found Drew and the eight-member staff to be topnotch professionals with high ethical standards. Although Everett stayed with Lever Brothers little more than a year, he learned much that was useful later in public relations, promotion, and personnel management.

Everett never felt really at home in Lever Brothers' corporate world, however. When Taylor telephoned out of the blue and asked if Everett would like to join the API staff, he accepted "immediately and joyfully" despite a reduction in salary of $5,000. Everett said that one way or another he would have left Lever Brothers, despite a promising future there, because he couldn't get excited about such public relations duty as announcing a new soap product.

The announcement of Everett's appointment was made by Ackerman on November 1, 1949. The New York Times carried a picture and story on the new associate director. A headline above Everett's picture read: "Soap Company Executive Appointed at Columbia."

When Curtis and Everett were later discussing ways of promoting API, Everett would sometimes make a suggestion. Curtis would grin and say, "That's an admirable soap company approach." In 1950, Everett took a three-month leave of absence from API under circumstances not of his own making. President Harry S Truman had appointed Nelson A. Rockefeller to head an International Development Advisory Board to implement the objectives of the President's Point Four Program, which called for aiding underdeveloped regions.

Everett's friend, Lubell, was hired to head a research and writing committee. Lubell needed a deputy and mentioned Everett's name to Rockefeller, who was impressed by the collaborative free-lancing of

Lubell and Everett. Lubell called Everett, who saw the job offer as an exciting opportunity. But he told Lubell he didn't feel he could ask for a leave of absence after being with API for only about a year.

Within an hour, Floyd Taylor called Everett into his office. Taylor said that Columbia's president, Grayson Kirk, had received a call from Rockefeller, a personal friend and Columbia benefactor, asking if Everett could be made available. Everett reported to 30 Rockefeller Plaza two days later and worked there five months.

Everett recalled that most of the advisory board's work was done at Radio City. He and Lubell sat in on all sessions and prepared the report. Rockefeller sometimes timed the board's work break with the performances of the Radio City Music Hall Rockettes, the dancing group.

A window in Rockefeller's office looked down on the stage through wall-to-wall glass. When the Rockettes came on, Rockefeller would raise a curtain, and his work group would watch the show. Later, Rockefeller thanked Everett and Lubell for "putting the ideas which the board wanted to get across into language that could be easily understood."

Everett devoted the rest of his career to API. When API severed its 28-year relationship with Columbia University, became incorporated in Virginia and moved to its own building in Reston, he was age 64, only one year from retirement.

He and his wife Beth owned a comfortable home in Hastings-on-Hudson, close to the commuter rail line in Westchester County, New York. They liked the community. Another person less committed to API might have taken early retirement rather than face the rigors of a move and the startup in Reston.

But no one saw any indication that quitting ever crossed the minds of Walter and Beth Everett. They sold their Dobbs Ferry home and rented a townhouse in Reston for API's maiden year there. Upon retirement, they moved to Newport, Rhode Island, close to where he had newspapered on the Providence Journal. The Journal Company appointed him to its board of directors, and he served until age 70 and mandatory retirement.

In 1967, when Monty Curtis resigned from API, scores of newspaper friends had given him a rousing party on the Columbia campus. They presented him with a silver bowl from Tiffany's and commissioned a British woodcarver to craft a mahogany plaque. That plaque, with the following words from a Curtis speech, hangs in the API building:

> *"Our job is to make tomorrow's newspaper better than today's. Daily discontent with the product has built every great newspaper."*

Now it was Everett's turn, and his newspaper friends responded with equal enthusiasm. More than a hundred friends from across the country gathered at the Sheraton Reston Inn on June 6, 1975, for the "Walter Everett Night to Remember," which featured the "Waltergate Trial," a word play on the national Watergate scandal.

After that fete, Everett's friends turned to the same British craftsman for a plaque similar to that made for Curtis. For his plaque, Everett chose these words:

> "All departments of a newspaper play
> important roles, but their common goal must
> be to serve the reader and the community."

For the "Night to Remember," Newbold Noyes Jr., former editor of the Washington Star and also a former API board member, wrote the script, which the obstreperous actor-journalists followed loosely. Appropriately robed, Turner Catledge played the judge. J. Allan Meath of Ottaway Newspapers was prosecutor, Noyes defense attorney, Monty Curtis bailiff.

Said prosecutor Meath: "We intend to impeach him (Everett) for conspiracy to improve the quality of the nation's daily press."

After witness upon witness, the trial ended like this:

Defense attorney Noyes: "Mr. Everett, have you ever in your life tried to help a newspaper to improve?"

Everett: "Never."

Noyes: "Has it ever crossed your mind to try to do such a thing?"

Everett: "Well, once I thought of writing a letter to the editor. But then I thought, what the hell!" (That was pretty strong language for Everett, but he was only reading his lines.)

Judge Catledge (after a voice vote of the jury found Everett guilty of conspiring to improve the nation's press): "Mr. Everett, you are hereby banished to Newport, Rhode Island. The court is adjourned. Waiter, bring me another drink."

13

How the Word Spread

At certain newspapers, the impact of the professionalism encouraged by API's seminars was evident from the beginning. But the spread of the API influence was uneven and often slow on newspapers reluctant to discard traditional and outdated ways.

Vincent S. Jones, executive editor of the Utica (New York) Observer and Dispatch and later editorial director of Gannett newspapers, was one of API's first and most frequent discussion leaders. Years later, he related his saddest memory of API: The comment of a young southern editor who listened to a Jones presentation on measuring reader interest in various kinds of news coverage.

"This is all fascinating," said the editor. "I can see how your staff must respond to such stimulating ideas. But what are you going to do on a newspaper which refuses to change anything—and is still very successful?"

A few months later, Jones was a discussion leader at a Seminar for General Reporters and noticed another barrier to change: Even when editors were current on promising developments, many didn't share their newfound knowledge with their staffs.

Jones had described to the reporters the continuing study of newspaper reading being made by the Advertising Research Foundation. Jones wrote to his Gannett boss: "The ignorance of the Continuing Study was pathetic. One boy (seminar member) said: 'Are these things state secrets? Is there any reason why we shouldn't know the survey facts about our own papers?' "

For a decade and more after World War II, newspapers in many communities reaped big profits although they lacked progressive management and gave readers inferior news reports.

At API's very first seminar—the one for managing editors and news editors—Louis Seltzer, editor of the Cleveland Press "raised the question whether the energies of newspaper executives were not too much taken up by problems of organization and labor relations, with the result that many newspapers had become mere assembly plants for syndicated news and features." That was reported by the Providence Journal.

In December 1951, an internal memo for executives of the Gannett group said, "API directors do take issue with people who argue that 'you can't quarrel with success.' This is tossed at people who argue for better makeup, livelier typography, readable writing, more illustrations...To the charge that some papers have succeeded in spite of outworn and obtuse policies and methods, this challenging argument can be advanced: 'Think how much more successful they might be.' "

This widespread newspaper failure to perceive how society and the larger media picture were changing burned into the memory of Monty Curtis. In 1971, he wrote his reaction to Mal Mallette, API managing director: "I used to become furious when I heard of seminar members—and there were many—who returned home and did nothing with their material."

He told of a member who returned to his newspaper in Ohio from the seminar for editorial writers in 1947 and inexplicably attempted no changes. This was not a case where the publisher resisted change. In fact, the publisher asked the returning editor what he had learned at API.

"Nothing," the editor replied, even though his fellow seminar members seemed to have reaped bushels of helpful information. The result, Curtis said, was that the newspaper and its parent group never sent another staff member to API. Significantly, that newspaper came to be regarded as inferior.

In 1972, Curtis disclosed a similar feeling to Barry Bingham Sr., a member and former chairman of the API Advisory Board and publisher of the Courier-Journal and Louisville Times.

"Be wary of comments by a certain kind of returning API seminarian," Curtis wrote. "This seminarian (tells) the boss what the seminarian thinks the boss wants to hear...The cure is for the boss himself to tell the prospective seminarian that he is to dig out all possible criticism for the improvement of the newspaper..."

Gannett's Jones referred to "Stone Age publishers and other bosses" and "ridiculous rules and practices" that shackled some seminar members upon returning home. That was sometimes the case. But not all resistance to change could be laid at the feet of publishers and other major executives.

Norman E. Isaacs, executive editor of the Courier-Journal and Louisville Times, appointed the first newspaper ombudsman in the United States and was among the first to adopt a six-column format for news content. He often told API seminar members that he found the most resistance not among fellow executives but among sub-editors and reporters.

Other patterns also formed. The first API seminar member from a given newspaper could be a lonely voice calling for change. But as others from the same newspaper returned from API the lonely voice often became part of a small chorus. Change was delayed but sooner or later triumphed. Then, too, editors who had been pressing with limited success for changes before attending API often found their staffs more receptive to the same ideas when they cited API discussions as a testimonial.

On the whole, API moderators thought that members of seminars on advertising, circulation, promotion and production were more receptive to new ways than news-editorial people.

One reason was built in. The progress or decline of advertising and circulation departments could quickly be measured by cold numbers. For news-editorial, measurement was delayed or difficult to separate from other factors involved in the complex equations of readership and circulation. Meanwhile, production departments leaped at innovation that would rescue them from the cumbersome technology dominated by the hot-metal Linotype machines first used in 1886.

For at least two decades after World War II, many newspapers comprised a collection of fiefdoms, with each department rarely communicating with the others. If there was disappointing growth in circulation, for example, it was not uncommon for the circulation department to blame the news department—and vice versa. By broadening its seminars to include not only news-editorial but also other departments, API began to carve windows in the interdepartmental walls.

In its first Management and Costs Seminar, in September 1949, API failed to include for the 20 members, all but one of whom lacked news-editorial experience, a discussion of news side problems and responsibilities. Six months later, for its second Management and Costs program, API brought in James E. Kerney, editor of the Trenton Times, to discuss "The Newspaper's Relationship with Its Readers." Similar discussions became a staple for all non-news seminar groups.

It must have been at least small comfort to certain editors when their non-news counterparts began perceiving that thorny problems were a part of newsroom existence.

Except for early sessions that briefed news executives on mechanical production techniques, however, API did not begin to open communication from the newsroom side of interdepartmental walls until the Publishers and Editors Seminar in January 1953. The seminar was designed for smaller newspapers. "Publishers" was included in the title because on small papers editors sometimes doubled as publishers.

API gave Alvah H. Chapman Jr., business manager of the Columbus (Georgia) Ledger and Enquirer, and Quinton E. Beauge, executive editor of the Williamsport (Pennsylvania) Sun and Gazette, a full morning to discuss "mechanical production; news room operation; hiring and training; and interdepartmental cooperation."

In program listings at least, the topic of interdepartmental cooperation in news-side seminars did not appear again until 1954 when a Managing Editors and News Editors Seminar heard Barney G. Cameron, circulation manager of the New York Herald Tribune, address "Circulation Department-News Department Cooperation." After that, seminar programs usually included a session on interdepartmental cooperation.

Looking back, Vin Jones said he had always regretted that so much of the "wonderful material developed at API seminars" was restricted to relatively small audiences and that the "confidentiality provision prevented publication or wider distribution of so many good ideas and success stories."

Actually, the confidentiality rule arose because Floyd Taylor and his successors wanted seminar members to be uninhibited in discussing problems. Taylor ruled that comments by members were off the record, that members were free to say what they wished without fearing an embarrassing breach of confidence. If a member felt that his boss was a thickhead and a penny-pincher, he could freely say so. Then fellow members would offer helpful suggestions on the best way to deal with that boss.

Except for that restriction, members were free to report seminar gleanings to their own newspapers. And they did, often with reports approaching the length of a small book. Some prepared separate reports for the different departments. Some held staff meetings, sort of mini-seminars.

During the first few seminars in 1946 and 1947, Jerry Walker of Editor & Publisher sat in and reported discussions. By agreement, he did not quote members or discussion leaders by name. He discontinued his attendance when it became obvious that his presence was discouraging discussion.

With rare exceptions, that's the way it was over the years—no outsiders in the conference room, no quoting of touchy comments, and no reluctance to speak out. A problem not described was a problem on which other members couldn't help.

The early hope of Sevellon Brown, Floyd Taylor, Grove Patterson and perhaps others had been that API would indeed share seminar information widely through publications. Patterson, editor-in-chief of the Toledo Blade, was the first chairman of the API Advisory Board. That publishing objective was not reached until 1950 and 1951, when API published two handbooks for editors and then ditched the project as impractical.

The first handbook, in hardcover, was titled "Food in Newspapers" and contained 20 pages. The second, with 74 pages, was "Fashion in Newspapers." Each was printed by the Columbia University Press and offered for sale at two dollars a copy.

Garrett D. Byrnes, Sunday editor of the Providence Journal, wrote the handbook on food. It grew out of a session on food coverage during an API seminar for Sunday editors. Byrnes also wrote the text for the handbook on fashion, which was profusely illustrated with pictures provided by the New York Times under supervision of Ben Dalgin, the paper's director of art and reproduction. Again the text was based on discussions at API.

In his introduction to the first handbook, Taylor described the plan for ongoing publication and the impetus behind it. He wrote that the handbooks would provide down-to-earth information that would help satisfy reader needs; a hoped-for byproduct was to strengthen newspapers as an advertising medium.

"It seems essential," Taylor wrote, "to grant the persistent requests of publishers and editors for publication of occasional handbooks based on material published at the Institute. The books will not be a substitute for attendance at seminars. Most of them, like this one, will contain only an expanded discussion of a subject covered in one session of one seminar."

API had indeed received requests for publications. But Sevellon Brown also had in mind a "quid pro quo," some way of rewarding newspapers for participating in API. In 1948, when API had visions of an endowment, there were quite grandiose plans for publishing.

Patterson wrote a promotional article for use in the endowment drive. Endowment income, he said, would enable "issuance of an Institute Quarterly containing articles for all categories of newspaper men and women on the techniques of their work and specialized assignments and upon the social, economic and political problems of the day with which they are dealing.

"These articles would not be a transcript of the seminar discussions but they would be suggested as to subject matter by the seminar proceedings...A plan for the distribution and sale of this Quarterly has been developed which it is believed will, after an experimental period, make it nearly, if not entirely, self-sustaining on the basis of a wide circulation in newspaper offices."

That plan died when the endowment campaign failed, but the publication goal lived on in a scaled-down fashion. In his introduction to the second handbook—the one on fashion which also covered beauty news—Taylor wrote: "Several other handbooks, now in preparation, will deal with more complex and difficult newspaper problems. The contents of one, for example, will be a summary of the large amount of material the Institute has gathered to aid newspapers in achieving high standards of accuracy."

Monty Curtis frequently led seminar sessions on accuracy. Perhaps his material was intended for the third handbook. For manifold reasons that handbook was never produced. Sales of the first two handbooks were disappointingly small, and their cost was not retrieved. The two-dollar price was high for such thin publications at that time. Also, coverage of food and fashion was not a leading concern of editors in that day.

Another reason may have been that, despite the reluctance of some newspapers to change, others were changing at a fast pace. They served in effect as daily, updated textbooks on topics like food and fashion.

Moreover, Taylor's death in August 1951, shortly after publication of the second handbook, left API with a staff of only Curtis and Everett until Bill Stucky was added in September 1955. Although some of the planned future handbooks would probably have been written by seminar members, they still would have required time from the API staff, time that could not be spared.

Requests for printed information continued to pop up. They were answered only after API moved to Reston and began publishing an occasional newsletter, the API Round Table. It often contained summaries of seminar topics.

Though publishing handbooks was abandoned, the teachings at API were distributed in ways other than the reports of returning seminar members. Seminar groups sometimes formed alumni associations. They kept in touch with each other for up to several years through newsletters or reunions at newspaper conventions.

The first alumni association was formed by the 21 members of the sixth seminar, for general reporters, in May 1947. Everett M. Smith of the Christian Science Monitor prepared a typewritten summary of 67 pages that was distributed to fellow seminar members and passed along in some cases to reporters at newspapers not represented in the seminar.

The summary contained myriad nuggets of advice. Columbia's journalism dean, Ackerman, for example, who had been both a reporter and press agent (the latter function is now called public relations), warned members that press agents were usually paid more to get a slanted story over than a reporter was paid for a truthful story.

Curtis, then a rookie discussion leader, advised: Insure against superficial reporting by always asking yourself if anything remains unexplained or unanswered.

Charles H. Hamilton of Richmond counseled that a good reporter must have a certain toughness—and a certain gentleness.

The celebrated Meyer Berger of the New York Times asserted: "The great weakness of many feature writers is to hunt with the pack, stopping where the others stop. I think that is where a feature writer might well begin."

Bernard (Barney) Kilgore, president of the Wall Street Journal, offered this: "You will never offend an expert (reader) by explaining something he already knows. Non-experts will like it. So forget the experts."

How long members of the May 1947 General Reporters Seminar remained in organized touch is not clear. But soon two permanent organizations that would have major impact on newspapers were formed as a result of API seminars. They were the National Conference of Editorial Writers (NCEW) and the American Association of Sunday and Feature Editors (AASFE).

Leslie Moore of the Worcester Telegram and Gazette later described in the Masthead, NCEW's quarterly publication, how NCEW developed from the four-weeks-long 1947 Editorial Writers Seminar.

Moore wrote that his publisher, George F. Booth, "was cheerful enough about getting up the small fortune for fees and expenses to send me to API for a month (and by parlor car yet!) but he was not at all convinced the results would warrant it.

"Anyway, the first day of the seminar...produced enough lively, solid stuff to stir several remarks among the lads to the effect that if this was a sample, please God, more editorial writers might be privileged to get together more often, and somebody even went to Floyd Taylor with the suggestion that this same bunch be convened at the same time the next year. (Floyd just smiled amiably; he had other seminars to run.)

"The last afternoon, as I recall it, Floyd Taylor suggested a small ad hoc committee meet in his office to think aloud about the future...We talked...Well, why not tackle Washington (as a meeting site) with an editorial conference for editorial writers from all over? No junket. No hoop-la. Strictly a working deal, patterned as nearly after the seminar as we could make it, trying to recapture its zeal and pragmatism for as many days as practicable—such was the scheme."

That's the way it was and has been, an annual NCEW convention of four days dominated by critiques of one another's editorial pages. At the outset, though, success was far from certain. Worcester publisher Booth, impressed by Moore's post-seminar enthusiasm, advanced $500 to mail an announcement-invitation letter to hundreds of editorial-page editors across the U.S. and Canada.

"Me," wrote Moore, "I couldn't believe anything until that final day when I hung around the Statler (hotel in Washington) for an hour and saw tall, short, lean, round, oldish, youngish types lugging in bags and saying they had come to a meeting of editorial writers. I thought a faint air of wonderment hovered around each."

In another article, Moore wrote: "If it lasts for centuries, I fancy the National Conference of Editorial Writers will always bear the stamp of that first API seminar."

NCEW's first meeting in Washington was attended by 103 persons. It welcomed all interested editorial writers into membership and by 1990 had grown to 575 members. In contrast, membership of the American Association of Sunday and Feature Editors, was purposely kept small for 25 years. Paul Neely, Sunday editor of the St. Petersburg Times, recorded some of the AASFE history in 1982, when he was its president.

The first API seminar for Sunday Editors and Feature Editors was held for three weeks in October and November 1947. On the final afternoon the 17 members were a tired lot, Paul Neely wrote.

With the discussion leaders, they had examined every phase of Sunday and feature coverage. They had heard from newspaper editors like Lester Markel of the New York Times and magazine editors like Raymond Carlson, editor of Arizona Highways, noted for its striking color photographs. On comics, they had heard Milton Caniff and Al Capp, creators respectively of Steve Canyon and Li'l Abner.

Though weary, Neely reported, the 17 members must have been sorry that the seminar was ending, for Garrett D. Byrnes of the Providence Journal proposed that the group reconvene annually. The other members welcomed the proposal, and AASFE was born, with Byrnes the first president. The association's first meeting was at API.

AASFE's original constitution required that new members be proposed, seconded and voted upon. Sentiment was to keep the group small. In the 1950s the limit was changed to 50 members; in 1967 that was raised to 60. The ceiling was lifted entirely in 1972. In 1989, membership totaled 140.

Other associations were formed as a direct or indirect result of enthusiasm crystalized by API seminars. One association, the Society of Newspaper Design, was established much later—in 1978—by members of the first API seminar devoted entirely to newspaper design. (API held a five-day Design, Makeup and Typography Seminar in 1956, but a third of the program was on improving printing quality.)

Ironically, Monty Curtis came to oppose the proliferation of specialized newspaper associations, although he may have welcomed them at the outset, when they were few in number. Then, too, in API's second year the American Society of Newspaper Editors, which had been founded in 1923, praised API for its role in improving newspapers. The resolution boosted API's stature and no doubt generated a number of seminar members.

But soon one new association seemed to encourage formation of yet another, whether API-associated or not.

In 1975, when Curtis was a Knight-Ridder vice president, he opposed the startup of the Investigative Reporters Association (IRE), telling its sponsors that "every service they proposed has already been performed competently...Still, they went ahead. 'Twas ever thus."

A Curtis letter to Mal Mallette, by then API director, referred to the Curtis opposition during his active API days. "Several times," he wrote, "I saw a movement start in the city editors seminars for a city editors association like APME (Associated Press Managing Editors) and others. Great God, how this business is over-organized...Someday somebody should do a piece on this, but it could not come from me because I am biased. The duplication of services, the horrifying total expense, and above all the wasted money on meetings from which there are no results would shock newspaper owners."

Although duplication was costly, it expedited the acquisition of new skills and understanding, much of which could be traced to API seminars. In the beginning, much of the expertise espoused at API came from the few newspapers that had introduced superior new techniques. API searched out the innovating newspapers and brought in their key people as seminar discussion leaders. The search included magazines, universities, government, industry and think tanks.

New techniques were challenged by the crossfire of seminar members. Ideas that survived the challenge spread like the ripples from a pebble tossed into a pond.

Lists of the members at early seminars show different patterns of influence. There were members already of great influence and others destined to ascend to high positions, where they had the clout to mandate change.

As a sampling, here are members who attended API in its first five years and became widely known for their achievement:

In 1946, Nick B. Williams of the Los Angeles Times, Eugene S. Pulliam of the Indianapolis News and Felix R. McKnight of the Dallas Morning News.

In 1947, George H. Beebe of the Miami Herald, Marshall Field Jr. of the Chicago Sun-Times, Martin S. Hayden of the Detroit News, J. Russell Wiggins of the New York Times, Murray Powers of the Akron Beacon Journal, Thomas L. Boardman of the Cleveland Press, and Arthur C. Deck of the Deseret News, Salt Lake City.

In 1948, Arville Schaleben of the Milwaukee Journal.

In 1949, Donald M. Reynolds of the Fort Smith (Arkansas) Times Record, Howard H (Tim) Hays of the Riverside Press and Daily Enterprise, Charles R. Buxton of the Denver Post, Lisle Baker Jr. of the Courier-Journal and Louisville Times, G. Prescott Low of the Quincy (Massachusetts) Patriot Ledger, Edward L. Gaylord of the Daily Oklahoman and Oklahoma City Times, Donald P. Miller of the Allentown (Pennsylvania) Morning Call and Evening Chronicle, and I. Z. Buckwalter of the Lancaster (Pennsylvania) New Era and Intelligencer Journal.

In 1950, Alvah H. Chapman Jr. of the Columbus (Georgia) Ledger and Enquirer, Bert Struby of the Macon (Georgia) Telegraph and News, Robert C. Achorn of the Worcester Telegram and Evening Gazette, Hugh N. Boyd of the New Brunswick (New Jersey) Daily Home News, and Phil A. Bucheit of the Spartanburg (South Carolina) Herald and Journal.

And in 1951, Buford Boone of the Tuscaloosa (Alabama) News, James H. Ottaway of Ottaway Newspapers, Carl A. Jones of the Johnson City (Tennessee) Press-Chronicle, and T. Eugene Worrell of the Bristol Herald Courier and Virginia-Tennessean.

As API expanded its seminars, its influence broadened and improved all aspects of newspapers—news gathering, writing and editing, commentary, advertising sales, manufacturing (printing), distribution, and management.

On the news side alone, API was a catalyst that brought about not only higher professional performance but also a landmark change in philosophy; newspapers began reporting topics that had been largely ignored in the past but were central to readers' lives. Business news is but one example. And newspapers began working harder to explain the meaning of the news.

In such manner, API helped newspapers gain strength against the gale winds of societal change. Regardless of the problems that newspapers would face almost a half century after API was founded, few would dispute that newspapers over that span had become infinitely better in every phase of operation and service to readers.

Monty Curtis, who favored Biblical allusions, described API as "an instrument for spreading the gospel."

And so it was.

14

Going Global

E arly in 1948, the API staff comprised just two: Floyd Taylor, the founding director, and Monty Curtis, the associate director who had come aboard the previous November. API had not completed its second annual cycle of six seminars and was still learning how to conduct successful programs. Taylor and Curtis were pondering the addition of new kinds of seminars as a way to build attendance. And they were increasingly troubled about the institute's financial health.

Although they already had their hands full, they leaped at a challenging new opportunity.

Germany, defeated in World War II, had been partitioned into four zones and occupied by military forces of the Soviet Union, France, Great Britain and the United States. In 1947, a group of American newspaper editors toured the American zone. Their number included Paul C. Smith of the San Francisco Chronicle and Frank Ahlgren of the Memphis Commercial Appeal. Smith was a member of the API Advisory Board, Ahlgren would be later.

General Dwight D. Eisenhower told the editors that the principal problems in building democracy in West Germany concerned schools and newspapers. He was receiving help from Columbia Teachers College on re-establishing the pre-Hitler school system, but needed assistance with the newspapers. After years of Nazi propaganda, the German citizens did not believe their newspapers.

In his Remembrance, Monty Curtis described what happened next. Ahlgren told Eisenhower that he should send a small group of good, young newspaper people to the American Press Institute for three months.

Ahlgren apparently felt that German newspapers needed a catalytic injection. Adolf Hitler had snuffed out free expression for 15 years. Few postwar German journalists understood the function of a free press or could shake off the years of subjection.

A year later, Eisenhower had become president of Columbia University, the long-sought prestigious successor to Nicholas Murray Butler. Eisenhower remembered Ahlgren's suggestion and broached it to API director Taylor. Taylor liked the notion of holding a seminar for German publishers and editors. But funds were needed.

Taylor's Long Island neighbor, Flora Rhind, worked for the Rockefeller Foundation. She suggested that Eisenhower apply to the foundation for a grant, and he did, on June 10, 1948. Eight days later, the Rockefeller Foundation awarded $36,246 to API, stipulating a post-seminar report, accounting of expenditures and return of money not spent.

With the grant, API held its first foreign seminar, for German publishers and editors, September 11-October 23, 1948. Fifteen German journalists attended, among them editors and owners of large and small newspapers. Annemarie Lagens, editor of Mosaik, a Berlin magazine, became the first woman to attend API, predating the few women who attended API domestic programs later that year.

The seminar, pretty much the model for later foreign seminars, had three parts: discussions at API, observation periods at newspapers and magazines, and independent travel.

That seminar was the first of 25 foreign seminars held by API between 1948 and 1971. From 1948 to 1951, four seminars were held for German journalists and three for Japanese journalists. All were aimed, as Taylor put it, at "study on an advanced level of the principles and techniques most desirable for a free press in a democratic society." Later, attention to a free press continued, but more emphasis was placed on techniques for improving newspaper quality.

The 25 seminars brought more than 300 foreign journalists, from 50 countries, to API. The first seven foreign seminars, for either Germany and Japan, were held at the request of the occupying U.S. Army. When that series ended, the Ford Foundation thought that similar programs for the economically underdeveloped nations would help their newspapers take a leadership role in social, economic and political reforms.

So seminars were held for Latin America, Asia, and the Middle East and North Africa. Starting in 1966, three consecutive annual seminars were held for European and North American editors or foreign editors, with one or two U.S. or Canadian members mixed in. The Rockefeller and Ford foundations were joint sponsors during five years starting in 1956. The Ford Foundation alone sponsored the final 10 foreign seminars.

Painful lessons on how to administer a foreign seminar were learned from the first program for Germans. Those 15 members were recruited and briefed on the seminar in their home communities not by API but by the U.S. military government. Taylor told the Rockefeller Foundation that insufficient care had been taken.

He listed eight members as "well equipped to profit from their visit to the United States." Two others, Taylor wrote, were qualified but had trouble with English (no translators were used in the foreign seminars). One member had "an enthusiasm for liquor that made him a problem child." Taylor described the other four members as "the least desirable." One of those was a "matter of constant concern...and seemed to be in a neurotic condition."

That experience caused API to send its own staff member abroad to interview seminar candidates as soon as it obtained grants with provision for the pre-seminar travel. For the first seven foreign seminars, API had lived with choices made by the U.S. military governments.

Subsequent interviewing trips by an API staff member lasted as long as seven weeks. Members for some seminars were sought in as many as 10 countries. Interviewing abroad had an advantage beyond member selection. The API interviewer became familiar with the needs of the newspapers and could plan the seminar program accordingly.

The foreign seminars created an especially exciting period for the API staff. Curtis went abroad six times between 1954 and 1966, three times to Asia and one time each to the Middle East and Northern Africa, Latin America, and Europe. Between 1956 and 1965, Everett interviewed candidates three times in Latin America and once each in the Middle East and Asia.

Russell W. Schoch, an associate director who joined API in 1961, sought foreign members three times between 1963 and 1970, in Latin America, Africa and Asia. Malcolm F. Mallette traveled to Europe in 1967 and to Asia in 1971. Associate directors William M. Stucky, William C. Sexton and Clarence Dean each went abroad once between 1958 and 1968.

API sought in 1959 to hold a seminar for Australia and New Zealand because journalists in those countries were so isolated. New Zealand newspapers were interested, but those in Australia were not. API substituted a seminar for Latin America.

The Rockefeller and Ford foundations wrote the checks and then stood back. The U.S. State Department provided round-trip transportation from the members' home countries to New York City for many of the seminars, and screened candidates for security. API selected or rejected on professional qualifications those not disqualified for security reasons. The U.S. Information Agency sometimes suggested potential interviewees, but that assistance was welcomed.

In all instances, API was unfettered in program planning and conduct. And, starting in 1954, it selected the members.

Sometimes API and the State Department did not agree. Everett visited a Latin American city where he wanted one candidate and the State Department representative wanted someone from a fringe newspaper, apparently because the paper was generous in using U.S. press releases. Everett and the man from State argued for two days without agreement. No one was invited from that country.

Another disagreement, in Latin America, went public. Everett invited and the State Department approved a travel grant for a young editor from a reasonably independent newspaper in a country ruled by a dictator. The editor was also a local correspondent for the New York Times, and the Times printed one of his stories that offended the dictator.

The dictator pressured the local publisher, who withdrew his sponsorship of the young editor. At that, the U.S. embassy canceled the travel grant.

Everett was at Kennedy Airport in New York City awaiting an early arrival for the seminar when he was paged by Frank Starzel, general manager of the Associated Press. The Times was breaking a story on the situation, and Starzel wanted Everett's comment. Everett withheld comment until he conferred with Monty Curtis back at API.

Curtis and Everett gained an emergency meeting with Columbia University President Grayson Kirk, who had succeeded Eisenhower and was a great friend of API. They proposed that API stand firm on the invitation and provide from its own funds the travel money the State Department had withdrawn. Kirk approved.

Furious, the Latin American publisher charged that API was interfering in the conduct of his newspaper and said he would make a formal complaint when the Inter American Press Association met in Havana. Everett attended the meeting prepared for a confrontation. But the publisher, either cooled or dissuaded, did not bring up the matter.

For API, it was important to stake out its independence in holding foreign seminars. It could not be beholden to either a government or a financial supporter such as a foundation. After all, API symbolized the independence of free newspapers. Despite its precautions, the possibility of foreign seminars projecting a harmful image was apparently the topic of recurring internal discussion.

This is shown by Floyd Taylor's letter of reply to Turner Catledge on December 14, 1950. Catledge, then assistant managing editor of the New York Times, was a member of API's Advisory Board. The Catledge letter does not survive, but Taylor's reply makes its contents clear. Taylor wrote:

"I received today your letter on foreign seminars and I have talked on the subject with Sevellon Brown and Dean Ackerman.

"Sevellon and the Dean have changed their minds and apparently would approve almost any foreign program while the international situation is so bad. As matters stand now, I find that I have more doubts about foreign seminars than they do.

"I am in general agreement with your point of view—that the question probably is one of degree. Your argument that we do not want to become known as an American propaganda agency seems to me to be valid. I am sure you are correct, too, in arguing that we do not want to spread the idea that we should rely on the government or foundations for financial support.

"The Institute is a newspaper project. If a time comes when newspapers will not support its programs it should be closed down. There is the further point, a practical one, that there would be no hope of long-term support from either the government or foundations. I would like to conduct a foreign program now and then, especially if it is financed by a foundation, but I am aware of some of the dangers and I am sure we should be cautious."

For the foreign seminars, API assembled impressive resources. One discussion leader for the first German seminar, Basil L. (Stuffy) Walters, executive editor of Knight Newspapers, told the members: "Never before has there been such a wealth of honest-to-God newspaper talent as you have had on this program."

API arranged for members to see actual practice of techniques they heard described in the conference room—such as reporting the activities of public officials. Several public officials led discussions. Taylor reported that Mayor William O'Dwyer of New York City gave a splendid discussion on the desirability of objective news reporting. At the same time, there was no attempt to conceal the faults of the American press.

Taylor's report on the first foreign seminar also illustrated the bumps a seminar can encounter. The Germans, three in particular, seemed less serious than Americans about time schedules. One member requested API to set up meetings with busy magazine editors, then failed to keep the appointments. One member "ridiculed the idea that the people of Germany as a whole should be informed through the press of issues of international politics so that democracy could be made to work."

A fellow member commented of the journalist in question: "He hates a free press." Taylor reported his concern that the man's "superior intellect may be used in the future for evil rather than good." Still another member had doubts that democracy would work under any conditions.

The presence of the sole woman member, Mrs. Lagens of Berlin, was no problem except on two occasions. As a woman, she was unexpectedly barred by both the University Club and the Harold Pratt House, sites, respectively, of luncheons given by the United Press and the Council on Foreign Relations. Also, because she had to be housed in a hotel and not the all-male John Jay Hall dormitory, she missed out on the informal dormitory discussions.

Most of the members had been affected by the Soviet Union's propaganda. This was most obvious in their interest in racial relations in the U.S. "Almost to a man," Taylor wrote, "they believed that discrimination against the Negro in America was much worse than it actually was and that many American Negroes were Communists."

To enlighten them, Taylor brought two black editors, George S. Schuyler, New York editor of the Pittsburgh Courier, and Joseph LaCour, manager of Associated Publishers, for dinner with the group.

The members, Taylor reported, also made "investigations of their own among Negroes in New York or Washington. Eventually, they became convinced that the position of the Negro in the United States, while far below what an enlightened man would want it to be, was far better than Soviet propaganda would indicate and was improving."

Preparing the German program took up most of the time of Taylor, Curtis, the two secretaries and some part-time help for two months. During the program, the full time of the institute staff was still needed because the Germans required much more help outside the conference room than a comparable group of Americans.

Several Germans, Taylor said, "arrived in the United States with the idea they were on a vacation." If it had been made clear to all the Germans in advance, Taylor wrote, that they were to take part in an intensive program some might not have come—but those who did would have been in the proper frame of mind. This was additional reason why API pushed for total control of future seminars.

The Germans found the program wearing even though it had been arranged in the belief that it would be less strenuous than programs already held for members from the United States and Canada. The unforeseen factors were some language difficulties, personal invitations that flooded on the members and the obligations to write for home publications about their adventures in America.

Surprisingly, some members among the more enthusiastic demo-crats were perturbed by the idea that clear writing on politics had a relation to the sound functioning of a democracy. Some, Taylor wrote, "shrank from the notion that clarity should be a major goal of journalists. One member repeatedly declared that he was educating the people of Germany when he forced them to read long, involved sentences."

The German cultural tradition of writing for the select few was pointed up during a conference in Providence with editorial writers of the Providence Journal. A seminar member expressed surprise that so much thought was given to editorials intended for an audience in which millhands predominated.

Most members of the German seminar, Taylor wrote, "had out-looks on life somewhat like those of men just released from long terms in prison...They had been living in a state of physical distress and intellectual starvation. They wanted to eat, drink and be merry; they wanted to look at well-dressed women; see plays; buy and read books; visit museums; talk shop; talk politics; go sightseeing...They obtained more than they expected—what most of them looked forward to was a comfortable vacation."

Taylor and Curtis were disturbed by the inability of the Germans to appreciate the good qualities of mass circulation papers in the U.S. The Germans found many minor errors and now and then major errors in articles based on interviews they gave in New York and elsewhere. American papers, they concluded, gave an accurate overall impression of an interview but erred frequently in details.

API urged seminar discussion leaders to avoid slang and unusual words. Language difficulties were amusing rather than serious.

One German, trying to order lima beans in a restaurant, could think of nothing to say except: "I want some beans from the capital of Peru." (In a 1956 seminar for Latin American journalists, one member kept a dictionary of American slang at his place at the conference table. It failed on the first test— "fat cat.")

The visits to newspapers proved beneficial. Those who observed at smaller newspapers seemed to benefit the most, because they could better examine the relationship of a newspaper to its community. Still, Helmut Meyer-Dietrich, chief editor of Der Tagesspiegel of Berlin, who visited the New York Times, wrote Times publisher Arthur Hays Sulzberger: "The time with the Times was teaching me more about American newspapering than all books written on this topic could give me."

In his Remembrance, Curtis wrote that a turning point for the West German press occurred when members of the first German seminar held during their visit to Washington a group interview with

Secretary of State Dean Acheson.

Acheson asked the visitors how they planned to establish free, responsible newspapers. Werner Friedmann, editor of Munich's Suddeutsche Zeitung spoke up. Newspapers in Germany were licensed by the military governments, and readers were suspicious of any licensed source of information. Friedmann proposed that licensing be continued for 18 months while he and his colleagues, using their newly achieved knowledge, started publishing excellent newspapers. Then licensing should be lifted.

That was done, Curtis wrote. When licensing ended, many partisan newspapers sprang up—Catholic, Lutheran, political party, labor—but advertisers did not respond, and they folded under competition with the improved non-partisan papers.

Taylor concluded his report by saying that he "had hopes that the German press will become a better instrument for encouraging the growth of democracy than it has in the past."

Foreign seminars posed various sensitivities. They were illustrated by a memo that Taylor sent to discussion leaders for the first Japanese seminar in 1949.

"We especially desire," Taylor wrote, "to avoid giving the impression that we regard ourselves as teachers and the Japanese editors as students...Japanese newspapers (modeled, to some degree, on the American press) are superior in technique to newspapers in many countries...The Japanese are being sent here (by the military government of General Douglas MacArthur) largely because...they are in need of a sounder philosophy of journalism than most of them possess..."

Taylor quoted experts on Japanese journalism. One said: "There are too many editors in Japan who regard newspaper work as nothing but a business and too few who believe they have a mission." Another said: "Japanese editors have too strong a tendency to print what they believe the people want, in order to build enormous circulations, and do not try hard enough to give their readers a sound picture of the world."

U.S. newspapers. Taylor said, were by no means free of faults. But Japanese editors for the most part had less respect for readers than did American editors, and API hoped that the Japanese would return home with "an enlightened professional self-consciousness."

After its early support, the Rockefeller Foundation dropped out of the picture. Ford Foundation, under a 10-year agreement, continued grants until 1971, when it switched priorities from foreign to domestic concerns and turned down various API proposals, including one to hold a seminar in Asia for foreign-news editors of American newspapers, many of whom had not traveled abroad.

Instead, Ford proposed a series of API seminars of three days to be held not only at Columbia but also at other domestic locations. The members would be "gatekeepers" on U.S. newspapers, that is, persons like the wire service and news editors, who would be briefed on China, the Middle East or whatever.

Curtis and Everett were not enthusiastic about the Ford proposal, but they knew that a negative response to the foundation could be sensitive. They discussed the matter with the Advisory Board, which decided not to accept.

Other factors also contributed to the ending of the foreign seminars. The seminars for developing nations had pretty much accommodated all qualified applications. After three seminars for Europeans, 1966-68, seminars for Europe were discontinued because they raised questions whether prosperous European papers shouldn't be paying for programs designed to improve their quality.

Then, too, in 1970-71 API held 19 domestic seminars and was not as dependent on foundation funds as it had been in 1948, when it held only six. In 1948, the first Rockefeller Foundation grant of $36,246 was heartily welcomed by the thinly financed young institute. Later grants averaged $35,000. As late as the 1960s, Monty Curtis remarked that the grants were enabling API to break even.

The foundation money also enabled the API staff to grow. Adding a second associate director, Everett, in late 1949 would have been too large a leap without the additional work (and income) posed by an annual foreign seminar. As Curtis put it in his Remembrance: "The foundations covered in their grants API's expenses, including staff salaries. API socked salary allowances in the bank."

Typically, the moderator of a foreign seminar devoted some 17 weeks to the project: a week or two preparing an itinerary, six or seven weeks of recruitment abroad, five weeks of arranging the program, three weeks in the conference room at API, a week with seminar members in Washington, D.C., and a post-seminar week writing a report and clearing odds and ends.

When Taylor died in August 1951, API was in the final phase of its fourth and last seminar for German journalists. API was heading into a 1951-52 schedule of six domestic seminars and the second program for Japanese journalists.

Much of the advance work for the Japanese program had been finished, a fortunate circumstance because now the staff numbered only Curtis and Everett. Staff size would remain at two until 1956, when William M. Stucky became an associate director.

Curtis wrote that he and Everett were hard pressed by the work volume after Taylor's death. By Everett's memory, however, he and Curtis carried the load comfortably for the five years before Bill

Stucky arrived.

Comfortable or not, the load would have been too much earlier, when seminars ran three or four weeks and API had not defined procedures or built a core of reliable discussion leaders.

The foreign seminars had value beyond benefitting the members, who reported vastly expanded skills and outlooks. The discussion leaders—there were 34 for the first German seminar, in addition to a dozen or so hosts—learned much about the press in foreign countries.

The same was true of host newspaper staffs. For example, members of the 1957-58 Seminar for Asian Journalists visited newspapers in 31 cities in 17 states and the District of Columbia, from Los Angeles and San Francisco, to Minneapolis to Miami; from Hutchinson, Kansas, to Troy, Ohio, and Lancaster, Pennsylvania. That was typical.

Frequently, the touring visitors fanned out into the communities. One year at Longmont, Colorado, publisher Edward Lehman of the Daily Times-Call arranged a news conference with the governor. A Latin American seminar group visiting Washington attended a news conference by Nikita Krushchev, who was on his famous trip to the United States.

Visiting public schools in Redondo Beach, California, an Asian group was astonished to find a teacher of Japanese origin in an American classroom. Everywhere, civic-club program chairmen sought the touring members as speakers.

At host newspapers, reporters wrote articles about the foreign visitors that gave readers a larger window on the world. In 1959, as illustration, readers of two host newspapers learned the perils faced by many foreign journalists; examples of imprisonment were legion.

Two members of the 1959 Latin American seminar from Colombia, Luis Gabriel Cano of El Espectador and Enrique Santos Castillo of El Tiempo, gained international acclaim 30 years later for their courageous resistance to attacks by the illegal drug cartel.

Dangers faced by journalists in some countries were again pointed up when Kamel Mrowa, editor and publisher of Al Hayat in Lebanon, a member of the 1965 seminar for the Middle East and North Africa, was shot to death at his desk a few months later by a political fanatic.

In Washington that year, U.S. Senator Hubert H. Humphrey of Minnesota spent two hours with the full seminar group, answering questions in his rapid-fire delivery. Afterward, a seminar member said to moderator Bill Stucky: "It's refreshing to find you have men like that in your Senate. Are there others?"

Visiting the Courier-Journal in Louisville, two foreign visitors were astonished by the high ethical standards. A Courier-Journal staffer could be dismissed for trying to fix a traffic ticket.

In 1967, at the height of the Vietnam war, members of a seminar for European newspaper executives were granted a 15-minute appointment with President Lyndon B. Johnson in the Cabinet Room of the White House. Six seminar members were from Denmark, Norway or Sweden, all strongly opposed to America's role in Viet Nam.

Johnson sought understanding for his sending more men and materiel to Viet Nam. "How," he asked, "can I tell the mothers of American servicemen that their president will not give them the best weapons?"

A chance remark was made about fishing. Johnson loved fishing. The editor of the Irish Press in Dublin, Joseph F. Walsh, saw an opening and moved in. "Mr. President," he said in rich Irish tones, "if you'll come to Ireland, I promise to show you the best trout fishing in the world."

Johnson grabbed a phone and barked to somebody that he'd be late. The scheduled 15 minutes stretched to an hour. Johnson may not have won over the Scandinavians on the Viet Nam war, but clearly all the members were captivated by the American president's personality.

The foreign journalists usually traveled in pairs and spent a week with each of two newspapers. Even before leaving New York, they could encounter memorable situations, which is not to say that domestic seminar members did not sometimes do the same. During an Asian seminar in the 1960s, Walter Everett was summoned to midtown Manhattan by the police on a Sunday morning to aid a seminar member.

On the Saturday evening, the member was walking along West 43rd Street when a gypsy fortune-teller persuaded him to come inside and learn what the future held. Following her directions, the member stood with eyes closed and prayed silently while the fortune-teller prayed for him and the success of his visit to America.

The member said later he thought he was touched near his back pocket, but he obediently kept his eyes closed. Some time later, he discovered that travel checks had been removed from his wallet.

While visiting newspapers away from New York, most members were hard-working and reliable. But there were exceptions. Vincent S. Jones, a host at Utica and later at Rochester, once recalled a Persian member who would arrive at the newspaper just in time to be taken to lunch and then would disappear until the cocktail hour. In Rochester, Jones found one universal request: "We must see Niagara Falls."

Harvesting the seminar benefits was a deserved reward for the seminar members. They were absent from their newspaper responsibilities for 60 days. Their absence required daunting advance work.

For example, in 1959 Manoel Francisco do Nascimento Brito of the Jornal do Brasil had been selected by API but a newspaper emergency arose and he thought he must withdraw. He telephoned a friend who had attended the 1956 Latin American seminar, Julio de Mesquita Neto of O Estado de Sao Paulo, to tell him of his decision.

"Before you cable the Institute," Mesquita told Brito, "I want you to fly to Sao Paulo and talk with me." In Mesquita's office, Brito found that his friend had arranged a table of exhibits— voluminous notes from the 1956 seminar and examples of how they had benefitted O Estado. Brito studied the exhibits—and did not send his cable of withdrawal.

For API staff members, the interviewing trips combined adventure and travail. Through its correspondents abroad, the Associated Press, United Press (later United Press International) and the New York Times were gracious and invaluable in helping to set up interviews.

Facing medical unknowns, the interviewer carried an Associated Press medical kit with remedies for everything from toothache to dysentery. An interviewer left New York burdened with luggage, camera, a portable typewriter on which to type interview reports, and a sheaf of airline tickets.

These possessions had to be guarded vigilantly. In Rome one year, Russ Schoch placed his briefcase on an airline counter and turned momentarily away. When he looked back, the briefcase, which contained briefing documents, was gone. Frantic, Schoch cabled API (a cablegram was then the major fast means of overseas communication). Somehow, probably by State Department courier, API quickly got replacement papers to Schoch.

In Hong Kong, Bill Stucky was riding in a rickshaw one evening when a knife-wielding robber appeared. The rickshaw driver fled, leaving Stucky alone. By the best of fortune, a policeman came onto the scene, and Stucky was unharmed.

In Rio de Janeiro in the late 1950s, Walter and Beth Everett were consoled by New York Times correspondent Tad Szulc before boarding a piston-engine plane for a night flight over the jungle to Venezuela. Szulc told the Everetts not to worry; he'd heard there were emergency landing strips carved out of the jungle.

Another time, flying into Rio on a small plane, Everett could see into the pilot's compartment. The pilot was reading a newspaper, and the stewardess was bringing him alcoholic drinks.

If spouses joined API staff members on the interviewing trips, as they often did, it was at their own expense. The non-expense-account tab was mainly air fare, though, because hospitality for meals, receptions and sightseeing often reached the point of embarrassment.

Sometimes different hosts in the same country had the same idea on successive nights. In Taiwan in 1971, Mal Mallette and his wife Eleanor survived three 10-course Chinese dinners, each course accompanied by toasts, on as many nights. Upon reaching the next stop, Hong Kong, they savored American-style hamburgers.

Selecting members was easier the second time that API foraged in a given continent or region, for members of the previous seminar paved the way. But it was always a challenge. In London in 1967, Mallette received a call from a sub-editor of News of the World, a British national weekly with a circulation of 1.5 million. The caller pleaded to be interviewed.

A meeting in a Fleet Street pub was arranged. There the sub-editor said that his newspaper's reputation for lurid content was unfair; it had carried exclusive articles by the likes of Winston Churchill and Field Marshal Montgomery.

Mallette, who knew nothing of News of the World, bought the current and previous issues. In both, the front page was dominated by the memoirs of the buxom actress, Jayne Mansfield, which even the most sensational American newspapers had found too lurid. The sub-editor was not chosen.

The foreign seminars did much to cement relations between API and the newspapers and newspaper-related organizations of the U.S. and Canada. The discussion leaders worked without fees. In many cases, their newspapers picked up travel expenses. Newspapers and wire services were hosts at excellent lunches and dinners and sometimes gave mementoes of considerable worth. Host newspapers away from New York City underwent considerable expense in entertainment and staff time.

Foreign seminar members were sometimes gathered for a final time after completing their visits to newspapers. Latin American members, for example, would rejoin in Miami or Puerto Rico, and Asian members would convene in Los Angeles or Hawaii. The regathering gave the members a chance to share experiences from their visits to newspapers.

There was often entertainment provided by local newspapers. In Honolulu, executive editor Bucky Buchwach of the Honolulu Advertiser, as only one example, became famous for his hospitality and especially the luaus.

The final gatherings, coming after weeks of close association, were an emotional time for members and moderator alike. In 1958, Stucky rejoined his Asian seminar members in Honolulu. They persuaded

Stucky to cancel a final round-table discussion on socio-economic topics because, they said, they were too exhausted to benefit. When the round-table was canceled, the members, suddenly re-energized, toured Pearl Harbor.

Stucky wrote: "The moderator can't stand airport goodbyes to friends he may never see again, so he took an easy way out. He arranged for a lovely young lady from the (Honolulu) Advertiser to bid them aloha in Hawaiian fashion as they boarded their chartered bus for the airport. And if there is any way to take the curse off parting, that's it."

When funds for additional foreign seminars could not be obtained after 1971, API staff members were disappointed not merely because of the loss of adventure, travel and friendships. The far more important benefits of those seminars for foreign journalists had been many, from the early attempts to bolster a democratic press in defeated Germany and Japan to subsequent efforts to foster both international understanding and improve newspaper quality and financial strength.

The battle for worldwide press freedom never ends. API was again reminded of this in 1971, the foreign programs' final year. Excellent candidates were identified in Singapore and Pakistan. But their governments would not permit them to apply. It was a lesson to remember.

The letters sent to API by foreign seminar members after they had returned home described countless improvements in their newspapers and outlook on their profession. A letter by Romulo O'Farrill Jr., manager of Publicacaciones Herrerias in Mexico City, well summarized the role of the API foreign seminars.

"It is impossible in a letter," O'Farrill wrote, "to tell you the many improvements that we have undertaken...But the biggest improvement, I believe, was to have a more matured definition on the philosophy of an independent and professional journalism and, in my opinion, this is the biggest item that modern newspapers must have...(and also) all of us who did not know each other before have now new and wonderful friends.

"I think that friendship and understanding among the people of the world is the most important thing to have, if we are ever going to have a peaceful and happy life."

15

The Quest for Solvency

Since API's establishment in 1946, its finances have been an almost constant concern. The founding newspapers contributed $142,000 to pay for a two-year experimental operation. But the question remained of how to pay the bills if the experiment was successful.

In a September 13, 1945, letter to Dean Ackerman, Sevellon Brown "contemplated" that after the first two years API would be financed through fees paid by newspapers for their seminar members and "by sustaining memberships (probably limited to about $3,000) from newspapers which would be privileged to send five or six staff men a year to the Institute for instruction and study."

By the time the first seminar ended in October 1946, further consideration had been given to the best way to raise funds. Robert U. Brown of Editor & Publisher editorialized that the men responsible for founding the institute had expressed concern as that first seminar closed whether publishers would continue their interest and financial support.

"When business conditions are such that publishers are no longer able to give financial assistance," Brown wrote, "is the Institute to die? It is too valuable an instrument for better newspapers to permit that, but it can happen under this arrangement (a founding fund) which was necessary at the start. The alternative is an endowment similar to the Nieman Foundation at Harvard—desirable but difficult to arrange."

Indeed an endowment was difficult to arrange. The first attempt to raise an endowment was headed by Grove Patterson, the first chairman of the API Advisory Board. In June 1947, after the first year of seminars, Patterson announced plans to seek an API endowment of $850,000, the equivalent of more than $5 million in 1990 dollars.

The $850,000, Patterson said, would produce income of $30,000 under yield rates of the day. Patterson and others, surely including Brown and probably Ackerman, had already been busy. Patterson said $100,000 was in hand and $20,000 more had been pledged.

Patterson did not expect that the sum could be found immediately. But he was convinced that publishers were prepared to give the necessary financial support after API's great success in its first year. "I am fully conscious," he wrote, "that we are raising our sights higher than any of the sponsors of the Institute contemplated when the first plans were made."

The sights, it soon became clear, were too high. After talking to Patterson, Brown wrote Ackerman that the major problem was "the doubt in the minds of publishers about the indefinite terms under which quite large endowment gifts were being asked...You will recall that in several instances...affiliation of publishers with other universities seemed an embarrassment for them in considering gifts to Columbia University."

It is not clear how much was eventually contributed toward Patterson's campaign because the funds were later mingled with API's reserves in its accounts with Columbia. By the end of 1948, the endowment drive had been abandoned.

When it became apparent that an endowment of sufficient size was beyond reach, Ackerman, Brown and probably several Advisory Board members decided to seek smaller annual contributions that would not embarrass publishers and would be funneled into the operating budget, not invested for their yield.

In December 1948, Ackerman announced that he had solicited contributions of $25,000 to API that year—apparently the minimum amount needed in addition to seminar fees once the founding funds were exhausted. Actually, newspapers contributed more than $25,000. API records show that they gave $39,500.

Under a Sponsorship concept (API always used the word with a capital "S") put into place in the early 1950s, API each year asked the newspapers that had sent members to the institute's seminars to contribute in addition to the tuition, then $180 a week. The hope was that altruistic newspapers would give enough money so that tuition could be kept below the full operational costs.

The plan was to obtain roughly two-thirds of operating costs from tuition and one third from Sponsorships. In that way, even newspapers with limited resources could afford to send staff members to API.

Walter Everett remembered the jubilation at API on the day when Floyd Taylor returned from a meeting with Columbia's acting president, Grayson Kirk, and told Everett and Curtis that the API staff itself would take over the solicitation of contributions. That was probably in early 1951.

The new policy was important because it removed Ackerman and Columbia from fund-raising for API and thus improved API's image at newspapers. Moreover, Taylor, Curtis and Everett thought they could do a better job of fund-raising than had been done—or at least they had the opportunity.

The change came after the Advisory Board, and probably Ackerman, failed with various plans. In 1948, for example, the Advisory Board decided to seek $1,000 annually for five years from 25 newspapers. It received, Bill Stucky wrote in 1957, 10 pledges of $1,000 annually for five years; eight contributions of $1,000 for 1948 with promises to renew annually; three five-year pledges of $500 each; and one contribution of $500 with a promise to review. "The Institute straggled along for the next three years," Stucky wrote. "By 1951, it appeared in desperate straits. Floyd Taylor was considering a State Department offer. Dean Ackerman was writing President Kirk (actually then acting president) that the Institute had to contribute to University overhead, although the Institute was barely able to make ends meet without contributing. Its operating balance at the end of the year was $139.67. Mr. (Sevellon) Brown was proposing an elaborate plan of membership with a specialist in solicitation on the (API) payroll."

None of that came about. The Advisory Board also discussed briefly a proposal to raise $50,000 for API's fifth anniversary. Brown's short-lived plan for memberships was apparently the only time memberships were considered.

The philosophy from the start had been to make API open to all newspapers. That philosophy led API in its fiscal crisis to Sponsorships, even though Brown had written in September 1945 to Ackerman that he thought API should be "very selective" in accepting seminar members. The strategy became that of seeking voluntary Sponsorships.

Nowhere except in Stucky's report was it recorded that Taylor considered a State Department offer. Everett did not recall any mention by Taylor of an offer and thought that if it was made it was quickly declined. Also, in 1950, Taylor had passed up an invitation to become the first director of the newly formed International Press Institute.

In its 1950-51 bulletin, API described the need for altruism this way: "Men from papers not represented at the Institute in the past are just as eligible to attend its seminars as those from papers that were among the original sponsors (that is, the founding newspapers). The same is true of men from papers not interested in making financial contributions."

Bulletins for the next five years devoted a page to a short item headlined: "Are You a Sponsor of the American Press Institute?" The wording changed a bit over that span, but always explained that tuition did not cover costs and the difference was made up by Sponsorships.

The first such item on Sponsorship asked that checks be made out to The Trustees of Columbia University and be accompanied by letters saying the checks were to support API. After that, API had apparently learned the peril of mentioning Columbia; the item said full information could be obtained by writing the API director. No mention was made of Columbia.

API's faith that some newspaper publishers would be willing to pay more than their fair share found sufficient response to keep the doors open.

The combined income of tuition, sponsor contributions, interest on reserve funds (reserves usually totaled about $200,000) and foundation grants for foreign seminars enabled API to maintain tuition at $180 a week (the fee included room and meals) until 1959-60, when it was raised to $390 for the two-week seminars that had become standard. Thus tuition increased only $15 a week over 14 years.

However, by 1973-74, API's last year at Columbia, tuition had been raised in two steps to $600 for a two-week program. The $600 figure reflected inflation, the limits of Sponsorship, and the rent paid to Columbia. The Sponsorship total was vital, and the staff worried over possibly budgeting for too high a figure.

"Each year," Monty Curtis once said, "we would send out the requests for Sponsor contributions and then pray." Such prayers were usually answered largely by the same newspapers and groups. In 1973-74, 398 individual newspapers and 24 groups contributed Sponsorships totaling $154,000. That reflected the newspaper industry's growing enthusiasm for API. Twenty years earlier, only 68 Sponsors were listed.

In API's 28 years at Columbia, its seminars were attended by members from 925 newspapers. Thus, about two-thirds of the participating newspapers became Sponsors eventually.

For its 1952-53 appeal, the staff printed a four-page message why annual contributions were needed. API had been asked, it said, to conduct similar work in the fields of television, public relations, trade paper publication and others. "Several of these proposals have been attractive financially. All have been rejected because the Institute was set up to be, and should always be, strictly a newspaper operation."

The institute operated on an annual budget of about $80,000, the message continued. Fees would provide approximately $38,000. Thus API was dependent on Sponsors for $42,000. Earlier, yearly contributions by a newspaper or a newspaper group ranged from $250 to $1,000. Contributions were deductible for income-tax purposes because Columbia University, the repository for funds, qualified for tax exemption under rules of the Internal Revenue Service.

Many newspapers and groups contributed faithfully year after year, with periodic increases. Other newspapers dropped out some years, then returned. Still others were beyond reach despite repeated supplication.

Sponsorship appeals succeeded in most years at least well enough to keep API solvent. On at least one occasion, however, a deficit threatened. In his Remembrance, Curtis told of a particular seminar, not identified, that drew few members and operated at a loss of $7,000. Edward Lindsay, editor of Lindsay-Schaub Newspapers in Decatur, Illinois, together with a few others, covered the $7,000. Small wonder that Curtis held such affection for API friends like Lindsay.

Occasionally, when budgets were tight, the suggestion was made to seek grants from non-newspaper foundations. Foundation support was probably available. API's foreign seminars were supported by the Ford and Rockefeller foundations. In 1950, the Ford Foundation provided seed money that led to formation of the International Press Institute. In the late 1960s, a Ford Foundation grant enabled the Southern Newspaper Publishers Association to form its own foundation and initiate three-day training workshops.

But serious discussion of foundation grants never developed. Turner Catledge and Ben Reese of the executive committee were particularly adamant about accepting only newspaper support. API was a newspaper project, they said, and if newspapers wouldn't support it, API should be dissolved.

Each year, API sent newspapers a summary of its finances. In 1975, Curtis wrote to James H. Ottaway of Ottaway Newspapers: "I remember how surprised Norman Chandler (publisher of the Los Angeles Times) was by our first report: 'This is the first time I ever had a report from anyone about what they did with the money.' "

In the same letter, Curtis said: "A byproduct of those financial reports was to stop all efforts by the administrators at Columbia to switch API money to other projects. The attempts were almost continuous. I remember one controller saying that API had no business returning the unexpended parts of foundation grants, but that these should go over to the medical school, and I told them to

SEVELLON BROWN: API's founder, a giant of his time.

FLOYD TAYLOR: API's first director set an enduring seminar pattern.

CARL W. ACKERMAN: Columbia's journalism dean gave API its first home.

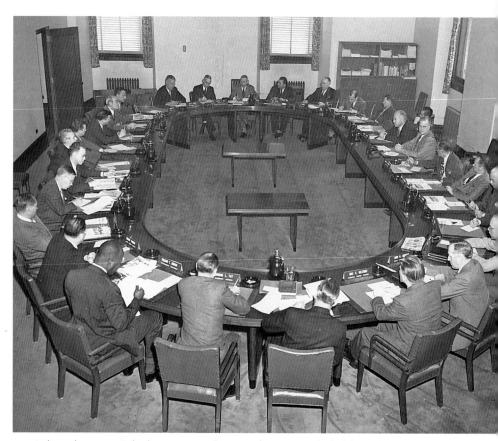

In the early years at Columbia University, the API conference room lacked the gold curtains that later shielded the windows.

J. MONTGOMERY CURTIS: The big fellow became known as "Mr. API."

A.H. KIRCHHOFER: Through Monty Curtis, his standards influenced API.

WALTER EVERETT: A deft administrator with impeccable judgment.

BEN REESE: Exemplified integrity and high purpose.

Four distinguished journalists recall their time as chairman of API's board: from left Paul Miller, Tim Hays, James H. Ottaway and Barry Bingham Sr.

GRAYSON KIRK: API had a firm friend in Columbia's president.

TURNER CATLEDGE: Quietly, he smoothed sometimes tense relations with Columbia.

For twenty-eight years, API was housed on the ground floor of Columbia's Journalism Building (far left)

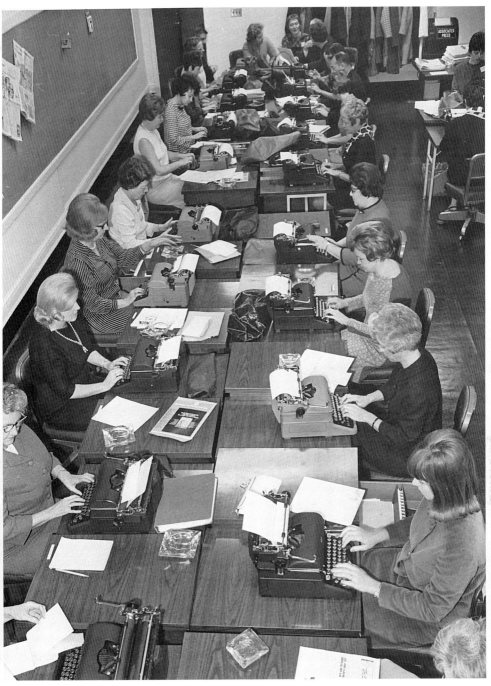
During a Women's Page Editors Seminar in 1967, members transcribe seminar notes.

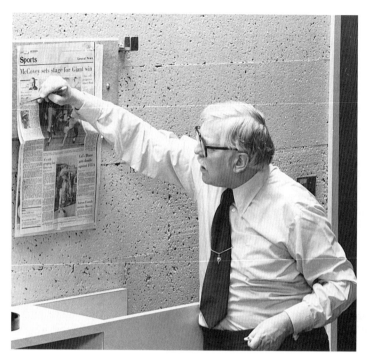

Edmund C. Arnold, the designer, makes a point during one of his record 208 appearances as a discussion leader.

Fourteen of the 22 discussion leaders honored in 1978 pose with board members and API staff. From left: Charles Young, Tim Hays (chairman), I. William Hill, Robert N. Brown, Frank Quine (managing director), Harry Lee Waddell, Edmund C. Arnold, J. Montgomery Curtis (board vice chairman), Robert D. De Piante, Vincent S. Jones, Walter Everett (retired API director) , Hal Neitzel, C. A. (Pete) McKnight, John Strohmeyer, John Dougherty, Don E. Carter, Ronald A. White, James H. Ottaway (chairman emeritus), Edward Bennett, and Malcolm F. Mallette, (director).

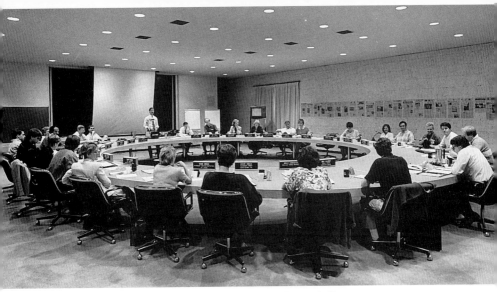

n API's building in Reston, the Red Conference Room offers comfort and efficiency.

In designing API's building, famed architect Marcel Breuer relied on his trademark pre-cast concrete.

MAL MALLETTE: Over 21 years, he filled all the chairs.

FRANK QUINE: Presided over eight years of growth and diversity.

WILLIAM O. TAYLOR: As fund-raiser, he earned his spurs as chairman.

BILL WINTER: Sought higher profile for API in a competitive era.

go to hell."

Sometimes such confrontations developed only because some Columbia officials failed to understand API's special situation. In 1960, for example, without notifying API, Columbia reduced from five percent to four percent the interest rate on API reserve funds invested through the university.

Interest on API reserves of $188,000 dropped from an expected $9,402 to $7,521. Curtis learned of this a month later through a credit memorandum from the controller's office. Invested funds remained the same, the interest was less.

Describing apparently unsuccessful attempts to get the decision changed, Curtis wrote of "previous efforts by University officers to get their hands on API monies," when one officer "tried to get all of our money and make us completely dependent upon the University," and another move when (the university) "tried to swipe our invested funds and throw them into some general pot which we could never touch."

Episodes like that infuriated Curtis and added to his protective stance. He often told or wrote about the unnotified lowering of interest. The lack of notification by Columbia was probably unintentional. Columbia administrators could hardly have understood how serious a loss of $1,881 in interest was to the struggling young institute on the ground floor of the Journalism Building.

But that's the way it was at API—a scramble for every dollar.

16

Tension and Divorce

On August 23, 1951, a Friday, the API staff finished another week of routinely preparing for its fifth annual series of seminars. A seminar for Japanese and Ryukuan journalists would begin in early October and would be followed by six domestic seminars, the last concluding in late June 1952.

Floyd Taylor, the director, and Monty Curtis, one of his associates, had been in the office all week, writing the many letters and making the countless phone calls necessary to set up seminars. Walter Everett, the other associate director, was vacationing at a salt pond in Rhode Island. Routine called for the office to remain closed until Monday. But by Monday routine had been shattered.

On Saturday, Curtis telephoned Everett. In the most difficult moments, Curtis could act with outward calm, an ability probably honed during his years on the pressure-packed city desk of the Buffalo Evening News. Speaking with precision as if dictating a news story, he gravely told Everett the staggering news.

Floyd Taylor, 49, API's founding director, the man expected to lead API for many more years, had died that morning at his home on Long Island, a victim of a coronary thrombosis. Everett was "completely shocked," as Curtis must also have been. Everett remembered sitting on a dock at the salt pond and thinking about Taylor, whom he admired. Then, devastated, he hurried back to New York City.

Everett and Curtis met at API to discuss their loss and to consider what had to be done. Sevellon Brown, chairman of the API Advisory Board, telephoned from Providence. Then Everett and Curtis went to Plandome, Long Island, to extend their sympathy to the widow, Marion Taylor, and to assist with funeral arrangements.

Following Taylor's wishes, he was cremated. Marion Taylor did not want the urn in her home, and Curtis arranged for the urn to be buried under an oak tree at Sunnyside, the home of the writer Washington Irving in Irvington, New York, overlooking the Hudson River. It was a fitting final resting place for a fine writer like Taylor.

With the API executive staff cut by a third and without a director, fast action was required. Curtis had been in place four years, Everett two. Curtis was age 45, Everett 41. Curtis at first proposed that he and Everett step forward jointly as candidates for co-director. But both realized that plan was impractical and agreed that Curtis should be the candidate.

In his Remembrance, Curtis gave his version of what ensued:

"Sevellon Brown rather favored me, but was not completely confident. He proposed this to (Dean) Ackerman, who replied: 'Good. I have Curtis right in my pocket.' This turned Brown away from me. But I had already moved to take the play away from Ackerman. A couple of years earlier I had dropped the 'affiliated with the Graduate School of Journalism' line on seminar programs. I avoided Ackerman. I used no journalism faculty members as seminar discussion leaders."

Actually, the decision to drop the "affiliated with" line from seminar programs had been made by Taylor after consulting both Curtis and Everett, even though the affiliation had not changed. And API had rarely used journalism faculty as discussion leaders anyway.

Everett doubted that Ackerman said anything as abrupt as having Curtis in his pocket. Ackerman did write to Brown saying: "I hope that the new director will be qualified to effectively represent API at the national level."

That could be taken as Ackerman's preferring a newspaperman of national prominence and thus a vote against Curtis. Moreover, the statement as quoted by Curtis seems inconsistent with Ackerman's manner. Though he could be quite direct, Ackerman was rarely impolitic. Beyond that, Curtis had written a beguiling precede to his Remembrance, a precede which signaled that his every word should not be taken literally. The precede read:

> "Caution to readers: This manuscript may be danger-
> ous to your memory. The 74-year-old author joined API
> 33 years ago and left 13 years ago. Isn't it amazing
> how as we grow older we were so much better? If an
> occasional paragraph raises an eyebrow, remember
> that honest fiction is often more accurate than
> unembellished fact."

Even before Taylor died, the tensions between the institute and the Graduate School of Journalism had been growing. Curtis described the situation bluntly: "Sevellon Brown doubted that I had the guts to oppose Ackerman and make API independent. Seeking strength, he (Brown) offered a co-chairmanship (of the Advisory Board) to Ben Reese, the just retired managing editor of the St. Louis Post-Dispatch."

Curtis was probably unfair to himself. Brown had known of Taylor's problems with Ackerman and how much time Taylor spent on those problems. It seems likely that, in enlisting Ben Reese, Brown hoped to free Curtis of such difficulty so that he could concentrate on running the institute.

By the Curtis account, he was the one who had alerted Brown to the probable availability of Reese. But if this was the case, it seems likely that Curtis did not foresee Reese's being designated co-chairman of the Advisory Board, only expecting that Reese would sit in on selected seminars.

Whatever his thoughts in advance, Curtis always bitterly resented what he regarded as Brown's lack of confidence in his ability to fend off Ackerman.

Everett saw the hiring of Reese in a different light. "His (Curtis') bitterness over Sevellon Brown's bringing in Ben Reese was unreasonable and hurt no one but Monty himself." Fortunately, Curtis and Reese became not only associates but also warm friends.

On October 8, 1951, the succession announcement came from Brown and Grayson Kirk, vice president and acting head of Columbia University.

(Kirk had been named acting president when Dwight D. Eisenhower, Columbia's president since 1948, took a leave of absence in 1950 to become commander of the North Atlantic Treaty Organization. Eisenhower resigned from Columbia after becoming U.S. president-elect, and Kirk succeeded him at Columbia in 1953.)

On recommendation of the institute's Advisory Board, the trustees of Columbia University had appointed Curtis director of API and Reese co-chairman of the Advisory Board. Everett continued as associate director.

The procedure was simpler than it may seem. Ackerman, who held the power of appointment, had deferred to Brown, who on his Providence newspapers followed a policy of promoting from within. Brown had recommended Curtis. The Advisory Board supported Brown, and when it forwarded the recommendation the result was assured.

Everett recalled that during the interregnum he, Curtis and Brown had convened several times, but Brown polled the Advisory Board only by phone and did not call a special meeting.

Taylor and Curtis fought their battles with Ackerman in different ways. No matter how heated his discussions with Ackerman might have become at times, Taylor kept his own counsel. He fought off, for example, an Ackerman proposal that API add seminars for broadcasters.

In contrast, Curtis spoke and wrote freely of his concern that Ackerman wanted to absorb API into the Graduate School of Journalism and, failing that, to use API as a bridge over which to reach newspaper contributors to his school. Even if Curtis had been less combative, inherent points of conflict between API and Columbia inevitably sharpened with the passage of time.

After five years of existence, API was no longer a novelty on the Columbia campus. Although API added to the Columbia lustre, Columbia had been hospitable in return. For API's first nine years Columbia gave API its space, utilities, financial management and janitorial services without charge. API did pay, of course, for the remodeling and furnishing of its quarters and for the meals and rooms for seminar members. Those payments were never in question.

After the first five years, though, Ackerman increasingly wanted relief for API's impact on his budget. He thought, for example, that his school deserved at least nominal payment for the hours he spent on API matters.

That issue was finally resolved in 1958, when API willingly began paying $5,000 a year as a token rent to the university. By the 1970s, that payment had escalated to $13,000, and API worried about the possibility of steep future increases from a university that was running up staggering deficits.

A second point of conflict defied simple solution. API existed on seminar tuition and contributions from newspapers. When attempts to obtain contributions beyond the founding fund fell far short of goals a major reason became apparent. Newspapers understandably gave first priority to journalism schools in their own states. They feared that funds given to an institute affiliated with the Columbia Graduate School of Journalism would be seen as a weakening of support for home-state schools.

Moreover, misunderstandings had arisen at newspapers over how API funds were handled. Because API had no corporate or legal existence—it was an affiliate of Columbia—fees and contributions received by API were deposited and disbursed by the university through accounts earmarked for API. This caused no problem except for some delay in paying bills.

But trouble came, curiously, in saying thank you. API always acknowledged contributions, but in the early years the university also sent its own acknowledgments to the same donors. Usually, this double acknowledgment did no harm. But on one occasion a batch of Columbia letters went out to API contributors mistakenly thanking them for a contribution to the School of Engineering. API learned of this from an indignant contributor. The accounts, Everett recalled, were not fouled up, only the acknowledgments.

Horrified, the API staff wrote apologetic letters. But they did not completely dispel the impression that API funds were handled carelessly.

Then, too, other Columbia activities sometimes displeased newspapers. The Columbia Journalism Review, a magazine of press criticism published under auspices of the journalism school, often criticized various newspapers for their coverage. Naturally, the targeted newspapers resented the criticism, even if deserved.

One such newspaper, in Pennsylvania, struck back by ending its support of API, which it mistakenly saw as somehow having a hand in the matter. On any number of occasions, API sensed animosity by other newspapers and sent letters explaining that it had no connection with the Columbia Journalism Review.

The annual Pulitzer Prizes awarded annually by Columbia were, surprisingly, another source of backlash against API. Newspapers coveted Pulitzer awards, the most prestigious in the U.S. When newspapers with strong entries were passed up by the judges, they sometimes laid their disappointment at the API doorstep.

Almost from the first day, Taylor and later Curtis and Everett worked, in Everett's words, "to have the newspaper profession perceive API as an independent entity, separate and apart from the J-school." There was irony in this because, after all, it was on Sevellon Brown's request to Dean Ackerman and Ackerman's endorsement that API found its first home at Columbia. Only 18 months after API's founding, the Advisory Board had become concerned about the institute's status as an affiliate of the Graduate School of Journalism. That concern stemmed from the failure of the endowment fund solicitations. And the Advisory Board tried unsuccessfully to change the arrangement.

On August 8, 1947, Brown wrote Ackerman, described the endowment obstacles and said, "It has seemed advisable to propose to the Trustees of Columbia University the incorporation of the Institute under the laws of New York State."

Five days later, Brown again wrote Ackerman. He said prospective endowment donors had told Grove Patterson of their belief "that the Institute should be exclusively of newspapers, for newspapers, and by newspapers, with Columbia affiliation as being very beneficial, but with the entity of the Institute clearly established as a newspaper proposition. With whatever arrangement the University considered fair as to the Institute's payment to the University to cover overhead costs, I, myself, believe that this arrangement of a separate entity for the Institute, with a formal affiliation with the University, would be best. I would like to hear your point of view...as soon as possible."

Ackerman sent an excerpt of Brown's letter to the university counsel's office, which responded that the proposal was feasible. On September 27, Ackerman sent the provost, Albert C. Jacobs, a copy of Brown's August 8 letter. Ackerman said he had no objection if Brown and Patterson wanted to seek endowment gifts to the American Press Institute, a New York corporation separate from Columbia University.

But then, in his cover letter to the provost, Ackerman said: "Although at the same time I would wish to make the following a matter of record in the correspondence: The American Press Institute is now and must remain affiliated with the Graduate School of Journalism and with Columbia University. The Advisory Board of the American Press Institute is an advisory board of Columbia University functioning through me as Dean of the Graduate School of Journalism...(If a separate corporation were formed) the articles of incorporation will have to make clear the affiliation with Columbia University, and we will have to retain the right to name a majority of the Board of Directors as representatives of the University."

Between September 27 and November 4, according to a document prepared by Associate Director Bill Stucky after research in the university's central files, John Godfrey Saxe, the university counsel, drafted a certificate of incorporation for API, and there was much conferring back and forth.

Finally, on February 28, 1948, Provost Jacobs wrote Saxe, implying that the matter had been dropped. He thanked Saxe for a memorandum on incorporation. The last paragraph of that memo read:

"This may suggest (in case the subject comes up again) that it may be advisable, in case you decide not to incorporate, of having some Articles or By-Laws which would definitely define membership for the future and, possibly, in addition, an agreement, in writing, with the University which would define the mutual privileges of the University and the Institute."

On March 15, 1948, Ackerman notified counsel Saxe that the matter of incorporation "will be dormant for some time." Five years later, according to Stucky's research, all other correspondence about incorporation had apparently been thrown away.

The perceived handicap in fund-raising imposed on API by its affiliation with the Graduate School of Journalism was a major cause of API's discontent.

But Everett noted another reason. "In the 1940s and '50s," Everett wrote, "journalism schools had many critics. Moreover, the school served beginners in the profession, API (served) mid-career men and women." Stucky noted: "Newspapermen objected to coming 'back to school' and every evidence of affiliation with the School of Journalism increased this feeling. Thus it became clear that a continued close association with the Graduate School of Journalism would discourage both financial support and seminar membership."

As an ally in combat with Ackerman, Curtis had Ben Reese, who could also be outspoken and blunt. But the most effective efforts on behalf of API were made quietly by Turner Catledge.

Catledge always declined to be named chairman of the Advisory Board. But he had a power base as, first, assistant managing editor, then managing editor, and finally executive editor of the New York Times. The Times and its ownership Sulzberger family were major influences on Columbia's administration.

In a 1979 interview with Mal Mallette, Catledge recalled a time when the API Advisory Board wanted to get a raise for Curtis and Everett. Of Grayson Kirk, Catledge said, "He was very, very partial to API. He saw it as a great way to popularize or to increase the service of Columbia University, the whole university establishment, to the public...We went to get raises for these people and told him what it would take.

"And he said, 'My Lord, that's more than our deans make,' and I said, 'Well, I can't help that.'

"I was always the one who had to run up there and butt up against Columbia because I was chairman of the (API's Advisory Board) Executive Committee...I told him (Kirk), well, that's just too bad because these people were highly professional people who could walk out the door and get more than 50 percent more than they were getting there. And they were supported by American newspapers, not by Columbia University...I told him that if this is what is going to happen we will just have to either close it (API) or move it off this campus because we can't get the people.

"He asked me, 'Well, what do we do?'...I said, 'Raise your deans.' He did raise his deans."

That conversation apparently occurred in 1956 or early 1957, for the minutes of a Columbia trustees meeting February 4, 1957, recorded approval of a salary increase for Curtis from $20,000 to $25,000, for Everett from $18,500 to $20,000 and for Stucky from $12,500 to $13,500.

The trustees also approved payment by API of 15 percent of those salaries to the Teachers Insurance and Annuity Association, the retirement fund. Earlier, the executive staff had paid half of that percentage from their own pockets. These changes were a major improvement in staff compensation.

Catledge, a soft-spoken native of Mississippi, was API's invaluable trouble-shooter. He almost certainly played a central role in persuading Kirk that the API director should report directly to Kirk and not through the dean of journalism. There is no record of exactly when the change took place, but it is described in Kirk's letter of December 6, 1954, to Sevellon Brown.

"I feel quite strongly," Kirk wrote, "that the present arrangement whereby the Director of the American Press Institute deals directly with me is best for all concerned. Accordingly, I reassured Monty Curtis that this arrangement will be continued after the appointment of a new Dean of the School of Journalism unless the API Advisory Board requests otherwise." Of course the Advisory Board did not request otherwise.

Kirk's action in removing the dean of journalism from the reporting chain was only one of his friendly actions toward API. His friendship may have had its roots in his early indecision whether to become a journalist or an academic.

As an undergraduate at Miami University of Ohio, he was editor of the student newspaper. Kirk once described himself as "just an ordinary Ohio farm boy who went to public school and on to college, thinking some of going into journalism. I thought it would be great to be a foreign correspondent." He became instead a scholar of international politics.

Forty years later, Kirk said, "It was my feeling that API was a highly desirable enterprise, and Columbia University should support it within reason." Kirk, Everett recalled, never interfered or even made suggestions on the operation of the institute. He frequently would come to the API conference room on the opening morning of a seminar and welcome its members.

Kirk's view that API was a highly desirable enterprise surely came in part from his own background. However, his thinking was probably reenforced by Robert Harron, director of the university news bureau and a former newspaperman.

"More than anyone else at Columbia," Everett said, "Harron recognized the great value of API to the university in terms of public relations and promotion." Harron called API a public relations man's dream. To API, he reported glowingly of incidents when he accompanied university officers on speaking trips in distant cities. Some of these trips were for fund-raising. Several times, someone came up from the audience, introduced himself and said, "I was at Columbia for an API seminar."

Dean Ackerman retired two years later, July 1, 1956, and was succeeded a month later by Edward W. Barrett. Although Curtis was reporting directly to President Kirk, Curtis and Barrett were battling within seven months.

Barrett was the son of Edward Ware Barrett, for many years publisher of the Birmingham (Alabama) Age-Herald. A Princeton graduate, he became a Columbia dean after work as a journalist that included high editorial positions at Newsweek magazine, the Office of War Information in World War II, service as an assistant secretary of state for public affairs and as executive vice president of Hill & Knowlton, the public relations firm.

Barrett resigned as dean in 1968 because he disagreed with Columbia's policies during the student demonstrations led by opponents of the war in Vietnam. Barrett said he had "no sympathy whatever" for Students for a Democratic Society, which led the campus demonstrations. Many other faculty members supported the dissident student organization.

Curtis said in his Remembrance that he thought the Graduate School of Journalism should have sought a dean with a practical news background. He spoke scornfully of Barrett as a press agent and public relations man, despite Barrett's varied journalistic background.

"Barrett's job," Curtis wrote, "was to run the School of Journalism, and that meant raising money. API looked like a choice platform. He tried to associate himself with API. This was resisted successfully."

The Barrett-Curtis tension can be seen in their emerging correspondence. Curtis wrote Barrett on February 28, 1957, outlining his views on the API-Journalism School relationship. The letter began amiably enough, with mention of cooperation. Then Curtis disclosed his underlying feelings.

"Had your predecessor (Ackerman) had his way," Curtis wrote, "there would be no Institute today, and the School would have lost much standing with newspapermen when his policies and methods became known...He asked at least one important seminar member to discourage his newspaper from contributing to the Institute."

Curtis listed reasons for keeping API and the journalism school separate and requested that his name be removed from the Faculty of Journalism. "It is flattering. But it is also fraudulent. I am not a Professor, I am embarrassed to say, either by training, record, achievement or current practice. So at this late date I am turning honest and asking you to discontinue my appointment."

Barrett replied that the journalism school had an important part in the birth of the Institute and, along with the university, "has played host and is playing host to the Institute...If the School, along with the University plays host to the Institute, it would seem gracious for the Institute to acknowledge this appropriately."

API complied with the request, as Walter Everett recalled, thinking it may have been heavy handed to edit out earlier references in API literature to the journalism school. Some time later, Barrett informed Curtis that President Kirk wanted Curtis to remain on the Faculty of Journalism. Curtis replied that if that was the wish of the president, he would continue.

Kirk hoped that the rift between API and the journalism school could be healed. He wrote Curtis October 1, 1957 that he had "taken the initiative in discussing with Dean Barrett possible means by which, without sacrificing any autonomy, the Pulitzer Prize activity and the American Press Institute could have some connection, however nominal, with the School of Journalism."

Kirk said he believed "there are values to be gained for all concerned if we can work out some arrangement whereby those who visit the University as members of API seminars are made somewhat more conscious of the School of Journalism...In view of the exceedingly choice space which the API occupies, I do not feel this is an unreasonable request and I am therefore writing to ask you to include some reference to the fact that the Graduate School of Journalism is your host in welcoming seminar groups and in the printed matter which you circulate to the various newspapers."

Turner Catledge in his 1979 interview said that Kirk had wanted Curtis to become the dean of journalism when Ackerman retired. Walter Everett confirmed that, recalling that Curtis had told him at the time that Kirk had offered Curtis the dean's job.

Kirk's proposal, as Curtis related it to Everett, was for Curtis to head both the Graduate School of Journalism and the institute, probably with a deputy to run API. If that had happened, Everett said, "Kirk would have solved all the problems of the two institutions in one master stroke."

How seriously did Curtis considered whatever proposal that Kirk may have made? Certainly, Curtis must have been flattered. But Curtis knew also how much time the dean of journalism spent on fund-raising—not that the director of API was free of such responsibilities. Then, too, the dean had to deal with the university bureaucracy to a far greater degree than did Curtis.

Most important of all to Curtis must have been the fact that the dean did not have the constant stimulation that meant so much to Curtis—the elbow-to-elbow relationship with working newspaper people.

Kirk's enthusiasm for Curtis became evident again in a November

5, 1955, letter. At the time, W. Emerson Gentzler, then provost, seemed to be pushing for an API contribution to general university overhead of as much as $20,000 a year.

Kirk explained to Curtis that Gentzler was making a study of overhead funds from all divisions, and correspondence from the provost was not intended to suggest such a large payment. Kirk wrote that he did not expect API to contribute to support of Columbia, but he wanted to be equally clear that API should pay its own way.

"May I suggest," Kirk wrote in his usual graceful manner, "that we leave the whole matter in suspense until some future time. You know that the University will never do anything which could be construed as being unfriendly to the best interests to the API."

Curtis passed the letter to Ben Reese, and next to the two quoted sentences by Kirk he wrote: "Ben, it never has.—Monty."

Nevertheless, Curtis had several blow-ups about Dean Barrett. They usually occurred during chance meetings. To the point of rudeness, Curtis would sound off against the dean, thinking that he was protecting API. Barrett would respond softly and turn away.

Everett wondered how Curtis would have responded if Barrett had stood his ground and asked: "What have I ever done to hurt you or the institute?"

When Curtis wrote his Remembrance of API in 1980, he included in the original manuscript a scathing passage on Barrett. He toned down the passage upon recommendation of the API staff. Still, Barrett felt he had been treated unfairly in the printed version and one day called API to express his reaction.

How to explain the enduring, even growing Curtis animosity toward Barrett? Part of the answer surely was Curtis' dedication to API, and his understanding that it had to be of, by and for newspapers or it couldn't survive.

In addition, though, Curtis once hinted to Ben Reese that he would like to be considered for an honorary doctoral degree from Columbia. Reese passed the word to Everett, who through discreet inquiries learned that honorary degrees could not be awarded to Columbia people currently on the faculty or administration.

Curtis grumbled over the explanation and may have seen Barrett as the obstacle. Later, Curtis coveted a Maria Moors Cabot Award, such as Everett received. Barrett was a member of the committee that failed to nominate Curtis.

Curtis was not the only person who made clear API animosity toward Barrett. Reese, brought in as additional strength against encroachment by the journalism school, delighted in telling the story of his reply when the newly arrived Ed Barrett asked him what he could do to help.

In his bullhorn voice, Reese relied: "You can keep your goddamn hands off API."

The API Advisory Board was surely well informed on the feud and the need for API to break away from the Graduate School of Journalism in a more formal manner than President Kirk's letter calling for the API director to report directly to him and no longer through the journalism dean.

In April 1957, the Advisory Board instructed the API staff to make a detailed study of the Institute's relationship with the university and the journalism school, the financial relationship with the university, and the status of the Institute's reserve funds. Bill Stucky's research resulted.

Based upon that research and its own feelings, the staff recommended that the Executive Committee of the Advisory Board "wait upon the President with the proposal that by appropriate official action the Institute be formally placed under the Office of the President for all administrative purposes."

Columbia trustees approved a resolution to just that effect, perhaps not fully understanding how much their action meant to API. On May 6, 1958, Curtis and representatives of the trustees signed an agreement that severed the institute from the Graduate School of Journalism.

The agreement had seven provisions: API and Columbia would continue their affiliation and cooperation. Columbia would furnish space in the Journalism Building for API's activities. Columbia would continue as API's fiscal agents, paying API obligations with money in API's accounts. Columbia would not be responsible for any API actions resulting from errors in judgment. API would pay Columbia $5,000 annually for overhead expenses incurred on behalf of API; if API was unable to make this payment it could request a postponement or waiver. And the agreement could be terminated at the end of any academic year upon one year's notice in writing from either party to the other. All of this was done quietly and smoothly and not during a time of special crisis. There was no public announcement by Columbia or API. The journalism school did not contest the move, and, Everett thought, probably was unaware of it.

Over the years, Everett wondered why Ackerman didn't resist API's several ex parte moves toward separation. After all, Ackerman had history, authority, and academic clout on his side.

"Perhaps," Everett wrote, "he thought API was going to be a problem or even a failure, based on declining seminar participation and financial support after the initial year. Perhaps he was following his natural inclination, which was to spawn a Big Idea and then leave the nitty-gritty to others. Perhaps he was deterred by the Advisory

Board, especially Catledge and Pulitzer (Joseph Jr.) and later by Ben Reese."

In any event, for API the May 6, 1958, action was, in Everett's phrase, a "charter and Bill of Rights," though for Kirk and the trustees it was hardly a blip on the agenda for the huge university.

In its 12th year, API had won a divorce from the Graduate School of Journalism. That divorce would be helpful when API faced the other problems forming just over the horizon.

17

Big Ben

Ben Reese retired as managing editor of the St. Louis Post-Dispatch on June 1, 1951. He was only age 62, a vigorous 62, and the assumption had been that Reese would stay in place until 65.

But he had been a newspaperman for 45 years, 38 of them at the Post-Dispatch, 25 as city editor and 13 as managing editor. Under his guidance, the Post-Dispatch had won four Pulitzer Prizes and started on a fifth. Reese had qualified for a pension of $12,000, a comfortable figure in those days, and a lifetime free subscription to the Post-Dispatch.

His only child, Ben Reese Jr., wanted him to move to the New Jersey shore and join him in the jewelry business. His professional reputation was certainly secure. Time magazine devoted almost a full page to his retirement, calling Reese a "legend" and a "bedrock newsman." And so he resigned and with his wife Estelle moved to Spring Lake, New Jersey.

Reese often told the story of how a few weeks away from active newspapering changed his outlook. On a beautifully clear summer day, he and his wife were looking out at the ocean when Reese turned to his wife. "Stell," he said, "if I have to spend the rest of my life looking at the goddamn Atlantic Ocean, I'll go crazy."

Stell Reese said she had known all along that her husband's idea of how he would spend his retirement would never work, even in a business association with their son. Ben Reese missed newspaper talk.

In the four or five months after Reese's retirement, Sevellon Brown and Turner Catledge had approached him about adding his journalistic lustre to API. The terms of their first blandishment are not clear, but Reese had replied in his usual blunt manner.

"Listen," he said, "you two slickers are not going to lasso me into any kind of a job. I am living where I want to live. I have earned retirement, and I am going to have it. Thank you, but the answer is 'no.' "

Now Brown and Catledge approached Reese again, with a modified pitch. They offered Reese a position as co-chairman of the API Advisory Board. Reese, Brown and Catledge would then form the executive committee. The clincher was that they wanted Reese to sit in on as many seminars as he chose to and also serve as a discussion leader on a topic he would call "The Newspaper's Responsibility for Public Service to Its Community."

Thus did the young API benefit for 15 years from the presence of a celebrated newspaperman from a celebrated newspaper. In the Reese years at the Pulitzer-owned St. Louis Post-Dispatch, the paper always was ranked among the country's very best. Under Reese as city editor or managing editor, the P-D won Pulitzer Prizes for such varied efforts as exposing voting frauds, exploring lax safety in an Illinois coal mine and political corruption.

Benjamin Harrison Reese was a man who commanded attention. He stood six feet, two inches and weighed 250 pounds. His heritage was partly American Indian, and facially he somewhat resembled a well-known portrait of the Indian chief Sitting Bull. Sometimes, but never in his presence, the Post-Dispatch staff referred to him as "The Indian."

His deep voice had bullhorn strength and terrorized Post-Dispatch reporters summoned to his desk. Yet Reese was in many ways the most kind and lovable of men. When he died in a Neptune, New Jersey, hospital in June 1974 at age 85 those who had worked with Reese at the Post-Dispatch described him as almost two separate persons.

"One," David R. Wallin wrote in the P-D, "was a man who was coldly detached where news was concerned and who drove his staff unmercifully when a big story was developing; who was passionately devoted to accuracy in the news; who frequently listened only briefly to reporters' descriptions of problems they were encountering and then snapped, 'I don't want excuses. Get the story.'

"The other was a man who stood solidly behind his staff; who rewarded good work with praise, pay increases and cash bonuses; who, away from the news, could be warm, understanding and generous. Universally, they paid tribute to his news judgment, to his devotion to the Post-Dispatch, and to his belief in the value and importance of complete and unbiased reporting."

Reese took home all editions of the Post-Dispatch and read every word. Arthur R. Bertelson, a successor to Reese as managing editor, recalled an instance when Reese found the word "irregardless" far back in an edition of the P-D. "He hit the ceiling," Bertelson said, and bellowed: "Somebody is trying to sabotage me."

If you made a mistake on the P-D, you were sure to hear about it. Alex Primm, who started as a reporter under Reese and rose to vice president of the P-D, said, "Ben could chew you out with a stare."

Bob Broeg recalled the time that his predecessor as sports editor, J. Roy Stockton, found a wire story in the P-D sports section that mistakenly referred to Joseph Pulitzer Jr. as Joseph M. Pulitzer. Reese spotted the error at about the same time and summoned Stockton to his office.

There Reese demanded loudly, "Just what in the hell, Stockton, does the 'M' stand for in Joseph M. Pulitzer?" Stockton removed his ever-present pipe from his mouth and shot back, "The same, Mr. Reese, as the 'H' in Jesus H. Christ."

"I used that in Stockton's obit," said Broeg, "and bless 'em, none of the readers claimed I was sacrilegious." Stockton had provided a rare instance when a staffer had a retort for Reese, one of the last of the old-fashioned, hard-nosed, hard-driving editors.

Reese once told an API seminar for editors: "If I owned a newspaper, I know what my platform would be. Suppose the town was Middleville, and the paper was the Gazette. My platform would read as follows: 'The Gazette is dedicated without fear or favor to making Middleville a decent place in which to live...It states an all-important objective with vast implications. It is the responsibility of the newspaper to the community it serves. If it is not the newspaper's responsibility, whose responsibility is it?' "

On his "without fear or favor" plank, Reese had documentation. One time, the May Company department store in St. Louis, a major advertiser in the Post-Dispatch, was in labor negotiations when a federal agency announced the 100 highest salaries in the U.S.

The president of the May Company chain of stores always made the list. Knowing that the announcement was coming, an executive from the St. Louis store asked Reese to spike the story or at least hold it until the labor negotiations ended.

Reese described his response at many API seminars and always when addressing advertising executives, who often were the target for advertisers when the newsroom reported such matters.

Monty Curtis quoted the Reese reply in his Remembrance: "Your store should be the last to impair the faith of readers in this newspaper. Our readers respond to your ads because they have faith in what we publish. They believe us. If we fail to use this story, the word will spread that the Post-Dispatch suppresses news when it concerns an advertiser. We will not let that happen. Because you have made this request, I will have to put the story on page one."

Another time, a friend of Reese called him to say that he was quietly going through a divorce, wanted to keep it private, and asked that it not be published. Reese replied that without the call he probably would not have learned of the divorce, but now because of the request to suppress news he was obliged to publish it.

When Reese joined API he made it clear that he would attend only those seminars at which he could make a contribution. At first he attended mainly the seminars for managing editors, city editors and investigative reporters.

Except when he was the discussion leader, he sat halfway along one side of the conference table and would break in with comments at any point. For a while, that sometimes presented a problem. In Riverside, California, editor Tim Hays of the Press and Enterprise began hearing from returning seminar members that Reese commented too frequently.

Hays wrote Paul Miller, then Advisory Board chairman, about the reaction of Riverside seminar members, but never received a reply. For one reason or another, though, Reese became more selective with his comments, which always reflected his intense interest and strong opinions on how a newsroom should be operated.

Seminar members soon recognized that they had a titan in their midst. They clustered around him during coffee breaks and at other opportunities. For a half day of such seminars, Reese would move to the discussion leader's chair and read his presentation of 20 or more typewritten pages. Then he would distribute copies of the text he had just read.

API strongly discouraged the reading of texts, because reading suppressed the desired comments by members. But Reese was never comfortable working from notes and insisted on the text. Seminar moderators, seeking to get exchanges started, soon learned to break in with questions of their own.

Though he had first planned to attend only news-side seminars, Reese became fascinated by the areas of newspapering— circulation, advertising, production—that he had seen little of as a managing editor. At the conference table, he grew and mellowed. But he never quite left his belief that the managing editor was a notch above other department heads on a newspaper.

Walter Everett recalled a seminar for advertising executives when members complained that their editors were aloof or even hostile to the advertising department. At that, Reese made clear his idea of the relative status of managing editors and advertising directors.

"When I was managing editor of the P-D," he said, "the advertising director was always free to knock on my door." A seminar member sitting next to Everett and at table's length from Reese muttered, "Timidly, I bet."

Often at the end of a seminar, the members would give Reese a standing tribute, causing him to wipe away tears. "If it weren't for API," he said on one such occasion, "I'd be dead by now."

Personnel matters soon drew Reese's interest, and he began including a list of "do's" and "don'ts" in presentations to city editors and managing editors. A favorite line was: "Praise in public, rebuke in private."

One time, a seminar member from the Post-Dispatch who had worked under Reese heard this latter-day advice. "My God," the P-D staffer told Everett, "You did something wrong in the old days, Mr. Reese would skin you alive in a voice you could hear halfway to city hall."

A frequent Reese anecdote disclosed that he recognized the impact of criticism. "When a reporter did something wrong," Reese would relate, "I would take him aside and say, 'This is not a matter of criticism, this is a matter of instruction.' Then I would give him hell."

Reese was a legend who followed a legend. At the Post-Dispatch, he succeeded Oliver Kirby (O.K.) Bovard, widely regarded as one of the greatest all-time managing editors. Although Bovard and Reese held some traits in common, the Reese approach to running a newsroom was largely inherent and not modeled after Bovard.

Reese reached the Post-Dispatch after starting his newspaper career at eight dollars a week on the Hobart (Missouri) Chief in his hometown. He had worked briefly on a paper in Fort Smith, Arkansas, and climbed to city editor on the Joplin Globe.

Reese told Editor & Publisher at age 80 that the meaning of the newspaper business was the same then as it had been in Joplin: You knew what went on in town because you made it your business to find out; your responsibility was to fight the bad when you found it; and your second responsibility was to favor the good; and it was important to keep it in that order.

That outlook apparently was pretty well crystallized by the time Reese joined the Post-Dispatch. He was hired there despite the lack of a college education. In that respect, he was like Sevellon Brown of the Providence Journal and Alfred H. Kirchhofer of the Buffalo Evening News. Still, it seems likely that working under Bovard solidified the Reese bent. Two anecdotes indicate the Bovard style.

When Bovard was a young reporter on the P-D, his close colleagues called him "Jack." In 1900, Bovard was named city editor. The next morning, a reporter named Harry James called the office, unaware that Bovard had been promoted.

The new city editor answered the phone. "Hello, Jack," said James. A cold voice answered. "This is Mr. Bovard, the city editor. Please keep that in mind, James." After that, Bovard signed memos "O.K.B."

Charles G. Ross, who became press secretary to President Harry S Truman, was a cub reporter under Bovard. One day, Bovard sent Ross to cover the story of a painter who had fallen from a smokestack in far southwest St. Louis. After several trolley rides and a long walk, Ross reached the scene. His return trip was equally arduous, but he thought he had the necessary information: name, address, age, extent of injuries, how the fall occurred, etc. He turned in a short item.

Bovard called Ross to his desk. "Ross," he demanded, "how tall is this smoke stack?" Ross could say only that it was quite tall. "Ross," said Bovard, " 'quite tall' is a relative term. I want you to go back and find out the exact height of that smoke stack." When Ross again returned to the office, his weary day had turned into night. But he knew precisely the height of the smokestack.

Bovard and Reese were alike also in the way they backed reporters. Irving Dilliard, the longtime editorial page editor of the Post-Dispatch, described Bovard as the reporter's friend. "He put himself in the reporter's place," Dilliard wrote. "When a reporter had proved his trustworthiness, Mr. Bovard placed full confidence in him."

That also was the Reese approach. Both threw resources into important stories. When Bovard resigned in July 1938, citing differences with Joseph Pulitzer, he did not suggest his replacement. And, according to Time magazine, Bovard made it clear that he thought Reese, the city editor, something less than a worthy successor. Shortly, though, Reese was named as successor to Bovard.

Bovard, however, apparently gave Reese plenty of operating room. The Post-Dispatch won its first Pulitzer Prize for public service—the most coveted of the several prizes—in 1936 when Reese sent a dozen reporters on a house-to-house canvas and exposed a fraud in St. Louis voting registration lists. And, Reese noted proudly to a Time magazine interviewer, "Bovard didn't know a damn thing about it."

For a number of years, Reese drove the 50 miles from Spring Lake to New York City to take part in API seminars. As he aged, the drive in heavy traffic became too much, and he rode the train.

As his health declined, he attended fewer and fewer seminars, but his enthusiasm never flagged. He attended the annual Advisory Board meetings for as long as he could walk. Old friends on the API staff found it painful to watch Reese make his way from the Journalism Building to the API dining room diagonally across the south campus quadrangle.

Just before his 80th birthday, Reese received a letter signed

"Punch." Arthur Ochs Sulzberger was inviting Reese to a birthday luncheon in the executive dining room of the New York Times. It was a touching occasion, and not all the tears were those of Ben Reese.

Monty Curtis, friend and colleague for 15 years at API, came up from Miami. Walter Everett, another close friend and by then API's executive director, was there with Mal Mallette, managing director, and Russ Schoch and Frank Quine, associate directors. Publisher Sulzberger and several other executives of the Times attended.

James H. Ottaway, chairman of the API Advisory Board, presented a tearful Reese with a framed resolution signed by the API Advisory Board and staff and the acting president of Columbia University, Andrew W. Cordier.

The resolution honored Reese as a "distinguished newspaperman for more than sixty years" and one who "exemplifies the integrity and sense of high purpose essential to the newspaper profession, and thus to the nation." More than 700 former API seminar members sent congratulations.

Ben Reese was still the warhorse. He told Editor & Publisher that he knew that a lot of people were preparing to celebrate his 80th birthday at a luncheon at the New York Times. He said he would go along with the "fool idea."

"But, hell, I hate birthdays! And 80—it's a challenge to all the things you mean to do—that you haven't had time to do until now. I hate it."

18

Selling the Mousetrap

PI Seminars attracted 151 members in the first year, 1946-47, but membership had fallen to 106 members two years later. The institute was clearly in trouble. What was wrong? The seminars had been enthusiastically received. Members returned to their newspapers and pushed through improvements. In 1947, the American Society of Newspaper Editors had praised API for its practical results.

API recognized that it must increase its enrollment or close its doors as an experiment that had failed.

Enter Monty Curtis in 1947 and Walter Everett in 1949. Curtis wrote of himself: "I am a promoter at heart." That he was. And Everett had learned the value and techniques of promotion during his stint with Lever Brothers.

"Promotion was needed," Curtis wrote in his Remembrance. "Floyd Taylor possessed many talents, but promotion was not one of them. He shunned ANPA (newspaper publishers) conventions. He appeared at ASNE reluctantly. He did not enjoy speaking to state or regional organizations. He often said to me and Walter Everett:'We are building the country's best mousetrap right here for newspapers. If they don't want to come to it, then we'll close up and go back to honest work.'"

Curtis mixed hyperbole and truth. He breathed promotion, and Everett, too, could and did promote, though in less flamboyant fashion. If Taylor was not a promoter at heart, he still exuded the essence of what a newspaperman should be and thus gave API its important image of solidness. Moreover, he made a number of speeches on the hustings. But his workload of getting API under way and writing editorials for the New York Herald Tribune was crushing.

Taylor's hand can be seen in such early promotional efforts as the literature used by Grove Patterson in 1948 when he started the doomed endowment fund campaign. Taylor, perhaps with help from the newly arrived Curtis, produced 24 handsome pages of text and pictures about the infant institute.

At the same time, in his determination to make API "the country's best mousetrap" for newspapers, Taylor typed a sentence that may have inhibited nominations for seminars. API's second bulletin, for 1947-48, contained these words: "Publishers are requested, however, to nominate only men who have sufficient ability and experience to make a material contribution to seminar discussion."

For emphasis, the sentence was set in italic type. The early seminars included so many journalistic luminaries from large newspapers that the italicized sentence could well have scared off others unsure of their own qualifications.

After that second bulletin, though, the annual publication was designed increasingly to build enrollment. The next year, it listed all newspapers represented at API the first two years. The total was 112, plus the Associated Press and This Week magazine, a Sunday supplement carried by many newspapers.

The listing of participating newspapers continued. In the 1950-51 bulletin, API began to blow its own horn with this muted toot: "As a result of Institute sessions, hundreds of changes have been made in the operation of daily papers...Papers report increased circulation, improvements in makeup and illustration, and use of ideas that saved money or increased income."

The 1954-55 bulletin carried in large type the text of the ASNE resolution of 1947 that endorsed API. (The resolution read: "The American Society of Newspaper Editors heartily endorses the work of the American Press Institute, established through the leadership of Sevellon Brown, of this Society, at the Graduate School of Journalism at Columbia University. We believe the American Press Institute is already helping immeasurably to raise the practical standards of operative journalism in the United States.")

Two years later, the 1956-57 bulletin listed the names of all seminar members for API's first 10 years: in 67 seminars, 1,578 members from 478 newspapers or newspaper organizations.

Each year thereafter until 1985 the bulletin listed all seminar members of the previous seminar year. With membership then totaling more than 1,000 a year, the listing required so many pages that it was subsequently dropped.

In the 1959-60 bulletin, Curtis and Everett asked rhetorically: Who comes to API seminars? "That's the question," they wrote, "most frequently asked by newspapermen whose newspapers have not yet made use of the Institute. The answer is: many of the ablest, most dedicated and most successful newspaper men and women in the United States and Canada." In that bulletin appeared 10 pictures of individuals—known on newspapers as mug shots—and 36 pictures of groups ranging from two to seven persons at various newspapers.

Those pictures required considerable planning. One group picture, for example, showed seven of the eight publishers from Southern California who had attended API. The various pictures were made at newspapers large and small, from the New York Times and Miami Herald to the Council Bluffs (Iowa) Nonpareil and the Corning (New York) Leader, for example. For potential nominators, the pictures demonstrated the breadth of newspapers that had sent staff members to API.

Each year the bulletin was sent to principal executives of all daily newspapers—the persons with inclination and authority to nominate for seminars—and also all former seminar members. As API participation broadened this meant that some newspapers received dozens of copies. Staff members who had not been to API could hardly escape seeing a bulletin.

API tried to include at least one picture from each kind of seminar. Thus many members could show colleagues pictures of themselves working at API next to someone from the Chicago Tribune or Los Angeles Times—or the Walla Walla (Washington) Union-Bulletin.

Although the bulletins with their pictures and list of seminar members fostered nominations, they lacked the personal touch. That was provided primarily by the charismatic Curtis and to a lesser extent Everett and other staff members.

Everett recalled many discussions among Taylor, Curtis and himself on how to broaden seminar participation. Taylor sent both Everett and Curtis into New England, separately and with different itineraries. They chose New England because it was close and API funds were sparse.

Everett visited both large and medium-size newspapers. He particularly remembered visiting Lowell and Lawrence, Massachusetts, because of a dingy hotel. In his third-floor room, he found a coil of thick rope by the window, one end tied to a radiator. By the radiator was a notice saying that in case of fire the guest should open the window, lower the rope and climb down. Everett stayed awake all night, worrying.

Everett and Curtis reported similar findings. Almost everywhere publishers and editors had expressed genuine interest in API. Most felt the three-week seminars were too long. That problem could be fixed. Shortly, two weeks became almost standard. Another issue could not be addressed, however. A few publishers were concerned about their seminar member being hired away by another paper, or comparing salaries with fellow seminar members, or after the seminar leaving for a better job.

Curtis and Everett found strong interest in a seminar for general managers, partly because of economic problems at many newspapers. Too, such a seminar could produce tangible, measurable benefits in contrast to less measurable results of a news-editorial seminar. And—although seldom stated—publishers had less fear of losing business-side executives, who were generally better paid.

Later came other promotional trips, most by Curtis. In January 1950, Curtis wrote Louis and Dolly Law, with whom he had boarded in Buffalo, and described his trip of the previous two months.

"The trip wasn't for fun, Dolly, and it wasn't much fun except for the few days in Cuba and part of a week in Miami. Almost all driving was done at night so Alma (Mrs. Curtis) got a view of the South after dark. It had to be that way because I spent the days with newspaper publishers and editors, interviewing and being interviewed. It was a joint mission for Columbia and the American Press Institute. We covered a little more than 3500 miles in 27 days, and I interviewed people at 29 newspapers."

The Columbia reference was not explained. Curtis may have been encouraging publishers to hire Columbia journalism graduates or doing a favor for Robert Harron, the Columbia public relations director and friend of API.

In his Remembrance, Curtis referred to his trips as playing a part in the decision to begin holding seminars on newspaper management that were called Management and Costs. Curtis wrote that among the newspaper men who most impressed him were G. Prescott Low of the Quincy (Massachusetts) Patriot Ledger, James L. Knight and Lee Hills of the Miami Herald, and Nelson Poynter of the St. Petersburg Times.

"I can quote Pres Low to this day," Curtis wrote three decades later: " 'The most serious threat to a free press is cost. We are being eaten up by production costs—especially labor costs. If we don't get out of the crazy way we are producing newspapers in factories, then the free press is doomed. We must develop better management, better sales methods and, above all, different production methods.' "

Curtis summarized other newspaper woes: "Newsprint prices were increasing every year. Labor costs were rising even more as postwar strikes shut down newspapers. Most contract settlements were costly. Meanwhile, newspapers, traditionally low-priced for subscribers and advertisers, were reluctant to raise rates. Newspapers then were selling at five cents a copy on the newsstands and even lower for home delivery, which never did make sense. Advertising rates were low. The feeling was that an increase in newspaper rates would lose subscribers and advertisers."

On the need for more efficient production methods, Curtis found Low's views echoed by Knight, Hills and Poynter. Even before Curtis trekked south, however, API held its first Management and Costs Seminar, in September 1949, a one-week program with 20 members from newspapers above 50,000 in circulation. Among them were publishers, general managers, business managers and circulation and production executives. These were men with clout. They could nominate seminar members from departments other than news-editorial, until then the exclusive source.

That initial Management and Costs Seminar was a turning point in the development of API. Notably, it was a departure from Sevellon Brown's founding vision that API seminars would be exclusively for news and editorial people. But the broadening of mission clearly could not have happened without Brown's approval. API remained his baby through those early years.

A Management and Costs program for newspapers under 50,000 circulation was held in the same 1949-50 series, in May 1950. Thereafter, Management and Costs became an almost annual staple. It remained a one-week program until 1957, when a two-week seminar opened with a full day of discussion on cost comparisons led by Fred W. Schaub of Lindsay-Schaub newspapers.

Until API added the Management and Costs seminars, editors often had to clear a seminar nomination with a general management executive who had no personal experience of the practical value of API attendance. Now those general executives themselves began returning home from API brimming with ideas for improving operations, obtaining more revenue and controlling costs. Their own seminar experience often led them to approve seminar nominations not only from news-editorial but also from other departments.

At API, the annual membership totals began a steady climb. Thus, API began to serve the total newspaper. Most years, some two-thirds of the seminar schedule was devoted to news-editorial, with its bevy of specialties (editing, reporting, the various departments) and one-third to non-news (general management, advertising, circulation, production, promotion and public relations). It was a happy and successful blend.

API promoted itself in various ways beyond its mailed bulletins and greater diversity of program. Starting about 1950, each seminar member received a handsome certificate of attendance, with the member's name and seminar attended, the seal of Columbia University, and signed by the Columbia president and the API director. Certificates were awarded retroactively, for Walter Everett's certificate on his 1946 City Editors Seminar attendance was signed by Grayson Kirk, who became president of Columbia in 1953. Members proudly displayed the certificates in their offices or homes.

A group picture was taken at each seminar, with members posing on the steps of the Journalism Building, in front of the imposing statue of Thomas Jefferson. Each member received a copy.

For the first few seminars, Editor & Publisher carried not only the list of incoming seminar members but also brief biographies. For many years after the bios were dropped, the list of members was continued.

John Hohenberg, the journalism professor and curator of the Pulitzer Prizes, wrote a laudatory piece for the Saturday Review, and API distributed reprints. Influential journalists like Earl Johnson, the United Press International editor, plugged API. Johnson wrote a newsletter directed primarily to telegraph editors and copy desk chiefs. He felt they were neglected by management. Johnson campaigned passionately, and after a while successfully, for an API seminar for those specialists.

Seminar members, their horizons broadened by API, expressed gratitude so frequently that the flow of resulting plaques posed a storage problem. When Floyd Taylor died, about 200 friends and members of the seminars he had conducted contributed $2,100 for a memorial library. Charles A. Fell, managing editor of the Birmingham News and Age-Herald, headed the contribution campaign.

The idea was to duplicate the kinds of books found in newspaper libraries. The library was set up in Room 201, across from the West stairway, a room into which as many as seven support staff members would later work in cramped space.

To API's chagrin, the library received little use. The books later filled shelves on a wall of the office of the API executive director. Though the library project failed of its goal—use by the busy seminar members—it illustrated the loyalty of former seminar members.

API also promoted itself within the university. In 1950, API sent Dwight D. Eisenhower, Columbia's new president, a file of letters from managing editors and news editors commenting on the institute. The idea was at least partly the idea of Robert Harron, the university's public relations man.

Eisenhower was impressed and suggested that Dean Ackerman prepare a summary for the university's trustees. Ackerman's letter of transmittal to the trustees represented one time when Ackerman was strongly in API's corner.

Ackerman forwarded parts of 100 letters, selected from the several hundred available. "A majority of these letters," Ackerman wrote, "including many of the most complimentary ones, were not addressed to the director or associate directors of the Institute." He explained that some had been sent to a newspaper's managing editor or other executive who had been making inquiries about seminar results.

"The letters obviously are frank and forthright," Ackerman wrote, "and are not of a promotional character." Anyone reading the letters, Ackerman said, might ask: "But doesn't the Institute receive any criticism?" The fact was, he wrote, that the API staff sought and noted criticism from seminar members, and therefore it had been "possible to produce continuous improvement in the planning and conduct of seminars."

Ackerman described the purposes of API and how it was financed. Then this closer: "Under the superb direction and management of Floyd Taylor and his associates, J. Montgomery Curtis and Walter Everett, the Institute is realizing this objective and also contributing to the nationwide prestige of the University."

The best promotions of all, of course, were successful seminars. But the charisma of Monty Curtis gave API an extra edge.

His first meeting with Robert W. Chandler, later owner and editor of the Bulletin in Bend, Oregon, provided an example. In 1949, Chandler recalled, he was working for the Denver Post. Curtis came to town to talk with Palmer (Ep) Hoyt, publisher of the Post. Hoyt invited Chandler and a few other staffers to lunch with him and Curtis at the Brown Palace Hotel.

"Here," Chandler wrote, "was this big guy talking plain talk, full of opinions and knowledge about newspapers, telling us exciting times were on the way for those of us who stayed with the business and who rose above the average of their fellows. It was a kind of second awakening for me. The Post never wanted to send me to an API session at Columbia, but I remembered it. As soon as I was able after I bought this (Bend) newspaper I went to Columbia and was able to learn at a seminar conducted by Walter Everett, with constant interruptions from Monty."

Curtis had many ways of making himself welcome in newsrooms he visited. Don Carter was city editor of the Atlanta Journal when he first met Curtis in 1952 at an API seminar. A few weeks later on a busy day in the Journal newsroom, Carter "glanced up and spotted a huge figure lumbering...toward my desk." It was, of course, Curtis. Carter was on deadline, working on copy and with no time to chat with a visitor.

"Monty," Carter recalled, "...without uttering a word, took a seat at an unoccupied desk...picked up a copy of the latest edition...began reading and making little notes on it."

A half-hour later, with deadline behind him, Carter walked over to

Curtis and apologized for keeping him waiting. "Don, old boy," said Curtis, "apologize no more. If you had not remained at your post and given your total attention to getting out your home edition on time, I wouldn't have thought you worth half the salary, whatever it is, that the Journal pays you."

Curtis glanced at Carter, then at the local section he had been scribbling on, and said: "Now, let's look at a few things in today's first edition that could have been done better."

Curtis' zest, humor and vantage location at API made him the guru of newspapering. Gilbert P. Smith, who became executive editor of the Utica Observer-Dispatch, recalled his impression that no other person knew so much as did Curtis about American journalism or journalists.

Others shared that opinion. When the New York Daily News brought in Rolfe Neill in 1965 as assistant to the publisher, he had never met Curtis. Neill went to Columbia "to meet this guy I'd heard about." They took an instant liking to each other. Later, as editor of the Philadelphia Daily News, Neill recruited Curtis to inspire young staffers. Telling his wonderful stories, Curtis was received avidly.

Scores of newspaper men and women remember Curtis for his encouragement. Robert N. Brown was a young electrical engineer freshly joined to his family's Indiana newspapers, Home News Enterprises of Columbus, when he met Curtis as an API seminar member. Brown's newspaper was the smallest in the Management and Costs Seminar.

"I expected to be thoroughly intimidated," Brown said later. But Curtis took a special interest in Brown, brought him back as a discussion leader on innovative production methods and praised the presentation as the best he'd ever seen. "Of course, this was gross exaggeration," Brown said, "but I shall never forget the measure of confidence it developed in me."

There was an unintended byproduct of Curtis' fame among newspaper people. From all directions, they turned to him for evaluation of job candidates. Rolfe Neill called Curtis a "one-man job bazaar." It was always important for API not to help one newspaper by hurting another, and it performed well in that respect. But Curtis, Neill quipped, could observe the letter of the law while breaking its spirit.

Once in a while, though, Curtis at least bent the law itself. When he retired in 1978 (it was a semi-retirement at most), Curtis received a "kind and thoughtful" letter from Warren H. Phillips, chairman of Dow Jones & Company, publisher of the Wall Street Journal. In reply, Curtis wrote: "The only time I ever broke an old American Press

Institute rule was to recommend Don (Carter) to Barney (Kilgore) when he was looking for someone to run the Newspaper Fund (which recruited college liberal arts students into newspaper work)."

But it is also recorded that when Paul Miller, chairman of the Gannett group, was looking for a successor he phoned Curtis for recommendations. Curtis named Al Neuharth, then with the Detroit Free Press, as either his only recommendation or as one of four or five.

Then there is the 1988 recollection of Alvah H. Chapman Jr., then chairman of Knight-Ridder. "Monty's most endearing trait," Chapman wrote, "was his ability to maintain a close personal friendly relationship with literally thousands of newspaper executives. I am told that Monty Curtis' recommendation to Nelson Poynter was one factor in Nelson Poynter's offering me a job to be executive vice president and general manager of the St. Petersburg Times. Whenever I asked Monty about this, he simply smiled."

With so many persons turning to him for guidance, it was not easy for Curtis—or other API staff members—to always observe both spirit and letter of their own law on personnel cross-checks. But any infractions may well have been outweighed by prudence and judgment. Curtis, according to Rolfe Neill, understood if a job-seeker was equal to a given newspaper's standards, "and he had a gentle way of channeling people of lesser talent to where they could make it. He gave a great deal to American journalism by rearranging the geography of personnel."

For two decades, there was scarcely a major newspaper meeting, state, regional or local, on which Curtis did not appear or had turned down an invitation because of earlier commitments.

In late 1950, writing to his former landlady in Buffalo, Dolly Law, he described his platform regimen: "Monday I fly to Atlanta to speak to a newspaper gathering. Did the same thing in New Brunswick, N.J., last week. Have to do it again in Maryland in February. Dates for speeches pile up. Think I'll quit it. Since I started making speeches, I've eaten enough clammy chicken a la king to poison a regiment."

During his time at API, Curtis rarely followed the advice he gave Don Carter 20 years later on how an editor must manage his or her time. "Do not respond to all calls for speechmaking," Curtis wrote. "In fact, be very hard to get. A very good turndown method is a letter which starts 'It is my misfortune to be unable to...' and then offer a substitute...If you are an easy-to-get speaker the word will soon get around. You will be deluged."

In 1960, the publisher of the newspaper Kayhan in Iran, Mostafa Mesbahzadeh, attended an API for newspaper executives from the

Middle East and North Africa. Greatly impressed by Curtis, Mesbah-zadeh invited him to Teheran to deliver lectures at the journalism school that Mesbahzadeh ran there.

Curtis lectured, had a private audience with the Shah of Iran, and was interviewed by the palace press corps. Mesbahzadeh's wife, who was a section editor of Kayhan, attended a second API seminar for the region in 1965.

But the Curtis travels, which usually were clearly promotional for API and beneficial to the newspaper industry, occasionally slipped into a gray area. For several years, Curtis served as a paid director on the boards of the Trenton Times and the Passaic (New Jersey) Herald-News. These duties took Curtis away from API work several days a year and fell outside the institute's goal of serving all newspapers.

Long after Curtis left API, Walter Everett, close to retirement himself, wrote Curtis for advice on an opportunity he had to join an unidentified newspaper board. (Everett did serve—after retirement—on the board of the Providence Journal.)

Curtis advised against it, saying such service required consider-able time away from API duties. If he had it to do over again he would not serve on a board of directors. Apparently, the API Advisory Board did not know of the board memberships by Curtis. Barry Bingham Sr., Advisory Board chairman, said he at least wasn't aware of the outside duties, and they never should have been permitted.

As an eat-sleep-and-breathe promoter, Curtis understandably disliked saying no to any request. That sometimes resulted in complications for other staff members in handling nominations. When a seminar was oversubscribed, as many were after the early lean years, the major criterion in accepting members into seminars was the order in which nominations were received.

A secondary criterion was called into play late in a seminar year. The staff, assembled to select the members at least six weeks before the seminar, would consider how many earlier nominees had been accepted from a given newspaper. In a close call, preference would be given to a newspaper that had not previously participated that year.

These discussions were frequently complicated by word from Curtis that some publisher had caught his ear at a newspaper function weeks before and that Curtis had promised a seminar membership, all other considerations notwithstanding.

One time, a newspaper group executive complained that several of his nominees had been deferred the previous year. Curtis wrote back and promised to accept into membership all nominees from the particular group. That skewed the selection process even more.

The most famous Curtis promotion endures in the API building in Reston. One version of the story went like this: Curtis and Turner Catledge, who enjoyed a laugh, were walking across the Columbia campus. They had downed a few martinis at lunch and were remarking on the memorial statues, busts and paintings on campus.

Catledge told Curtis that the latter should be fittingly memorialized for his work with API. When Curtis agreed with that idea, Catledge handed him five dollars and said, "Here, I'll pay for it."

Sometime after leaving API, Curtis came up from Miami to attend a meeting. Without telling anyone, he glued onto the wall in the API lavatory a small photoengraved plaque. In 1974, when Mal Mallette and Frank Quine were the rear echelon at Columbia and moving vans bound for Reston were being loaded, Curtis called from Miami to be sure the plaque had not been forgotten. It was already packed.

Mounted above a urinal in the API building in Reston, the plaque mystified new generations of male seminar members—and the few females given special entrance. It read:

American Press Institute
J. Montgomery Curtis Memorial Can
Here He Always Knew What He Was Doing

With Curtis in the forefront, the promotions worked. By 1974, when API left Columbia, 925 U.S. and Canadian newspapers had been represented at seminars. That was close to half of all dailies. Two categories were underrepresented. Only 70 of the participating newspapers came from the under-10,000 circulation category. Those very smallest dailies lacked funds for training or couldn't spare a staff member for two weeks and still get the paper out.

Then there was a hard core of larger newspapers, usually owned by a handful of chains, where profit was the overwhelming force and training was haphazard or non-existent. A frequent lament of API staff members was that they couldn't get some of the worst sinners into the pews.

In 1977, after 31 years and 375 API seminars, membership totals from different newspapers were compiled.

When a morning-afternoon newspaper combination was considered one nominating base, the all-time leader was the combined Norfolk Virginian-Pilot and Ledger-Star with 110 seminar members.

In second and third place, respectively, again based on a morning-afternoon combination, were the Providence Journal and Evening Bulletin with 109 members, and the Courier-Journal and Louisville Times with 97 members.

The single-cycle newspaper with the most members was the Record of Bergen County, New Jersey, with 92 members.

Nine newspapers or combination newspapers had sent 75 or more members, and 32 newspapers had sent 50 or more members.

The promotions by API had clearly been successful. Floyd Taylor's mousetrap had survived.

19

Devotion and Discussion

In the early 1950s, Monty Curtis, Walter Everett and two secretaries made up the API staff. Both Curtis and Everett lived in Westchester County, north of New York City, and commuted on the New York Central trains. Often they rode the same trains to New York's 125th Street station and shared a taxi to Columbia on 116th Street and well to the west of the railroad line.

One morning, with Curtis and Everett aboard, the train ground to an unexpected halt between stations, an occurrence not unfamiliar to New York commuters. Away from a station and with no options for alternate transportation, Curtis and Everett were captives. They fretted. What would happen to the morning session of the seminar?

When they finally reached 125th street, they scurried for a taxi and bade the driver to step on it. They rushed into the API conference room—and found that they had hardly been missed. The discussion leader that morning was C.A. (Pete) McKnight, a Charlotte, North Carolina, editor who had appeared at several earlier seminars. McKnight had sized up the situation and started his presentation right on time.

Another time, in Reston, a snowstorm snarled transportation out of Rochester on a day when John Dougherty, managing editor of the Times-Union, was scheduled to be the afternoon discussion leader. He had planned to fly to Reston that morning. Tracking the storm through telephone calls, the anxious API staff learned that the airlines had canceled flights.

One more call was placed to Dougherty to learn when he thought he might break through the snowdrifts. Within limits the staff could juggle the schedule, substituting roundtable or clinic group sessions that required no discussion leader. The call reached Dougherty's secretary. She reported that Dougherty had chartered a plane and was on his way.

Staff worries shuttled between the seminar schedule and the likely cost of chartering a plane from Rochester to Dulles International Airport, five miles from API. But not to worry. The intrepid Dougherty, another veteran discussion leader, had somehow found a pilot with a small, single-engine plane who had decided to brave the weather and was flying to or close to Washington anyway. The charter's cost to API was modest.

In 1979, planning a seminar that would begin in mid-February, Mal Mallette factored in the possibility of weather problems. As opening discussion leader, therefore, he scheduled Walker Lundy, executive editor of the Tallahassee (Florida) Democrat, over another possible choice, an editor from Idaho. Better to invite the Idaho editor in a warmer month.

On the morning of arrival Sunday, when members would be welcomed and briefed for Monday's start, Lundy called from Tallahassee. The Atlanta airport, then the hub of the Deep South's air transportation, had been closed by fierce ice and snow. Soon there were similar calls from seminar members in the Southeast. Knoxville had 12 inches of snow, Asheville eight; nobody could get through stormbound Atlanta.

In Virginia, the Blizzard of '79 was about to begin. By Sunday evening, snow was falling heavily in Reston. But 30 of 36 members, none from the South, had arrived, as had John H. McMillan, editor of the Oregon Statesman and Capital Journal in Salem, the discussion leader scheduled for Monday afternoon.

By Monday morning, 21 inches of powdery snow blanketed Reston, where even a dusting of snow brought roadway panic and the road-grading machines of summer doubled as snowplows. Nothing moved. Mallette, carrying a change of clothes in a knapsack, slogged the two-plus miles from home to API. McMillan and the 30 arrived seminar members burrowed the 400 yards from the Sheraton.

The schedule was juggled. McMillan handled the opener, and clinic groups were moved up to Monday afternoon. At noon, having trudged two miles in the snow, Frank Quine arrived to answer jangling phones. No other staff members reached API that day.

The saviour was Eugene R. Miller, publisher of the Evening Sentinel in Ansonia, Connecticut, the discussion leader scheduled for Tuesday morning. He left Ansonia Monday morning, reached the Sheraton Inn at 3:45 a.m. Tuesday after catching a snow-stalled Amtrak train, and spent three hours at Union Station in Washington to find a taxi driver willing to take him into the snowbound countryside. The limited-access highway to Dulles International Airport, which bisects Reston, was one of the few roads that had been plowed.

The schedule juggling continued. Walker Lundy, who had been scheduled for Monday morning, didn't reach Reston until midday Thursday. But no sessions were missed, though their order was scrambled for four days.

Juggling options decrease as a seminar nears its end. So on a Thursday in 1987, on the fourth day of his five-day seminar on newspaper design, Associate Director Don Lippincott began sweating out his two Friday discussion leaders. If they couldn't make it through a Northeast blizzard, Lippincott's program would suffer. Both discussion leaders were to present redesign case studies.

In Syracuse, the flight of Nancy Tobin, a member of the Syracuse University journalism faculty, was canceled. She took a train west to Buffalo, hoping to catch a flight. After cancellations there, one flight took off for Washington. Tobin was aboard. Meanwhile, Edward Henninger, assistant manager editor of the Dayton Daily News, could get only as far as Pittsburgh, where he overnighted. He reached API 30 minutes before Tobin finished her presentation.

"The point was," said Lippincott, "that they never gave up and almost willed themselves to get here."

No recounting of such episodes—many more could be told—conveys adequate credit to the hundreds of discussion leaders who shared their expertise for the betterment of newspapers. When preparations for a seminar have been made by the staff— preparation that usually require six weeks—the program's success depends almost totally on the discussion leaders.

With rare exceptions, API discussion leaders—not only those who coped with snow and ice—accepted their assignments with pride and prepared accordingly.

Discussion leaders who returned several times derived not only the satisfaction of helping newspaper brethren but also concrete rewards.

Charley Young, sports editor of the Buffalo Evening News, appeared as a discussion leader 46 times. "I never—not once— contributed nearly as much as I came away with," Young said. "First, there were the contacts. I met perhaps a hundred of the nation's top sports editors. When a story broke in their area, they were there for me to contact. And it was on a first-name basis. I can't tell you how many insights into major stories I managed to get from those contacts."

Frank J. Savino, an advertising executive of the Record in Bergen County, New Jersey, described a typical reaction: "(Being a discussion leader) certainly made me feel great, but it also imposed a great burden, because you had to prepare for three hours of discussion, and you had to keep it moving and lively...The nervousness lessened as you did it over and over, (but) it never truly left you...You got to become friends with many, many more associates in the business. The networking grew even more because they looked on you as an expert..."

Seminar members who returned to API as discussion leaders found themselves in an entirely different situation when they sat in the discussion leader's chair. The members turned expectantly toward them.

Gloria Biggs remembered her initial fright when API brought her from the St. Petersburg Times, where she was women's editor, to lead a session in 1961.

Midway in the session, Biggs told members that she could take the rest of the presentation in one of two directions, as they wished. One male member—the program was for women's editors— said, "I don't care which direction you take as long as you keep talking." With that, Biggs knew she had an attentive audience, and her jitters left.

API's discussion leader lineups changed with the years. Monty Curtis noted in his Remembrance that one reason API located at Columbia was the resource of a distinguished faculty. Columbia had 18 Nobel Laureates at the time, and API used many of them.

They included John R. Dunning, the physicist who developed the gas-diffusion method used in making the atomic bomb; Jacques Barzun, a famed scholar, writer and educator; and historians Alan Nevins and Henry Steele Commager. Later there were others like Zbigniew Brzezinski, the expert on the Soviet Union and geopolitics, and Amitai Etzioni, the sociologist.

Drawing from the treasure house of metropolitan New York, API brought in not only journalists but also politicians, academics and other experts. Such resource people contributed greatly to one of the API objectives—illuminating the social, economic and political problems of the day.

When API seminars were two or more weeks in length, so-called mind-stretching sessions were included, with a variety of discussion leaders like Marya Mannes, the author and critic; Herbert Mayes, editor of Good Housekeeping; Paul N. Ylvisaker, the educator; Dr. Herman Hilleboe of the World Health Organization; and Patrick J. Murphy of the Police Foundation. These mind-stretchers were usually great successes.

Walter Everett recalled that in API's first few years, the staff was inclined to hold Columbia faculty members in awe. When he was preparing his first seminar, City Editors in 1949, Everett leaned heavily on Floyd Taylor and Monty Curtis for advice. For a session on hiring and training reporters, Taylor and Curtis recommended a professor in the Columbia psychology department whom they had used several times.

"This gentle soul," Everett related, "showed up with two white mice in a cage, which he placed on the conference table, and alluded to them frequently." After the session a seminar member said to Everett, "I can't relate my reporters to those mice." Everett, himself perplexed, thought he must have missed the significance and asked Taylor and Curtis. "They smiled, shrugged and spread their hands, as mystified as I was."

Curtis loved to tell of the time he brought in a political science professor from Dartmouth for an editorial writers seminar. The professor began by saying he had observed state legislatures for many years, and "the increase in intellectual attainment, high purpose and knowledge on the part of state legislators has indeed been remarkable...Now I find them far superior in their conduct, their manners and their attitudes."

Curtis turned to Luther Harrison of the Oklahoma City newspapers, a seminar member, who had observed legislators in Oklahoma and had served as a legislator in Mississippi. "Have you, Luther," Curtis asked, "found that this description of today's legislators is characteristic of the ones you know in Oklahoma?"

"I can answer that by a case very much to point," Harrison replied by Curtis' account. "During the last session, two of our legislators got into a fist fight while drunk in a street in our red-light district. A gentleman stepped out of a whorehouse and stopped the fight."

After that, Curtis reported, "The discussion became more realistic."

Working closely together as they did, the API moderators and the more frequent discussion leaders became close friends and enjoyed joshing each other. On a gray winter afternoon, a discussion leader whose name is lost to history noticed that Curtis, the moderator sitting at the opposite end of the conference table, had dozed off.

"Monty," the discussion leader said loudly, "why are you sleeping?"

Startled into wakefulness, Curtis replied with equal volume: "Because you're so goddammed dull."

In 1970, Ronald C. Anderson, director of circulation for the Rochester newspapers and the discussion leader that day, learned that the moderator, Associate Director Frank Quine, was observing his first anniversary with API.

Unknown to Quine, Anderson conspired with the seminar members. When Anderson was describing how a newspaper subscription price is shared with the youth carrier, he asked Quine how the latter's former employer, the St. Petersburg Times Company, shared the price. Quine replied that he did not know.

At that, Anderson pounded the table, and the members hooted derisively. "You don't know!" Anderson thundered. "How can we work with a moderator who doesn't know that?" In unison, Anderson and the members, every last one, marched from the room, leaving Quine alone and bewildered. It was several moments before he realized he had been had.

Just as the performance of discussion leaders determined the quality level of a seminar, so, too, did the selection of those discussion leaders. In no other area did the API staff work harder than in identifying discussion leaders. Every seminar was examined for members with discussion-leader potential, and members were asked to list prospective discussion leaders whom they knew.

In 1971, Curtis mentioned discussion leaders in a letter to John Hohenberg: "A problem in the early days was to find experts who would lead discussions and not make speeches. Also, we had to constantly emphasize the practical nature of API (to provide material a newspaperman could take back home and put to work right away)."

Looking for discussion leaders, API searched for diligent, articulate persons whose newspapers—or at least departments—were on the cutting edge.

API cross-checked recommendations it received before issuing invitations, but the approach had its perils. One time API turned to the head of a newspaper association and received several names. To its sorrow, API learned that the names were offered more for political reasons than ability.

Discussion leaders varied greatly in style. Humor and personality, the staff soon discovered, could mask a lack of substance. Seminar members sometimes found that a flamboyant discussion leader left them with less information than did one of serious mien.

Nobody excelled William T. Jardine, associate circulation director of the Minneapolis Star and Tribune, in blending showmanship and substance. On the eve of his presentations on newspaper sales, Jardine, alone, worked hours in the API conference room.

Next morning, members found a carnival atmosphere. A colored balloon hovered over each chair. Other balloons were fastened to dart boards promising jackpot prizes. In a corner, a separate table was laden with beribboned packages. Sealed envelopes dangled mysteriously from a string.

And a wall was festooned with boldly lettered posters. "Make Your Carriers Proud," one poster read. Another proclaimed: "Enthusiasm Is Like Measles—If You Haven't Got It, You Can't Spread It." Jardine knew that youth newspaper carriers responded to excitement.

A telephone jangled, and Jardine pulled a telephone from an inside pocket. "Hey, it's for you," he would say, passing the phone to a seminar member. Guffaws. "Great with carriers," he said, "but I also use the phone at football games. You should see the mouths fly open."

Jardine would talk about his white shirt. He paid two dollars more, he said, to get a collar that wouldn't wear out. Three hours later he would remove his suitcoat and reveal a shirt pocked with holes. Great collar, he said, but not much of a shirt.

Sometimes luck played a role in finding top discussion leaders. Ronald A. White, then a production engineer for Scripps-Howard, recalled that he had only a day's notice when he filled in for Wilmott (Bin) Lewis of the Washington Star. White became API's most frequent discussion leader on newspaper production systems when computers were revolutionizing the manufacture of newspapers.

Over time, API identified dozens of persons who could handle various discussion leader assignments. In part, this resulted from the increasing number of seminar members. Newspapers usually sent their best people, staff members already in responsible positions or those ticketed for promotion. In API seminars, they came under the scrutiny of the moderator, always seeking future discussion leaders.

In its early years, API was sometimes hard put to find a certain kind of specialist who could lead a discussion and whose paper was progressive. One such scarcity occurred when newspapers began to revamp what had long and widely been known as the society pages, and broadened content so that they could then be called women's pages. Most papers were locked into the society-pages philosophy and published in those pages mostly news of the upper class.

From 1949 until the late 1950s, API turned again and again to Marj Heyduck of the Dayton Journal-Herald, a forward-looking women's page editor with a sense of humor. On the 25th anniversary of joining the Journal-Herald she presented the paper with a clock, instead of waiting for the usual gift of a watch by her employer. The paper deserved the clock, she explained, for putting up with her.

In those years, API also called occasionally on Jean Mooney of Newspaper Enterprises Association, a syndicate, to discuss women's interests. Starting in 1956, API began bringing in other women's page editors whom it had identified as espousing something other than wedding and engagements and news of society parties.

Dorothy Jurney of the Miami Herald (later with the Detroit Free Press) led the relief column, followed by Gloria Biggs of the St. Petersburg Times, Maggie Savoy of the Arizona Republic, Marie Anderson, Jurney's successor at the Miami Herald, and gradually a few others as more newspapers belatedly recognized the range of needs and wants of women readers.

Being selected as an API discussion leader often advanced a person's career; the bosses back home had evidence of high marks being awarded by API moderators who could compare a given discussion leader against scores of others from across the country.

The steadily acquired ability to pick a discussion leader on a given topic from a sizable list was a comfort to moderators as they built seminar programs. Sometimes the first, second, third, or even later choices were not available on a given date. After all, these men and women worked full schedules at their papers. In such cases, the moderators worked through the list until they found a person who could leave home base on the requisite day.

These longer searches could be frustrating for the moderators. But they also could bring elation when a rookie discussion leader came through with a smashing session. In such fashion did the API faculty grow.

Curtis called a seminar program the tip of the iceberg. Like the ice below the surface, the work that preceded a seminar didn't show. Not infrequently, a seminar member, even after watching the long parade of discussion leaders, would say to a tongue-biting moderator: "Do you work here full time or is conducting seminars all you do?"

API learned not to rely on star quality. A case in point occurred in the late 1960s, when the advertising director of a major newspaper was highly recommended as possessing the qualities API sought. He was certainly a great success on his own newspaper. But at API, he bombed.

Totally unprepared despite the usual advance instructions from API, he also failed to understand his audience and spoke in useless generalities. Within the API offices, where moderators let their hair down, the moderator of his session proclaimed that he had just worked with API's all-time worst discussion leader.

As guidance in planning future seminars, the API moderators developed post-seminar reports. For a number of years, these reports were skimpy. Seminars and discussion leaders were so few that staff members could work from memory.

With growth, though, elaborate critiques evolved, to the point that discussion leaders were graded on a scale of ten. In general, a rating of eight was good and acceptable, nine was very good, and ten was excellent. Rarely was a discussion leader rated below a seven. But one day in the 1970s, Associate Director David A. Roe, outraged because a discussion leader had failed to prepare and thus failed miserably, told his colleagues: "I've just awarded the first zero."

In New York City especially, seminar members sometimes wanted to hear celebrity discussion leaders, journalists or otherwise. They often did meet celebrities, but usually on occasions like the luncheon at the Associated Press, where one group chatted with actress Gloria Swanson and comedian Red Buttons.

API took selective chances with celebrities as discussion leaders. Yogi Berra, catcher for the New York Yankees, appeared on a panel during a sports editors seminar. Red Barber led a discussion on the effect of broadcasting on sports coverage. One sports editors seminar heard Red Smith, the celebrated columnist.

API quickly learned to make unmistakably clear to discussion leaders what was expected of them. Weeks before their scheduled appearance, first-time discussion leaders were sent API's detailed guidelines on preparation and presentation. The guidelines concluded by emphasizing that members expected instruction on the cutting edge of the newspaper industry and were interested in an elevated level of understanding about trends, issues, ideas and techniques.

Sometimes a prospective discussion leader initially said yes but backed off when API spelled out the assignment. Experience with the author of an acclaimed book on writing technique provides an illustration. The author, in promoting his book, had spoken from many platforms and may have initially seen API as another opportunity for his set speech. At the telephoned invitation he accepted readily, perhaps not really hearing the description of preparation expected. When those details were sent in writing, the author withdrew, pleading the illness of in-laws.

Some API friends and supporters served as unofficial scouts in identifying discussion leaders. Among them was Malcolm (Mac) Borg, publisher of the Record in northern New Jersey. Borg was one of several persons who urged API to make more use of the case method that Harvard used successfully in its 14-week management development programs. A number of newspaper executives, including several from the Record, attended the Harvard programs.

In October 1972, Walter Everett attended one of the Harvard programs for two days under arrangements made by Borg. After sitting in on two case-study presentations, Everett wrote in a lengthy report: "By API standards, both sessions would be called complete failures. Applying the API basis of evaluation—what did the member get that would be truly useful in his job—the answer would have to be nothing...Can the case method be used successfully in API seminars? Dr. Flowers, administrative director of the Program for Management Development, insists that it can. But I am not convinced."

For API, the problem was lack of time. The case method required time. Nonetheless, the idea was not discarded, and API later began building in hands-on exercises and mini-case histories. But the main thrust remained tightly packed discussion leader presentations, with members interjecting as they would.

Usually, API sessions reflected the best work being done on newspapers. But at times it developed important new material of its own, through the staff or by assignment to discussion leaders.

Writing improvement was a case in point. In the very beginning, API brought in experts on writing. Robert Gunning, who developed the "fog index" to evaluate writing clarity, was one. Another was Rudolf Flesch, the Austrian immigrant who taught himself English and wrote the best-selling book, "The Art of Plain Talk." It recommended that average sentence length not exceed 17 words.

Many well-known newspapermen disputed the Flesch teaching, but API found in James H. Couey Jr., Sunday editor of the Birmingham (Alabama) News, a discussion leader convinced of the importance of short sentences.

Preparing for API sessions on writing improvement, Couey took copies of stories from the newspapers of the scheduled members to all kinds of civic meetings in Birmingham. He distributed copies of the stories to everyone in the meetings, gave them 10 minutes to read, then asked on a form 10 questions about the specifics of the stories.

Grading the answers, Couey proved that Flesch was right: comprehension did increase as average sentence length decreased. API charted the results from 410 newspapers. The chart not only was used at API but also was reproduced by Ted Bernstein of the New York Times in his directive to the paper's reporters and editors, "Winners and Sinners."

Among the API discussion leaders who appeared at several seminars were a number of colorful figures who gained measures of fame in the newspaper business. Two examples support the point.

Edmund C. Arnold, who ultimately led the all-time API high of 208 sessions on newspaper design, layout and typography, was editor of the Linotype News in Brooklyn. He had conducted various workshops on design across the country before his first API appearance in 1959. Harry Lee Waddell, scheduled to conduct a typography session for a women's editors seminar, was ill. Monty Curtis called Arnold on short notice.

That was the beginning of an Arnold-API association that continued during his professorships at Syracuse University and Virginia Commonwealth University.

Arnold was a master teacher. He espoused finding the principles and articulating them. "Principles do not change," he said. "Teach others to look for and follow principles." Arnold's guiding principle in design was that of functionalism: Every typographical element should serve a useful purpose or be discarded; if the element already served a useful purpose then the challenge was to find a way to serve the purpose better.

Arnold not only taught. He also entertained. In his deep voice that rattled the windows, he made famous the town of Frankenmuth, Michigan, where residents were of German extraction and where he once ran the weekly Frankenmuth News.

When Arnold began making long presentations, he turned to humor to prevent possible monotony. He concentrated on yarns about Frankenmuth, and giggles would start when he would say, "And that reminds me of Frankenmuth." His Frankenmuth characters, which he told about in a Bavarian accent, were "all real, and they are all fictional."

There was, for example, Ludwig Pfaffelhuber of the Frankenmuth News. "Ludwig," Arnold would say, "was not really my right-hand man; he was my only man. And he was my second choice; anyone else would have been my first."

Then there was Waldemar Veitengruber, who ran Waldemar Veitengruber's Emporium & General Store. "He was our biggest advertiser, two-by-five ad every week. He was the only man I ever knew who would mark 'Wrong Font' on a period. And he did it, regularly. But he never did it on a proof. He waited until the paper came out. Every week without fail, at 12:54 Thursday noon he would walk in our front door. He had stopped at the post office and picked up the Frankenmuth News.

" 'Boys, the Frungenmoot Noose have made a small mistake on my adwertising. I think you better take a little off my bill.' "

Arnold the master teacher, the stand-up comic, the author of a string of books, the wearer of outrageously loud jackets, contended in 1988 that he was always "basically shy—you'll find that hard to believe." And he told how when working as a salesman for the Linotype Company he would sit in his car for 45 minutes, screwing up courage to make a call.

None of that showed at API, where he once made 11 presentations in one year. In 1980, after conducting his 200th API session, Arnold was honored by the API staff at a luncheon. (With 115 appearances, Robert D. De Piante was the only other discussion leader to surpass 100.) Arnold said he had met so many persons in so many places that recall was often a problem. Perhaps, he said, "I should take the advice of Jack Dempsey and call everybody 'Champ.' "

Another especially colorful discussion leader was Eugene C. McGuckin Jr., general manager and later associate publisher of the Duluth Herald and News-Tribune. McGuckin was a high-strung mathematical genius who for years conducted the all-day confidential revenue and costs study, held with the cooperation of the Inland Daily Press Association.

Inland assigned a secret code number to figures submitted in advance by each seminar member, and McGuckin marched the members through a gruelling analysis that told each member where his newspaper stood in relation to other newspapers of similar size.

Frank Quine, then an API associate director, had never met McGuckin when preparing a Management and Costs Seminar. McGuckin was scheduled all day on the first Tuesday.

On Monday afternoon as a session neared its end, Quine recalled, "the large doors of the API conference room were suddenly pushed open. I noted out of the corner of my eye a tall, incredibly skinny and long-necked fellow wearing a white T-shirt and shorts. He was dripping with perspiration and breathing quite hard, indeed even had a wild look in his eyes. He resembled Ichabod Crane, on foot.'Better be careful; might be a drug addict,' I thought. 'Looks like he's in his underwear. I think I've got to throw this guy out of here.' "

Quine left his moderator's chair and, walking as tall as possible, confronted "this intruder who gave new meaning to the word spindly. He looked at me through glasses that had slipped down on his sweaty nose, smiled and said, 'McGuckin here. Been jogging around the campus and thought I'd say hello.' "

Though bone thin in his later years, McGuckin had played football at Princeton. Once he ran in the Boston Marathon. He said he had gotten so thin working long hours to learn how to make a living.

Before his API sessions, McGuckin was a basket case. His first time working with McGuckin, Mal Mallette found him 10 minutes before the session with head hung below his outspread legs."I'm deathly sick," McGuckin croaked to the alarmed moderator. Then he added, "But don't worry, I'm always this way."

In the discussion leader's seat, McGuckin was a martinet. Woe to the member who didn't pay attention. Fiercely, he protected the secrecy of the origin of each set of figures. One day, William Eckenberg, a soft-spoken former New York Times photographer, entered the conference room on assignment to take candid pictures for the annual API bulletin.

"Get that man out of here," McGuckin shrieked. Despite explanations by the moderator, McGuckin relented only reluctantly and after some delay.

But everyone adored McGuckin. He was mentor to a string of assistants, one being Roger Grier, later vice president of the Hearst Corporation. McGuckin was business manager in 1957 when Grier joined the Duluth newspapers as a classified advertising salesman. Grier remembered McGuckin as a stern taskmaster, for himself and others, with an ability to encourage potential.

"When I thought I had done poorly," Grier recalled, "he would say, 'You did a great job on that.' When I thought I had done well he'd kick me in the tail and ask why I hadn't done this or that."

One day McGuckin didn't hire a seemingly qualified job applicant and explained his reason to Grier: "The person's shirt and tie didn't match. As he said that, he took off his own tweed jacket, which had elbow patches. His shirt collar was frayed and its elbows were out."

McGuckin cracked the whip, but between cracks he deprecated himself. Of his beanpole figure, he said, "I wasn't born, I was extruded." A chain-smoker, he coughed frequently. "The doctor said the cough is good for me," he explained. "It's the only exercise I get."

Adjoining the staircase in the API building in Reston is a mosaic of the nameplates of newspapers, groups and foundations that contributed funds for construction of the building. When Ridder Publications, which owned the Duluth newspapers before merging with Knight to form Knight-Ridder, contributed it specified that these words be added to the plaque noting its donation: "In memory of Eugene McGuckin, Jr."

When McGuckin died of cancer in 1971 at age 59 a Duluth News-Tribune editorial said: "...at times (he) seemed to be a long-lost Knight from King Arthur's Round Table. He had a code of ethics that would have shamed the angel Gabriel." Such was the measure of admiration and respect for a man who would stay up all night figuring percentages on a Frieden calculator for his presentations at API.

API continually searched for new discussion leaders. Prospects were measured against the proven superior performers. Prudently, a seminar program often mixed outstanding veterans with a rookie or two. Accordingly, certain discussion leaders like Ed Arnold and Gene McGuckin were brought back again and again.

API kept calling on certain prized discussion leaders as they climbed the career ladder. A few climbed swiftly to such responsible positions that they had to turn down API invitations. Among them were Alvah H. Chapman Jr., Allen H. Neuharth, and Stanton R. Cook. They became chief executives of, respectively, Knight-Ridder, Gannett and the Tribune Company.

Virgil Fassio, who was destined to become publisher of the Seattle Post-Intelligencer, came to API first as a seminar member and then as a rookie discussion leader from the Valley News-Dispatch of Tarentum, Pennsylvania, where he was circulation manager. He continued to be invited as he moved to larger and larger newspapers, to the News-Journal of Wilmington, Delaware; the Detroit Free Press; and the Chicago Tribune, all in circulation executive capacities.

Fassio typified the intense preparation of the most successful discussion leaders. Recalling his first discussion leader assignment, in 1958, Fassio wrote: "I never worked harder in my life...I spent evening after evening going through all the clippings on circulation that I had accumulated. I didn't want it to be a discussion of the Valley Daily News circulation operation. I wanted it to be a discussion of the field of circulation, with many options and drawing on other newspapers' experience, since no two circulation operations are alike."

Fassio contacted the circulation directors of papers in the seminar to learn about their operations. Finally, he developed an outline in a booklet, with room for notes on each facing page. He remembered the token honorarium: $75. API always considered its honoraria as tokens. It could not afford to reward discussion leaders fully for their work. For a small-paper circulation manager, though, $75 was an appreciable sum in those days. And of course Fassio had an expenses-paid trip to New York City.

In 1978, its 33rd year, and after several hundred persons had served as discussion leaders, API honored the 22 who had led 25 or more seminars.

Six of the 22 honorees were deceased. The others attended a luncheon in Reston. API Chairman Tim Hays presided. James H. Ottaway, the immediate past chairman, presented certificates of appreciation. Monty Curtis and Walter Everett joined in. Speeches were supposed to be short, but some were long. Mal Mallette, API director, said, "It would be difficult to find 22 persons who have contributed more to the improved quality of newspapers than the 22 persons we are honoring."

The honorees, listed with the number of their seminar appearances at the time, one or more of their newspaper or other affiliations, and their areas of expertise were:

Edmund C. Arnold, 193: Linotype Company, Syracuse University, Virginia Commonwealth University (design and typography).

Robert D. De Piante, 92: Toronto Star, Charlotte Observer (photography).

E. Douglas Hamilton, 81: New York Herald-Tribune, Columbia University Graduate School of Journalism (libel).

Don E. Carter, 70: Atlanta Journal, Newspaper Fund, the (Bergen County) Record; Macon (Georgia) Telegraph and News (news-editorial).

Ronald A. White, 67: Scripps-Howard; Gannett Company (production).

Harry Lee Waddell, 57: McGraw-Hill (design and typography).

Virgil Fassio, 48: Valley News-Dispatch (Tarentum, Pennsylvania); Wilmington News-Journal; Detroit Free Press; Chicago Tribune (circulation).

Charles E. Young, 46: Buffalo Evening News (sports).

Edward L. Bennett, 42: (Bergen County) Record, Newark News, Norfolk Ledger-Star (circulation).

Vincent S. Jones, 41: Utica Observer-Dispatch, Rochester Newspapers, Gannett Company (news-editorial and photography).

John L. Dougherty, 41: Rochester Times-Union (news-editorial).

James J. Doyle, 39: Providence Journal and Evening Bulletin (editorial page).

I. William Hill, 32, Evening Star, Washington, D.C. (news-editorial).

C. A. (Pete) McKnight, 31: Charlotte Observer and News (news-editorial).

Robert N. Brown, 31: Home News, Columbus, Indiana (general management and production).

Norman E. Isaacs, 27: the Courier-Journal and Louisville Times, Columbia University Graduate School of Journalism (news-editorial).

John Strohmeyer, 27: Providence Journal, Bethlehem Globe-Times (investigative reporting).

Willard C. Worcester, 27: Muncie (Indiana) Star and Evening Press (general management and labor relations).

Clarence Dean, 26: New York Times (writing and editing).

Marj Heyduck, 26: Dayton Journal Herald (women's pages).

Eugene C. McGuckin Jr. 25: Duluth (Minnesota) News-Tribune and Herald (financial management).

Hal B. Neitzel, 25: Decatur (Illinois) Herald and Review, Cincinnati Enquirer, Easton (Pa.) Express (advertising and marketing).

Responding for the honorees, Vin Jones recalled the early days at API:

"...The seminarians were encouraged, not to say incited, to interrupt us at any time with questions or disagreement. Thus the collective expertise of the group was as important, or more so, than the input from the so-called authorities... Leading a discussion before such a group was a rugged experience."

Rugged it was, and Jones and the others did learn much in the process. But those 22 discussion leaders—and many others like them—were brought back not so they could learn, but because in their presence seminar members learned.

20

Hard Work and High Jinks

Nick B. Williams of the Los Angeles Times was one of the 25 members of API's first seminar, the one for managing editors and news editors of large newspapers. He later became editor of the Times. In 1988, 42 years after that first seminar, the retired Williams wrote of his API experience.

"I recall Floyd Taylor," Williams wrote, searching a memory that he said often failed him. "I think I was among those attending the API's first get-together. Floyd, as I recall, was our guide and director, gently steering us toward achieving the purpose of API when some of us were more boisterously inclined. True, there was some after-hours roistering, but for some, such as I was, the over-all tone was one of opportunity to see and study journalism at its best—and better than I had been accustomed to. Certainly that exposure led to major improvements in the quality of my own newspaper, the Los Angeles Times."

A symbiosis of hard work and humor, high jinks and burning the candle at both ends became the natural condition for seminar members. Freed of daily deadlines and family responsibilities, they became immersed in an intense, memorable learning experience and devoured ideas that would make their newspaper labors more effective.

James J. (Jimmy) Doyle, a former chief editorial writer of the Providence Journal, recalled the serious part some 30 years after he had led 39 sessions as a discussion leader.

"The members I talked to," Doyle wrote, "were invariably sharp, sometimes demanding and even cranky. I was moved by the way they responded to the opportunity of API. They were there on business, by God, and if anyone, such as myself, presumed to be a Barney Baruch (the financier and adviser to presidents), he had better be prepared to fight for his life."

Many newspaper men and women learned with mixed anticipation and anxiety that they had been selected to attend API. In the seminar, they would be compared with peers from across the U.S. and Canada. It was only natural for them to wonder how they would stack up.

When a seminar began, the members usually concealed their concern. But as seminars were ending, members frequently confessed that they had arrived at Columbia or Reston with a stomach full of butterflies.

API staff members soon perceived this butterfly syndrome and attempted to put the new arrivals at ease. They studied pictures of seminar members sent in advance and usually could greet every member by name at the first meeting, even though the moderators and members had not met previously. Because they wrote and distributed brief biographies of members, the moderators also knew each arrival's background.

At Columbia, Monty Curtis delighted in delivering at the welcoming dinner on Sunday evenings his warnings on "Manners and Morals on Morningside Heights." He admonished seminar members to stay out of Morningside Park, just east of the campus; to understand that subway trains that looked almost alike could take members from downtown either to Columbia or to Harlem; to take a taxi back to Columbia from mid-town when in doubt or fuzzy from midtown imbibing.

The need for a warning on the different routes of the 7th Avenue IRT (the one with a station stop at Columbia) and the 8th Avenue subways was apparent early. At the first City Editors Seminar, in 1946, fellow seminarians with I. William (Bill) Hill of the Washington Star awarded him the John Jay Hall Award for Vehicular Retardation. Three times during the three-week seminar, Hill boarded the wrong train and wound up nowhere near Columbia.

API recognized that its members were adults. It demanded only that members be punctual and diligent in attending all program sessions. Those who didn't would be reported to their publishers, who, after all, had a stake in the required attendance.

Rarely was that extreme step necessary, but the prospect, emphasized on arrival Sunday and also printed in the API bulletin, once brought a hilarious moment. That was in 1976, when James F. (Jim) Hurley III, publisher of the Salisbury (North Carolina) Post, attended a Publishers Seminar at Reston.

In his pre-publisher days, Hurley attended an Editors Seminar in 1962 and a Management and Costs Seminar in 1966 and knew well

API's insistence on punctual and total attendance. Still, one morning Hurley hurried into the conference room several minutes late.

Hurley could relate an anecdote with the flair and intonations of another North Carolinian, Andy Griffith. His fellow seminar members, having enjoyed a stream of Hurley anecdotes, demanded an explanation.

It went something like this: "I overslept and I rushed down to breakfast and hurried through the line. I kept thinking I had to get to the seminar on time or API would report me to my publisher.

"Then a thought suddenly hit me. 'Hurley, why are you rushing like this—you ARE the publisher.' "

During a Managing Editors and News Editors Seminar in 1961, moderator Curtis scanned the rim of the conference table one morning and saw that the chair assigned to Harry G. Burnham Jr. of the St. Paul Pioneer Press was vacant. Curtis knew that Burnham had struck up a friendship with another member, James H. (Rags) Raglin of the Lincoln (Nebraska) Journal.

"Rags," Curtis asked, "do you know why Harry is not here?"

"Beats me," Raglin replied. "He seemed fine when we got back to the hotel two hours ago."

In his Sunday evening oration, Curtis, switching from serious mien to a high-wattage smile, would conclude in this manner: "Ladies and gentlemen, in brief we don't care what you do outside the seminar. Just don't do it here (on Morningside Heights)." In other words, don't cause any problems between API and Columbia University.

Newspaper folks are not without curiosity. So the admonition about avoiding Morningside Park usually caused them to stride beyond the King's Crown Hotel on East 116th Street and peer through the wrought-iron fence at the seemingly placid but dangerous park at the foot of an escarpment.

The Sunday night warnings were not capricious; API felt a responsibility for the welfare of its seminar members. And it recognized that many members came from communities where the safety of person and property was never at risk.

Once in a while, though, a seminar group took the Sunday night warnings on personal safety too seriously. In 1971, Walter Everett learned after a day or two that most of the members of his Newspaper Librarians Seminar had holed up evenings in the King's Crown Hotel.

Twenty-one of the 28 members were women, and they were reluctant to venture forth and enjoy the nocturnal delights of New York. Everett told them that only prudence was required. In response, the librarians thereafter matched the most explorative of other seminar groups.

For its first 25 years or so, women members were always a small minority in all seminars except those for librarians and women's page editors. When Judith W. Brown of the New Britain (Connecticut) Herald attended a Publishers, Editors and Chief News Executives Seminar in May 1960 she was the lone woman in a membership of 28.

Almost three decades later she wrote: "I am now forced to recognize that I didn't implement all of the wise things I learned there. Of course, some of my attention was focused on trying to keep up with the boys, who, for the most part, were cordial enough but refused to allow me to accompany them to those places designated as 'off limits' by Walter Everett."

Punctuality was important to efficient discussion in a way that seminar members sometimes failed to appreciate for the first day or two. Of time, there never seemed to be enough, a fact well known to the moderators. Invariably, a tardy member would break in with a question on a point that had been covered before his or her arrival. Almost invisibly, peer pressure would then exert itself with this message: "Hey, get here on time, and we'll not have to backtrack just for you."

At Columbia for many years, API used a silver bell, the kind with a tapping button on top, to assemble members into the conference room from their writing desks or the coffee bar. Herding members was an important part of the moderator's duties, and the tinkle of the silver bell was often drowned out by the chatter.

After he attended a Circulation Managers Seminar in 1970, Robert L. Holt of the Houston Chronicle solved that problem by sending API a Texas cowbell whose clang rivaled a pneumatic drill. The cowbell filled the need until 1980 when, in the newly enlarged building at Reston, API held for the first time two concurrent seminars, in the conference rooms at opposite ends of the elongated building.

One cowbell, two seminars. The cowbell was assigned to the red (for the carpet color) conference room, there to be used in the first-ever Journalism Educators Seminar. That left the Circulation Managers Seminar, in the blue conference room (also named for the carpet color) without a bell. Those members knew about the cowbell, donated by another circulation executive. The cowbell mysteriously disappeared from the red room and appeared in the blue room.

One member of the Journalism Educators Seminar was Douglas Ann Newsom of Texas Christian University. Upon returning home, she sent a badly needed second cowbell, inscribed as being from TCU.

On punctuality, patterns soon developed. Most punctual of all were members of the circulation and advertising seminars. A moderator could count on all members of those seminars to be in their chairs five or ten minutes before the scheduled start of a session. In fact, those seminars sometimes started early on the spur of the moment.

For news-side seminars, the patterns were less precise. Managing editors and other department heads were usually prompt except for a straggler or two. In seminars for non-supervisory personnel like reporters, the number of stragglers increased, and calls were often made by a secretary to an absentee's room. Moments after such calls, a flustered latecomer would arrive, sometimes without breakfast.

Seminar moderators were occasionally seen at first as stuffy or inflexible for insisting on punctuality. But they knew from experience that not confronting one straggler invited more stragglers.

Although routine reminders usually sufficed, there were exceptions. One came in a seminar moderated by Associate Director Clarence Dean, a gentlemanly former reporter for the New York Times.

Despite the usual modest measures by Dean, tardiness was endemic by early in the second week of the two-week program. Worse, two or three members had missed a full session. Dean asked Curtis to intervene, to bring the word from the executive director.

Curtis did—with a vengeance. In a voice just short of a bellow and with language not found in a family newspaper, Curtis laid down the law: be here for every session, be on time, that or be sent home followed by a full report to the publisher. The miscreants got the message.

Another sort of problem popped up now and then because of over-enthusiasm. Clustered with 30 other persons around the conference table, all of whom had been urged to comment and question, an occasional seminar member would simply talk too much, describing in exhaustive detail how his or her paper did this or that.

Peer pressure would often take hold. In one way or another, fellow members would convey the message: "Shut up unless you have something to say." But once in a while moderator intervention was required, and the goal then was not to embarrass the offending member.

About 1970 in a Sports Editors Seminar, Russ Schoch encountered a member who talked non-stop. Failing to get his message across in subtle fashion, Schoch called the loquacious member into his office and asked him to trim back on comments. That worked—for two or three days. Schoch cringed to think what it was like to work on the same sports staff.

Despite the rare overly talkative member or stragglers, the moderators almost always became fond of their seminar groups and watched sadly as members left for home. The internal critiques tell of one outstanding group after another. But once in a while the mix of 30 or more personalities produced another reaction.

"Never," one moderator wrote after a seminar for reporters, "have I been forced to spend so much time with people who cared so little about anything else other than their own little worlds...With their overwhelming tunnel vision, they seem to have lost sight of the reader. No one had much to say about him (the reader) except for discussion leaders."

But that was a rare exception. The prevailing atmosphere of a seminar was captured by Vincent S. Jones in 1979 when API honored the 22 discussion leaders who had appeared at 25 or more seminars.

"Some genius had set up this operation," said Jones. "He, or they, realized that the 'students' were well past their teens. They were used to good food, and drink, and adult company. So while Columbia's undergraduates were herded into a huge, clamorous hall, with about as much privacy as Grand Central Station, the seminarians gathered in a cozy private dining room where they were fussed over by old family retainer type waitresses serving superb food. There was no incentive to slip out to one of the sleazy saloons along Upper Broadway. API cocktails were strong, plentiful, and free—or at least prepaid."

To say that members never slipped out to a saloon was overstatement, of course, but at both Columbia and Reston, many members gathered at night in someone's room for newspaper talk. At Reston, API set up a hospitality room at the Sheraton Inn. API provided the room, the members provided food and potables.

In his Remembrance, Curtis wrote: "It is unfortunate that the rollicking humor which developed through seminar camaraderie has not been preserved. The uproarious resolutions, poems and parodies have been countless. Anyone who has worked on a newspaper will understand this creativity, which usually gushed forth in the closing moments of a seminar as new-found friends said reluctant good-byes."

Curtis quoted lyrics sung by members of an Executive Editors and Managing Editors Seminar in 1979. To the tune of the "Battle Hymn of the Republic," the members chorused these words:

> *We all came out to Reston,*
> *Where they trapped us for 10 days,*
> *We heard it, and we noted it,*
> *We learned to mend our ways.*
> *They sent us reeling homeward,*

Stuffed with knowledge and buffets,
A-P-I we salute you.

We learned a lot, we talked a lot,
We paid our Reston dues.
We laughed a lot, we gawked a lot,
We drank a lot of booze.
We bitched a lot, we moaned a lot,
And talked about the news,
A-P-I we salute you.

Most of the high jinks developed on the final day of a seminar. At Columbia, where each member had a water carafe at the conference table and seminars ended in mid-afternoon of a Friday, a person or persons unknown would sometimes sneak back early from lunch and fill one or more carafes with vodka.

On one occasion, Everett recalled, two seminar members hired a Bunny from the midtown Playboy club. They brought her to Columbia in a taxi with a raincoat over her scanty costume, and hid her in the API stockroom. When the final afternoon session started, the woman appeared in the conference room doorway, dropped the raincoat, danced, circled the table and gave each member a graduation kiss.

In a more serious mode, members would call Mrs. Edna Brennan into the conference room and give her a present. For 19 years, from 1951 to 1970, Edna Brennan was, in her term, API's house mother. In the writing room adjacent to the conference room, she presided over the coffee bar, dispensed aspirin when needed, sharpened pencils, sewed on buttons and kept the place shipshape.

Members often called her "Mom," and she looked the part, a diminutive woman who wore her gray hair in a bun. She called the seminar members—some 5,000 in her years at API—her sons and daughters.

The press, she said at retirement, was made up of perfect gentlemen: "They're neat and never throw matches on the floor, and they cover their typewriters." And an interviewer said: "Mrs. Brennan glows when she talks about the women attending: 'The men always sit up and take notice.' " She was, to be sure, shocked that time when a Playboy Bunny appeared.

Ripostes and monkeyshines were not all saved for the final hours of a seminar. About 1970, the moderator of a Women's Page Editors Seminar thought the members were unusually vocal in afternoon sessions.

He stumbled on the reason: The members, mainly female, had

perceived that the dining room supervisor, a jovial fellow named Tony Crespo, was vulnerable to a feminine smile. So, at the members' request, he was spiking the luncheon iced tea with vodka.

Though the spiked tea and the carafes surreptitiously filled with vodka deserve mention, API encountered remarkably few problems where alcohol was concerned. The occasional serious problems always involved a long-time alcoholic who could not stay sober away from home.

There were cases in the Curtis-Everett era when they sought help from the university psychiatrist. Everett said they always held off telephoning the nominator of an excessive imbiber until it was absolutely necessary, concerned that the incident might impair a career. When they did call, they usually found that the nominator was not surprised but concerned. One newspaper doubled its sponsorship in appreciation of API's special help to its seminar member.

Discussion leaders and seminar members who knew each other sometimes jousted amiably. A Sports Editors Seminar in 1969 brought together two friendly journalistic rivals, member Cooper Rollow of the Chicago Tribune and discussion leader Charles R. (Chuck) Johnson of the Milwaukee Journal. At that time, the Tribune carried a box on page one calling itself the world's greatest newspaper. During a three-hour session in which he made several references to the Tribune, Johnson never failed to add: "Which by its own admission is the world's greatest newspaper."

Sometimes the target was the discussion leader. At one seminar, a member passed the word that a particular discussion leader was extremely hard of hearing and reluctant to admit it. The member urged his fellow members to speak out loudly so that the discussion leader would be able to hear. So questions and comments were practically shouted.

In truth, the discussion leader had normal hearing. Afterward, the puzzled discussion leader wondered why the members had been so loud-voiced.

Perceptive discussion leaders received instant feedback on how well they had done. If members were silent at the end, the discussion leader had bombed. Performance from acceptable to brilliant could be gauged by applause ranging from polite to ringing. Another gauge was how members clustered around the discussion leader at the end, seeking answers on individual problems.

Discussion leaders soon knew when they had struck a responsive chord. Gloria Biggs, who became Gannett's first woman publisher, recalled when she was women's editor of the St. Petersburg Times and led a discussion on personnel relations at a Women's Page

Editors Seminar with 31 members, only four of them male. The feminist movement was still gestating, and most newspaper women were stationed in the women's news department.

Why, Biggs asked rhetorically, were so many publishers so weak-kneed about changing their newspapers while the needs of women were changing so greatly? Biggs said the women's pages were captives of the women's clubs, whose members were friends of the publishers' wives. Thus, she said, newspapers in many ways were pawns of the women's clubs, and the inflexible publishers were "pusillanimous characters." When Biggs ended her presentation, the applause "went on and on and didn't stop."

One time at Reston, Woodrow (Woody) Shadid of the Bloomington (Illinois) Pantagraph received the ultimate accolade after his presentation on selling techniques to an Advertising Executives Seminar. Like Knute Rockne exhorting his Notre Dame football players, only with humor added, Shadid had whipped up member enthusiasm over sales opportunities. At the end, the members hoisted Shadid to their shoulders and carried him from the room.

Changes in student attire developed at Columbia and a few other universities before spreading to the hinterlands. Seminar members arriving from more conservative locations were often astonished by their first glimpses of the Columbia students and sometimes wrote about it for their newspapers.

In 1965, Don Wasson of the Montgomery (Alabama) Advertiser, attending a Managing Editors and News Editors Seminar, wrote: "There are many odd things about Columbia, especially for a Southerner, but the oddest of all is the undergraduate...The Columbia undergraduate wears denims, chino or corduroy trousers, all of the peg-leg type, faded, unpressed and in most instances too short. Almost any sort of outer wear on the top half of the torso is acceptable.

"...A barber from the deep South...would probably kill himself upon one glance at these undergraduates. Hair, it seems, is 'in' and Columbia undergraduates are hirsute to the point of absurdity. They have beards, goatees, moustaches and sideburns...The girls at Columbia appear to be doing their level best to look like ugly boys..."

This ambience was inspirational to certain seminar groups, including a Classified Advertising Managers Seminar in 1965 attended by Earle DuBois of the Record in Hackensack, New Jersey. A DuBois colleague, Leonard Goldblatt, remembered the DuBois account of a resulting practical joke.

Taking their cue from student apparel, the members showed up at a morning session of the seminar dressed in scruffy jeans, torn T-shirts and ratty sneakers, all somehow acquired. Faces were unshaved, hair uncombed. The moderator—Goldblatt thought it was Walter Everett—and the discussion leader played it cool, making no reference to the new look. The members were disappointed in this lack of reaction.

Just after the mid-morning coffee break, the university president, Grayson Kirk, entered the conference room together with several visiting dignitaries. Kirk had wanted to show the visitors some normal activity at a time when student demonstrations were mounting. Kirk did a double take and quickly shepherded his visitors from the room.

Curtis once cooked up a gag with John Hohenberg of the journalism faculty. Curtis knew that the seminar members would not recognize Columbia president Kirk. One morning he brought in Hohenberg and introduced him as being Kirk. Hohenberg proceeded to dress down the members for alleged (but not real) misconduct at the King's Crown Hotel. It was a while before the members caught on.

Inevitably, seminar members compared salaries, either through a seminar-wide survey they took quietly on their own or in the small clinic groups, where members were placed according to the circulation of their papers.

Moderators knew that raw figures could be misleading because they did not factor in the varied living costs, employee benefits and level of responsibility. When moderators learned of surveys, they tried to offer perspective. Sometimes a member with a lesser salary had buying power superior to that of another member with a higher salary.

Curtis once wrote that he was able to stop most salary comparisons with these remarks:

"Comparisons of salaries, fringe benefits and many other factors are unreliable...Go back home, do the very best job you can, and if you have a fair employer you will be rewarded. Give yourself a year or more. If by that time you feel that your progress has not been recognized, you know what to do. On the other hand, go back home and show your boss that another man with your job on some other paper is making a lot more money and you are giving yourself a very weak basis for progress."

Seminar members came to API with a range of understandings on what they could put on the expense account. After all, their publishers had incurred an appreciable sum for tuition, room and meals (which were stated separately in Reston but at Columbia were part of a flat fee) and travel. Was a night or two on the town eligible for expense accounting? Nominators were sometimes generous, sometimes tight-fisted.

A great contrast in expense latitude surfaced at a Women's Page

Editors Seminar at Columbia in the early 1970s. A member from a Southeastern paper asked the moderator the policy of most newspapers on non-required expenses. On the expense account, other members were enjoying the attractions of theaters and nightclubs. With little personal money to spare and no expense-account permission, she was being left out.

She cited the case of a fellow member from a prairie province of Canada. As a reward for her good work and knowing this was a rare opportunity to enjoy New York, her publisher had authorized a generous flat sum, so generous that the Canadian member had taken the other members of her clinic group to a Broadway play. Encouraged by the moderator, the Southeastern member called her newspaper and was granted modest extra expense money.

A major challenge to a moderator to maintain a schedule and reasonable order often came on field trips. In Columbia days, some 190 seminar groups visited the New York Times for a social evening and discussion with Times editors and other executives. Scores of groups lunched at the Associated Press in Rockefeller Center and attended a United Press International reception in the New York Daily News Building on East 42nd Street.

The all-time test for a moderator probably came during the New Methods of Producing Newspapers Seminar, January 23-February 3, 1961. At the time, photocomposition—also called cold type—was rapidly replacing the hot-metal slugs of type produced by Linotype and other linecasting machines.

A Linotype operator averaged 10 lines a minute. The earliest photocomposers in the U.S., Photon about 1954 and Linofilm about 1958, could produce 60 lines a minute and that production speed soared in later models. Offset presses, which printed with greater quality than the traditional letterpress, were also sweeping into the newspaper industry.

To keep its seminar members abreast of this revolution, API not only arranged a demonstration at the seminar of early phototypesetting but also took both New Methods and Management and Costs groups to watch actual production at several plants in or reasonably close to New York City. In the 1961 New Methods Seminar, Curtis was the moderator, but he asked Everett to pinch-hit on a two-day excursion for the 29 members.

On a chartered bus, the members left Columbia at 10:30 a.m. on a Sunday for Chicopee Falls, Massachusetts, where they visited the new plant of the Wall Street Journal. The Journal was host for dinner, and at 6 p.m. the group headed for Boston. There on Monday they observed a Linofilm operation at the Boston Globe, lunched courtesy of the Globe, and then journeyed to nearby Quincy, where publisher G. Prescott Low and the Patriot Ledger were pioneering Photon operations.

Everett recounted what happened next. Pres Low was host at a dinner preceded by a "long and free-flowing cocktail hour. Wine accompanied the meal, and the seminar members were in high spirits when they boarded the Campus Coach (the charter) for return to New York.

"To my dismay," Everett continued, "I found that Pres (Low) had provided a farewell gift for his guests—a case of beer and several bottles of assorted liquors, stashed near the bus driver's seat. The seminar members descended on this with whoops of joy. It took considerable time to round up stragglers, and by the time the bus departed Pres's liquor had been largely consumed. Immediately, there was a cry from the back of the bus for the driver to stop at a package store for more."

Everett, seated behind the driver, whispered to him to keep driving until he reached the turnpike. He knew that the franchised restaurants on the turnpike served no liquor.

Meanwhile, the bus was rolling along suburban streets with plenty of bars and package stores. Each time, a bar or package store appeared, some seminar members would rush forward and implore Everett and the bus driver to stop. Two or three others came forward and urged Everett to hold his ground. Said one member, "If you don't keep going, you'll deliver a busload of drunks back to Columbia." Everett called it "a wild and raucous scene."

On the interstate highway, the bus stopped at the first Howard Johnson's restaurant. Members rushed off the bus, unaware that no liquor was available. Most, however, were content to use the rest rooms—there was none on the bus—and have coffee. Everett pretended not to see the seminar member who had the driver open the luggage compartment and retrieved a bottle of liquor he had farsightedly stored there. He shared the bottle with his friends and, said Everett, "all of us were friends again by the time we reached Columbia."

The seminar members wrote a poem about the adventure and read it on the closing day. Lamentably, Everett did not keep a copy. Perhaps the poem mentioned that Monty Curtis, knowing the bus would not reach Columbia until late hour Monday—or early Tuesday— had not scheduled a seminar session for Tuesday morning.

Curtis had his own memorable way of relating to seminar members. Bill Hill of the Washington Star, a member of API's third seminar, wrote: "Back in those old-old days, there were several Star executives who were critical of Monty. They said he talked too much."

On the other hand, the story goes that Curtis became so miffed with members of one seminar that he would talk with them only while actively moderating and went to lunch separately.

Joseph Pulitzer, Jr., never a seminar member but an occasional seminar visitor during his 28 years on the Advisory Board or Board of Directors, said of Curtis that he "enjoyed his wit, of which I was somewhat in awe. He was so forbidding a raconteur that I felt like rehearsing anything I might launch into."

Then there were the memories of Ted Durein, managing editor of the Monterey (California) Peninsula Herald, who first came to API as a member by paying his own tuition and transportation.

Durein returned several times as a discussion leader, once when a blizzard had seized New York. Curtis decided to stay overnight at the King's Crown Hotel. Moderators usually did that during winter storms and kept extra clothes in their offices. Always one to seek conversation, he persuaded Durein to join him, though Durein was registered at the Taft Hotel in midtown.

Curtis loaned Durein a pajama top which on Durein became a floor-length nightshirt. In their shared room, Curtis began reading aloud from "The Wapshot Chronicle," a bestselling novel by John Cheever.

The occasion, Durein recalled, was hilarious to start with, but it became more so. "We laughed until the tears rolled down our cheeks."

In 1962, Curtis moderated what came to be known as the Super Seminar. The 26 members included some of the most prominent editors in the country. Among them were:

Donald K. Baldwin of the St. Petersburg Times
Charles L. Bennett of the Daily Oklahoman and Oklahoma City
    Times
Brady Black of the Cincinnati Enquirer
Creed C. Black of the Wilmington News-Journal
Tom Boardman of the Cleveland Press
Larry Fanning of the Chicago Sun-Times
William J. Foote of the Hartford Courant
William H. Hornby of the Denver Post
Norman E. Isaacs of the Courier-Journal and Louisville Times
Earl J. Johnson of United Press International
Herbert G. Klein of the San Diego Union
C. A. (Pete) McKnight of the Charlotte Observer
Al Neuharth of the Detroit Free Press
Newbold Noyes Jr. of the Washington Evening Star
Michael J. Ogden of the Providence Journal and Evening Bulletin
Eugene S. Pulliam of the Indianapolis News

It was a formidable gathering of editorial talent—and loquacity. Creed Black recalled that Pete McKnight was the one who talked Curtis into holding such a seminar, with members invited by name instead of soliciting nominations.

Curtis was reluctant, Black said, because he felt the participants would all know each other from APME and ASNE meetings and the two weeks would turn into a non-stop bull session and party. Black remembered that in fact the prestigious members were hard-working, and there was much more partying at a Management and Costs Seminar he attended two years later. But Herb Klein remembered the group as "a wild bunch."

Hard working or not, wild or not, the members provided at least one difficult moment for Curtis. That came on the third day when the discussion leader—on the topic of solving cost problems—was Mark F. Ethridge, chairman of the Louisville newspapers and one of the most respected and best-liked newspaper executives in the country.

When Ethridge ended his presentation at noon, he insisted that seven or eight seminar members, by the recall of Norman Isaacs, "join with him at the West End (a Broadway saloon) for a popper." The contingent included Isaacs, Ogden, Klein, Fanning, and some others.

One popper led to another and then a few more. "We dragged into the afternoon seminar 'way late," Isaacs recalled, "to face a near-apoplectic Curtis." A couple of days later, Isaacs asked the still fuming Curtis how they, the West End contingent, could have said no to "one of the most charming (and still wise) old brigands in journalism." Curtis puffed out his cheeks and said something like: "Oh, hell, let's forget the whole damned bit."

In that seminar, Curtis read aloud to members several examples of fine newspaper writing. One he began to read without identifying the source. It was a 1944 story out of Naples, Italy, about a British general hospital and "a pale, slender English girl with dark hair and eyes", a nurse called Miss Mac who was constantly teased by the volunteer ambulance drivers. Then one day German bombs fell on the hospital, and Miss Mac's "coffin looked incredibly small as they lowered it into the ground."

Curtis paused and looked across the conference table to where Newby Noyes sat. Tears glistened on Noyes' cheeks. For it was Noyes who had spent several weeks in that hospital and written the story.

Much of the character of API seminars can be found in two experiences at a City Editors Seminar in December 1960. It opened December 3 with an all-day discussion on organization and operation of the city desk led by Al Neuharth, assistant to the executive editor of the Detroit Free Press. One point Neuharth stressed was the need for newspapers to have two city editors—a "working" city editor and a "thinking" city editor. The latter would be freed of daily routine in order to think and plan.

On December 16, on the seminar's final morning, Douglas E. Hamilton, counsel of the New York Herald Tribune, was leading a session on libel when an API secretary entered the room and whispered a message to a seminar member. The member hastily left the room, as Walter Everett, the moderator, recalled. Soon the secretary returned with messages for two other members. They left, too, but first they explained the reason.

At 10:33 a.m. that morning, in a heavy snowstorm, a TWA Constellation was flying inbound from Dayton to LaGuardia Airport, and a United jet from Chicago was headed for Idlewild, now John F. Kennedy Airport. The two aircraft collided over Staten Island. The TWA aircraft disintegrated and plunged to the ground. The United jet staggered several miles, then crashed in the Park Slope section of Brooklyn. All 128 persons on the two-planes were killed, as were five persons on the ground, struck by falling wreckage.

Some of those newspapers with city editors at API called to order them to cover the disaster. Ten or more of the city editors rushed out to Broadway, yelling for taxis and searching for their police passes. One seminar member, lacking a police pass, got through police lines by frantically waving his Columbia University bursar's receipt, which showed that API tuition had been paid. All of them telephoned in byline stories.

In the API conference room, the discussion on libel continued. One of the remaining seminar members commented grimly: "This is the day that separated the working city editors from the thinking city editors."

The day held was symbolic for API and its seminar members. They worked hard, they played hard, but always they were newspaper men and women.

21

The Staff Grows

Although the six chief executives of API—Floyd Taylor, Monty Curtis, Walter Everett, Mal Mallette, Frank Quine, and Bill Winter—guided the institute's growth and slowly changing character, much of API's work was done by men—and later men and women—who labored as associate directors.

Moreover, they were responsible for planning and conducting most of the seminars. Their status was much like partners in a law firm, not that of assistants.

Seminars of high quality were the key to API's success, and the associate directors steadily sought the right formula for that quality. As API grew and added associate directors, it found several factors that sharply narrowed the field of prospects.

To begin with, associate directors could be discovered only at respected newspapers where they had earned the respect of peers and superiors. Then, too, they needed a broad knowledge of newspaper operations because they would conduct a variety of seminars.

There was rarely time to orient a new associate director. So it helped immeasurably if the new arrival had attended API as a seminar member and, better yet, had also served as a discussion leader and thus witnessed the behind-the-scenes preparation.

Associate directors not only managed all details of preparation but also were expected to relate smoothly with members and discussion leaders.

API sometimes felt it had to ask permission from a prospect's employer before making an offer. After all, API could not be seen as raiding employees from the newspapers it served.

Associate directors usually faced a salary cut in joining API, either in dollars or in buying power in high-priced New York City and suburban Washington. But there were inducements: prestige in the profession, a vantage point from which to observe the newspaper industry, an opportunity especially in the early days to join an exciting experiment, the relief much of the time from daily deadline pressure, and until 1971 travel abroad for the foreign seminars.

In his Remembrance, Curtis wrote: "One reason for API success was the practical experience of the API staff on excellent newspapers." He mentioned that fact repeatedly. In 1971, for example, in a letter to John Hohenberg, Curtis wrote: "Note that every API staff member has been an experienced newspaperman."

Perhaps the reason for the reiteration was disclosed in a letter Curtis wrote in 1972 to Murray Powers of the Akron Beacon Journal: "...When I took over from Floyd Taylor there was University pressure to hire associate directors who had PhDs and use journalism professors for lecturers. My answer was that if Columbia University wanted this they could find themselves a new boy because I was not going to preside over a failure. A great many PhDs are wonderful at the true disciplines of learning—philosophy, the sciences, the humanities—but newspaper journalism ain't one of them no matter how hard some journalism educators try to pretend that it is."

That passage puzzled Walter Everett, who encountered in his tenure no such pressure. Perhaps Curtis' comment was based on a remark by Dean Ackerman or an inquiry by a member of the journalism faculty.

For three years after Taylor's death, the API staff comprised Curtis and Everett—then the sole associate director—and their secretaries. The workload, comfortable for two years with a schedule of one foreign and six domestic seminars, became progressively heavier starting in 1954-55 when a seventh domestic seminar was added.

The seminars for non-news/editorial departments that API began working into the schedule in 1949 generated increasing interest. API measured potential seminar membership each year with a questionnaire to newspapers, stating the seminars it was prepared to hold the following year if interest was expressed.

The questionnaire for 1955-56 showed that it was time to expand the seminar schedule again. API scheduled a leap from seven domestic seminars to ten. Clearly, a second associate director would be required.

Increasing staff size demanded careful timing. Thin financial reserves mandated that staff growth be linked to increased seminar tuition and additional Sponsorship contributions. And there was no guarantee that API could find the person it wanted on short notice. Several times during the years under Curtis offers were turned down.

Twice, for example, Curtis approached Don E. Carter, who had attended a City Editors Seminar in 1953 and returned again and again as a discussion leader, usually on how to develop a news staff. But the offers came at times when Carter's career was advancing nicely. So he declined.

Kenneth E. Johnson was another who declined an offer from Curtis after agonizing over it. Johnson first came to API as city editor of the Grand Junction (Colorado) Sentinel and became publisher and editor there. He returned several times as a discussion leader and as a member attended six API seminars between 1960 and 1978.

Ted Durein, who attended API in 1950 as managing editor of the Monterey (California) Peninsula Herald, recalled how Curtis offered him an associate director's post in 1961, after their stay at the King's Crown Hotel when a blizzard struck New York City.

"Monty," Durein said, "you have to be kidding. Here I am, a California native in galoshes, with dirty snow over my shoe tops, with earmuffs in my pocket, and you offer me a job in New York."

Curtis replied with typical humor: "It's worse in the summer time."

Nonetheless, Durein discussed the offer with his wife Lib before turning it down. "Had I taken the job," Durein said years later, "and somebody asked me how I landed (it), I would have had to say: 'By sleeping with Monty Curtis.'"

By the time Curtis and Everett knew they needed a third staff member to help handle the enlarged 1955-56 schedule, they had worked with scores of some of the best newspaper men and women. Among the prospects was William M. Stucky, Sunday city editor of the Louisville Courier-Journal, who had attended two seminars, City Editors and Management and Costs.

Curtis received strong recommendations on Stucky from Barry Bingham, publisher of the Courier-Journal and a member and future chairman of the API Advisory Board, and Louis Lyons, curator of the Nieman Foundation. Stucky had been a Nieman Fellow at Harvard in 1949-50. Stucky became an associate director in September 1955.

As an API seminar member, Stucky had come from his hometown paper, the Lexington (Kentucky) Leader, where he was city and executive editor. The fact that the Leader sent him to a Management and Costs Seminar suggests that he was being groomed for a general management assignment. But the Courier-Journal beckoned, and he left Lexington.

On scholarships, Stucky attended Phillips Exeter Academy and Yale University, where he graduated in 1940 after majoring in drama and writing a column for the Yale Daily News. He worked six months as a "junior writer" for Metro-Goldwyn-Mayer in Hollywood, then served on Navy destroyers in the Atlantic, commanded the destroyer escort USS Naifeh, and rose to lieutenant commander.

Stucky's favorite subject was news writing. He led 21 seminar sessions on writing in addition to his full share of moderating duties. In those years, the API staff members often served as discussion leaders. Curtis was the staff expert on accuracy, Everett on matching news content to reader interest. Ben Reese, not as a staff member but as co-chairman of the Advisory Board, frequently led sessions on community service and investigative reporting. On a few occasions, all four men led discussions in the same seminar.

For five years and four months API rolled along with a compatible, talented staff of Curtis, Everett and Stucky, holding nine or ten seminars plus a foreign program.

Then, after spending a quiet New Year's Eve at home in Tenafly, New Jersey, with his wife Robyn and sons, William Jr. and Robert, Bill Stucky died in his sleep January 1, 1961, of a coronary thrombosis. He was 44, the same age at which his father, a doctor, also had died of a coronary thrombosis.

Everett recalled his reaction to the news: "complete shock...I couldn't believe it." Only a decade had passed since he and Curtis had learned of Floyd Taylor's equally unexpected death of a heart attack.

Stucky's death was a major loss for API. Curtis called Stucky "one of the great ones who built API." Everett remembered him as "an exceptionally fine person, newspaperman and associate director. He added literary and intellectual dimensions to the work, and his enthusiasm was contagious."

Stucky's death pointed up a gap in API's employee benefits. Starting in 1957, API had paid 15 percent of the executive staff members' salary into the Teachers Insurance and Annuity Association, the nationwide retirement fund for college faculty members. The amount accumulated for Stucky was small. In five years at API he had received raises, but his initial salary had been only $12,500.

Equally difficult for his wife and children was the lack of API group life insurance. Other than the small pension, his widow Robyn recalled, Stucky had left only his $10,000 military service life insurance policy.

Paul Miller, president of Gannett Newspapers, was then chairman of API's Advisory Board. Curtis wrote that Miller "knew what pay and security meant to employees" and was distressed to find the lack of provision for Stucky's family. Miller subsequently arranged for group life insurance up to $50,000 each for the API staff.

Once again, Curtis and Everett needed help. On file was a job application from Russell W. Schoch of the Des Moines Register and Tribune. Russ Schoch attended a Women's Page Editors Seminar in

1957, when he was feature editor of the Register and Tribune. He had been a discussion leader in 1959. He was a native of St. Paul and a cum laude graduate of Carleton College in Minnesota. He joined the Des Moines Tribune as a reporter in 1937 and later worked on the city, pictures and copy desks.

Curtis and Everett were impressed that Schoch had applied to join API. They brought him aboard in April 1961, returning the moderating staff to three. Schoch remained with API for 15 years.

Schoch was an outgoing fellow equally at ease at a blue-collar bar or embassy reception. A physical culturist, he often spent the lunch hour swimming in the Columbia pool. He wore his hair clipped almost to the point of shaving, and he kept his face tanned the year around, sometimes using a reflector to focus the sun's rays. He enjoyed a good joke and could tell a few himself. The threesome of Curtis, Everett and Schoch scheduled 10 domestic seminars in 1961-62 and 11 in 1962-63. Twelve seminars were scheduled for 1963-64, and Curtis brought in another associate director, upping the moderator staff to four.

In several years, API held at least one more seminar than had been announced in the annual bulletin. Additional seminars accommodated nominations for the one or two seminars with the largest oversubscriptions.

Each so-called Seminar X minimized time between nomination and seminar attendance. In striving to keep pace with accelerating demand, API was limited not only by staff availability but also by the number of usable two-week periods in a year.

The second associate director—Everett had become managing director in 1958—was William C. Sexton, the 30-year-old day editor of United Press International in New York City. He attended the 1961 Managing Editors and News Editors Seminar that included two others who would later serve, one long term, one briefly, on the API staff. They were Malcolm F. Mallette and Samuel G. Blackman.

A clergyman's son and native of Baltimore, Sexton had grown up in Cincinnati; Culver City, Indiana; and San Diego. He dropped out of the University of North Carolina to join the United Press (soon to become UPI) in Raleigh. He later worked for the wire service in Charlotte, Detroit, New York and London, sandwiching in military service in Germany.

He was in London 1953-59, part of that time as bureau manager, before returning to New York in 1959. For a 30-year-old, he had exceptionally broad wire service experience, and he bubbled with ideas. After his seminar attendance as a member, API brought him back three times as a discussion leader.

With a four-man executive staff, API scheduled 12 domestic

seminars in each of the next two years.

API added a third associate director for 1965-66, Clarence Dean of the New York Times, and stretched to 14 domestic seminars. Dean's arrival put the moderating staff at five. Not until 1980 in Reston, would the executive staff grow beyond five.

In contrast to the youthful Sexton, Clarence Dean was 55 years old. He was a 1933 graduate of Trinity College in Hartford who attended a City Editors Seminar in 1951 as assistant city editor of the Hartford Times, where he spent 10 years.

After that, during 11 years with the New York Times, he reported, worked rewrite and filled in occasionally for columnist Meyer Berger. At least eight times while with the Times he led sessions on writing at API. He continued to handle that subject occasionally after joining the staff, in all a total of 26.

Always meticulously tailored in conservative suits, Dean quietly enjoyed the shenanigans of his associates but did not participate. In his sessions on writing he railed against cliches and journalese and plugged for accuracy and clarity.

But nothing is forever. Bill Sexton enjoyed moderating seminars, but soon became bored with the back-shop details of preparation. That became apparent to Curtis and Everett. Early in 1966, the executive editor of the Louisville Courier-Journal, Norman E. Isaacs, was searching for a young managing editor brimming with ideas for breaking away from tradition.

Isaacs asked Curtis if he would mind an offer being made to Sexton. Curtis did not object. Shortly, Sexton was on his way to Louisville, paring the API executive staff back to four during a year of 15 domestic seminars and a foreign seminar that would take Russ Schoch out of the rotation for an eight-week interviewing trip in Africa.

Curtis phoned Mal Mallette, managing editor of the Winston-Salem (North Carolina) Journal, who had been in that 1961 seminar with Sexton and Sam Blackman. Mallette had returned to API a dozen times in five years as a discussion leader.

He was a native of Syracuse who sometimes said he had been raised in a snowdrift and enjoyed the mild climate of the mid-South. He also liked Winston-Salem and the Journal. But after a three-week courtship by Curtis he signed on as an associate director.

Mallette was a magna cum laude graduate of the Syracuse University School of Journalism. As a communications officer in the Air Force during World War II he rose to captain. He returned in 1946 from service in Germany not to journalism but to a seven-year career as a lefthanded pitcher in professional baseball. The New York Yankees had covered most of his college expenses, and he played for

Yankee farm clubs at Norfolk, Newark and Kansas City before ending up in the Pacific Coast League.

After the 1949 season he was drafted from Sacramento by the Brooklyn Dodgers and looked forward to playing a major role on a team that included Jackie Robinson, Roy Campanella, Gil Hodges, Duke Snider and PeeWee Reese.

But calcium formed in his left shoulder. He underwent surgery in early season and resultingly appeared only briefly as a relief pitcher in Dodger box scores for 1950. Mallette pitched two more years, for the pennant-winning Montreal Royals in the International League, and made the league all-star team in 1952 with a 13-2 won-lost record.

The surgery, though, had depleted the fast ball he needed to climb back to the major leagues. So he turned back to his vocation of original intent—newspapering, starting on the Asheville Citizen-Times in North Carolina.

Mallette reported to API in late April 1966 and conducted his first seminar, for editorial page editors and writers, only five weeks later. Help had arrived in the nick of time.

Mallette remained with API for 21 years, until his retirement in 1987, with a length of service on the executive staff exceeded only by the 26 years of Walter Everett. He served three years as an associate director, six years as managing director, four as director and eight as director of development.

Staff turbulence was not ended. A year later, in late winter of 1967, Curtis dumbfounded the API staff—and much of the newspaper business—by announcing that he would leave API on July 1 to become vice president/development of Knight Newspapers (later Knight-Ridder) in Miami.

Everett, who was usually in Curtis' confidence, learned the news only a day or two before the rest of the staff.

To Mallette, Curtis said: "I've got to get away from this telephone." He meant the calls that poured in—requests for a speech or an article, a personnel evaluation or leads on a new job. When in doubt, when in need, everyone called Monty Curtis.

But his decision stemmed from more than a desire to escape a jangling telephone. His wife, Alma, was arthritic, and the warmth of Florida may have been seen as alleviating her condition. Curtis had shrugged off other offers over the years, including a 1951 proposal from Lee Hills that he join Knight Newspapers.

Hills, later editorial chairman of Knight, recounted that for a while "I thought I had made a sale. But eventually he (Curtis) decided his commitment to API was too strong to interrupt it at that stage."

Sixteen years later, though, Hills "began to sense that Monty had

API in fine shape and might be looking for a new challenge before retiring. I talked with him during Christmas week of 1966. My hunch was right. Perseverance paid off."

Curtis told Hills he "had virtually decided to take early retirement, not to vegetate but to try something different. It would have to be connected with newspapers."

"That," Hills said, "was all I needed to know." The job title meant that "Monty would help with our expansion program and especially with the development of executive talent...He became our own critic-at-large...He was not just respected—he was downright popular."

The question of a successor as executive director was never in doubt. To help make certain, Curtis had written Columbia president Grayson Kirk some time earlier, saying that at his retirement or departure he wanted API to avoid the confusion that preceded his own ascension after Floyd Taylor's death. He recommended that Walter Everett be his successor.

In June, scores of Curtis friends gathered at Columbia for a rousing sendoff party arranged by a committee headed by Don Carter. It was a bash. The head table resembled a Who's Who of newspapering.

Publisher Jim Kerney of the Trenton Times chartered a bus, loaded it with food, Tuborg beer, and every one of the 36 persons still on his staff who had attended API. Among the passengers for the joyful trip to Columbia was the Times metropolitan editor, Donald E. Lippincott, who became an API associate director 13 years later.

Curtis, ever the deadline worker, wrote his farewell remarks that morning, saying that he was the undeserving recipient of exceptional good fortune.

Curtis was given a silver bowl from Tiffany's, and the party-goers paid for the API mahogany plaque containing the Curtis quote about making tomorrow's newspaper better than today's.

So Monty Curtis left his beloved API—but only in day-to-day presence. For academic year 1967-68, the Advisory Board expanded itself from 13 to 15 members. One of the new members was J. Montgomery Curtis, vice president/development of Knight Newspapers.

When API incorporated in Virginia, and the Advisory Board was replaced by a Board of Directors, Curtis became a member of the corporate board and was later elected one of two vice chairmen from 1976 to 1978, when he retired but remained with Knight-Ridder as a consultant until his death in 1982. On the API board, he was succeeded by Don Carter, then a vice president/news for Knight-Ridder.

In 1967, it was appropriate for the Advisory Board to add a

member from Knight Newspapers. A major source of seminar members and a strong financial supporter, Knight Newspapers had not previously been represented on the Advisory Board. That was not unusual, because there were no term limits and board vacancies were minimal.

Turner Catledge, for example, served on the Advisory Board from its inception in 1946 until he retired from the New York Times in 1970. Joseph Pulitzer Jr., editor and publisher of the St. Louis Post-Dispatch, joined the Advisory Board in 1956 and served until 1982 on the subsequent Board of Directors, when he had completed the permissible nine years on that board. With 26 years to his credit, Pulitzer led all others in total service on the two boards.

For the API staff, having a former executive director on the corporate board was a mixed blessing. In Reston, API faced problems that often differed from those Curtis faced at Columbia. The staff spent many hours explaining that reality to a Monty Curtis who called or wrote frequently. "I cannot avoid a sort of proprietary interest in API," Curtis wrote in a 1977 letter to Rolfe Neill.

The appointment of Everett as executive director came quickly and routinely. But API was back to a four-person staff. Everett was scheduled to interview foreign seminar candidates in Europe, starting in April 1967. Knowing he could not be away for six weeks, Everett transferred the assignment to Mallette.

For two years, Everett, Schoch, Mallette and Dean conducted the seminars, first 14, then 15, plus the foreign programs and any late-added seminars.

Late in 1968, Clarence Dean suffered a mild stroke that slurred his speech and required therapy. Everett shuffled seminar assignments, hoping that Dean could return to work after a few weeks.

One day, Dean tested his now weak and distorted voice on an amplifier Everett brought into the conference room. Even amplified, Dean's voice could not be understood. To everyone's regret, he took early retirement at age 58.

In 1975, fire broke out in Dean's apartment in midtown Manhattan, perhaps from a dropped cigarette. Groping in the smoke for his small dog, Dean was asphyxiated.

Before that tragedy, while Dean's ability to return to work was still in question, API was left with an overloaded staff of three. The prognosis on Dean had to be waited out. Then bringing on a replacement associate director would take time. As a temporary measure, Everett turned to Sam Blackman, who at age 65 had retired November 1, 1969, as general news editor of the Associated Press.

Blackman, one of the most popular executives ever to work for API, lived in Teaneck, New Jersey, and had commuted to AP headquarters

at 50 Rockefeller Center. By exiting at a different subway stop, he could commute to API. Blackman, who attended a 1961 seminar with Sexton and Mallette, knew API well. He had been retired only two months when he accepted API's call for help. He conducted four seminars over six months, giving API just the lift it needed.

In the search for a new associate director, a passing comment counted. Francis E. (Frank) Quine, then sports editor of the St. Petersburg Evening Independent, attended a Sports Editors Seminar in 1967. During the seminar Quine mentioned to moderator Mallette that he would enjoy being involved in mid-career training or journalism education. Meanwhile, Quine had been named news editor of the Independent. He accepted Everett's offer and reported to API in mid-1969.

Quine was a native of Cuyahoga Falls, Ohio, and a graduate of the Kent State University School of Journalism. Four Christmas-break trips to Florida during college showed him there were warmer places than the suburbs of Akron.

Upon college graduation in 1959, he went job hunting in Florida, where he could play his beloved game, tennis, outdoors the year round. He found a job as a sports writer with the Jacksonville Journal. After three years there he became a sports writer for the Evening Independent in St. Petersburg in 1962. He moved up to sports editor in 1965 and to news editor in 1967. He joined API at age 31.

Quine became API's managing director in 1977 and its director in 1979, when Mallette was reassigned by the board from director to a new position of director of development as preparations began for expansion of the API building.

Quine was director eight years and served with API 18 years before becoming director of development for the College of Journalism at the University of Maryland.

When Paul Swensson became an associate director in 1971, API was finally back to its former executive staff complement of five. Twenty years earlier, in 1951, Swensson had been an API discussion leader when he was managing editor of the Minneapolis Tribune.

A native of Mitchell, South Dakota, and a graduate of Gustavus Adolphus College, Swensson started his career on the hometown Mitchell Republic in 1930. He joined the Minneapolis Tribune in 1935 and remained in Minneapolis until 1961 except for Army service and a brief stint on the San Francisco News. He was managing editor of the Minneapolis Tribune, 1950-55, and of the Minneapolis Star, 1956-61, when he became executive director of the Wall Street Journal's Newspaper Fund. In that capacity he had again been an API discussion leader.

Swensson was director of the Temple University journalism department's reporting and editing program just before he joined API. He retired in 1975 at age 67.

In 1971, then, API had in place this executive staff: Walter Everett, executive director; Mal Mallette, managing director; and Russ Schoch, Frank Quine and Paul Swensson, associate directors. It was a staff that would remain unchanged for more than five years, the five tumultuous years leading to and including migration to a new home in Virginia.

22

The Big Apple Sours

When Monty Curtis became an associate director of the American Press Institute in 1947, he moved into a spacious and inexpensive university-owned apartment two blocks from the Journalism Building on Morningside Heights, the so-called Acropolis of America. Its streets, as in many other sections of New York, were safe.

Walter Everett found similar circumstances when he arrived two years later. He, too, lived at first in a spacious and attractive university-owned apartment on Claremont Avenue, a block west of Broadway. His daughter attended an excellent school operated by Columbia University Teachers College primarily for the children of faculty members, and there was the assurance of a subsidized college education.

Children of faculty members could attend Columbia College, the undergraduate component, free of tuition. If they attended college elsewhere, Columbia paid half the tuition.

When Everett and Curtis later moved to the suburbs, Columbia provided mortgage loans a point or so below commercial interest rates. Later arrivals to the staff received the same advantageous loan rate.

The staff found other benefits, too. The API executives held the same privileges as faculty members, including routine health care at the university dispensary, a standard privilege for Columbia employees.

The supporting staff, mainly secretaries, also had several perquisites, including waived tuition for a certain number of class hours. For such benefits together with Social Security and disability insurance, API paid Columbia an amount equal at one time to 22 percent of salaries.

API salaries, though, were substantially below those prevailing on newspapers for persons of similar experience and position. Both Everett and Curtis had taken substantial salary cuts to join API, even though New York City's living costs were among the nation's highest.

Still, for its first two decades or so, API, in the midst of the communications center of the nation, was an exciting place to be. As Everett recalled: "The institute then was unique, and joining its staff was a high professional adventure."

In those first two decades, personal safety was rarely a concern. But Manhattan gradually became dirtier, more hazardous and expensive. Retired faculty members recalled that serious personal security problems arose by the mid-1960s.

On the Sunday evenings when they briefed arriving seminar members, Curtis, Everett and the other moderators began warning the newcomers of dangers not only in Morningside Park to the east but also in Riverside Park, a lovely strip of greenery two blocks west of upper Broadway along the Hudson River. Even in the daytime, brutal muggings took place in Riverside Park.

At the same time, housing and commuting costs soared. Curtis developed a standing gag on the paralysis of public services that often afflicted New York. He asked seminar members if they knew the significance of a certain day in 1912. When seminar members fumbled for an answer, Curtis gave his own. That date marked the last time New York City was without a strike by its subway or bus transit workers, police, firefighters or garbage collectors.

The hyperbole stemmed from fact. The Big Apple seemed to many to have turned sour.

Moreover, Columbia University itself was frequently afflicted by turbulence for a mix of reasons. One reason was pushed into the background by subsequent events: widespread dissatisfaction among students with the educational curriculum. At Columbia, many students had long been critical of the educational offerings. They felt the university had become austere and remote. Restless, the students were easily stirred into protest for other motives.

The war in Vietnam provided a central motive for disturbance. Many other campuses shared that turbulence, but Columbia's geography made it particularly vulnerable. The campus was flanked north and east by urban ghettos.

Columbia added to its own woes when it sought to build a new gymnasium on two acres in Morningside Park. Both the citizens of Harlem and Columbia students reacted angrily to that proposal, calling it insensitive aggression.

That was not totally fair to Columbia perhaps. It had spent

$250,000 to reclaim garbage-littered land and build a Columbia-Community playing field there in 1957. A hundred teams of Harlem youths competed on that field. But the tenor of the late 1960s was protest, and Columbia was an easy target.

Serious episodes began as early as May 1965, when student protesters formed a human chain to block the Naval Reserve Officers Training Corps from entering Low Library for final review ceremonies. City police were summoned to break up the demonstration.

Later, students physically protested campus interviews by recruiters from the Central Intelligence Agency, the Marine Corps and Dow Chemical Company. The latter manufactured napalm being used in Vietnam.

Racial tensions soared, too. When the most serious violence ended in 1968, Columbia appointed a fact-finding commission headed by Archibald Cox. In its 222-page report, "Crisis at Columbia," the Cox Commission said this about racial tensions:

"Situated on Morningside Heights, the University looks down on the flats of Harlem, one of the most depressed of all urban ghettos. Millions of black people must have looked up at the institutional buildings as symbols of the affluence of a white society; remote, unattainable, and indifferent. Hundreds of Columbia students…(who) went down into Harlem with high ideals of social justice, but little prior experience with the realities of urban poverty, have been shocked by immersion in the ghetto."

In the week of April 23-30, 1968, the predominantly white Students for a Democratic Society and the Students Afro-American Society led 700 to 1,000 students in seizing five university buildings, including Low Library where they rifled the files of President Grayson Kirk. They, and their supporters, some who were non-students from the surrounding community, barricaded themselves inside the buildings for six days.

After six days, the buildings were reoccupied with the aid of more than 1,000 New York City police. President Kirk, on the advice of colleagues, called in police, although Columbia, like many other universities, had a tradition that municipal and state police do not belong on campus.

One police unit moved into Hamilton Hall, headquarters for the undergraduate college, about 2:20 a.m. on Tuesday, April 30, by traversing utility tunnels that connected campus buildings. There they freed Acting Dean Henry S. Coleman, a hostage.

Other helmeted police made direct assaults. The students resisted in all places. At the Mathematics Building, students wet the entrance stairs with soap and water to make them hazardous for police.

The Cox Commission reported 692 arrests, of which 75 percent were Columbia students. The statistics largely dispelled contentions that the demonstration was the work of outside agitators. At two nearby hospitals, 103 persons, including eight faculty members and 13 police, were treated for injuries ranging from heavy bruises and lacerations to sprains and two fractures.

As the string of demonstrations developed before the occupation, the API staff watched with growing concern. The early demonstrations did not infringe on API seminars, although some seminar members were overly skittish because TV coverage usually magnified what had actually happened. Press cameras zoomed in on protesters, whose chantings and facial distortions increased at the sight of a camera, for broadcast or print.

One day, Mal Mallette led his seminar members to lunch by walking through a demonstration in front of Hamilton Hall. Seminar members were astonished to find only desultory picketing. Next day, a New York newspaper carried a close-cropped picture of one demonstrator, his face seemingly twisted in anger.

With the occupations, the campus exploded into an uproar. The students not inside the occupied buildings milled about outside those buildings and at campus entrances, especially the one at 116th Street and Broadway, at the northwest corner of the Journalism Building.

Carrying signs of protests, the students shouted and chanted. Campus security guards uneasily stood watch. City police patrolled just off campus. There were frequent scuffles, because not all students agreed with the protests.

The faculty, too, was split in its opinions. Classes remained open for two days, but attendance was minimal. Then the university vice president and provost, David B. Truman, emerged at 3:15 a.m. from a meeting of university officials and faculty and announced to a milling throng that the university would be closed until after the weekend. The hour of the announcement was not unusual; protests continued at all hours.

Because the Journalism Building housed only graduate students (plus of course API and the bookstore), it escaped occupation. The occupations started on a Tuesday, the second day of API's two-week seminar for Telegraph Editors and Copy Desk Chiefs, scheduled for April 21-May 3, 1968.

The API seminar numbered 30 members, including one woman, Ruth A. Wilson of the Milwaukee Journal. Mostly, the members were fascinated by the closeup view of campus discord. For the first week, the program proceeded on schedule despite the distractions. On the first Friday of the seminar—and the fourth day of the occupation of five buildings with most of the university shut down—Everett and

Mallette, the seminar moderator, and other staff members returned from lunch in John Jay Hall, diagonally across campus. Rumors flew that police were about to storm the occupied buildings.

While Mallette started the Friday afternoon session—the discussion leader was William B. Dickinson Jr. of Editorial Research Reports in Washington—Everett identified several Manhattan hotels that might have the facilities to accommodate a transplanted API seminar.

API needed at least 30 single rooms, a conference room, space for clinic group meetings, and a private dining room for lunches and dinners, all at reasonable cost. The New Yorker Hotel at 34th Street and Eighth Avenue offered all the needs except a private dining room. It was no time to quibble.

At the Friday afternoon coffee break, API instructed seminar members to vacate the King's Crown Hotel before dinner and check in at the New Yorker Hotel. Seminar supplies were shuttled, and new instructions went out to the discussion leaders for the second week.

On Monday, April 29, the seminar convened in an unused barroom at the New Yorker. Timothy A. Blagg, a seminar member from the Delaware State News in Dover, recalled that the lights were dim, the room smelled of stale smoke, and everyone at the hotel expected to be tipped for every move.

Somehow matters worked out, even though on the final Friday morning the hotel unexpectedly mandated a move to a smaller, poorly ventilated room. The discussion leader, Edmund C. Arnold, rescued the morning with his humorous tales of his onetime paper, the Frankenmuth News.

Only later did Mallette, who commuted from Paramus, New Jersey, learn why by Friday these seminar members became the most exhausted he had ever seen.

At night, some members had returned to Columbia to watch the protests. In fact, Blagg and Ronald A. Britzke of the Evening News in Newburgh, New York, had checked back into the King's Crown Hotel, a half block from campus.

Blagg possessed a Delaware State Police press pass, with his name and picture. Covering the word "press" with his thumb, he used the pass to get through the police barricades around campus. Blagg recalled seeing a policeman "wipe out" a demonstrator with a billy club blow to the solar plexus. Blagg and some other members filed stories for their papers.

All of the member fatigue, however, did not result from reporting at the barricades. Seminar members reveled that week in being in mid-Manhattan.

Joseph F. Kane, who supervised AP's general desk in New York and was a seminar member, lived in mid-Manhattan. Members took to gathering at Kane's apartment about 3 a.m. and compared their night's activities before grabbing three or four hours of sleep. They reported that they vastly preferred their New Yorker rooms (as little time as they spent in them) to those at the King's Crown.

Despite the police bust of April 30, the issues at Columbia remained. They touched off more violence May 21-22, 1968, after protest leaders pushed for a university-wide strike. By May 2, 340 faculty members had signed a petition backing the strike.

Protesting students again occupied Hamilton Hall. On the night of May 21-22, up to a thousand students milled about the campus. Hearing that the university had again requested police intervention, some students barricaded the Amsterdam Avenue entrance to campus.

The Cox Commission report described what happened at 4:20 a.m. "The police came. Hell broke loose." As police advanced, most students fled toward their dormitory rooms. "Some police first warned the students; others chased and clubbed them indiscriminately...Some (students) who fled came back out to attack the police. Bottles and bricks were hurled by students...The action grew fierce...They (police) charged into Livingston and Hartley Halls (dormitories), clubs swinging. In Furnald Hall they chased and clubbed students as high as the fourth floor landings. By 5:30 a.m. the campus was secured."

That violence exploded scant hours after moderator Russ Schoch had welcomed the 25 members of his Editorial Page Editors and Writers Seminar. This time, API stayed on campus. James J. Doyle, a discussion leader from the Providence Journal, passed through police lines and was horrified to discover that the brick walkway leading to the Journalism Building had been torn apart. Students had used the bricks as missiles.

Two years later, for the first week of a two-week Advertising Executives Seminar, API again moved its seminar operation to the New Yorker Hotel when student dissidents were protesting. During that week, pickets blocked the entrances of several buildings, including Journalism. API staff members shouldered their way past semi-resistant pickets.

By then, threats of a shutdown on campus had been so frequent that Everett had prepared a three-page memo on procedures for a quick transfer to an off-campus site.

The threat to API was clear. Student protests might shut down seminars at any time. Seminar members should not be asked to shoulder their way through picket lines. True, many other campuses had suffered violence. There was no telling how long war in Vietnam, the main source of student discontent, would last. And both Columbia students and citizens of the bordering community nurtured other anti-Columbia grievances.

Even if campus violence and neighborhood crime had not become concerns, API had other reasons to ponder what the future might hold at Columbia. The most pressing reason was lack of space. Members for the 15 domestic seminars of 1968-69 totaled 511, more than a three-fold increase over the first year, 1946-47.

The executive and support staffs totaled 12 persons. Room 201 near the bookstore entrance, which once housed the Floyd Taylor memorial library, now provided cramped space for the supporting staff—the secretaries and a bookkeeper.

To alleviate its space crunch, API fashioned a tiny office for an associate director in the anteroom to the writing room. Then in that high-ceilinged space another office was cantilevered overhead for use by Agnes Lister, the assistant to the director, who shepherded seminar nominations and other records. Her office was reached by a steep stairway.

Space was at a premium all over campus. To slash per-student costs, the Graduate School of Journalism had increased enrollment from the 65 or so of early years to about 160. Understandably, the journalism faculty envied the API space they once had held.

The university had neither the money nor the space for construction. The plan for a new gymnasium in Morningside Park backfired, though negotiations had begun as early as 1958.

In 1968-69, using the sidepiece extensions to the conference table, API accommodated an average 34 members for its 15 seminars. Still, a backlog of nominations was growing, and newspaper men and women were not best served when their API attendance was delayed a year. Over the remaining pre-Reston years, API boosted its seminars to as many as 19 a year, using all available two-week periods.

A precipitate decline in food quality posed another problem. For years the meals served API seminar members had been excellent. Because students had several nearby restaurant options, Columbia had to provide tasty meals at reasonable costs or students would eat elsewhere. But faced with university-wide deficits, Columbia about the mid-'60s contracted out its former in-house food service. That's when quality plummeted—and complaints from seminar members soared.

At one time, campus food service was available almost all weeks. Now the commercial firms declined to serve API during weeks when the students were away. To fill in, API tried several schemes. For a while, seminar meals were taken at the Faculty Club on Morningside Drive, but that arrangement became too costly. As a stopgap measure, API arranged a few times for members to eat at the West End, a cafe and bar across Broadway.

Seminar members returning to their newspapers told colleagues about the sag in food quality. As a result, future members often came to API ready to complain about the food.

During certain stretches, API's monitoring restored something akin to the food quality of old. No matter, many of the preconditioned seminar members complained. Whether low quality was real or imagined, perceptions were a problem.

Meanwhile, the concern about crime on the campus deepened. Thefts there became so common that API kept its doors locked. Staff members moved from office to office with door keys in hand. Because of the bookstore, heavy foot traffic traversed the journalism lobby.

Clarence Dean left his office door open one day during a quick visit to Room 201, only 50 feet away. On return, he discovered that his wallet had been taken from his suit jacket, hung in his office closet.

With his office door closed, Frank Quine was conversing with a discussion leader, James Scofield of the St. Petersburg Times, when a heavy object slammed into the door. They found that a campus security guard and two city policemen had hurled an armed intruder, discovered on the fifth floor, against the door. The man had been carrying a sawed-off rifle and ammunition.

Spunky Edna Brennan, API's den mother to seminar members, frequently shooed suspicious-looking persons from the building lobby. Over a weekend, the journalism school was burglarized of newly bought equipment. In 1973, a journalism student was robbed at 2:30 p.m. in an elevator of the Journalism Building.

To little avail and at great cost, financially beleaguered Columbia doubled and redoubled its security force. On foot and on motor scooters, security officers patrolled round the clock.

An API secretary taking night courses fought off a would-be rapist on a campus walk. API secretaries who lived near campus traded stories of burglaries of their apartments. Mallette's pocket was picked on the subway as he escorted his Women's Page Editors seminar members to a dinner at the New York Times.

Everett was walking on Broadway toward the bank on 113th Street when a chunk of concrete as large as a garbage can crashed to the sidewalk 10 feet in front of him. He glimpsed two boys who had pushed it from the top of a four-story building.

In November 1970, Russ Schoch and his dog Doc were crossing Claremont Avenue at 116th Street on their evening walk. Forty feet away, under the Barnard College dormitory windows, a Columbia student was jumped by two teen-agers, one carrying a knife. Schoch, who was carrying a can of Mace, ran to the rescue. The assailants sped away in a waiting automobile. Barnard dormitory windows opened, and shortly a police car arrived—too late.

"There is nothing," Schoch wrote in a memo to colleagues, "like an experience of this kind within rods of your own home on a street flanked by faculty apartments and Barnard dormitory rooms to bring the problem of personal safety to mind...Certainly no one should venture anywhere after dark alone in this area."

To be sure, New York City was not alone in facing rising crime. Schoch vacationed each year in Clear Lake, Iowa. Fearing that his Claremont Avenue apartment would be burglarized in his absence, he packed his car with items like cameras and TV sets. One summer, he and his wife Mary overnighted in a motel in Hammond, Indiana. While they slept, their car was stolen in one of the ironies of safety problems at Columbia.

Still, the API staff coped with their personal concerns. A deeper concern was the safety of seminar members and discussion leaders. In 1970 a Florida publisher, though stating his interest in API, wrote that he declined to nominate because he was "hesitant to subject any of our people to the possibility of personal harassment which I understand some nominees have experienced." Other potential nominators almost certainly made the same decision without telling API.

The same year, Cleve Rumble of the Louisville newspapers turned back from a walk near campus to stay clear of a gang of milling youths only to find a bloodied youth near the King's Crown Hotel. Police told Rumble the injured youth had been beaten by the gang with pieces of chain.

Gordon Parker of the Trenton Times, a seminar member, was entering the King's Crown Hotel at 2 a.m. on a Saturday when two assailants brandishing knives robbed him of his wallet. API learned of the incident only some time later, from another Trenton Times seminar member. A number of times, that was the case. So API was never able to determine how many serious incidents occurred.

The muggings were not solely the work of youths from nearby ghettos. The New York Times reported a new kind of crime on the college campuses of New York and even at Princeton. The new crime, a product of the drug culture, pitted student against student and frequently went unreported. At one time the dean of Columbia College reported that in three months at least 15 Columbia students had been robbed in their dormitories—"robbed at gunpoint, pistol-whipped, threatened with knives or physically assaulted."

This was not the Columbia that had welcomed API in 1946. API needed more space and reasonable safety for its seminar members, discussion leaders and staff. It was time to find a new home. But where?

23

Chairman Ottaway

E arly in 1959, Walter Everett telephoned James H. Ottaway, president of Ottaway Newspapers-Radio in Endicott, New York, to ask if he would be interested in serving on the API Advisory Board. Everett recalled Ottaway's response:

"Well, I'll tell you," Ottaway said, "anything I join I like to get involved in." Everett assured Ottaway that involvement was exactly what API sought, and Ottaway joined the Advisory Board effective July 1, 1959. Ottaway could not have realized just how involved he would become with the institute. He not only would serve on the Advisory Board but also would become its chairman in 1968.

There was more—much more. When API incorporated in 1971, preparing to strike out on its own on Columbia property or elsewhere, Jim Ottaway was one of the five incorporators. Two years later, at the first annual meeting of the new, non-profit corporation, Ottaway was elected the first chairman of the corporate Board of Directors. He remained as chairman until 1978 and continued as a board member until June 30, 1984, when he resigned after 25 years of service to API.

His fellow members honored him with a bronze plaque mounted in a first-floor hallway of the API building. It stated that Ottaway's "foresight, leadership and dedicated effort contributed immeasurably to the construction of this building and to the American Press Institute."

The display of the plaque followed a "Jim Ottaway Appreciation Night" in 1977, when more than a hundred friends of API honored Ottaway with a dinner at the Mayflower Hotel in Washington, testimony that they understood how much he had contributed.

API had also been blessed earlier in the leadership of its Advisory Board. Grove Patterson, editor-in-chief of the Toledo Blade, was the first chairman, in 1947-48. Patterson led the first effort to raise an endowment for the infant API.

Next came Sevellon Brown, 1948 to 1956, API's founder and publisher of the Providence Journal and Evening Bulletin. Brown continued the effort to place API on a sound financial basis and, along with Floyd Taylor, API's first director, helped fight the battles with Dean Ackerman of the Graduate School of Journalism.

Ben M. McKelway, editor of the Evening Star and Sunday Star in Washington, D.C., followed Brown and continued the string of chairmen with national prestige. McKelway was appointed to the Advisory Board in 1947. After two years as Advisory Board chairman, McKelway asked to be replaced.

"I think that with my other jobs I should turn over the chairmanship to someone else," McKelway wrote to Monty Curtis. "Frankly, I think I am making a fool of myself in the number of things I have undertaken and I think I am the biggest damn joiner in the United States."

Paul Miller, chairman of Gannett Newspapers, with headquarters in Rochester, New York, joined the board in 1953. He succeeded McKelway and served as chairman, 1958 to 1963. Miller was especially helpful in adding to staff benefits.

Then came Barry Bingham Sr., the urbane editor and publisher of the nationally renowned Courier-Journal and Louisville Times. Bingham was chairman from 1963 to 1968, stepping down because he thought the institute should have periodic turnover in its Advisory Board chairmanship. Bingham remained on the board three more years, however, and played an important role when API searched for a new home.

The procedure for finding new members of the Advisory Board was informal. The API staff recommended persons who had been active in sending members to API and also provided financial support. Almost routinely, the Advisory Board forwarded the recommendations to the Columbia trustees, and approval there was equally routine.

On operational matters, the Advisory Board deferred to the API director and staff. It had no authority to do otherwise, and was not so inclined anyway. Curtis once said he feared that if the Advisory Board had more authority some less-informed members might regard API as a "plaything" and make capricious decisions.

Still, the Advisory Board was important in various ways.

In the earliest days, the prestige of the board members and their newspapers gave the fledgling API credibility. Board members helped promote API, spreading the word in their home regions and at newspaper meetings. The board was usually effective in dealing with the university administration, often with Turner Catledge of the New York Times as principal emissary.

Then, too, benevolence notwithstanding, the board was a stabilizing influence. The staff director reported to it annually. The annual meetings, often held in the richly paneled Trustees Room of the university, were relaxed affairs that generated more good fellowship than hard business.

The staff director reported on seminar participation and financial support. He discussed plans and asked for comments on certain proposals. The board would elect a chairman, and he would name the executive committee and possibly other committees. Seldom were there changes, and never any contests.

But API's situation was changing, and it was both logical and fortunate that API turned to James Haller Ottaway when it sought an Advisory Board candidate in 1958.

The Ottaway group had grown to eight newspapers in New York, Pennsylvania and Connecticut. Both Ottaway and his wife Ruth had attended API seminars, and 98 seminar members had come from Ottaway newspapers. His newspapers were small, and it was important that small newspapers be represented on a board weighted toward large newspapers.

An extra advantage would emerge from having Ottaway as Advisory Board chairman in the years leading to the departure from Columbia. Ottaway, moving from Endicott, established headquarters for his group in Campbell Hall, New York, a crossroads near Goshen only some 70 miles from Columbia. Time and again, Ottaway would drive to Columbia to confer with the API staff, architects, attorneys and others.

Jim Ottaway was a newspaperman through and through. He once wrote that he had "been born alongside a drum of ink" and "it rubbed into my veins." His father, Elmer James Ottaway, co-founded the Port Huron (Michigan) Times-Herald in 1900. Young Jim moved from delivery carrier to press flyboy (taking stacks of freshly printed papers off the press) to classified and national advertising manager.

For 18 months he was assistant general manager of the St. Petersburg Times, of which the Ottaway family owned 20 percent. In 1936, the Ottaway family sold its interests in St. Petersburg, and Jim Ottaway spent six months as classified manager of the Grand Rapids (Michigan) Herald.

But Jim and Ruth Ottaway were determined to strike out on their own. With a modest down payment and promissory notes, the Ottaways in 1936 bought a semi-weekly of 4,000 circulation, the Endicott (New York) Bulletin. From that base, the Ottaways began a group that had grown to nine newspapers by the time it merged in

1970 with Dow Jones & Company. The story was written by Charles A. King in "Ottaway Newspapers, the First 50 Years," published in 1986.

Best of all from an API standpoint was Ottaway's philosophy on newspapering. Later, at age 71, he described the early struggles of his young company: "We were not arrogant. We tried hard to serve our readers and our communities...Our watchword was quality—editorially and in every department of the newspaper. We believed we had a public trust and we did our best to discharge it by publishing interesting newspapers and being good local citizens."

When he joined the API Advisory Board, Ottaway began informing himself in depth about the institute. He always studied the available material and, Everett recalled, "asked questions, but always in a quiet and self-effacing way." In that respect, he and Everett were similar. Everett had been executive director for a year when Ottaway became Advisory Board chairman in 1968.

API was approaching its 25th year. It had been operating at or near capacity for five years and unable to meet the demand for some of its seminars. The campus violence, random crime and complaints about food quality were joined as problems by deteriorating conditions at the King's Crown Hotel. Once the source of mirth, the hotel had become a nagging irritant.

But API still had no formal legal existence, only that 1958 agreement with Columbia trustees which either party could terminate on a year's notice.

Ottaway thought it was time for a thorough study of API, both its successes and frustrations. The vehicle for that study, a seven-member Development Committee appointed by the Advisory Board, was announced August 1, 1969. The committee comprised three persons from the 15-member Advisory Board—Ottaway himself; Turner Catledge, executive editor of the New York Times; and James E. Sauter, vice president/operations of Booth Newspapers in Michigan—and four other newspaper executives.

Ottaway appointed two subcommittees: Facilities and Finance, and Programs and Services.

Over eight months, the subcommittees considered ways to improve the quality of seminars, to increase the number and variety of seminars as demand warranted, to provide other services that might be helpful to the newspaper profession, and to improve physical facilities for the institute and for housing seminar members.

Allen H. Neuharth, executive vice president of Gannett Newspapers, chaired the Facilities and Finance Committee. Other members were Robert W. Chandler, president and editor, the Bulletin, Bend, Oregon; William F. Kerby, president, Dow Jones & Company; and

William O. Taylor, general manager, Boston Globe.

Don E. Carter, executive editor, the Record, Hackensack, New Jersey, chaired the Programs and Services Committee. Other members were: Robert P. Clark, managing editor, Louisville Times; Derick Daniels, executive editor, Detroit Free Press; Sauter; and John Strohmeyer, vice president and editor, Bethlehem (Pennsylvania) Globe-Times.

The Programs and Services Committee queried scores of former seminar members on their evaluation of seminars and recommendations. A report from Daniels to Carter pointed up the need for stronger financing.

"Money," Daniels wrote, "...will of course be needed if we expect API to have the flexibility not merely to implement the suggestions...but also to generate its own self-sustaining flow of ideas."

Daniels suggested that API move beyond the job-oriented seminars that had been its cornerstone and add fresh approaches. The hard reality of competition had become "no longer just one newspaper against another, or against TV, but each newspaper alone against the collective total of all media in the war for reader time and advertiser dollars."

Newspapers, Daniels wrote, had urgent need to train "renaissance generalists," and API should make the conference room a furnace to convert pure knowledge instantly to practical advantage. He said that the API staff was restricted by budgets and time and needed to reach beyond seminar members for helpful knowledge. Given the imperfect state of the newspaper art, newspapers might know what they wanted but might not know what they needed.

"This suggests to me," Daniels wrote, "that API must play God, at least to the extent of assessing the given newspapers in advance and then designing programs to reflect both the desires and the needs of seminarians."

Daniels ended with these words: "As we stare forward into a transitional future which may see API physically uprooted and financially uncertain, we might all remind ourselves...that API built its foundation of accomplishment in one cramped conference room and will never be judged on performance anywhere else."

With input from Daniels and the others, Don Carter fashioned the report of the Programs and Services Subcommittee in November 1969.

The subcommittee, Carter wrote, "found no serious complaint or challenge to its present format or overall method of operation. However, in looking for new directions "we find almost unanimous agreement that API should increasingly concern itself with the identification and analysis of the changing function of newspapers...We find also a sharp need for developing better management skills within our industry...API should be a forum for stressing the interdepartmental relationships within newspapers."

There were 22 discrete recommendations, including: emphasis on the problems newspapers would face in the future, an experimental regional seminar away from Columbia (this was not unanimous), occasional short seminars on pressing newspaper problems, publishing newsletters and occasional papers on significant newspaper trends, improving opportunities for blacks in journalism, occasional brainstorming and blue-sky sessions, better housing and a lounge room where members could gather, seminars for general reporters and news editors, reducing some two-week seminars to a week or ten days, more planned activity in the evenings, inviting a journalism school dean or faculty member to many seminars, getting more feedback on seminar results, using more visual aids in the conference room, creating a library and extensive files for staff use, feeding more management training into the regular seminar schedule, and providing adequate time and funds for the staff to visit newspapers and newspaper meetings so as to bring back fresh approaches.

"Our subcommittee cautions against taking new directions solely for the sake of doing something new," Carter wrote. "We think API is a highly effective and successful influence in journalism, and we oppose any change without good reason and demonstrated need. We think, however, that API can and should try new approaches to meet the developing needs mentioned in this report. We make the recommendations as a long-range blueprint for change that can be put into effect only over a period of time and on an order of priority established by the API staff and the Advisory Board."

Six months later, in May 1970, Walter Everett reported to the Advisory Board the progress made by the API staff on the Carter subcommittee's recommendations.

Seminars had been modified to add emphasis on management training, sessions had been held on enlisting and training blacks, seminar members were being exposed to newspaper problems outside their current responsibilities, and efforts were being made to include in seminars one or two members with responsibilities different from the majority to promote interdepartmental understanding.

Too, the traditional Wednesday afternoon off had been eliminated, staff members were attending more newspaper-oriented meetings, and three alternate proposals had been presented to the Ford Foundation for continuing API seminars for foreign journalists.

Everett also reported plans to implement other recommendations. They included an increase if possible in the number of seminars for specific circulation categories, inviting a journalism school dean or faculty member to each appropriate seminar as interest warranted, and devising a system for checking more thoroughly on seminar results. Further, he promised an effort to begin a modest publications program with the present staff.

On the recommendation for reducing some regular two-week seminars to a week or ten days, Everett wrote: "I and the rest of the API staff feel that we should be very sure before offering any such seminar that the subject can be adequately covered in the shortened time. This was not true of the one-week seminars the Institute held years ago, for example Management and Costs. Upgrading them to two weeks was a big step forward in the quality on which API's reputation depends."

Monty Curtis was also a strong advocate of two-week seminars and objected strenuously when, after moving to Reston, API shortened its programs to 10 days by holding conference table sessions on Saturdays and clinic group meetings on weekday evenings.

Curtis despised programs that ran one week or less. He thought that such short gatherings did not permit covering the essential material. And he also valued the camaraderie and friendships that members developed in longer programs and used to the advantage of their newspapers.

Thus parts of the "long-range blueprint for change" prepared by the Program and Services Subcommittee were quickly transformed into concrete actions. Other items had to await a move to larger quarters. Such a move was much on the mind of Al Neuharth's Facilities and Finance Subcommittee.

In November 1969, Neuharth's subcommittee submitted six recommendations:

1. API should continue to be located in or near New York City. Second choice would be a location within 50 miles of Manhattan. Other possibilities (Chicago, Miami, St. Louis, Washington, Atlanta, Los Angeles) had been investigated, but unanimously the subcommittee agreed on New York City as the best choice.

2. API should continue to be affiliated with a prestigious institution of higher learning.

3. If satisfactory long-term business-like arrangements could be made, API should continue to be located at and affiliated with Columbia University. Those arrangements would have to include: physical facilities adequate for present needs and future growth (including housing and capacity for two simultaneous

seminars), physical separation of API and the Graduate School of Journalism—ideally an API building of its own on Columbia property or floors of API's own in a Columbia high-rise building, greater operational autonomy spelled out in a long-term contract, and API control of its assets and disbursement of funds.

4. If the foregoing arrangements could not be made with Columbia, API should explore the possibility of affiliating with another institution of higher learning in or near New York City.

5. Whether API's future location was at Columbia or elsewhere, the Advisory Board should commit to raising funds in the range of $500,000 to $2 million and approach Columbia or other institution with its requirements and willingness to finance the proper physical facilities.

6. If recommendations of the Programs and Services Subcommittee were adopted, an Endowment Fund campaign should be undertaken to help finance that programming, rather than sharply increasing API seminar tuition. Any endowment campaign should be subordinated to the capital-fund campaign that might be necessary for long-term arrangements on facilities. The subcommittee said that past API fund-raising through sponsorships had been so low key that capital or endowment campaigns, "properly planned, timed and conducted, would be highly successful."

On December 10, 1969, the Advisory Board decided that action could best be taken by a smaller group and authorized the Executive Committee—Ottaway, Bingham, Catledge, Curtis and Ben Reese—to carry the ball.

To the extent that API had to break out of its circumstances, the Facilities and Finance Subcommittee had defined the future. But the manner of breaking out took directions the subcommittee could not possibly have predicted.

24

A Decision to Move

Despite the problem of safety for seminar members and the API staff, the institute's Executive Committee recognized the great advantages of keeping API at Columbia University. Its first priority was to explore finding larger quarters at Columbia.

Some years earlier, API had discussed with Columbia President Grayson Kirk the concept of a separate building for the institute. Kirk approved the idea, but the time was not appropriate for a major fund drive, and space needs were not then as pressing. Now the needs were pressing.

Walter Everett sent a seven-page memo on API's needs to the new president of Columbia, Andrew W. Cordier. Grayson Kirk had retired as university president in 1968 at age 65.

Kirk's retirement was timely from Columbia's standpoint because his decisions to call in city police when students occupied buildings had made him a lightning rod for student protests.

Cordier, dean of the Faculty of International Affairs, was a former United Nations diplomat. At first titled acting president, he became president in 1969, but in 1970, William J. McGill, president of the University of California at San Diego, a psychologist and former Columbia faculty member, would begin 10 years as Columbia's president.

Thus API dealt in succession at a critical time with two new presidents, Cordier and McGill. They struggled with huge deficits, student violence, a divided faculty, and an antagonistic neighborhood. API's problems drew scant attention.

Moreover, some faculty members and administrators had come to see the Graduate School of Journalism as a vocational school that lacked intellectual validity. That led them to question whether the school itself should remain at Columbia. That view often included API, too.

On March 24, 1970, the API Executive Committee and Everett met for 45 minutes with President Cordier. The meeting was cordial but unproductive, though Cordier said the university held API in high regard and wanted to ensure its future growth.

This discounted reports API had received from lower-level administrators that Columbia might wish to sever its connection with API. An assistant vice president, Alex Stoia, had told Everett that Columbia might want to reclaim API's space within five years. Precedent existed for that. Also pressed for space, two or three small institutes of the think-tank variety had already broken away from Columbia, which had been glad to recapture the space.

Joe Nye, the university business manager, had commented in a conversation with Everett that eventually Columbia would need API's quarters for other purposes. The comment became known at API as "the friendly eviction notice." Years later, Nye said that in the eyes of many at Columbia, "API didn't quite belong."

Still, Everett felt no immediate threat of eviction. API probably could have stayed indefinitely in the Journalism Building, operating at capacity but still falling short of newspaper needs for mid-career training.

And that training world had become competitive. For nearly a quarter of a century, API, the pioneer, had been almost alone in the mid-career training field. Now, several regional newspaper organizations, following API's seminar format, had begun training programs of shorter duration.

When API vacated its quarters in 1974, the journalism school welcomed the return of the space it once held. Ironically, however, in 1985 Columbia awarded the ground floor of the Journalism Building to the newly established Gannett Center for Media Studies, later renamed the Gannett Foundation Media Center and then the Freedom Forum Media Studies Center.

The key fact in March 1970 was that Columbia President Cordier could offer nothing specific. He gave no encouragement on the possibility of providing land, on or off campus, on which API could erect its own building. Nor did he see any hope of constructing a university building in which API could have space. Cordier agreed that the King's Crown Hotel was inadequate, but the university then had no plans to replace or renovate it.

Despite Cordier's assurance that Columbia wanted to help ensure API's growth, the university made no real effort to keep API, on or off campus. Its only suggestions were two white-elephant properties that had been willed to Columbia.

One was an aging mansion in the Riverdale section of the Bronx bordering the Hudson River. The estate was in danger of losing its tax exemption. Use by API would have assured that exemption but the building required major alterations and construction of rooms and dining facilities for seminar members.

Hesitant from the start, API quickly backed away when it learned that the Riverdale neighbors would oppose construction.

The second suggestion was an old apartment building on Riverside Drive that had zoning and eviction encumberments. It was not remotely suitable for API.

After meeting with Cordier, the Executive Committee asked the Advisory Board for authority "to explore in a quiet and entirely preliminary way" the possibility of relocating and affiliating with another institution of higher learning in the New York City area and, if necessary, extending the search to other areas. The committee also recommended that the search at Columbia be continued after McGill, the incoming Columbia president, arrived.

Any move to change API's legal status, the committee said, should be delayed until the matter of location was settled. There was no point in seeking incorporation in New York State when a new home might be found in another state.

Through the efforts of Jim Ottaway, whose newspaper group had just merged with Dow Jones & Company, publisher of the Wall Street Journal, services of the Journal's law firm, Patterson, Belknap and Webb, had been made available to API without charge. For nearly four years, Christopher H. Stoneman of the law firm worked closely with API. API never learned the amount of the legal fees it saved through the intervention of Jim Ottaway.

On August 23, 1970, the Advisory Board unanimously approved the Executive Committee's recommendations on seeking new affiliations.

Seven Advisory Board members were re-elected to three-year terms. Turner Catledge, who had just retired from the New York Times, resigned. James B. (Scotty) Reston, vice president of the Times, was recommended to the Columbia trustees to replace Catledge. Chairman Ottaway, after his unanimous re-election, appointed Newbold Noyes Jr. of the Washington Evening Star to succeed Catledge on the Executive Committee.

The Advisory Board presented Catledge with a framed resolution written by Monty Curtis and signed by board members and the API staff. Curtis always scorned formal resolutions and prided himself on writing resolutions without the word "whereas." The Curtis resolution said in part:

"Diplomat, strategist, and tactician, as Boardsman in Residence, you smoothed relations with our associates and rustled nary a feather.

"Orator, kindly mimic and teller of tall but purposeful tales, you touched wisdom with merriment, and graced both."

With such good-natured praise did Catledge leave the Advisory Board, not knowing that in three years he would be asked by API to head a critical fund-raising campaign.

There was no inclination to disclose the confidential recommendations on relocation to the Columbia administration through the minutes. The version sent to the university secretary, Edward B. McMenamin, a standard transmittal after Advisory Board meetings, made no mention of the relocation decision.

In fact, explorations for a new home were already under way. The president of Princeton University, Robert F. Goheen, and Barry Bingham Sr. were close friends. They owned neighboring summer places in Chatham on Cape Cod. Bingham had sounded out Goheen on the possibility of API's moving to the Princeton campus in New Jersey, some 50 miles from New York City.

To API's delight, Goheen expressed interest. On the Princeton campus was a building about the right size for API. It was occupied by the Institute for Defense Analysis, which was preparing to leave because students had protested its presence. The API staff visited the beautiful campus and discussed possibilities with a Princeton vice president.

Everett later dispatched Frank Quine to Princeton to make a transportation study: How would seminar members reach the campus from major transportation centers such as Newark International Airport 35 miles to the northeast? It looked as if API would have to operate its own shuttle limousine to the Newark airport, a prospect it did not relish.

Still, it was beginning to look as though Princeton would be API's new home when Goheen disclosed that he would step down in 1972, after 15 years as president. With that announcement, talks with API collapsed. Clearly, other administrators at Princeton did not share Goheen's interest in API.

With mounting tension, API's search began anew. On a map, it plotted all the newspapers that had sent seminar members. Though members had come from all across the U.S. and Canada, the preponderance had come from the north and east of the Mississippi River, simply because there were more newspapers there. Purely on the basis of average travel distance, Pittsburgh would have been the choice.

But API sought a major metropolis, a major transportation hub. Chicago was eliminated for fear that its blizzards would close too many seminars. Los Angeles was too far from too many newspapers. Boston was too far east.

Gannett Company invited API to look at property adjacent to the new plant for its Westchester Rockland newspapers in White Plains, New York. The site was too small.

Then Curtis called from Miami to say that the University of Miami in Coral Gables was interested. James L. Knight, a principal of Knight-Ridder Newspapers, planned to fund a continuing education center near the Miami campus, and perhaps quarters for API could be built into the center.

API held reservations about Miami purely because of its distance from most newspapers. But Ottaway, Bingham, Everett, and Mallette flew to Miami and met on September 11, 1971, with officials of the university and the Miami Herald.

Even before the site visit, however, the staff and board were concerned that Miami would be seen as a sun-and-fun location. One advisory board member, for example, asked how a nominator would react when his seminar member returned from a winter seminar with a deep tan.

The depth of that concern was never tested. Miami was crossed off because the timetable for constructing the James L. Knight center was uncertain, as was housing for seminar members. Years later, the Knight center was built in downtown Miami, a departure from early plans.

In June 1970, Fred W. Stein, editor and publisher of the Binghamton (New York) Press and an Advisory Board member, died. Allen H. Neuharth, president of Gannett, was appointed to fill the vacancy. He would play a major role in API's decision to move to Reston.

The search continued. API looked at a mansion in Washington, D.C., once occupied by Eugene Meyer, the financier and publisher of the Washington Post. It was too small.

Charles L. Bennett, executive editor of the Oklahoma City newspapers, a frequent discussion leader, suggested a site in Oklahoma City and a tie with the University of Oklahoma. But API felt the location would be too geographically remote.

Columbia, Maryland, the young planned community being developed between Baltimore and Washington, began a courtship but did not offer suitable property. Moreover, the new community seemed more oriented to Baltimore than Washington.

While API searched, the American Newspaper Publishers Association, the trade group for the newspaper industry, was also planning to move from New York City, where the rent of its Manhattan offices had been raised sharply. At one point, ANPA asked API if it was interested in sharing space in a new ANPA building or, as an alternative, locating an API building on property acquired by ANPA.

ANPA, too, had looked around. Thomas C. Fichter, an ANPA vice president, remembered one day when the ANPA search committee left New York by limousine to inspect a possible building site in New Brunswick, New Jersey. Just outside New York, the limousine drove past smelly chemical plants and oil refineries.

Revolted by the sights and smells, the committee turned back. Said one member, "We could never get the board to come through this to get to a meeting."

Neuharth, API's new Advisory Board member, was also on the ANPA relocation committee. When ANPA was settling on Reston, Neuharth learned that other property was still available in Reston in a nearby area reserved for associations and educational organizations.

Dulles International Airport, supposedly the region's airport of the future but still underutilized, lay five miles west of Reston. The limited access highway from the Capital Beltway to Dulles bisected Reston.

Best of all, a Sheraton hotel was being constructed only a quarter mile from the available property and was eager for business. API wanted to avoid having to construct and operate facilities for member rooms and meals. Alerted by Neuharth, API focused on Reston.

One of the first and perhaps the most highly publicized of the planned communities developed after World War II, Reston was started in 1962 by Robert E. Simon. His initials suggested the name Reston. Simon had bought 7,500 acres of wooded Virginia countryside in Fairfax County 18 miles from downtown Washington. He forged with the county an agreement for orderly development according to a long-range plan.

Short on capital, Simon had sold his holdings to a subsidiary of Gulf Oil Company, Gulf Reston, by the time API entered the picture.

At its annual meeting on April 23, 1971, the Advisory Board weighed the factors. Once the annual meetings had been relaxed and routine. Now the atmosphere changed. Some sentiment remained for somehow retaining affiliation with Columbia, even if API relocated. Affiliation with another university, if not Columbia, was deemed important.

Joseph Pulitzer Jr. asked if API could house seminar members away from Columbia and bus them to seminars, thus minimizing campus security problems even if not adding operating space. It was possible, Everett replied, but at greater costs.

Eugene S. Pulliam thought Reston was better for ANPA than for API and suggested that the Chicago area and Northwestern University be considered. Ottaway and others noted that, whatever the decision, API would have to find income other than tuition and sponsorship contributions.

James Reston and Pulitzer said that API should make it clear (it subsequently did) to Columbia's newly arrived president, William J. McGill, that API would have to move unless better quarters could be obtained. Ottaway asked Reston and Pulitzer to join him and Everett to so inform university president McGill.

Less than five months later, at an Advisory Board meeting on September 14, 1971, Barry Bingham reported that the Development Committee recommended Reston as API's new home. He cited the advantages of being in the Washington suburban area, the certain growth of Reston, the attractive countryside, the variety of housing choices, other newspaper enterprises planned to locate there, and the proximity to Dulles and National airports.

There was uncertainty in the room. Neuharth, chairman of the Facilities and Finance Subcommittee, said three members had no objection to Reston, one was less than enthusiastic, and he shared this lack of enthusiasm (even though he was the one who had learned of available suitable property in Reston).

Chris Stoneman, the attorney, described the legal aspects of API's obtaining tax-free benefits. First, API would form a non-stock corporation in Virginia, and an agreement would be made between the American Press Institute, Inc., and Gulf Reston.

Then he would seek tax exemption, which might take two or three months. He saw no big problem, although affiliation with Columbia University would be "enormously helpful."

Stoneman would need authorization for a board for the new corporation. He advised keeping the incorporating group small so that documents could be passed along for signature. And the application to the Internal Revenue Service must show that the new corporation was successor to API and give API's entire financial history.

Someone on the Advisory Board thought that API might be able to use an "affiliated with Columbia University" line in its literature even if it moved to a non-university site. Everett reported that Alex Stoia, the Columbia assistant vice president, had told him that such an affiliation with Columbia was not viable. Stoia also had said that separation from Columbia might be difficult.

Stoneman said Columbia had no grounds for that attitude. The central question was release of API's reserve funds held in special accounts by Columbia.

Board members still favored a university affiliation, preferably with Columbia. Neuharth suggested the possibility of affiliating with the University of Virginia or a Washington area consortium of George

Washington, Georgetown, Catholic and Howard universities. Otta-way, Noyes and Edward Lindsay favored Columbia only. Bingham favored an affiliation but with a university without a school of journalism.

The Executive Committee was authorized to explore the possibility of a university affiliation. It would prove impractical.

Then, point by point, the Advisory Board unanimously approved these actions:

1. Incorporate the American Press Institute as a non-profit corpo-ration and seek tax exemption from the Internal Revenue Service.

2. Enter into an agreement with Gulf Reston, Inc., to buy up to four acres of land at not more than $80,000 per acre, on which API would erect a building for its occupancy. (Gulf Reston had initially sought $140,000 per acre, but lowered the price after Neuharth berated Gulf Reston's top executive for trying to take advantage of a small training institute. ANPA had earlier bought ten acres just a thousand feet away for $50,000 an acre.)

3. Enter into an agreement with the Sheraton Inn at Reston to provide rooms and meals for seminar members.

4. Undertake a campaign to raise funds to buy land, to construct the API building, and to cover other costs of relocating the institute to Reston.

How much money should API seek to raise? Should there be separate drives for land and building and for an endowment? Specific mention of a $3.5-million goal was removed from an early proposal. Bingham thought it would be necessary to name a figure. Noyes thought $3.5 million was out of reach and urged that endowment money not be sought at the time. Jack Kreuger of the Dallas Morning News agreed with Neuharth that a figure not be set. Ottaway suggested a minimum of $2.5 million.

The board split on whether to seek an endowment. Everett was disturbed at the notion of making a move without knowing exactly what funds would be needed.

In the end, all agreed to proceed in two steps, first a building fund and later an endowment fund. Curtis said he would be unable to head any fund campaign but would be happy to serve in an advisory capacity.

It was time to hire an architect. In Reston, Everett interviewed several firms. Everett had said at a board meeting: "We are looking for quality and distinction but not luxury." Several firms were at work in young and bucolic Reston. None impressed Everett, who had sought advice on area architects from Newby Noyes, editor of the Washington Star. Noyes turned to his arts editor, Frank Getlein. Why not seek the best nationally, Getlein asked? He named five prestigious firms, including Marcel Breuer and Associates of New York City.

Breuer, whose buildings such as New York's Whitney Museum were internationally acclaimed, usually accepted only projects much larger than what API envisioned, about 25,000 gross square feet. But he was intrigued that the building would be for newspaper training and situated in a planned community. By early October 1971, Breuer became API's architect. He assigned Hamilton Smith to head the project, but participated himself in the conceptual phase.

On December 6, 1971, the Executive Committee met at API. Barry Bingham Sr., who had been so active to that point, could not attend. His son, Barry Jr., was starting treatment (it proved successful) for Hodgkin's Disease. Also, Bingham Sr. was chairman of Berea College in Kentucky, which had embarked on a fund drive.

Attorney Stoneman was seeking the critical IRS exemption. The charter as an educational corporation in Virginia was issued October 22, 1971. Ottaway had named himself, Bingham, Curtis, Noyes and Everett as the incorporators, and thus the first Board of Directors. Later, when there were fewer documents to sign, other members of the Advisory Board would be added to the new corporate board.

With receipt of its Virginia charter, the institute began two and a half years of dual existence, still operating in historical fashion at Columbia but with a corporate life in Virginia.

As Ottaway described in his foreword to this book, Turner Catledge, though retired at his home on Prytania Street in New Orleans, had consented to head the campaign to raise funds for construction of an API building.

In Catledge, API had the fund campaign chairman it needed, a person of national prestige, almost a symbol. For although Catledge would make a few solicitations, mainly in his memorable jaunt through the southeast with Ottaway, the vast bulk of the work would fall on the shoulders of Ottaway and several other Advisory Board members and the API staff.

After consultation with Neuharth as chairman of the finance committee, the Executive Committee decided to limit the fund-raising to the cost of acquiring the land and constructing and furnishing the API building in Reston. Based on preliminary information, that figure was set at $1,936,200.

The figure was as low as prudence permitted. Still, reaching the goal seemed much in question. Ottaway scheduled an Advisory Board meeting for January 28, 1982. The date presented a conflict for one board member, Otis Chandler, publisher of the Los Angeles Times. To Walter Everett, he wrote: "I think raising almost $2 million is going to be tough." He referred to the fact that the ANPA had just started a $10 million campaign, and many newspapers had already contributed to it.

In reply, Everett summarized why the Advisory Board felt that a properly mounted campaign could succeed:

1. Funds were being sought for a specific, tangible objective, essentially "bricks and mortar," with needs itemized to the last dollar.

2. The amount sought, while large, was substantially less than had been raised in recent years by other newspaper service organizations.

3. API's need for increased work facilities and assured permanency was supported by 26 years of service to newspapers, during which time the number of seminars had tripled.

Then, too, API had the advantage of pledges already in the collection basket. The Nicholas B. Ottaway Foundation, the contributions vehicle of the Ottaway family, had pledged $100,000. And through the efforts of Edward Lindsay, Lindsay-Schaub Newspapers had pledged $10,000.

During this sequence of deciding to leave Columbia, working through a list of possible sites until choosing Reston, and determining a building fund goal that might or might not be achievable, API received the all-time scare of its life.

Stoneman, the attorney made available by Dow Jones & Company, had applied for an Internal Revenue Service tax exemption for corporate API, confident that the exemption would be granted if he supplied the institute's complete financial history, which he did.

Then one day in late February 1972, Stoneman called Walter Everett to say that the IRS had rejected API's application for tax exemption.

Everett recalled his reaction: "I was stunned. In all of the staff and board discussions of real and imagined problems arising from incorporation, this possibility hardly had been touched. In hindsight, this seems incredibly stupid. But in all of the years since the institute's founding its non-profit, tax-exempt status never once had been questioned. We had come to take it for granted.

"Thus we were totally unprepared for the IRS turndown. For my part, I thought the decision meant the end of API. Financially, the institute barely had been keeping its head above water, and loss of the tax-exempt incentive for supporters seemed like a death blow. Although Stoneman tried to be reassuring, it seemed to me highly unlikely that IRS would change its mind.

"All of us on the staff went about our work in the deepest gloom. We had no contingency plan...All we could do was wait. How Stoneman managed to reverse the IRS ruling I never knew, but to me it was like API had been brought back from the dead."

The IRS letter of February 24, 1972, said it was not clear from API's application for a tax exemption that its purposes were exclusively educational. Further, the certificate of incorporation did not provide for distribution of assets upon dissolution.

Stoneman wrote back to the IRS four days later. He addressed the question of distribution of assets in the event of dissolution by quoting Article 6 of the Virginia Non-Stock Corporation Act of 1956 to the effect that assets on dissolution could be transferred to "one or more domestic or foreign corporations, societies or organizations engaged in activities substantially similar to those of the dissolving corporation..."

Stoneman also wrote in the same letter: "The Institute's educational program will have as its sole objective the improvement of the journalistic skills and capabilities of the individual participants and will not be designed or conducted to provide benefits to the newspapers by which those individuals are employed..."

That letter, hand-delivered to the IRS district office in New York City, brought a reversal the very next day, February 29, 1972. The IRS determined that API was exempt from federal income tax under section 501 (c)(3) of the Internal Revenue Code.

The key fact was that IRS had at first determined API to be an organization that was not a private foundation. After Stoneman's appeal, an initial tax exemption for two years was granted. That exemption became permanent two years later after API documented its corporate operations.

The IRS ruling meant that contributions to API by U.S. newspapers, foundations and individuals were tax deductible. Small wonder that Everett felt as if API had been brought back from the dead.

Almost three decades later, Stoneman said: "The only real light I can shed on the matter is that the (Internal Revenue) Service was primarily concerned that API might be intended more as a trade association serving constituent newspapers' commercial interests than as a truly educational organization."

After that scare, API made certain that its bulletin and other literature emphasized the training of the individual seminar members.

By March 1972, with the tax-exemption in hand, API was working full bore to obtain pledges and contributions. The Advisory Board had ruled that money or pledges totalling $1.5 million must be obtained before a construction contract could be signed. Ottaway had received assurances from Bankers Trust in New York of willingness to lend at favorable rates if API had pledges but not cash.

Everett brought back Sam Blackman, the retired AP executive who had helped API through a staff crunch, as an acting associate director. Blackman took charge of two seminars previously assigned to Mallette, the managing director, so that Mallette could devote more time to fund-raising.

On a brisk morning in March 1972, Ottaway and Mallette flew in the Ottaway Newspapers plane to Pittsfield, Massachusetts, and made the first on-site solicitation of the campaign, at the Berkshire Eagle. In two days, almost hedge-hopping across Massachusetts, they also called on newspaper publishers at Worcester, Quincy, Lynn, Salem, Beverly, and Lawrence.

They started the trip with considerable trepidation. From the response to their visits they would pretty much know if the building fund drive would succeed. To their delight, they were cordially received everywhere, and pledges were made.

Ottaway and Mallette especially remembered the manner in which they were greeted by Richard C. Steele, publisher of the Worcester Telegram and Evening Gazette.

With a smile, Steele welcomed the two supplicants as "pickpockets." Then, he said quickly, "But sit down, I've dealt with pickpockets before." The visitors left with one of the most generous pledges of the campaign.

In the Ottaway Newspapers plane, Ottaway and Everett solicited in Virginia and North Carolina. Mallette made three major swings, through New Jersey and eastern Pennsylvania on one, Indiana and Ohio on another, and Wisconsin and Minnesota on a third. Several Advisory Board members, among them Bingham, Edward Lindsay, Neuharth, Gene Pulliam, William O. Taylor and Tim Hays, aided Ottaway in calling on prospects. Catledge kept in close touch and made a few contacts to supplement his work on the trip with Ottaway.

Everett directed the solicitation letters and brochures that spilled from the API offices. Agnes Lister, his assistant, tracked totals on pledges, which extended as long as five years.

On July 18, 1972, cash and pledges totaled $1,650,425 and

another $953,856 was anticipated—for a final total of $2,604,281. Given that good news, the Advisory Board unanimously accepted that day the low bid for construction of API's building-to-be.

Architect Hamilton Smith had issued 29 invitations to bid. With construction booming in the Washington area and most builders fully committed, only five bids were received.

The general contract went to Sharpe and Hamaker of Arlington, Virginia, which bid $1,173,000 and offered to complete construction in 365 calendar days. That schedule proved far too optimistic.

In those sometimes frantic months, one watershed change had taken place almost unremarked. For more than two decades, the Advisory Board had been mainly just that—advisory. Its recommendations were always subject to approval by Columbia University, although approval was almost always routinely granted. But it was the API staff director who mainly called the signals.

With API's incorporation and adoption of by-laws, the chairperson/president of the Board of Directors, rather than the staff director, became the chief executive of the institute.

The Ottaway-Everett relationship remained pretty much the same through Everett's retirement in 1976. But incorporation had changed the rulebook, and later chairmen would exercise varying degrees of authority.

25

Farewell, Columbia

The decision by the Advisory Board on September 14, 1971, to move the American Press Institute from Columbia University to its own building in Reston, Virginia, marked the beginning of three hectic years for API.

In those three years, API would incorporate in Virginia, obtain an IRS tax exemption, buy land, raise $2.6 million for the building fund, hire and monitor an architect and contractor, make countless decisions about the building and its furnishings, sign a 25-year contract for seminar member rooms and meals with the Sheraton Reston Inn, hire a new supporting staff in Reston, move, bid a nostalgic farewell to Columbia, and begin holding seminars in Reston in September 1974.

During all this, the seminars at Columbia not only continued without pause but also grew in attendance. In the final three years at Columbia, API held 54 seminars with membership totals of 492, 553 and 566, respectively. The 566 was a record for API's 28 years at Columbia.

Through much of this period, the schedule for the move was vague. Sharpe and Hamaker, the general contractor, had won the contract both on low bid and its forecast of completion in 365 calendar days. In contrast, another bidder had wanted 700 days. The bid was accepted July 18, 1972, an indication that API might move as early as late summer of 1973.

That was not to be. Building construction fell behind schedule. The general contractor had not previously worked with pre-cast concrete panels that were the hallmark of the Marcel Breuer design, and that was one cause of delay.

The six professional staff members all had decided to move. They were Walter Everett, Mal Mallette, Russ Schoch, Frank Quine, Paul Swensson and Agnes Lister, the assistant to the executive director. All wrestled with the question of when to sell their homes in metropolitan New York and buy or rent in Virginia.

The other members of API's Columbia staff had strong ties to New York and did not plan to leave. Of course they deserved to know when their API employment would end. Loyally, most of them stayed until the final days.

Other questions arose. At Columbia, API was paying the university $13,000 annually as reimbursement for its offices, utilities, and accounting and custodial services. Preparing the yearly budget was a relatively simple matter, with the unknowns being the number of seminar members and the total of Sponsorship contributions.

But those unknowns could be predicted with considerable accuracy. At least API knew for certain its fixed costs.

But when Jim Ottaway, Everett and the API staff looked ahead to operating in Reston they saw only a string of unknowns. They needed fairly accurate forecasts on which to base financial planning.

To help with those forecasts, Ottaway made available to API William C. Lundquest, who first worked for Ottaway as a reporter in 1939 in Endicott, New York, and became a publisher and headquarters executive with Ottaway Newspapers. Recently retired, Bill Lundquest lived on Cape Cod.

Lundquest was an ideal choice, experienced in budgeting and easy to work with. He huddled with Everett and Mallette and the associate directors. Then he was off to Virginia to learn about local wage levels, insurance premiums, utility costs, fuel oil prices, state and local fees and anything else that would have bearing on the API budget.

Fortified with Lundquest's findings, Everett estimated that operating costs for fiscal 1974-75, starting July 1, the first year in Reston, would total $684,000, approximately $180,000 more than at Columbia University in 1972-73, the last period for which final figures were available.

At Columbia, the seminar tuition included payment for the member's housing and meals. Looking ahead to Reston, both the staff and Advisory Board favored billing separately for the rooms and meals at the Sheraton Inn, because those costs would be higher and members could choose a single room or share a double room at lower cost.

The contract with the Sheraton Reston, signed in 1973, stipulated a single room rate of $18 that would be adjusted annually according to the national consumer-price index. Just ahead were several years of high inflation that would cause that base price to soar.

The Executive Committee looked over the Everett-Lundquest

budget projection in December 1973 and recommended a tuition in Reston of $500 for a two-week seminar plus a separate charge of $351 for a shared double room and meals. Thus the total cost to a seminar member would be $851, an increase of $251 over the 1973-74 tuition at Columbia.

On January 21-22, Ottaway, Curtis, Everett and Mallette reviewed the Executive Committee's December recommendations. A total cost of $851 might drastically reduce seminar nominations. After all, previous tuition increases, always established with trepidation, had been much smaller—$30 in 1959, $60 in 1965, $60 in 1969, and $90 in 1971.

All agreed that such a large increase in the first year in API's new location risked turning away potential participants before they could experience the improved working facilities.

A smaller tuition increase, though, would mean that a Sponsorship increase of about $100,000 would be needed. For many sponsoring newspapers that would require doubling their contributions.

Nonetheless, Everett suggested that a more vigorous Sponsorship campaign be mounted, rather than risk a loss of seminar participation or goodwill in the first Reston year. That was the direction taken. Tuition was set at $400 for two weeks and $275 for one week.

Meanwhile, staff members found housing in newborn Reston more expensive than in the New York suburbs. Builders could not keep pace with buyers excited by the concept of a planned community. The Reston housing costs caused a couple of staff members to buy houses in nearby less expensive communities rather than in Reston itself.

The Advisory Board approved bridge loans from API reserve funds to staff members who needed short-term help in buying a new home before they could sell in greater New York City. By winter's end in 1974, several staff members were signing, with trembling hand, two mortgage checks each month.

With new furnishings ordered for Reston, API had its Columbia equipment appraised. Staff members bought much of the furniture at the appraised value. For sentimental reasons, Everett bought some of the bookcases acquired years before for the Floyd Taylor Memorial Library.

The big oval table in the conference room was left to the journalism school. Norman Isaacs, once executive editor of the Louisville newspapers but by then a journalism professor, used it first for editing and media management courses. That left little to be moved except the files.

Paul Swensson, the first staff member to move to Reston, served as advance man for a few days, then returned to Columbia to conduct API's final program there, a Telegraph Editors and Copy Desk Chiefs Seminar, June 16-28, 1974.

Fittingly, the final discussion leader at Columbia was Joseph M. Ungaro, managing editor of the Westchester Rockland Newspapers in White Plains, New York. Earlier, Ungaro, had been managing editor of the Providence Evening Bulletin, whose one-time publisher Sevellon Brown had founded API.

Ungaro's topic was electronic tools in the newsroom, including pagination systems then emerging. So, symbolically at least, the final presentation at Columbia dealt with both the past and the future.

The 33 members of that final seminar at Columbia brought the total over 28 years to 8,785. In all, the members had attended 321 seminars and had come from 925 newspapers in 50 states, the District of Columbia, nine provinces of Canada, Puerto Rico and occasionally from abroad.

Appreciative of all that Columbia had done for it, API wanted to depart graciously. In April 1974, members of the Advisory Board had signed a letter to university president William J. McGill to thank him and the trustees.

"We and the API staff," they wrote, "hope to continue many of the associations the Institute has had with Columbia and its faculty." Of course, those associations became lost to distance and time.

In May 1973, the Advisory Board had decided that any formal continuing affiliation would be, as Scotty Reston put it, "bogus," only a "paper" affiliation perhaps symbolized by having the president or another officer of Columbia on the Board of Directors of the American Press Institute, Inc.

As the time of API's departure neared, Columbia was also gracious. Joe Nye, the university business manager, was host to the API staff at a lunch in the dining room API had used for all of its years. Nye presented API with a mounted bronze lion, symbol of Columbia athletic teams. The attached plate read:

The American Press Institute—Columbia University
1946-1974
In recognition of lasting and profound contributions
to the profession of journalism
during 28 years of association with Columbia University

In Reston, the Columbia lion was placed in a niche near the front entrance, a reminder of API's earlier existence.

Other goodbyes and thanks were said. The Advisory Board held a lunch at the Hotel Pierre for publisher Arthur Ochs (Punch) Sulzberger and a number of his New York Times associates, those who had most often been hosts on the 191 evenings when seminar groups had visited the Times for cocktails, dinner and newspaper talk.

In its busyness, API failed at one amenity. Columbia's journalism school learned of API's impending departure by way of the grapevine. Elie Abel, then the dean and later dean at Stanford University, remembered the communications gap years later. Thus the happy partnership of journalism education and mid-career education, envisioned by Sevellon Brown and Carl Ackerman, ended without ever having been achieved.

Mal Mallette and Frank Quine, along with others, had moved to Reston in mid-June. When the final seminar ended, they returned to Columbia and directed the loading of files and office equipment into a moving van.

Then they took a last nostalgic look around, locked the office doors, gave the keys to campus security and grabbed a cab for LaGuardia Airport and the shuttle to Washington.

In Reston, newly hired secretaries awaited a reporting date. Joyce Scott already had gone to work as secretary to Walter Everett, and as the office manager she went to Columbia and observed office procedures there. Her Columbia counterpart, Eileen McEvoy, then spent two weeks in Reston instructing the other secretaries in the mysteries of helping to prepare seminars.

Also hired were a business manager, a building superintendent, and a person to keep seminar facilities neat and serve coffee during the session breaks. Nightly cleaning was contracted. API was taking on housekeeping and other maintenance formerly supplied by Columbia.

Maston (Matt) Ballew, the building superintendent, began work in May. With construction ended, he logged in the sporadic arrival of furnishings and tracked down delays. He needed help, which came in the person of Mallette's son, Bruce, who had just finished his college semester. He lived in the family's still-vacant Reston house, slept in a sleeping bag and bicycled to the API building.

The Reston API structure at 11690 Sunrise Valley Drive offered 24,000 gross square feet with seminar-related working space of 16,000 square feet. Space at Columbia had been only 4,900 square feet.

The Breuer design was striking. For months, photographers from architectural publications came to record images. In the two-story building, the ground floor was devoted to offices and general work and storage space. The second story contained seminar facilities: the huge conference table with a circular table for up to 36 persons, a library, a writing room, a lounge with a coffee bar, four rooms for clinic groups and an amphitheater with tiered seating for closeup viewing of newspaper pages or other material being used by a discussion leader.

Before going to his drawing board, the Breuer architect Hamilton Smith had spent several days at Columbia learning seminar procedures. He wanted to understand the functions and make the form follow. Then there was the API wish list. A bulging folder held ideas filed for the glorious day when new facilities would be constructed.

Columbia facilities combined the functional and the makeshift. The big conference table was impressive, but its straight long sides made it difficult for one seminar member to see another seated along the same straight edge. At Reston, the circular conference table provided easy sight lines.

At Columbia, for a closeup look at pages during sessions on layout and design, members clustered their chairs in the back of the conference room, and the discussion leader tacked displays on a mobile corkboard. Now there was the compact amphitheater.

At Columbia, a slide projector was perched on the conference table, a situation so awkward that audiovisuals were seldom used. At Reston, audiovisuals were projected from a raised booth at the back of the conference room to a screen that retracted into the ceiling.

So it went, convenience after convenience, including swivel chairs of exceptional comfort. For the handicapped, a ramp led from the entrance to the first floor, several steps below, and an elevator to the second floor. Several members in wheelchairs attended seminars without difficulty.

The API staff had pored over Hamilton Smith's preliminary design and raised a number of questions. Several modifications resulted. One question, however, was not pressed sufficiently.

In 1973, only a small percentage of seminar members were female. Noting that, the architect did not provide a women's restroom on the second floor. While men used a large men's room on the second floor, women descended to the first floor and a small women's room.

That misjudgment was fixed when an addition was built for 1980 occupancy. The addition included a large second-floor women's room.

Furnishings throughout the building were functional and generally bright—with one notable exception. The conference room struck many persons as a bit drab. When Robert N. Brown, publisher of Home News Enterprises in Columbus, Indiana, joined the Board of Directors in 1976, he at his own expense commissioned architect Marcel Breuer to design a wall tapestry.

Using the first three and last three letters of the alphabet, Breuer created a colorful design, the basis for a huge tapestry. Handwoven in India, the tapestry supplied the needed visual lift.

Along the staircase inside the front entrance, the so-called credit wall gave permanent recognition to those newspapers, newspaper groups, foundations and associations that had contributed to the building fund.

Contributions from these professional associations merit individual mention as evidence of the industry-wide recognition API had achieved: American Society of Newspaper Editors, Associated Press Managing Editors Association, International Circulation Managers Association, International Newspaper Advertising Executives, Inter-State Circulation Managers Association, Mid-Atlantic Circulation Managers Association, New England Association of Circulation Managers, Pacific Northwest International Circulation Managers Association, and the National Conference of Editorial Writers.

From slick proofs of newspapers' nameplates—the page-one flags—Amos Press, which published the Sidney Daily News in Ohio, made reverse zinc engravings, assembled them by states and provinces, and mounted them on three wooden frames designed by architect Hamilton Smith and an art student in New York. The frames were laid out so that seminar members could quickly find the names of their newspapers as they climbed the stairs.

Later, nine other newspapers, influenced by the credit wall, contributed to the building fund. For their nameplates, a small postscript panel was added at the top of the stairs.

The credit wall extended thanks to some 725 contributing organizations. In the small first-floor lobby, a calligraphic volume listed the 848 seminar members, discussion leaders, Advisory Board members and other friends who made personal contributions in amounts ranging from five dollars to a thousand dollars.

Contributions to the building fund totaled about $2.6 million. Relocation to Reston cost some $2 million, including land, architectural fees, site development, construction, equipment and furnishings, moving, fund-campaign expenses and incidentals. That left a welcome surplus of $600,000, which was placed into a building fund to generate yield for maintaining the building.

On a mid-July day in 1974, when API held its first staff meeting in Reston, the choice of that planned community seemed wise beyond question. There was still the matter of meeting increased operating costs as well as other problems. But there were satisfactions beyond the splendid building facilities.

A short walk to the west stood the Sheraton Reston Inn, where seminar members were housed and took meals, a vast improvement over the King's Crown Hotel.

A quarter-mile to the east along Sunrise Valley Drive stood the one-year-old headquarters of the American Newspaper Publishers Association. Soon it would be called the Newspaper Center because of its added tenants, starting with the International Circulation Managers Association and the International Newspaper Promotion Association. Gathering in Reston, a number of newspaper-related organizations would create a form of synergy.

When the chips were down, the newspaper publishers, newspaper foundations and organizations and former seminar members had come through handsomely, their generosity a testament to what API had contributed toward increasing newspaper quality over its first 28 years.

Now API was part of a vibrant newspaper community with an exciting future.

26

Broadway to Boondocks

When API began a new existence in Reston in 1974, it had much to offer members of its staff. Those who had endured commuting hardships in New York City could now reach the API building in a few minutes. Amenities included neighborhood swimming pools and tennis courts and a public golf course just across Sunrise Valley Drive.

The major shopping center at Tyson's Corner lay eight miles east, about halfway to Washington with its attractions. Reston's population, planned for an eventual 60,000, had reached 15,000 and was growing steadily.

There was a palpable pride of community—because the concept of this planned community promised lasting escape from stringtown development and had attracted nationwide attention.

For seminar members, however, starting with the first Reston seminar—City Editors (for newspapers under 75,000 circulation)—on September 8, 1974, Reston was the boondocks.

Dulles International Airport five miles to the west possessed long runways, a stunning terminal building—and only a scattering of flights, most of them transcontinental. Most seminar members, except those who drove, arrived at bustling National Airport in Washington and rode infrequent buses to Dulles. Then they waited for a van from the Sheraton Reston Inn.

Once they made their way to the inn, a short walk from API, seminar members found themselves almost isolated for two weeks from urban life and amenities. Compared to life in New York City, it was almost like being on the moon.

From the standpoint of attentiveness in seminars, the isolation held certain advantages. But, for the first three or four years, that argument faced a hard sell to seminar members, particularly in winter when the hotel's outdoor pool, lighted tennis courts and nearby jogging trails held no attraction. Seminar members jested that an API seminar meant 12 days and a hundred nights.

API supplied sheafs of information on how to catch buses, rent cars at Dulles or share taxis. But in fact weekday evenings over two weeks presented few convenient options. There was no subway to midtown Manhattan, no lively West End bar just across Broadway, as in Columbia days.

On Saturday and Sunday, the middle weekend of the two-week seminars, members visited Washington, knowing that if they missed the last bus they would have to dig deep for taxi fare. Members who had driven to a seminar never lacked for weekend passengers.

John Strohmeyer, the editor of the Bethlehem (Pennsylvania) Globe-Times who had served on the API Development Committee, later expressed again his disappointment that API had decided to leave New York. Though recognizing the increasing problems at Columbia, Strohmeyer wrote: "The experience of being in New York for two weeks was an educational dimension of going to API and could never be duplicated in sterile Reston."

For seminar members, sterile was an appropriate word for the Reston of API's early years. Roger Sovde of the Rock Hill (South Carolina) Herald had attended four seminars at Columbia and became the all-time attendance champion by attending three more at Reston—a total of seven. He remembered a winter-time seminar at Columbia when he stuffed newspapers into the cracks around the windows of his King's Crown Hotel room.

Of his first seminar in Reston, in 1976, he recounted: "Our excitement included watching a tire being changed and watching landings and takeoffs at Dulles."

For several years, before an office building was constructed between the Sheraton Inn's parking lot and API, seminar members often took a path through a patch of oak trees rather than the sidewalk along Sunrise Valley Drive. One day a copperhead snake was seen sunning itself at the edge of the path. That wasn't the kind of excitement seminar members had in mind.

The 306-room Sheraton Inn opened scant weeks before API moved to Reston. Its own startup troubles exacerbated API's problems. Food quality fluctuated as the Sheraton worked its way through a succession of chefs, one of whom doused with oregano almost every dish but chocolate mousse. The unpredictable food quality brought a brief boycott during API's third Reston seminar, for investigative reporters. No doubt the isolation presented time to dream up the protest.

Mainly, though, seminar members alternately complained and

joked. During the frequent spoofs of API staged by seminar members on the eve of the final seminar day, the isolation and the hotel provided fertile material.

Slowly, the isolation eroded. One by one, restaurants opened in Reston. Flight schedules at Dulles airport languished for several years, then burgeoned until many non-driving members could arrive and depart at Dulles, obviating the long trip from National.

By the late 1980s, Reston's population had exploded to 55,000. High-technology companies swarmed to Reston and the so-called Dulles corridor, causing the area to be called Silicon Valley East. Suddenly, Reston boasted office space equalling that of downtown Baltimore. In 1990, the Reston Town Center opened, giving the community the entertainment and big-ticket shopping cluster it had lacked.

In API's early years at Reston, the Washington newspapers helped greatly to relieve the isolation. In the first two years alone, the Washington Post was host to some 25 seminar groups for a plant tour, dinner and discussion with editors and other executives.

Several seminar groups were lunch guests of the Washington Star. Visits with leaders of Congress often followed. The White House gave seminar groups tours that far exceeded the rush-in, rush-out visits for tourists. Briefings by high administration officials were tied in. A few groups met with Presidents Ford, Carter or Reagan, others with the wives of those three presidents and also Barbara Bush.

Later, USA Today, first published in 1982, was host for dinner to dozens of seminar groups in its dining room 17 floors above the Potomac River in Arlington. Just across the Potomac lay Georgetown, and many groups ended up there for a nightcap or two. One or two field trips were made to the Free Lance-Star in Fredericksburg, Virginia. The Baltimore Sun, which had a high-technology mailroom, was host to several seminars on newspaper production. Other trips were made to the new printing plant of the Washington Post in Springfield, Virginia.

Resources of Washington and vicinity were steadily worked into seminar activities. Evening boredom was lessened by bringing members back to the API building after dinner for clinic group meetings that often continued until 11 p.m.

A major breakthrough came with establishment at the Sheraton of an API hospitality room. API supplied the parlor room, members supplied refreshments, food, shoptalk and conviviality.

To Reston came some seminar members who had earlier attended API at Columbia. At mention of the King's Crown Hotel, the alumni of New York days guffawed, puzzling those who had never endured that hotel. It was the returning seminar members who felt the relative isolation most troublesome.

But, comfortably housed in the Sheraton Inn, they weren't nostalgic for the King's Crown. And they appreciated the comfort, efficiency and flexibility of the new seminar facilities.

During the settling-in at Reston, the steps to API's new corporate existence were completed. The initial Board of Directors, which had no officers and was limited to five persons for ease of signing documents, comprised Jim Ottaway, Barry Bingham, Monty Curtis, Walter Everett and Newbold Noyes Jr. Bingham resigned before the April 27, 1972, meeting at Columbia at which the first officers were elected, and Al Neuharth replaced him.

The four remaining incorporators plus Neuharth elected officers from their midst: Ottaway, president and chairman; Curtis and Neuharth, vice chairmen; Noyes, secretary and treasurer.

On April 26, 1974, the new Board of Directors enlarged itself from five to 18 persons. The additional members were mainly carryovers from the Advisory Board, which had continued to exist until API left Columbia. By-laws stipulated that at least two board members come from each of the four regions defined in the U.S. and one member from Canada. The other nine members were at-large.

The first 18-member board comprised the officers together with:

Frank Batten, chairman, Landmark Communications, Norfolk
Robert W. Chandler, president and editor, Bulletin, Bend, Oregon
Walter Everett, executive director, American Press Institute
Katharine Graham, publisher, Washington Post
Howard H (Tim) Hays, editor and co-publisher, Press and Daily
   Enterprise, Riverside, California
Edward Lindsay, vice president of planning, Lindsay-Schaub
   Newspapers, Decatur, Illinois
Rollan D. Melton, president, Speidel Newspapers, Reno, Nevada
John E. Motz, president and publisher, Kitchener-Waterloo Record,
   Ontario, Canada
Joseph Pulitzer Jr., editor and publisher, St. Louis Post-Dispatch
Eugene S. Pulliam, assistant publisher, Indianapolis Star and
   News
James Reston, vice president, New York Times
James E. Sauter, president, Booth Newspapers, Ann Arbor,
   Michigan
William O. Taylor, treasurer and general manager, Boston Globe
John Troan, editor, Pittsburgh Press

Except for current or past chairmen, board members were limited to nine years, three terms of three years. The nine-year limit brought measured turnover in board membership so that API was governed over time by a broad cross-section of leaders of the newspaper industry.

In the final year at Columbia, 421 Sponsors had contributed $153,000 to API. (Because some contributions came from newspaper groups, the number of newspapers represented far exceeded the number of Sponsors.)

In 1974-75, the first year at Reston, API pushed hard for Sponsorship increases and set a goal of $259,000, explaining why its costs were up and stressing the advantages of the new facilities. The total received, from 440 Sponsors, was $212,489, short of the goal but still a heartening increase of $60,000.

The result was a deficit of $28,000. Much of that was one-time expense associated with the move from Columbia. Nevertheless, API needed Sponsorships totaling $249,000 for the second year in Reston. Such were the realities of costs outside the Columbia umbrella. Inflation made matters worse.

In response, API would soon resurrect the idea first broached at Columbia in 1948—that of raising an endowment. For the time being, it had the security of the approximately $600,000 surplus in the building fund.

Meanwhile, API began using its splendid new quarters to advantage.

In May 1975, API held its first Publishers Seminar, designed for publishers, presidents and chief executive officers of newspapers or groups over 75,000 circulation. At Columbia, API had thought top executives would balk at the King's Crown Hotel.

At Columbia, to be sure, API had held several seminars titled "Publishers, Editors and Chief News Executives," but the word "publishers" was added as an inducement to those on very small papers who served as both publisher and editor.

Heartened by the success of the initial program for publishers, API conducted seven months later a Publishers Seminar for newspapers under 75,000 circulation. It was doubly oversubscribed, and a second such program was added later in the year. In November 1976, API held a third Publishers Seminar, again for larger newspapers.

In quick succession, then, these seminars for publishers gave some 120 top-level newspaper executives the experience of a Reston seminar and a chance to judge the facilities against the new level of Sponsorships that API was seeking.

At Columbia there had been requests for a seminar for non-daily newspapers, so-called weeklies, some of which publish two or three times a week. But Floyd Taylor's measurement of potential nominations showed a disappointing total. So no weekly seminars were held in the Columbia years.

In the first Reston year, however, API measured again—with guidance from the National Newspaper Association and several weekly publishers—and found encouraging interest.

The first weekly seminar, Management of the Weekly Newspaper, was held in February 1976. Frank Quine moderated, and 35 members attended. An oversubscription resulted in a second such seminar the following April.

Adding weekly seminars presented a problem of how to categorize members. Membership of the initial seminar comprised one-third from small community-oriented papers, one-third from medium-sized newspapers or multi-paper groups, and one-third from large multi-paper groups that published in suburban markets rather than communities remote from a large city.

Quine concluded that the member mix brought a learning experience that would not have resulted if members had come from just one of the three segments. API quickly scheduled seminars on Editing the Weekly Newspaper and broke the management curriculum into separate programs for community weeklies and suburban weeklies even though a mix had worked fairly well.

When it began seminars for weeklies, API stipulated that only members from newspapers of paid circulation were eligible. The reason was the proliferation of shoppers, publications devoted almost solely to advertising and delivered free.

But many free-distribution weeklies with serious news content were beginning publication. API changed the rule to require only that a member come from a newspaper and not from a shopper.

An API concern with the weeklies was their limited ability to provide sponsor contributions. API operated on roughly two-thirds seminar tuition and one-third Sponsor contributions. A number of weeklies that used API subsequently made Sponsorship contributions, but few at a level commensurate with the dailies. The Board of Directors voted to continue the weekly seminars but limited them to two a year.

Meanwhile, the entrance of several other newspaper organizations into the mid-career training field and using the API format placed API in an uncomfortable position.

API recognized some of the new activities as a logical supplement to its own programs. But it was concerned that some training newcomers needlessly duplicated what API had been doing for years and siphoned off support API needed to conduct programs of the highest quality.

The ANPA Foundation seemed a primary challenger. While API was still at Columbia, the ANPA Foundation, formed by the American

Newspaper Publishers Association, undertook a $10 million fund-raising campaign (which fell short) with the intention of using a large part of the contributions for training.

API's Walter Everett and Mal Mallette met in New York with Joe D. Smith Jr. of the Alexandria (Louisiana) Daily Town Talk, ANPA's president, and Stewart MacDonald, executive director of the ANPA Foundation, to express API's concern over the possibility of inefficient duplication of training.

They described how in 1969 the API Development Committee checked closely with all users of API before drawing a blueprint for API to enlarge its services to newspapers. Everett and Mallette received assurances of non-duplication, but subsequent developments did not lessen their concern.

At the April 15, 1975, meeting of the API Board of Directors, Chairman Jim Ottaway reported that on March 22 he and Vice Chairman Al Neuharth had met with Harold W. Andersen of the Omaha World-Herald, then ANPA's chairman, and Richard Steele of the Worcester Telegram and Evening Gazette, chairman of the ANPA Foundation, and discussed ANPA Foundation training proposals that would duplicate API's work.

Ottaway read portions of a letter from MacDonald to the ANPA Foundation's program advisory committee which said that the ANPA Board of Directors urged the foundation not to hold seminars that competed with API programs.

The meeting described by Ottaway was one of several with various organizations in which API outlined its efforts to supply needed training and preserve its operating strength without seeking a monopoly or acting like the dog in the manger.

The effort was delicate. API could only present the story of its pioneering, how it had conferred industry-wide on policy and how duplication would be detrimental. Sometimes organizations were receptive to the API story, at least for a few years.

A case in point arose in December 1975 with the Inland Daily Press Association, the largest and oldest regional association. When API began its Management and Costs seminars, Inland had helped greatly through its revenue-and-costs studies. It also contributed to API's building fund.

In 1975, Inland formed the Inland Foundation and began exploring possible educational projects. Its educational committee invited Ottaway and Mallette, who in mid-year had succeeded Everett as director, to meet with it and minimize the possibility of overlapping effort. Ottaway and Mallette met in Chicago with Warren G. (Spike) Wheeler of the South Bend Tribune, president of the Inland Foundation; Robert N. Brown of the Columbus, Indiana, Home News

Enterprises and Inland board chairman; and several others.

To his own board, Mallette reported: "The Inland Foundation Committee was most cordial and seemed receptive to our presentation."

From Miami, Monty Curtis watched the inception of some new non-API seminars with disdain. This was clear from a 1971 letter he wrote to his former neighbor in Westchester County, Buren H. McCormack, executive vice president of Dow Jones & Company:

"Seminars. They are all over the lot. API adopted the dictionary definition of a respectable word—'seminar.' It has become so corrupted over the years that whenever two or three newspapermen gather at a bar they have a printed program saying that they are holding a seminar and thus achieve a tax-deductible expense. I have little respect for these seminars, regardless of who holds them. You can't do anything worthwhile in two or three days. You have to have a professional staff to do all the planning and conducting."

Then in 1975 he wrote to James H. Ottaway:

"Eventually, the cheap imitators of API will learn that the preparation, conduct and completion of valid seminars requires special skills, devotion, experience, and willingness to learn. Some of my closest newspaper friends have always taken the attitude that there is nothing to this business of conducting seminars. They should try it."

Despite the growth of training elsewhere, the demand for API seminar attendance continued in its first year at Reston. Nineteen seminars were held, and 552 members attended. The third highest membership total of all API years had been achieved despite the increased cost of attending API.

Walter Everett moved to Reston even though he knew he would serve only one year there and then retire to Rhode Island. At the board's meeting in April 1975, two and a half months short of his retirement, Everett reported that many of the problems involved with the move from Columbia had been solved.

Operating expenses were up substantially, and a deficit was likely, but he said he was pretty well satisfied with the year in general. It was a modest summary of his exceptional accomplishments.

Cognizant of Everett's achievements over 26 years, the board invited him to serve as a non-resident consultant. And, together with other members of the staff, the board went forward with plans for its "Walter Everett Night to Remember."

Years later, Everett later concluded that he had held the best job in the world at the best of times.

The executive staff stability that endured while API moved to Reston was ending. Not only would Everett leave on June 30 but so, too, would Paul Swensson, an associate director. Swensson was 67. The usual retirement age was 65. But under a waiver available to all staff members with board approval, Swensson had chosen to stay two additional years.

As expected, the board elected Mallette as director effective July 1, 1975. He had been an associate director three years and managing director six years. The board decided that no managing director would be named at the time. Mallette was also elected to the board. Russ Schoch and Frank Quine were reappointed as associate directors.

With a professional staff reduced by retirements to three persons, API was approaching its second year in Reston. But the staff would soon be replenished, and 1975-76 would bring new highs of 21 seminars and 644 seminar members.

27

Adding On

In 1946, the year of API's founding, the circulation of daily newspapers in the United States totaled 50.9 million copies. From that level, circulation climbed slowly to its all-time zenith of 63.15 million in 1973. That was the year when API was packing for its move to Reston.

After 1973, daily circulation dropped as low as 60.65 million (in 1975) and only again surpassed 63 million in 1984, when the fledgling national newspaper USA Today provided a boost.

In the large cities—New York, Boston, Chicago, Detroit, Milwaukee and Los Angeles among them—some newspapers were dying. But elsewhere newspapers were prospering, at least economically. Most publishers looked at robust bottom lines and saw the demise of several large papers as a problem peculiar to the big cities.

Before long, however, many publishers abandoned complacency and faced a sobering, even chilling fact: circulation continued to slip despite a surge in household formation. Each household was a potential customer, and occupied households increased 40 percent between 1950 and 1975. At the same time, penetration of households—the average number of daily newspapers sold per household—plummeted from 1.23 copies to .85 copies. By 1990, the average had sagged to .67 copies per household.

Recognition of threats to newspapers led publishers to demand even more of API; major growth of API seminar schedules and attendance resulted. Only five times in API's Columbia University years did API seminar membership exceed 500. In Reston, annual membership had risen to 644 in the second year. Three years later, in 1979-80 with 25 seminars, membership had reached 817.

Not only were membership totals climbing. So, too was the

number of members per seminar. Only once in Columbia years did the average exceed 30—30.7 in 1972. At Reston, with its larger conference table and other facilities, an average of 30-plus members became commonplace.

In short, API found that it had moved to its larger Reston home just in time to respond to the burgeoning newspaper training demand. Publishers recognized that to bolster circulation they had to improve the product (a word that newspaper men and women abhorred but slowly came to accept). Only better-trained staffs could improve newspaper quality. Publishers turned more and more to API for that training.

As a result, API steadily increased the number and variety of seminars. In two respects, though, plans for adding new dimensions to seminar programs did not work out. They related to a library and a videotaping studio.

On the second floor was a large library. And on the first floor was a room designed to become a studio for producing video tapes.

The plan for the library counted on only a modest collection of books—journalism texts quickly go out of date—but it was thought seminar members could make use of a large selection of newspapers, special sections, marketing guides, stylebooks, and other examples of excellent work. How those works were to be collected, indexed and displayed brought such a divergence of opinion that a Library Committee was formed with Robert N. Brown as chair.

In the end, the plans were scaled back for practical reasons. For a while, API employed a librarian, but finding a person who understood the specialized needs of seminar members was difficult. Moreover, a librarian added to payroll expense, and API was struggling to stay in the black.

Then, too, seminar members found little time for a library. With morning and afternoon sessions in the conference room and two or three evening activities such as clinic group meetings and a trip to a Washington newspaper, few members sought opportunities to browse. So the library collection was reduced to a level that various staff members could maintain.

When the Reston building opened, the proposed videotaping area resembled a small TV studio. The plan was to record interviews with leading newspaper figures on every topic from the principles of publishing to writing to newspaper delivery routes. Extra lighting required for videotaping had been built in. Behind a glass partition, a control room awaited the necessary equipment.

There the plan collapsed. Equipment bids exceeded $80,000. API did not have the money. For years the room lay empty. Eventually, it was put to other use.

While still at Columbia, API had begun acting on recommendations of the 1969 Development Committee. At Reston, it made additional responses. One was a newsletter, the API Round Table. Since its founding, API had printed only one publication on a recurring basis—the annual bulletin. More and more, API alumni had requested a publication to keep them posted on the institute.

The API Round Table appeared three or four times a year. The first issue was Fall-1975. Items included a summary of API's first year in Reston, excerpts from the Waltergate Trial, part of the "Walter Everett Night to Remember"—his retirement party—and names of the 193 discussion leaders in the first Reston year of seminars.

API began scheduling some one-week seminars. At Columbia, two seminars had been loosely structured: Picture Editors, and Newspaper Promotion and Public Relations. They were cut back to one week. Scheduling evening clinic group meetings facilitated the downsizing. The new seminars for weeklies and publishers of dailies were one-week programs from the start. When API tackled programs on particular topics, as opposed to job-related seminars, it scheduled them for five days or fewer.

The first short seminar addressing a specific topic came in July 1976, a three-day program on The Newspaper and Tomorrow's Readers. Objectives were twofold: (1) to examine reading and writing skills in the society, and (2) to seek ways in which newspapers could reverse declining readership by becoming more interesting and useful.

Attendance was by invitation, and the 33 members represented a broad spectrum of geography, circulation, age, experience and responsibilities. This was fitting to the objectives; it was increasingly clear to many newspaper executives that falling readership could be attacked only through closely coordinated effort by all departments of a newspaper.

This was API's first attempt to help solve a newspaper problem in a manner beyond imparting skills in seminars of job-related scope—circulation manager, city editor and so on. Others followed.

API distributed widely a 44-page summary of the discussions. One member, editor Robert M. Stiff of the St. Petersburg Evening Independent, summarized how falling readership had to be attacked from all directions: "The answer, of course, is that there is no single answer. It is more likely a series of small answers that will vary from city to city."

API continued to test the interest in various proposed seminars. The resulting seminar schedules revealed the areas in which newspaper publishers were placing training emphasis.

For its first decade in Reston, API usually held two or three seminars a year for circulation executives. Starting in 1977, API also held a series of one-week seminars titled Training the (circulation) District Manager.

Clearly, newspaper leaders had concluded that the job of circulation manager had transcended the traditional role established when almost every household bought one daily newspaper and some bought two. Old-guard circulation managers needed new skills if they were to succeed. The seminars for district managers emphasized training the seminar member to train colleagues back at the home newspaper.

Publishers recognized the need for improved news writing. Starting in 1977, API responded with one-week seminars on Effective Writing and Editing. News-side seminars had always included a half-day or full-day session on writing, going back to the first-year presentations by Robert Gunning and Rudolf Flesch. Now API found that writers and editors would eagerly discuss writing for a full five days.

Another thrust by publishers was for expanded training of advertising executives. API had offered Advertising Executives Seminars since 1952, programs attended by a newspaper's top advertising executive. Now publishers recognized the potential in training second-level advertising executives. As a result, API added a Retail Advertising Managers Seminar in 1976-77 and a National Advertising Managers Seminar in 1977-78.

In a 1976 issue of the API Round Table, Mal Mallette described the tenor of the time:

"The pervasive feeling one senses at API these days is of a profession that has identified its several problems, decided they must be solved and is girding itself for a tenacious effort to solve them.

"Firmly held opinions are not rare among newspaper men and women. We are a confident breed, usually certain that we know what is best for newspaper and reader.

"Who, then, can recall a time when newspaper people seemed more willing to question traditional beliefs and try new approaches?"

Some new approaches were evident in the ages of seminar members. The average age had dropped sharply in the 1970s. Once it was unusual to find, say, a managing editor under age 40, and editorial writers were almost always grizzled veterans. Now managing editors barely into their 30s began to appear. So did younger editorial writers.

Publishers were clearly turning to younger editors and executives, cognizant that newspapers were failing to attract young adult readers. Younger editors, some publishers concluded, would produce newspapers with more appeal to younger readers.

API tracked for several years another major change: the surge of women into seminars. In its early years, API seminars included only a scattering of women except in seminars for women's page editors and librarians. API took its first count by gender for the 1976-77 seminars. There were 710 members, and 82 of them—or 11.5 percent—were women.

That percentage climbed steadily until a record was reached for fiscal 1986. Total membership was 1,145, and 293 or 25.6 percent were women. After 1986, the breakouts were not continued, but it's likely that the 25.6 percent has been exceeded. In 1982, Barbara S. Williams, editor of the Charleston (South Carolina) Evening Post, became the first woman to attend four API seminars.

By 1978, Jim Ottaway had completed 10 years as chairman of the Advisory Board and the subsequent Board of Directors. He stepped down at his own request, though he remained on the board until 1984. To succeed him, effective July 1, the board elected Howard H (Tim) Hays, editor and co-publisher of the Press and Enterprise in Riverside, California.

Hays had long been close to API, which he attended as a seminar member in 1949 and 1953. He had been editor of the Riverside newspapers since 1949 and co-publisher since 1965. In 1973 he had been elected to the first API Board of Directors when it expanded to 18 members.

Although Riverside was across the continent from Columbia and Reston, his newspapers had sent 52 seminar members by the time he became chairman. He was already known nationally in journalism; in 1974 he was president of the American Society of Newspaper Editors.

As Ottaway did when he became Advisory Board chairman at Columbia, Hays appointed study groups, a Professional Training Survey Committee and a Policy and Programs Committee, with William O. Taylor and Don E. Carter as chairs.

Taylor was by then president and publisher of the Boston Globe. Serving with him were Barry Bingham Jr., editor and publisher, Courier-Journal and Louisville Times; James E. Burgess, vice president of newspaper operations, Lee Enterprises, Davenport, Iowa; Robert W. Chandler, president and editor, the Bulletin, Bend, Oregon; Donald E. Graham, executive vice president and general manager, Washington Post; Marjorie B. Paxson, publisher, Public Opinion, Chambersburg, Pennsylvania.; Michael E. Pulitzer, publisher, Arizona Star, Tucson; George W. Wilson, president and publisher, the Monitor and New Hampshire Patriot, Concord, and Malcolm F. Mallette, director, API, ex-officio.

Carter, then a vice president of Knight-Ridder Newspapers, Miami, undertook as chairman of the Policy and Programs Committee an assignment similar to that which he carried out at Columbia in 1969. On his committee were Robert N. Brown, publisher, Home News Enterprises, Columbus, Indiana; William J. Carradine, vice president/administration, Southam Press, Toronto; Clayton Kirkpatrick, editor, Chicago Tribune; Rollan D. Melton, senior vice president, Gannett Company, Rochester; Perry Morgan, publisher, Virginian-Pilot and Ledger-Star, Norfolk; Donald A. Nizen, vice president, New York Times, and Stephen W. Ryder, publisher, Medford (Oregon), Mail Tribune.

The committees reflected Hays' desire for studies involving a broad range of geography, experience and newspaper size.

Hays instructed the Professional Training Survey Committee to compile information on all in-service training programs, present and projected; appraise the utility of these programs and determine the extent to which they were unnecessarily overlapping or duplicative; and recommend how API could best respond to the increasing demand for training.

Noting that in-service training programs under all sorts of auspices had proliferated, Hays said: "In many respects, this is encouraging. It's a response to an increasing interest in professional training and an increasing willingness to pay for it. But some caution signs are in order. The lengthening list of training programs is a mixed bag, including some programs that were started with no apparent concern for duplication of existing programs and without examining how they fit into the overall picture of in-service training."

The Policy and Programs Committee was asked to examine the current work of API, to explore its effectiveness in identifying and serving the training needs of newspapers, and to make recommendations for the long-range development of the institute.

Both committees reported to the Board of Directors in November 1978, after four months of work.

Taylor reported these findings: Other training programs were proliferating, but there was no deliberate attempt to duplicate API. There was strong regional loyalty to the programs of the Southern Newspaper Publishers Association and the Inland Daily Press Association. Overall, API had an outstanding reputation.

Committee members differed on the possibility of API's holding some seminars away from Reston. Taylor favored concentrating efforts in Reston. The committee favored shortening seminars. It also favored an advisory board to give guidance on seminar topics—but make no policy decisions.

Carter's report for his Policy and Programs Committee was

bittersweet. The committee had reached scores of individuals on newspapers that had been involved in API's work.

The API building, the quality of the staff and the popularity of the seminars provided the sweet side. On the bitter side, Reston itself was perceived as dull and boring. Lack of transportation remained a sore spot. Members needed a place in the evenings to talk shop other than the Sheraton Inn's disco lounge. (This part of the report led to opening the API hospitality room at the hotel.)

API already had introduced a number of one-week seminars. The 1978-79 schedule listed 15 two-week programs and eight of one week. Carter's committee recommended even more streamlining. Seminar length was a topic of debate from the time of the four-week marathon for editorial writers in 1947, and the periodic shortening stemmed from efforts by newspapers to lower training costs and time away from the job.

Floyd Taylor, Monty Curtis and Walter Everett had all wrestled with the question. After a meeting of the Policy and Programs Committee, their successor, Mallette, then director, described his views to Carter.

It seemed likely, he wrote, that API would hold more and more one-week seminars because many programs were on a specific subject and the material could be covered in a week. A few other seminars should be shortened by a day or two, but not arbitrarily chopped to one week. But 10 days were essential for broad-ranging seminars like managing editors and city editors.

"Over 13 years," Mallette wrote, "I have watched seminar members come to API and over two weeks grow in skills, confidence and perspective. Many are almost literally transformed...This kind of change takes time. Two weeks is both long and short, depending on whether you're thinking of the work piling up back home or the lifelong benefits being reaped...My approach would be to consider modifications rather than drastic shortening for many programs."

Carter's committee reported findings beyond a tilt toward shorter seminars. API participants in the western U.S. and Canada had urged that API hold periodic seminars in western cities. API staff members needed more time in the field to identify problems and trends. Some discussion leaders placed too much emphasis on "how we do it," and too little thought to how problems could be solved by a broad range of newspapers.

API needed to develop more Washington-area resource people—stimulators, mind-stretchers, generalists—and work them into the seminar experience. In addition to the proven discussions at the conference table, API should try other instructional methods like case studies and role-playing.

API, Carter's report continued, should teach more about management in terms of motivating and training people, in exposing executives to seminal thought in brainstorming sessions, and in breaking down interdepartmental walls and building institutional teamwork. And API had not moved rapidly enough into the emerging area of newspaper marketing, it said.

Those two committee reports offered an updated blueprint. Several recommendations on program changes were quickly placed into effect. The report on the proliferation of other training programs underscored that the years of a virtual API monopoly were gone.

Some recommendations—getting staff members into the field more frequently, for example—were desirable but beyond the budget limitations. However, several staff vacancies occurred in this period of 1975-1980, providing a chance to broaden the staff's outlook.

Between 1975 and 1979, API hired five associate directors, always to fill vacancies. The executive staff remained at five persons despite the growth in seminars and members per seminar. Only one of the five newcomers remained more than about three years. Three left for immediate or promised executive posts on newspapers. The fourth became publisher of a national magazine. The fifth, Laurence S. Hale, remained with API more than 12 years, until retirement.

The five new associate directors during 1975-79 were Allen H. Swartzell, Arthur E. Mayhew, David A. Roe, Hale, and Janet C. Sanford. Swartzell and Roe were the first to bring general management experience to the API executive staff. Sanford was the first woman.

Al Swartzell held a degree in journalism/government from Indiana University. After seven years as a government reporter for the Elkhart (Indiana) Truth and the La Porte (Indiana) Herald-Argus he became advertising director and assistant publisher at Elkhart, then general manager of the Bloomington (Indiana) Daily Herald-Telephone, then business manager and later general manager of the Boston Herald American.

He joined API July 1, 1975, after the Herald American ceased publication and API faced two staff vacancies at Reston upon the retirement of Everett and Paul Swensson. Swartzell left after a year to become general manager of the Colorado Springs Sun.

Arthur Mayhew filled the second vacancy in Fall 1975. A Texan with a journalism degree from Texas Tech, Mayhew was sports editor of the Pampa (Texas) Daily News before moving to the Delaware County Times in Chester, Pennsylvania, and rising from reporter to city editor to associate editor to executive editor. In 1978, Mayhew returned to Pennsylvania as general manager of the Beaver County Times.

David Roe joined API late in 1977 from Paddock Newspapers in suburban Chicago, where he was vice president and general manager. Roe received B.S. and M.S. journalism degrees from Northwestern, and rose to publisher with Hollister Newspapers, then a weekly group in suburban Chicago. Next, at the Washington Post, he held various positions including assistant to the president. He worked briefly for Park Newspapers as vice president/operations and then Paddock before coming to API.

Roe was named managing director of API several months before he went to the U.S. Chamber of Commerce in 1980 as publisher of its magazine, the Nation's Business.

Larry Hale, who joined API January 1, 1977, was a journalism graduate from the University of Missouri. He worked on the Jamestown (New York) Post-Journal. As a radioman, he was aboard the U.S.S. Augusta with President Truman when Truman announced the dropping of the first atomic bomb. In 26 years with the Binghamton (New York) Press, Hale moved up from reporter to city editor, managing editor and editor.

Janet Sanford joined API in the spring of 1979 from Farm Journal magazine in Philadelphia, where she was managing editor of the company's book division and editor of the magazine's farm family living section. Earlier she was women's editor for the Mesa (Arizona) Daily Tribune and women's editor of the Arizona Republic in Phoenix. She attended Phoenix College and instructed part-time at Arizona State University. Sanford resigned from API in July 1982 to become senior states editor for the nascent USA Today and later was named publisher of Gannett's Visalia (California) Times-Delta.

Despite the frequent staff openings, API failed to attract associate directors who were either marketing specialists or members of a minority group. A high priority of the staff and board was to hire an associate director with general management and marketing experience. Staff backgrounds were mainly news-editorial. Another priority was to hire a minority member, a black in particular.

Several times, first Walter Everett, then Mal Mallette, then Frank Quine sought to bring aboard a marketing or management expert and a minority group member. Budget limitations foiled the bids for a general executive/marketer. The prospects were often earning twice the API salary for associate directors. Several blacks expressed interest but withdrew, believing upward mobility in their careers was better where they were.

As seminar members increased, the quest for a stronger financial base continued. In 1976, the board authorized establishment of an endowment fund, with the hope that endowment income could brake seminar tuition increases. But the board decided against a formal campaign or setting a goal in dollars. Nonetheless, contributions reached $262,000 within a year. The endowment fund would languish at about that level for four years.

API had reached another crossroads. The board turned its attention to raising funds for another purpose: constructing an addition to the building.

In 1978-79, API held 24 seminars, using all available weeks except August, the month when the staff prepared for the next schedule of seminars. A record attendance of 788 members was reached. Still, some 300 applicants were to be deferred to later attendance because of lack of space. The number of deferrals had increased sharply, from 128 two years earlier to 187 a year earlier.

The board faced a difficult decision. Only five years earlier, API had asked the newspaper industry to pay for a move from Columbia University to Reston. Then API had pressed for increased Sponsorship because of higher operating costs in its own building. The board was controlled by those factors when it had authorized the endowment fund without a formal campaign.

Thus board members were concerned that they might be asking too much of the newspaper industry too quickly if they sought more construction money. Yet there was the comforting memory of the oversubscribed building fund drive in 1973 that brought in $2.6 million.

One possibility was to start seminars elsewhere. The Policy and Programs Committee had found sentiment for an API western presence, periodic seminars in the west to minimize travel expense for seminar members from the region. Holding a seminar or two annually in the west would give API additional capacity without construction.

The board's executive committee met for five hours, November 5, 1978, at the Sheraton Reston Inn, on the eve of the full board's meeting. Chairman Hays presided. Others attending the full meeting were committee members Monty Curtis, Donald E. Graham, Edward Lindsay, Jim Ottaway and Bill Taylor. Also Mal Mallette, then both a board member and the staff director, and Frank Quine, who had been promoted to managing director September 1, 1977.

Don Carter attended as chairman of the Policy and Programs Committee. Hamilton Smith of the architectural firm of Marcel Breuer and Associates, who had directed design of the original API building, also attended. Smith made a presentation on building expansion and explained his fee schedule if API decided not to go ahead with construction.

Uncertainty marked the meeting. An addition of 13,000 square feet to the existing building of 24,000 square feet would permit holding two seminars at the same time. API had already bought a 40-foot strip of land adjacent to its original property, so there was room to build. A second conference room would give API more freedom to innovate, experiment and schedule proposed seminars that were then marginal in demand and did not make the schedule.

But costs seemed close to prohibitive. Inflation and the Washington area boom had driven the estimated price up to $1.2 million.

Ottaway asked if API was becoming too ambitious. Would expansion be enthusiastically received by the industry once fund-raising began? Graham asked about additional operating costs and whether too many eggs would be placed in the Reston basket. Taylor also asked about increased operating costs.

Quine said that the break-even point after hiring an additional associate director and secretary would be reached by scheduling only five additional seminars a year. Mallette said that current nominations justified adding three—possibly four—seminars if facilities were available. He said that when API moved to Reston it knew that it might have to add a second conference room later.

But new facilities would not be used full time in the foreseeable future, probably only 25 to 30 percent the first two or three years. Carter urged API to "tough it out" on the current abundance of nominations and look for options other than building expansion.

Hays, though a Californian who was interested in API establishing a "western presence" that would accommodate some of the nominees, still pushed for the addition. API was turning away too many nominees, he said, and publishers had always responded to API needs. A motion by Taylor, seconded by Graham and unanimously approved, called for constructing an addition. Next day, the full board concurred.

Announcing the decision, Hays said: "The decision to expand our facilities was forced on us, and we're happy it was. We don't like to turn people away. We don't like to ask them to wait. We applaud the publisher who is seeking more training for his staff. We're complimented that he turns to API...There isn't anything that promises more for journalism than the increasing interest of publishers in career education."

The addition was designed so that two concurrent seminars could be held entirely apart from each other. Facilities included a conference room (called the red room for its carpeting), small clinic rooms, a writing room for members, that missing second-floor women's restroom, additional office space, and a separate mechanical room.

Hays appointed Ottaway to head a nine-member committee to raise funds. A campaign to obtain $1.228 million began in March 1979. As building costs rapidly escalated even more, the goal was lifted to $1.5 million.

The general contract was awarded to Associated Builders of Hyattsville, Maryland, with completion specified in time for the 1980-81 seminar series.

Once again, the newspaper industry recognized the need and responded. Contributions totaled $1.929 million. Of the total, $1,874,350 came from 769 newspapers and 58 groups or related foundations and four newspaper organizations. In addition, 140 former seminar members made personal contributions totaling $54,907.

During this time of growth and adjustment, the Board of Directors, on the initiative of Tim Hays, reassigned Mallette from director to the new post of director of development, with responsibility for the building expansion, fund-raising, publications and newspaper and professional relations. To succeed Mallette as director, the board named Frank Quine, managing director since 1977. The managing director position was abandoned.

Quine became the fifth person to serve as director or executive director. He would hold the top staff position during an eight-year period of growth made possible by the building expansion and newspapers that turned to API as they continued their efforts to retain readers.

28

Monty's Legacy

In 1976, Monty Curtis and George Beebe were flying from San Jose to Wichita to hold a workshop for the news staff of the Eagle Beacon.

Beebe, associate publisher of the Miami Herald, had attended API's first seminar for Sunday and Feature Editors in 1947. That was the first seminar moderated by Curtis. Now, Beebe and Curtis conducted periodic workshops for Knight-Ridder newspapers. "This," said Beebe later, "was heaven-made for Monty. It was American Press Institute on the road."

Then age 71, nine years after he resigned as API executive director, Curtis had lost none of his zest for conversation.

In the first-class section of the United Air Lines plane, there was only one other passenger. "Monty was his usual jovial self—joking one minute, talking seriously the next," Beebe said.

When Curtis went to the restroom, the stewardess asked Beebe: "Please tell me, who is this man? I have had movie and TV stars aboard, as well as corporate executives. But I've never met such a fascinating man."

Never again would Curtis take such a carefree flight, but he was about to add to his legend with a courageous fight for life.

The next day, November 22, 1976, in the conference room of the Wichita Eagle Beacon, Curtis warmed up his audience for a Knight-Ridder news seminar with humorous remarks. Suddenly, Davis (Buzz) Merritt, the editor, nudged Beebe. "Something's wrong with Monty," he said.

Although Curtis kept talking, his head slowly drooped to the table. His voice ceased. Beebe, Merritt, publisher Eugene Lambert and others pulled Curtis to the floor, ripped open his shirt and began to massage over his heart.

Within seconds, Steve Zluticky, a maintenance employee, clamped an oxygen mask on Curtis, an action that undoubtedly prevented brain damage. Months later, Curtis learned that publisher Lambert recently had portable oxygen equipment placed on each floor of the building.

An ambulance rushed Curtis to St. Francis Hospital. A surgeon, operating immediately, found a ruptured aneurysm on the aorta. Curtis remained hospitalized 12 weeks, nine in intensive care.

He spent five hours a day for several weeks on a kidney dialysis machine. A pacemaker was installed to speed his faltering heartbeat. In crisis still a man of humor, Curtis jested that the pacemaker had a Diehard battery. He referred to his three doctors as his plumbers. His weight, usually 220 pounds, dropped to 180.

He became a favorite of the nurses and gave them nicknames like Bubbles. When he later returned to Wichita to thank them for their loving care, they ran to his side and hugged him. The Eagle Beacon ran a picture of the towering, beaming Curtis being hugged from three sides.

A story with the picture carried the headline: "Miracle Man Visits His Saviors." The story included this quote: "You know, it's the most egotistical thing—but it never occurred to me that I wouldn't recover."

Jim Ottaway, Don Carter and George Beebe were among his many visitors. Letters and cards poured in. Mal Mallette telephoned Curtis and found him hoarse from throat tubes but eager to receive news on anything going on in the newspaper industry.

Curtis was out of touch and wanted to catch up. "Tell them (the API Board of Directors)," he said, "that I am the luckiest guy in the world because of the people I work with."

Visitors related stories of his spunky battle. Lee Hills of Knight-Ridder asked Curtis later to set down some of the tales. Curtis did, including the purported words of Dr. Hugo Weber Jr. about Curtis' arrival by ambulance:

"You were flat on your back on a table. I was trying to get some clues of what was wrong with you. Suddenly you sat straight up and said, 'Who in the hell is in charge around here? I speak only with the top man.' "

Apocryphal though that story may have been, it probably resulted from the banter that flowed from Curtis once he regained consciousness.

On February 14, 1977, he flew to Miami with his wife Alma and a physician in the Knight-Ridder corporate jet. Knight-Ridder executives, including John S. Knight and Alvah H. Chapman Jr. welcomed him at the airport. He spent a few more days in a Miami Beach hospital and then recuperated further at his home on LaGorce Island.

When Curtis returned to his Knight-Ridder office in the Miami Herald building, he looked up the advance obituary that the Herald had prepared when it was doubtful that he would survive. He found four errors, thought the obit was too long and suggested ways to trim it. Smiling, he told one and all about the rare privilege of reading one's own obituary.

Although his sense of humor never faltered, Curtis apparently knew how his body had been weakened. In September 1978 he wrote this to Mrs. A.H. Kirchhofer, wife of his former boss at the Buffalo Evening News:

"My long siege in the hospitals changed my thoughts about many things, including the end of our stories, which all of us face. And my values changed. For some years I strove only to be good at my work, my highest goal. No longer is this true, and it should not have been for many years earlier. It seems to me that our highest goal should be the finest service we can render to those we love. Once that is established it becomes so much easier to accept the end of the story when it comes."

Curtis retired as a Knight-Ridder vice president on December 31, 1978, at age 73, but stayed on as a consultant, usually working a half-day in the office after a morning of swimming and reading newspapers.

He fired off long letters to newspaper friends, urging them to greater efforts. After stepping down from the API board (he was elected honorary vice chairman), he continued to write and telephone API.

One reason that Curtis wrote the long letters, said his friend Rolfe Neill, "was that once a man no longer has a newspaper he has lost his pulpit." Through the postal system, Monty Curtis clung to his pulpit.

On a diminished scale, his work remained pretty much what it had been just before his illness. He described his typical pre-illness work in a letter to John Lux, publisher of the Grand Forks (North Dakota) Herald:

"Do you remember Thornton Lee and Monty Stratton, who pitched for the White Sox? They remind me of myself. They were called junkmen because they did everything which came their way.

"I have checked and rechecked a new K-R telephone directory, critiqued some Duluth newspapers in preparation for a visit, written a speech for Jim Knight, helped prepare a budget, talked with a lady who is writing a book, done a couple of personal jobs for Lee Hills, chatted with several visiting firemen here for meetings, sympathized with an insulted subscriber and I don't know how he ever got on my phone but I never transfer anyone, dictated a number of letters to good friends in our business, counseled with some newspapermen who want help on how to counter hostility to their newspaper, and spent even more time looking out across Biscayne Bay and cursing all the gods of all religions for permitting the rain to interfere with a truly significant activity like golf or swimming."

In August 1982, physicians discovered cancer in Curtis' left knee. The leg was amputated at Massachusetts General Hospital. Curtis adjusted to an artificial leg, saying he was already able to "kick reluctant editors with great vigor."

When he returned to Miami October 14, friends met him at the airport with a 12-piece brass band.

Curtis was in surprisingly good spirits as he hobbled on the artificial leg. But he contracted pneumonia two weeks later and died of complications at 11:30 p.m. November 25 at Miami Heart Institute. It was Thanksgiving Day 1982. He was age 77.

Curtis had told friends that he wanted a memorial service held for him at the American Press Institute. On February 1, 1983, nearly 100 friends and relatives gathered in API's Red Room and celebrated Monty Curtis.

They came from as far as Alberta, Minnesota, California, Massachusetts and Florida and told Monty Curtis stories during and after the service.

The celebrants filled chairs in the hollow center of the huge conference table. On the rear projection screen, a series of pictures of Curtis changed with each speaker. Tim Hays, Frank Quine and Mal Mallette offered remarks. Then Barry Bingham Sr., Jim Ottaway, Edmund C. Arnold, John C. Quinn and Rolfe Neill delivered "reflections." Walter Everett and others spoke from the audience.

In his benediction, Don Carter said: "Please make us, as he taught, reverent in the use of freedom, fair in the exercise of power, and courageous in the exposure of wrong."

As the crowd departed, someone said, "There was love in that room today." The reason for that love, Rolfe Neill said later, was that "they knew Monty was for them (as newspaper people). It's kind of like your mother; she's for you always."

Alma Curtis, stricken with arthritis, could not attend. Barry Bingham Sr. wrote her, saying: "I don't know when I have seen such a demonstration of regard and affection."

When Curtis died, stories and columns about him appeared in newspapers across the country as friends tried to tell readers, who didn't know Curtis, what one man had meant to newspapers. In the

Charlotte News, Bob Colver painted Curtis with these words:

"Monty Curtis worked from an old, but solid, principle: What makes good newspapers is good reporting, and what makes good reporting is good reporters.

"He worked over newspapers; he worked with newspaper people. He was a teacher, a preacher, a coaxer, an exhorter, a pounder and a stroker. He was, in short, the best friend a newspaper person could have..."

Curtis was such a master of humorous anecdote that a few deserve preservation in this history of API. To record them all would require a separate volume. A sampling, quoting or paraphrasing, follows:

A delegation of undertakers visited the Buffalo Evening News and requested that they be called morticians. That seemed reasonable, what with the beauty parlor girls insisting on being called beauticians. And in those days bootleggers wanted to be called booticians.

The editor ruled that from then on undertakers were to be called morticians. A couple of weeks later, a gangster was found in a ditch in North Tonowanda with his throat slit from ear to ear. He was known in gangland and to the police as "Mike the Undertaker."

We rushed that story through for the first edition, and you can imagine my reaction when the first copy arrived on my desk with an eight-column (full width of page) headline that said: MIKE THE MORTICIAN FOUND MURDERED.

The copyreader who changed the text to mortician from undertaker and wrote the headline insisted that he was only following orders.

With Knight-Ridder, Curtis joked about being vice president in charge of memorials, tributes and resolutions. Once he was asked by Ohio State University to write a tribute that could be read when John S. Knight, founder of Knight Newspapers, was awarded an honorary degree. A few weeks later, Knight walked into Curtis' office and said he was to receive an honorary degree from Ohio State; they wanted him to deliver a talk and would Curtis write one for him. Without mentioning the tribute he had prepared for Ohio State, Curtis again obliged.

When Paul A. Poorman was interviewed for the editorship of the Akron Beacon Journal, he went to Miami for psychological tests, as everyone seeking to join Knight-Ridder did at the time. One test required a lot of free association, mostly designed, as Poorman put it, "to see if I was homicidal enough to run a newsroom." Poorman was waiting to begin the tests when Curtis entered the room. They hadn't seen each other in years. Curtis advised Poorman on how to handle the tests:

"You'll do fine if you remember that it was your mother you loved and it was your father you respected. Get it backward and you're outta here."

The late editor of the Minneapolis Tribune, Gideon Seymour, answered his own telephone. His office door was open. He urged people to write. At 3 o'clock one morning the telephone rang by his bedside, and an elderly voice said:

"I am an old lady, and I do not sleep well. When I am awake, I read. I am reading your Tribune, and every other page is blank."

Seymour replied: "Give me your address, and I will have a good paper delivered to you."

Came back the old lady: "But you do not understand. I like your paper better this way."

A managing editor once told me: "Make yourself useful, son, but don't be a damn nuisance about it."

(On heavy pollution in the upper Ohio River during his boyhood in West Virginia):

Now, sir, I swam in that river 82 miles south of Pittsburgh. I swam daily, and believe me, it was exercise because the water was almost solid. It did not splash. It crunched. This was slow going, but it built muscles. At that time I did not know that there was any other kind of water. So you can imagine my astonishment when at the age of 16 I dived into a clear, clean mountain lake, began my usual stroke, and began skimming over the water like a ruptured duck.

With the American Press Institute, I traveled considerably abroad, mostly to the former colonial nations. Time and again, the native newspapermen would say: "But you do not know what it means to live in a colonial country which is ruled by an absentee power." And I could always reply accurately: "Yes I do. I come from the State of West Virginia, which indeed is a colonial possession ruled by absentee power."

I sat next to an elderly lady at a New York Philharmonic concert. Under the master conductor, Toscanini, that superb orchestra performed Beethoven's Ninth Symphony, an unquestioned master-piece. The performance was brilliant, flawless. When it concluded, the old lady leaned over to me and said: "It was just the same old thing again."

(A bit of whimsy about expense accounts and budgets):

Don't think that I have (not) ever budgeted. In fact, I kept perfect budgets. The only trouble is that I made them up at the end of the year for the 12 months just ended. This is called the Curtis retroactive system.

Ted Bernstein (the New York Times expert on grammar and syntax) and I used to play double negatives, only Ted would make them triple by adding another negative, like: "He never was no good for nothing nohow neither."

(On the ultimate in sentences that end with a preposition):
A little boy says to his father: "Why did you bring that book I don't want to be read to out of up for?"

(His dreamed-up reminder not to use the verb "to get" in any form):
When I got your meaning I decided to get up and go out to get busy and get all those things I should have gotten by first getting them down on paper so I would get better and better and thus get used to the way you want things gotten. It's amazing how well we have gotten along together by getting to understand each other. Do you get my meaning? If not, let's go out, get ourselves to a bar, and get drunk.

My boss on the Buffalo Evening News was a bear on localizing. His telegraph editor missed many local angles in wire stories. I wanted to shock him into action. One day my car radio told me that 14 children had frozen to death in a stranded school bus in Wyoming. One other child survived. At 10 o'clock, a batch of copy came from the wire editor to the city desk. The wire editor had circled any mention of Western New York. Then I found the Wyoming bus story. The word "buffalo" was circled. The sentence read: "A 15th child survived because the boy was covered by a buffalo robe."

What ever happened to short editorials? My favorite was by Mike Barry of the Kentucky Irish American, who wrote of Governor Happy Chandler: "Anyone who calls our Governor a thinker, lisps!" Later Mike wrote of Happy: "Anyone who writes that our Governor is a favorite son has written an incomplete sentence." Where are the paragraphers of yesteryear?

Turner Catledge of the New York Times once instructed the staff to seek balance in writing stories of violence in New York City schools. After all, while a few students were violent, thousands of others were not. This caused Clarence Dean, then on the rewrite desk, to compose the following (and never published) lead:
"While 4,296 students at (a certain high school in Brooklyn) went quietly about their studies yesterday, another student murdered

the principal."

While waiting for a $12-a-week job to open on the Savannah Morning News, and having failed as a Chevrolet salesman, I kept alive by shilling for a freak show at Tybee Beach. With a buddy, I stole a watermelon each night. By eating a large, 10-cent, spongy, highly absorbent Dutch cake with an entire watermelon we would be so filled and distended that we would not be hungry again for 12 hours. When I landed a job on the Savannah paper, I could eat at least one meal a day in Morrison's Cafeteria. Them (sic) were the days, my friend, and I resent them not.

(His favorite story, as recalled by several API seminar members): Waynesburg College in Pennsylvania was dedicating a statue in memory of the school's namesake, General Mad Anthony Wayne. The general was astride his gigantic and hollow bronze horse, waving his cavalry sword. The statue, awaiting dedication, was covered by a huge tarpaulin. Some students sensed historic opportunity. During the night, they crept under the tarpaulin, sawed off the tip of the horse's penis and inserted a cork, which they attached to the covering with a cord. Then with a garden hose they filled the empty shell of the horse with water, thousands of gallons of water.

On dedication day, dignitaries gathered on a platform surrounding the statue. "Now," said the college president at the appropriate moment, "we unveil this memorial to our founder." He pulled the cord to remove the covering. The cord in turn also pulled out the critical cork. The horse, uncorked, began wetting down the platform.

Though mortified, the dignitaries waited for a while, then left. The wetting down continued for hours.

Always something of a philosopher—remember that Curtis was a philosophy major at West Virginia University—he expressed with humor, sometimes with hyperbole, sometimes with rancor what he saw as the enduring truths of newspapering.

Excerpts from his speeches and letters form an almanac of newspapering, a guide for neophytes and a collection at which the best of the old-timers can nod their heads in agreement—or occasional dissent:

ON REPORTING

The great need of newspapers is better reporting. Slicker writing, better makeup, more sophisticated production, better features—all that is needed. But all pales before better reporting.

When reporters or anyone else says, "Oh, we had that (in the paper) before," look out. Maybe you did have it before, a long time ago, but there are a lot of readers who might have missed it, and you must have many new readers. This is one of the most tiresome excuses news departments make for not working.

Another old lesson that can never be taught too many times is that, when a big story breaks, write it for all you've got with plenty of people and space.

When you assign an ordinary non-business reporter to a business subject you invite disaster. That's the first mistake—the assignment. The next mistake is caused by the reporter who does not have brains enough to ask simple questions and balance all sides. The third mistake is made by the editors who are equally ignorant and use the story.

When you can get to someone who has been involved in an unusual happening, the direct quotes are always fascinating. I don't see that done much anymore.

Show me a reporter who groans at the word "obits," and I will show you a reporter who can't write a good obit. Show me a reporter who says, "Oh, God, another meeting of the zoning board," and I will show you a reporter who cannot write a decent story about any government meeting.

ON WRITING

Good writing has always been the concern of good newspapermen. We have always had at any time at least a few brilliant writers. It is the general average of writing which has so improved in the last decade and a half.

Q. What is the dullest way to tell an action story?
A. By a rewrite of a story from a reporter who talked with a battalion chief who was not on the scene but received a report from a police lieutenant who also was not on the scene but received a report from a desk sergeant who had his information from a patrolman who heard it from a fireman.

Nothing, but nothing equals quotes in giving the reader the impression that the newspaper was on the scene and is doing its best to give the reader an accurate picture. Quotes must be absolutely accurate. For sensitive cases, there is nothing like a tape recorder.

There is no substitute for quick, constructive criticism of writing immediately after it is done. Do this job tactfully but forcibly. Do it every day. Improvement will result.

Why are the best-written things around a newspaper office always the memos written by reporters and editors? A reporter will come back from an assignment and write a story. Then an editor may ask him to write a background memo on anything he could not include in the story. And what happens? The reporter relaxes and turns out a highly readable job, describing personalities, injecting humor, and generally having a good time. The readers never see this kind of writing.

ON ACCURACY

How can errors be stopped? I could write a book from my files on accuracy. It would be useless. Memos, speeches and all that are a waste of time and effort. Mistakes will continue to increase until we start firing people who make them.

Good newspapermen will strive for years to earn a respected image, and then one careless, thoughtless step will ruin all that for a considerable number of readers. How do you prevent these wounds? Publication comes only after complete thought and a decision by the man at the top. Never hesitate to withhold publication for a day. Be fair. Be right, and you will win.

If the readers perceive you as biased, then you are biased in their minds, although the record may prove otherwise. An early newspaper boss told me: "No matter how fair and accurate you are, whatever you print will be resented if the facts disagree with the reader's hopes."

ON EDITING

(Apply) the vacuum principle of newspaper editing. Leave a vacuum of interest for your readers and somebody else will fill it.

Nothing is so effective as concise, precise copy editing. You offer variety. You have many more stories and pictures so your reader spends more time with your newspaper.

Take times of sensitivity and typify them—a funeral, a graduation, a wedding—so that everyone who has been through these experiences can share the moments and say: "That is the way it happened to us."

If I were running a newspaper today, and I am thankful that I am not, I would insist that all stories be fairly balanced, not only in content but certainly in presentation.

Where, oh where, are the obituaries which are read because they are beautifully written, the facts are complete, they teach a lesson or two and, above all, they involve nobodies just like most readers—except there is a lot of good reading in the interesting nobodies of the world.

It is easy to prove that people do not buy a newspaper because they love it for what it has not done. During the course of a year, a good newspaper will offend thousands of people.

An editorial page which attempts only to please is not only a bore—it's a wicked waste of money, and it doesn't sell newspapers.

Guilt is individual. Make guilt institutional, as our editorials and news stories have done, and nobody pays a damn bit of attention.

(On teen-age sections). Teen-agers do not like to be segregated. And teen-agers aren't teen-agers very long. That's the lovely part about oldsters. They just keep on getting older, and may the Lord preserve their eyesight.

For 40 years, readers puzzled me. They no longer do so. Print what they need. Print what they want. Print what they damn well should want in less space than for what they do want.

A newspaper can be a true success only if it is warmly and deeply in touch with its readers. All expertise will not prevail without the touch.

In every competitive situation I have watched, I have never seen the paper with the lowest story count win.

Every successful newspaper emphasizes news. Why state the obvious? Because some newspapers forget it. We are NEWSpapers. Failures, some recent, took the magazine approach to news. News is our cake. We need icing, but in proportion.

If your editor has to hire an outside consultant to tell him about his readers, isn't it time you got yourself a new editor? I will go for the marketing survey that analyzes populations, income classes and so on, but I still cannot convince myself that an editor needs a management consultant who never worked on a newspaper.

Encourage opposing viewpoints. On important local issues, do not fail to consult with knowledgeable reporters. I have seen many situations when a reporter would have saved the situation had he been consulted.

Some newspapermen have become just too damned big for their britches. They want to write and present articles of enormous length, analyzing this or that, raising great questions and offering few answers.

ON STAFF MANAGEMENT

(Employees) want to know someone they can go to talk to about their careers. They have got to relate to someone in management.

Be sure that each person knows at all times where they stand with you as a result of their work. If someone is doing badly, let them know at all times. Nothing so disturbs a staff as a surprise firing.

No newspaper I can recall ever beat its competitor by raiding its staff. A newspaper that meets its competition by copying and matching and raiding is a newspaper without initiative and talent at the top and good morale through the ranks.

ON THE CITY DESK

You cannot conduct a good city desk unless the operating details are licked. Future files, methods of making assignments, inter-person relationships, expense accounts, overtime, and all the myriad details are vitally important. Unless they are reduced to an absolute minimum of time consumption and are not allowed to dominate, how in the hell can anybody get out a good newspaper?

ON NEWSPAPER DESIGN

The great difficulty with some of the (newspaper) designers is that they are in love with the "impression" created by the design. They pay no attention to reading matter, and that is why some well-designed papers are losing circulation.

ON CIRCULATION

We gain circulation when we invest money in the product, have editors who are sensitive to their readers' needs, encourage habit-forming content and back that up with intelligent, hard-driving marketing by the new type of circulation director.

Circulators are wrong when they insist on deadlines so early that the newspaper is missing late-breaking news. And editors are wrong when they insist on deadlines so late that the reader does not get his paper on time.

ON ADVERTISING

No one wants puff stories for advertisers. Neither should any newspaper penalize its advertisers by playing down or rejecting legitimate news of them.

Ad salesmen and especially ad art departments are notorious for squeezing deadlines. In many shops, I found that the ad departments violated production schedules more than anyone else.

ON FREEDOM OF THE PRESS

Why aren't newspapers regulated? We are regulated—by the standards of the owners, the ethics of the editors and business managers, the tastes and interests of the readers. Press councils and review boards? So far, their record of incompetency is high. They should remain powerless. Let the press be criticized severely by readers. That's all the regulation we will ever need.

ON THE OLD DAYS

My incentive (on newspapers) was fear of losing my job. Maybe that's the trouble today. No fear. What we need in this world is more fear—not simple respect, but good old, downright, shivering and quaking fear.

You (could) smell as well as see the newsrooms of those days. To me there is nothing so nostalgic as the odor from a stereotype foundry with its scorched mats. Can you get that from film or plastic plates? The whole damn world is going to hell.

Newspapers in those days were a lot of fun. We were serious, but we did enjoy ourselves. Today's crop is not enjoying itself nearly so much, and Jack Knight agrees with me. I guess it was inevitable. When you are a billion-dollar corporation answerable to stockholders it just can't be the same.

There were always a few principled and accomplished newspapers and newspapermen. But most of us, especially when I started in the 1920s and throughout the 1930s, were a scruffy, underpaid lot serving publishers who were really counterfeiting on their printing presses and should have been hauled in for taking money under false pretenses.

ON PUBLISHING A NEWSPAPER

Ownership. Everything starts with that. If the owner wants a good newspaper and knows what a good newspaper is, all he has to do is hire the right people, pay them well and guide them. Inheritance can wreck a newspaper or improve it in quality and profit. Incompetent heirs have let newspapers die. Brilliant heirs have done the opposite.

The chief obstacle to the progress of many newspapers is that most of their executives will not listen, are uninformed, place the bottom line above the importance of content, and occasionally are just plain stupid.

Today's successful newspaper is produced by a team which knows where it is going. If the contemplated action agrees with the philosophy, you go ahead. Otherwise, otherwise. It's just that simple.

Readers and advertisers don't give a damn who owns the newspaper as long as it delivers what they want and what they pay for.

It is the non-news publishers sitting in their cloistered towers and their dull clubs who produce boring newspapers, unless they have the sense to hire good editors and let them alone.

The most difficult job in the world must be to conduct an institution so fearless that it takes minority positions early; so dedicated that it indulges in no search for mere popularity; so fair that it prints local news which over a year's time must personally displease thousands of readers, and yet retains their respect; so skillfully written and edited that it retains their subscriptions; and so superbly managed that it remains solvent and independent by its own efforts.

The whole thing is a miracle.

* * *

After Curtis died, the Knight Foundation approved a $75,000 challenge grant to API toward establishment of an annual J. Montgomery Curtis Memorial Seminar. In short order, other foundations, newspapers and newspaper groups matched the challenge grant. With income from the corpus of some $150,000, API in 1984 began holding an annual seminar of two or three days on a topic of major concern to newspapers.

Attendance was by invitation, usually 22 or 23 members who in the view of API were best positioned to find ways to solve the problem. Members paid no tuition or room and board, only their travel, thanks to income from the corpus.

The first seven topics were: credibility and the public perception of newspapers, new strategies for newspaper advertising growth, attracting and retaining readers, the role and responsibilities of the press in covering political candidates, the future of newspaper design, improving service to customers, and covering the drug crisis.

Discussions were summarized, printed and distributed in the industry.

Through the memorial seminars, then, Monty Curtis continued his crusade for better newspapers.

29

More Training, More Choices

During Frank Quine's eight years as API director, from 1979 to 1987, the institute's service to newspapers expanded not only in the enlarged building in Reston but also in seminars in the West and in three-day workshops at nearly 20 locations across the continent. New highs were set in the number of seminars and members, and API achieved a measure of financial stability.

Even while construction of the new wing to the building was still pending, API announced a record-high 25 seminars for 1979-80, together with the major change of trimming the former two-week seminars, which were Sunday through the second Friday, to nine working days, Sunday through the second Wednesday.

Thus members of these seminars could return home two days earlier than in the past. The reduction in days away from home was accomplished by scheduling a full work day on Saturday and adding more evening sessions. Nothing was subtracted from the program.

Fifteen of the 25 seminars for 1979-80 were set for 10 days, the others for five working days, Sunday through Friday. Moreover, experimentation with seminar length continued. In 1985, the seminar for classified advertising managers was condensed to six days, Sunday through Saturday.

Reducing the length of seminars without sacrificing content benefitted newspapers through lower costs for hotel rooms and meals. Moreover, members were away from their jobs fewer days, a factor especially important on small newspapers.

On the other hand, members sometimes complained that they suffered from information overload—too much new knowledge too quickly. Similar reactions had been reported in the very first year or two of API programs at Columbia University, when most seminars were three weeks. Those reactions were the reason that at Columbia API sometimes left a mid-week afternoon free: to give members time to catch their breath.

In Reston, despite the possibility of information overload, the shortened seminars had an advantage beyond lower costs and less time away from the job. That was the lack of free time that could engender a feeling of isolation in a Reston without much nightlife. The energies of seminar members were consumed by day and often evening seminar sessions, meals, shoptalk in the hospitality room, and a modest amount of sleep.

Other major changes were also being made. API's first "western presence" seminar, Managing the Changing Newspaper, was held July 13-18, 1980, in the amphitheater of the law school at Stanford University in Palo Alto, south of San Francisco.

The program evolved into the popular Developing Management Skills Seminar. Frank Quine, who usually took his regular turn conducting seminars, moderated the program. Bob Chandler, a board member and Stanford alumnus, arranged a lunch at the Stanford Faculty Club to acknowledge API's first western seminar. Among the Bay Area publishers who attended was Dean Lesher of the Contra Costa Times and Lesher Communications, who along with Tim Hays had pushed for a western presence. Several other board members, including Hays, also attended.

Among the Stanford officials on hand was Elie Abel of the School of Communications who had been cordial to API as dean of Columbia's Graduate School of Journalism.

The members were housed in Stanford's Florence Moore Residence Hall, with no room telephones, TV or private baths. Quine reported that the beautiful Stanford campus and weather won out over the spartan housing. But he also found that the Stanford facilities, though adequate, did not offer the "same climate" as the API building.

That reaction would be echoed by other API staff members when they took a seminar onto the road. They missed the supporting staff, the facilities for easy photocopying, and so on. For Stanford and all other on-the-road programs, advance work had to be accelerated to allow for shipping large boxes containing discussion leader materials, member name signs and other necessary items.

Publisher Ted Natt of the Longview (Washington) Daily News, a seminar member, rode his Harley-Davidson motorcycle the 700 miles from Longview to Palo Alto and parked it in the residence hall laundry room overnight. Next morning, Quine received a message that the motorcycle was illegally parked and must be moved.

On Thursday evening of the one-week program, the other members plotted to haul Natt's motorcycle up to the second floor of the residence hall, start the engine and drive it down the corridor. Ringleaders were talked out of the prank, which would not have helped API's relationship with Stanford. The motorcycle remained chained to a bicycle rack.

The attendance of 22 at Stanford was disappointing. In general, attendance at western seminars would fall below the average of programs in Reston. Also, the members did not come solely or even mainly from the West, as anticipated. Nominations came about equally from newspapers east of the Rockies.

Stanford facilities were available only during the summer academic break. Summer break coincided with the preponderance of newspaper vacations, and probably contributed to the modest membership totals.

API began holding two western seminars in 1983, selecting the Kellogg West conference center at Pomona, California, 50 miles west of Los Angeles, as the second usual location. With long advance reservations, the Kellogg West facilities were normally available most months.

In 1985, however, API could not provide sufficient advance notice to Kellogg West. It shifted the seminar to Reno, which had helpful folks at the School of Journalism at the University of Nevada-Reno. Seminar sessions were held in a campus building.

Members were housed at the nearby Ramada Inn and Conference Center where the lobby, like most Reno lobbies, was packed with slot machines. The biggest loser at the slots was a discussion leader. Woody Wardlow, the API moderator, played only the dime slots and lost less than $10 for the week.

Memories of the personal safety concerns at Columbia had faded when a 1983 incident at Pomona reminded API that perils lurk everywhere. Several members of a seminar for reporters were enjoying an evening drink at a Pomona restaurant when four or five armed holdup men appeared.

Patrons were forced to lie on the floor. The intruders robbed the bar and took the wallets of several patrons but somehow not those of the API seminar members. A shot was fired, but no one was hit.

The new wing of the API building was dedicated Sunday, October 25, 1980. The first Journalism Educators Seminar began that evening. Next day, for the first time, there were sessions held simultaneously at opposite ends of the expanded building. In the blue conference room on the eastern end, the circulation managers began the second week of their program. The journalism educators convened in the red room on the western end.

Because many journalism schools and departments worked with

tight budgets, the API staff had doubted over the years whether enough academics could afford to attend. That concern was eliminated in 1983 by a grant from the John Ben Snow Memorial Trust that enabled API to waive tuition for the educators. Snow had been chairman of Speidel Newspapers, which later merged with Gannett.

In addition, newspaper associations in Oregon, New York and New Jersey established one API fellowship each for journalism educators at schools in their states. Beyond that, all-expense fellowships for selected journalism educators were formed through various contributions honoring Jim Ottaway and Rollan D. Melton, former president of Speidel. The Melton fellowship and another established by several contributors were limited to educators who were members of a minority population group.

Each year three or four working newspaper men or women attended the journalism educators seminar as associate members, giving the educators additional opportunity to update themselves on current newspaper problems. The associate members usually left with a heightened appreciation of the educators.

In 1982, API began announcing its seminar schedules for the calendar year rather than the academic year, a carryover from Columbia days. The change was made as a convenience to nominating newspapers, most of which budgeted on a calendar year rather than a fiscal year and began the annual budgeting process as early as August. API's aim was to have its schedule for the next calendar year in the hands of budget-makers from the start of the process. The change in scheduling rhythm reflected another change in newspaper management since the early years of API. In those years, many newspapers operated rather informally from a loosely stated budget. Some had no budget at all.

With two conference rooms available in Reston and two western seminars held each year, API climbed to its peak all-time year of seminars and members—37 seminars, 1,203 members—in 1984-85. (Though API had converted to a calendar-year announcement of seminars, its own budget remained on a fiscal July-through-June basis).

Before that, API survived a recession. Membership first exceeded 1,000 in 1981-82, when 35 seminars were held, but the total fell to 29 in 1982-83 with only 732 members. Thus API again was reminded how newspapers, like many other companies, cut training budgets when the economy soured.

"Those were dark days at API," Quine later recalled. "Seminar tuition revenue was down $100,000 in that year alone. We somehow matched that by cutting expenses. We did things like eliminating styrofoam cups in the staff coffee lounge and restricting the number of discussion leaders with long-distance travel costs."

In 1984, API became a landlord when its board approved a request by the newly formed Center for Foreign Journalists to rent about 1,000 square feet of available office space on the first floor of the new wing. The vacant space was being held for future expansion of the API staff.

The Center for Foreign Journalists (CFJ) was founded to provide a training base primarily for Third World journalists visiting the U.S. on fellowships or grants. The founders were Thomas Winship, retired editor of the Boston Globe; James E. Ewing, president of the Keene (New Hampshire) Sentinel; and George A. Krimsky, former news editor of world services for the Associated Press.

The center sought not only office space but also occasional use of an API conference room when the room was not being used by API. In two or three years, though, CFJ shifted its objectives and in the main began sending trainers abroad rather than holding programs at Reston.

Another major addition to API's service to newspapers came in 1985, when it initiated three-day workshops for reporters, soon adding workshops for copy editors and advertising sales personnel. These workshops, all held at regional sites away from Reston, gave newspapers low-cost training opportunities for front-line staff members.

These workshops were, to some degree, a renewal of an initial API mission. In its early years, API held occasional seminars for reporters—city hall reporters, political and government reporters and the like. In fact, the fifth seminar ever held was for reporters of municipal affairs, and the sixth was for general reporters.

But most newspapers chose to send API mainly department heads such as city editors or copy desk chiefs, relying on them to in turn train their staffs. Accordingly, seminars for reporters disappeared from the seminar schedule for many years except those for investigative reporters.

API had responded to a newly resurgent interest in training reporters two years earlier, in 1983, by scheduling at Reston two five-day programs titled Improving Reporting Skills. Because newspapers of appreciable size have anywhere from a dozen to scores of reporters, the five-day seminars were not a full answer from a cost standpoint.

Thus the three-day regional workshops for reporters and, shortly, for copy editors and advertising personnel. The strategy was to hold workshops at sites surrounded by a cluster of newspapers within a four-hour drive.

Taking API workshops on the road threatened to step on toes.

Many state press associations had begun holding training sessions, some as short as one day, and those sessions had become an important revenue source for the associations. To the relief of the API staff, objections were expressed by only one regional and one state association. API adjusted its schedules and sites to minimize overlap with those two groups.

The first regional workshop was held July 14-17, 1985, at a motel near the Indianapolis Speedway. John G. Finneman, who had just been named senior associate director by Frank Quine, moderated the workshop. As senior associate director, Finneman coordinated planning for all seminars and workshops. He had joined API in 1979 as an associate director.

The 36 members at Indianapolis illustrated the merit of the cluster concept in selecting sites. Members came from six states: 13 from Indiana, seven each from Kentucky and Ohio, six from Michigan, two from Illinois and one from Tennessee.

"Can API be taken on the road with success?" Finneman asked rhetorically in his internal report. "Definitely, yes. Good planning and programming are the keys."

Nationwide, newspapers had lauded the announcement that API would begin holding regional workshops. Now Finneman wrote that the workshop members shared that enthusiasm: "They were eager to learn, eager to share, and appreciative of this opportunity."

Larry Hale, an associate director, conducted the second workshop, that same September in a hotel in Tulsa. He, too, had 36 members. API, Hale wrote, had "provided training to a group that thirsted for it, and needed it very much."

Ten days later, Don Lippincott, another associate director, held a reporters workshop in a motel conference center near Stroudsburg, Pennsylvania. "We have begun a valuable new service," Lippincott reported.

API staff members heading out solo to conduct workshops learned to expect adventure, not all of it welcome. From his pioneering Indianapolis workshop, Finneman remembered clattering dishes in a kitchen just beyond the thin wall of the workshop conference area. Others remembered noisy air-conditioners, balky audio-visual equipment, cleaning crews that failed to appear, and hotel or motel staffs that couldn't comprehend the precision API required.

Between 1985 and 1990, API twice held as many as seven workshops in one year, a total of 30 in the period that drew 1,041 members.

Meanwhile, back in Reston, API continued to introduce new seminars to meet newspaper needs. In the mid-1980s, they included: Coverage of Entertainment and the Arts, Newspapers and

Telecommunications, Suburban and Community News Coverage, Technology and the Newspaper Library, Newspaper Systems and Data Processing. Most were for five days, but two were only three days in length: Marketing the Daily Newspaper and The Newspaper Budgeting Process.

In 1986, API augmented its efforts to help newspapers improve their minority hiring and advancement efforts. For several years, many seminars had included a session on hiring and training minorities. Now, in cooperation with the ANPA Foundation and an industry-wide task force, API held a two-day seminar on Minorities in the Newspaper Business.

For most of its existence, API had built a limited measure of cross-training into its seminars, hoping to increase interdepartmental cooperation. Non-news seminars, for example, included a session on selection of news content, and news-editorial seminars included a session on general management problems.

Cross-training efforts were expanded in 1985 with two new seminars: The Non-News Side of Newspaper Publishing, and News-Editorial Management for Non-News Executives. The first was designed for editors and other newsroom managers seeking a working knowledge of how non-news departments function. The second was for those in advertising, circulation, marketing or general management who had never worked in news.

Another major innovation was approved in 1986, when the board earmarked some $300,000 for development of a computerized newspaper management simulation that would become the center-piece of a five-day program for senior executives and candidates for key publishing or upper-management responsibilities—the Executive Development Program.

Development of the computer simulation was contracted to the Sterling Institute of Washington, D.C. The project involved gathering market information and newspaper publishing cases and building an econometric model to drive the simulation.

API planned separate programs for members from large and small newspapers. Accordingly, the Sterling team developed two mythical newspapers, the Zenith Advocate and the Westfield Journal, for large and small papers, respectively.

During the simulation portion, seminar members had access via computer screens to financial reports, revenue and pricing data, historical trends, market and demographic data, critical operating ratios used to measure the newspaper's performance, and so on. In addition there were memos, letters and reports on internal and external events affecting the newspaper and its market.

In competing teams of five or six, seminar members made their decisions. The computer tracked the likely impact of those decisions on performance of the newspaper and projected the company's publishing status six years out at the conclusion of the simulation.

Objectives were to increase executive effectiveness in establishing priorities and setting long-term goals, to improve understanding of how management groups make decisions, to develop better insight into interdepartmental dynamics, and to assess the effect that management practices and styles have on the performance of subordinates.

The Executive Development Programs, first held in 1988, were a hit. Tuition was set at $1,500 to recoup the cost of the simulation.

As API expanded its programs, it also expanded its list of publications. A publication with especially strong impact appeared in 1985, the 60-page booklet: "Effective Writing and Editing: A Guidebook for Newspapers."

It was written by Woody Wardlow, who pulled from the API files the best writing and editing advice developed during 39 years of seminars and also drew from his own experience—31 years as a reporter and editor. API sent the booklet to newspapers and journalism schools throughout the U.S. and Canada. It went through five printings—a total of 31,000 copies. In 1991 it was still being distributed to members of appropriate seminars.

With the new seminars and workshops, API's impact on the newspaper industry burgeoned in its first dozen years or so in Reston. The extent of the burgeoning can be shown by recalling that in 28 years at Columbia University, API seminar membership totaled 8,875.

In 1976, two years after settling in Reston, API welcomed its 10,000th member, William R. Sanders, retail advertising manager of the Tribune-Democrat in Johnstown, Pennsylvania. Ten years later, it welcomed member number 20,000. She was Karen Storey, classified advertising manager of the San Jose Mercury News.

As the needs of newspapers changed, so did the needs of individual staffers as their careers progressed. As noted earlier, Roger Sovde of the Rock Hill (South Carolina) Herald attended a record seven seminars and Kenneth E. Johnson of the Grand Junction (Colorado) Daily Sentinel attended six. Close behind were several who attended five seminars, including Richard T. Bentley of the Merced (California) Sun-Star, William Dwight Jr. of the Holyoke (Massachusetts) Transcript-Telegram; Stephen W. Ryder of the Medford (Oregon) Mail Tribune, and Warren H. Koon of the Natchez (Mississippi) Democrat.

In 1981-82, Robert A. Sproat of the Dallas Times Herald built a unique record as he moved from director of consumer services to director of advertising by attending four API seminars within 15 months: Circulation Managers, Management and Costs, Advertising Executives and Marketing the Daily Newspaper. Thomas R. McCartin, publisher of the Times Herald, said the flurry of attendance gave Sproat exposure to the full context of his position.

H. Hurtt Deringer of the Kent County News in Chestertown, Maryland, became in 1984 the first weekly representative to attend four API seminars for weeklies, a mark that seemed likely to stand for some time.

In making the many changes and additions to its training services, API often had strong encouragement from its four Regional Advisory Boards. The idea of establishing advisory boards had been discussed from time to time. Two years after he became chairman of the Board of Directors, Tim Hays appointed the first advisory boards.

"...we think it appropriate," Hays said, "to involve more of (API's) friends in its activities and give it a broader base of professional counsel and support."

There were four regional advisory boards: Eastern, Central, Southern and Western. Initially, each had ten members. Soon they were expanded to 11. Terms at first were set at six years, but that was later reduced to four years. The boards met separately in their own regions one year and jointly at API in Reston in alternate years. Four-year terms gave members opportunity to attend two meetings in the home region and two at Reston.

The first chairmen were: Eastern, Charles McC. Hauser of the Providence Journal and Evening Bulletin; Central, Maxwell McCrohon of the Chicago Tribune; Southern, Wayne T. Patrick of the Rock Hill (South Carolina) Herald; and Western, Stephen W. Ryder of the Medford (Oregon) Mail Tribune.

Members were drawn from a wide range of newspaper expertise, circulation and geography, and a flow of suggestions resulted. Frank Quine and Mal Mallette attended all of the in-region meetings between 1980 and 1987, and the full API executive staff sat in on the joint meetings in Reston.

By any measure, the Regional Advisory Boards were a success, though they imposed administrative work for an already busy API staff. The boards were dissolved after 1988 to give the staff time to study the recommendations. However, there was soon discussion of reviving them.

Through the 1979-87 span, staff changes occurred from time to time, with a pattern of associate directors leaving for jobs of good standing and presumably greater income.

During the period, these persons joined API as associate directors:

John G. Finneman. A journalism graduate of the University of Minnesota, Finneman worked for his hometown Duluth Herald and

News-Tribune three years as a reporter, then joined the Racine (Wisconsin) Journal Times as a reporter. He became Sunday editor in 1971 and Sunday and feature editor in 1973. He joined API November 1, 1979, expanding the executive staff to six persons as API prepared to hold two concurrent seminars upon completion of the new building wing then under construction. With Finneman's arrival, David A. Roe, an associate director since 1976, was named managing director.

Elwood M. (Woody) Wardlow. Wardlow began his newspaper career with the Journal-Standard in his native Freeport, Illinois, after graduating from the University of Wisconsin. He later served 27 years on the Buffalo Evening News, as a copy editor, copy desk chief, assistant managing editor and managing editor/administration. In 1979, he took early retirement at Buffalo to write and teach. In June 1980 he joined API at age 56, filling a vacancy opened when Roe resigned and became manager of the publishing division of the U.S. Chamber of Commerce. Wardlow remained with API until his second retirement, in 1989.

Donald E. Lippincott. After graduating from the Rutgers University School of Journalism, Don Lippincott became editor of weekly newspapers in Point Pleasant and Toms River, New Jersey, before joining the Trenton Times in 1953 as a suburban beat reporter. He was later city hall reporter, statehouse correspondent, city editor, metropolitan editor and—from 1969 to 1979—managing editor. He was deputy editor, 1979 to 1980, then joined API in October 1980 at age 53, bringing the executive staff again to six.

Becky B. Smith. A native of Charlotte, Smith graduated as an English major from Salem College in Winston-Salem, North Carolina. She was an editor for TV Digest magazine in Fort Lauderdale and a reporter and editor for the Marietta (Georgia) Daily Journal and the Winston-Salem Journal and Sentinel before joining the Greensboro (North Carolina) News & Record, where she worked 11 years. She was assistant managing editor/features when she left to join API in January 1984. Smith filled a position that had been open since mid-1982, when Janet Sanford joined the founding staff of USA Today. Smith returned to Greensboro in July 1986 to become publisher/editor of a weekly specialty magazine published by Landmark Communications, owner of the Greensboro News & Record.

Carol Ann Riordan. Riordan, the daughter of Thomas A. Riordan, who served several years at managing editor of the Jackson (Michigan) Citizen Patriot, graduated from St. Mary's College of Notre Dame, where she majored in speech and theater. She then worked as a reporter for the Niles (Michigan) Daily Star and as a feature writer for the Clearwater (Florida) Sun and the Belleville (Illinois)

News-Democrat. Next at the Madison (Wisconsin) Capital Times, she became editor of the feature/entertainment section. She joined API in August 1986.

Jeffrey A. Cowart. Jeff Cowart graduated in journalism at Louisiana State University, then was a reporter for the Fort Lauderdale Sun-Sentinel and the Alexandria Daily Town Talk and Plaquemine Post in Louisiana before joining the Baton Rouge State-Times in 1977 as a layout and copy editor. He was city editor, 1980 to 1983, then moved to the Rock Hill (South Carolina) Herald as city editor and became managing editor in October 1986.

Cowart joined API in January 1987 so that API would be at full complement when Mal Mallette retired June 30, 1987. Cowart resigned from API in November 1988 to become press secretary to the governor-elect of Louisiana, Buddy Roemer.

During the 1980s and despite the recession early in the decade that saw brief training curtailment, API's financial resources became significantly stronger. For its first three and a half decades, API had operated with thin reserves and occasional deficits.

At Columbia, reserves totaled about $200,000. The first breakthrough came when the building-fund campaign for the original construction in Reston raised some $2.6 million, about $600,000 beyond its goal.

In October 1980, Chairman Tim Hays thought the time right to seek more contributions to the endowment fund, which then stood at $427,540. He appointed an Endowment Fund Committee of William O. Taylor (chairman) and Robert N. Chandler and James H. Ottaway, members. Hays said a larger endowment would add long-range strength and make it easier to keep seminar tuition at reasonable levels. The goal was to build the fund to $1 million.

With Taylor leading the way, the committee brought in additional contributions and pledges that pushed the principal up to $1.16 million by mid-1983.

With inflation biting into the buying power of the reserves, the board voted on December 1, 1981, to hire Pacific Financial Research Company of Beverly Hills, California, as investment manager. The decision was timely. API's portfolio value grew from some $2.2 million in 1983 to $4.5 million in 1987. After trailing off a bit in 1988, it reached an all-time high of some $4.7 million in 1989. In 1990, a chunk of that portfolio would be cashed in to refurbish and repair the 16-year-old API building.

Yet another change relating to finances was inaugurated in 1987. API had never tried to relate the amount of Sponsorship contributions to the circulation size of a sponsoring newspaper. The result was that amounts donated by newspapers of the same general size varied widely, depending on the level of generosity, historical pattern and the value publishers placed on API.

Some years, API received more than 400 contributions from a mixture of groups and individual newspapers. During the 1970s and 1980s, groups acquired formerly independent newspapers at an accelerating rate. As a result, though total Sponsorship increased most years, the number of contributors decreased.

This was troubling, because if a sizable newspaper group should decide not to be a Sponsor the dollar total of contributions would plummet. Fortunately, all the larger groups and most of the smaller ones continued their support. A related problem was persuading groups to add to their Sponsorship the amount that had been given by papers they acquired.

So the board approved a formula to recommend to all Sponsors: $15 per thousand of circulation. The formula system caused publishers of a few historically generous papers to cut back because they had been giving well above the formula. But the formula resulted in 1987-88 Sponsorships totaling $579,000, an increase of $100,000 over the previous year. Within three years, though, the board became concerned that a formula established a finite ceiling on contributions because newspaper circulation was not growing and API operating costs were continuing to increase. So the board began looking at other fund-raising options.

In 1983, Hays completed five years as chairman and asked the board to name a successor, although he wished to remain as a non-officer. Hays had crossed the continent from California any number of times to carry out his duties as chairman.

Effective July 1, 1983, the board elected William O. Taylor, chairman and publisher of the Boston Globe, as API's third corporate chairman. Taylor, who moved up from vice chairman, had won his spurs. At Columbia, he had served on Al Neuharth's Facilities and Finance Subcommittee of the Development Committee. In 1978, he chaired the Professional Training Survey Committee that studied the work of other, emerging training efforts. And he had led the Endowment Fund Committee that increased total contributions to $1.156 million.

Between 1961 and 1975, Bill Taylor had attended four API seminars. His newspaper, the Globe, had contributed generously to Sponsorship, the two building funds and the endowment. And at the time of his election as chairman the Globe had sent 142 staff members to API.

Taylor would serve as chairman until 1988, when like Hays he chose to step down after five years.

The next major personnel change at API was the retirement June

30, 1987, of Mal Mallette, the former associate director, managing director and director who had been director of development since 1979.

Mallette had reached age 65, the usual retirement age for the executive staff. He would leave after more than 21 years with API. But first, on February 17, 1987, about 170 API friends and supporters gathered at the Sheraton Inn for a humor-filled retirement party.

Mallette's distant past as a pitcher for the Brooklyn Dodgers provided barbs for the master of ceremonies, Vince Spezzano of the Rochester Newspapers, and others. Frank Quine and party co-chairman Steve Ryder of Medford, Oregon, arranged for a one-time Dodgers broadcaster to create a fantasy sports tape on which Mallette faced sluggers Mickey Mantle and Yogi Berra of the New York Yankees in the final game of a World Series.

Mallette "just knew" that Mantle or Berra or both would hit tape-measure home runs. But fantasy was kind: he struck out both.

Mallette's departure was long planned, but a surprise change came in mid-year with the resignation of Quine as director after 18 years on the staff. He was age 49. He joined API in 1969 as an associate director, moved up to managing director in 1977 and to director in 1979.

Privately, Quine had told colleagues that he didn't plan to remain with API until retirement, but clearly his departure was premature. Accepting Quine's resignation, Taylor praised him for "conscientious service and administrative leadership." Quine said, "The board felt it was time to bring a fresh perspective to API. For me, it was a terrific run, right in the center of newspapering's most pressing issues of the '70s and '80s."

Quine later became director of development of the University of Maryland College of Journalism and vice president of Washington Journalism Review, a monthly magazine of press and media analysis published by the college.

Eugene Patterson, chairman and chief executive officer of Times Publishing Company in St. Petersburg, where Quine once worked, was appointed to head a search committee and find a successor.

Reviewing the change in directors at a later board meeting, Patterson said the board sought a director who would be "innovative, bold, unorthodox, exciting, creative, experimental."

30

New Directions

William Lawrence Winter entered Arkansas State University in his hometown of Jonesboro intending to follow the pre-medicine curriculum. Winter really didn't know what he wanted to do. But many of his friends were in pre-med, so he tried it.

His first college chemistry course, however, told Winter that his future lay elsewhere. "I just could not do college chemistry," he said later.

Where to turn? A remembered comment by a high school English teacher pointed the way. Winter wrote a light-hearted essay, and the teacher scribbled in the margin: "If you don't become a professional writer, I will come back and haunt you, and there's nothing more disconcerting than having a fat ghost hanging around the house." So Winter switched to journalism and received his undergraduate degree from Arkansas State in 1965.

By the time Bill Winter, then 43, reported to work September 1, 1987, as the sixth director in the 41-year history of the American Press Institute, his career had taken unusual twists.

The resignation of Frank Quine, the previous API director, had been announced in May 1987. In June, meeting in Las Vegas, the Board of Directors discussed criteria for selecting the next director, and Chairman Bill Taylor appointed a Search and Screen Committee.

Gene Patterson chairman of Times Publishing Company, St. Petersburg, chaired the committee. The other members were: Larry D. Franklin, executive vice president of Harte-Hanks Communications; Robert G. McGruder, deputy managing editor, Detroit Free Press; Madelyn P. Jennings, senior vice president/personnel, Gannett Company; and Taylor, ex-officio.

In addition to its own efforts, the committee hired a personnel search firm. It was the firm that recommended Winter as a candidate.

After graduating from Arkansas State, Winter earned a master's degree in journalism at Ohio University and became a journalism instructor at San Antonio College, a junior college. Three nights a week, he also shot film and wrote scripts for KENS-TV in San Antonio. After 18 months, he joined the journalism faculty at Central Michigan University.

But then a tornado in his hometown Jonesboro demolished several houses in which his parents held investments. With resulting insurance payments, they loaned money to their son so that he could pursue a doctoral degree. At Syracuse University, Winter began a doctoral program in mass communication.

In Syracuse, however, he disliked the heavy snowfalls and leaden winter skies. After a year, he learned through a trade magazine ad that the Bozeman (Montana) Daily Chronicle, a newspaper of 8,000 circulation, was seeking a combination sports editor and county government reporter.

Sports were not alien to Winter. In Jonesboro, he twice had been city junior tennis champion, and he also played on the Arkansas State tennis team. Winter called the Bozeman managing editor and was hired on the spot.

He remembered the Bozeman job as the most satisfying he ever had. There he was allowed to "do my thing," or more accurately the several things demanded by small newspapers.

From Bozeman, Winter signed on in 1970 with the Associated Press in Helena, Montana's capital. Nominally state sports editor, he also covered non-sports news, including a trial for cannibalism. Near Yellowstone National Park, two young men were accused of killing a social worker while spaced out on LSD. One cut out the victim's heart and ate it.

"It was the story of a lifetime," Winter recounted. But nationally, it competed for display with the even more grisly story of the Manson mass murders in California.

In 1971, Burl Osborne became the Associated Press chief of bureau in Louisville. He brought Winter there as state sports editor. Sixteen years later, as president and editor of the Dallas Morning News, Osborne would be on the API Board of Directors that appointed Winter as the Institute's director. And a year later, in 1988, Osborne would succeed Bill Taylor as API chairman.

Those who work for AP know to keep their bags packed. After a year in Louisville, Winter became the AP correspondent in Cincinnati. A year later, he was off to Jackson, Mississippi, as AP correspondent.

In 1975, he returned to Louisville as chief of bureau, when Osborne transferred to Columbus, Ohio.

The promotion to chief of bureau was a major step up for a journalist. But two years later Winter decided it was time to confront another passion: country music.

At Arkansas State, he had played and sung in fraternity musical groups. Now with a little money in reserve, he could risk learning how far his singing voice and guitar chords could take him.

Winter took a leave of absence from the AP and spent three months learning songs, building a repertoire. Then he scrounged for bookings, often as the night-off substitute for established performers in Louisville clubs and restaurants.

"I never got over how difficult it was to be a performer," he said. He cited the long hours of practice, the indignities of dealing with "arrogant agents and troglodyte club owners, and, often, of being ignored by the club and/or restaurant customers for whom you perform."

One night, when a drunk heckled him and Winter replied in kind and later led a sing-along, the customers gave him a brief standing ovation. "One night like that," he said, "makes you understand why people endure the music business."

But nine months of occasional bookings depleted Winter's bank account. In 1978, he put his guitar aside and returned to newspapering as executive sports editor of the Louisville Courier-Journal and Times. A year later, he moved to the Akron Beacon Journal as assistant managing editor/news.

During five years in Akron, he attended night classes at Kent State University and received his doctor of philosophy degree in the administration of higher education.

Also during his years with the Akron Beacon Journal, Winter attended a 1980 API seminar on Sunday and weekend newspapers. The moderator, Janet Sanford, identified three of the 34 members as potential future discussion leaders. One was Bill Winter, whom she described as "solid, but still too new to newspapers."

In 1984, Knight-Ridder moved Winter from Akron to its Pasadena (California) Star-News as executive editor. There, three years later, the API board found the man it believed could give the institute the new directions it wanted but had not concretely defined.

Winter was interviewed individually and collectively by members of the Search and Screen Committee. The nature of those interviews is pertinent here because the board had decided to change directors even though the years leading up to the decision had been marked by positive change, growth and economic health.

No committee member spoke precisely about institutional directions, Winter recalled, but he drew several conclusions.

The board, he inferred, thought API was too heavily weighted to its tradition of independence. The board valued that independence, but also thought it was time to become "a more welcoming partner" in working with other newspaper organizations.

The board, he thought, wanted API to present a higher profile and become more visible in the increasingly competitive training field. The board also wanted more long-range planning. And it thought the best time to change directors was during a time of success.

Winter was in his third month as director when chairman Bill Taylor asked the board to discuss emerging issues in the newspaper industry and how API should respond to them. Board members variously pitched in with these observations:

• More racial diversity was needed, not only in newsrooms but also in newspaper business departments.
• Training for managers needed increased emphasis.
• Newspapers needed to learn how they could use product quality to better competitive advantage.
• The newspaper industry should try to get ahead of the information business curve, and in the attempt API should challenge newspapers to send their brightest people to its seminars.
• API should increase its target marketing and promotion of new seminars.
• API should continue to offer bread-and-butter programming but continue to add increasingly creative new offerings in increments.
• API should increase its efforts to reach out to small dailies, weeklies and journalism schools.
• API should seek ways to better share its information and ideas.
• API needed to be perceived as a center for new ideas.
• API should not abandon its tradition.
• API needed to redefine its direction and mission.
• The API staff and the board were not far apart in their concerns.
• API needed additional resources if it was to expand its efforts.

Those far-ranging—and sometimes contradictory—expressions came from newspaper executives concerned over declining newspaper readership and, in some cases, revenues. Board members clearly hoped that API could supply remedies beyond those that had so enormously improved newspaper quality and operations since that first API seminar in 1946. They wanted even more from API.

API had always served newspapers in part by identifying progressive practices and spreading awareness of those practices. Now, if discussion in the "emerging issues" board meeting was an accurate measure, the newspaper industry also looked to API to generate seminal ideas, ideas to stem the scary slide in newspaper readership and advertising market share.

Such was the splintery baton passed to Winter. He called the time one of great opportunity for API. API's thrust, he said, would be the continuing education of newspaper men and women through extensive seminar programs plus additional activities through which the institute could show "real leadership in the industry."

In this period of expanded expectations, the API executive staff continued to change. As it did, certain long-standing goals of diversity and skills were reached.

Malcolm K. (Mike) Hughes became an associate director in January 1988 after 30 years with United Press International. In his final months with the wire service, Hughes had been editor-in-chief and executive vice president.

Earlier, he was European sports editor, executive sports editor, news editor for the U.S. eastern division, editor for the Canadian subsidiary (United Press Canada), vice president and general manager of the international divisions and executive editor. He also taught journalism at Baylor University.

Hughes was born to British parents serving in India and was educated at St. George's College in Mussoorie, India, before living 17 years in Great Britain. At API, he succeeded Jeffrey Cowart, who resigned to return to Louisiana.

Robert L. Secundy joined API in August 1988 with the title of associate director/finance and administration. Previously, those duties had been held by Eileen Owens Friedman (who moved from the Washington area) under the title of business manager.

Secundy, who is black, was the first minority member on the executive staff. He held a degree in electrical engineering from the University of Pennsylvania and an MBA degree from the Wharton School of Business and Finance. He began his career as a financial analyst for Sun Oil Company, then was assistant circulation manager of the Washington Post and president of his own computer training company before joining API.

Sherry Brown joined API as an associate director in January 1989 in anticipation of Woody Wardlow's retirement two months later. Brown, a journalism graduate of Indiana University, worked for the Bloomington (Indiana) Herald-Telephone before spending 12 years with the Lafayette (Indiana) Journal and Courier, the first 10 as a reporter and departmental editor, the last two as marketing support director.

Terri Dickerson-Jones joined API in April 1989 as an associate director, ahead of Larry Hale's retirement in June 1990. She brought to seven, a new high, the number of persons who conducted seminars. (Winter, among the seven, limited the seminars he conducted to some of the Executive Development Programs.) Dickerson-Jones also represented other changes. With Sherry Brown and Carol Ann Riordan, she increased to three the number of women associate directors.

Dickerson-Jones, who like Secundy is black, was the first associate director without experience at a daily newspaper, but she brought strong ties to the newspaper industry. She held a B.S. degree in education from the University of Virginia and had worked earlier as a publications editor, fund-raiser and program development specialist before serving three years as manager/minority affairs for the American Newspaper Publishers Association.

API's board also underwent significant change. In 1989, chairman Taylor resigned from the Board of Directors, effective July 1. He had served six years as chairman.

Taylor's resignation came at a time when the nine-year term limitation had brought several newcomers to the 18-member board. Several more veterans were close to the time limit. For its chairman, the board turned to Burl Osborne, president and editor of the Dallas Morning News, who had been elected to the board in 1986.

This was the Burl Osborne who Bill Winter had succeeded in the Associated Press bureau in Louisville. Osborne's exceptional energy had taken him from his native coal town, Jenkins, Kentucky, to a peripatetic 20-year career with the AP that included assignments in Bluefield and Charleston, West Virginia; Spokane, Washington; Denver; Louisville; Columbus, Ohio; Washington, and New York City.

While AP bureau chief in Columbus, he attended a 1973 API seminar for managing editors, and he had served on discussion leader panels on wire service reports.

In 1974, Osborne became assistant chief of bureau in Washington. Three years later, he was called to New York as AP's managing editor. He joined the Dallas Morning News in 1980 as executive editor and rose to publisher.

Osborne's energy enabled him in 1990 to serve not only the Dallas Morning News and API but also the American Society of Newspaper Editors as president.

Like earlier API chairmen, Osborne was committed to quality. He described his philosophy in the ASNE Bulletin:

"Put simply, the news product must be fair, accurate, balanced and straightforward, presented as objectively as can be managed. The quality of the content is the foundation for everything else that happens."

Under Osborne and Winter, the API stream of innovations contin-ued. After two years of preparation that began under Frank Quine, the computer-based newspaper management simulation had been tested and found ready. With the simulation as its nucleus, the first Executive Development Program (for newspapers over 75,000 circu-lation) was held February 28-March 4, 1988.

Despite a glitch that forced a computer programmer to work through the night, the initial program was pronounced a ringing success, as was the one for smaller newspapers a few weeks later. The Executive Development Programs (EDP), which initially ran Monday through Friday, set a new level for intensity. The competing teams, usually four teams of five to seven members each, were graded by the relentless computers on the effectiveness of their decisions. Electronically squeezed into a week, the decisions repre-sented six years in the life of a newspaper—imaginary, but realistic in its market responses.

The competition generated workaholics. When moderating one EDP, Winter arrived at the API building at 7:28 a.m. Other kinds of seminars usually start at 9 a.m., sometimes at 8:30. But waiting at the locked entrance were four EDP members. Within 10 minutes, the full teams, each assigned to a different room, were at work.

As newspapers in the real world faced new challenges, API commissioned the computer experts to update the simulations.

The EDP five-day program was so intense that, in response to the recommendation of members, API added a sixth day to give members time to talk with one another and digest what they had learned. So that the members would be away from their newspapers only one work week, API started the programs on Sunday mornings.

API stepped up its publications program, especially in connection with the J. Montgomery Curtis Memorial Seminars. After the 1988 Curtis seminar on the future of newspaper design, API published, under direction of Senior Associate Director John Finneman, a handsome summary of the proceedings at a cost of $65,000. It recouped the expenditure by selling the book to newspapers and colleges and universities throughout the world.

API also stepped up staff production of articles for trade publica-tions as an effort toward both visibility and additional sharing of seminar-generated information.

In June 1988, API held its first seminar in Canada, where only five years earlier the Board of Directors had met for the first time outside the U.S. Both the board meeting and the seminar—Developing Management Skills—were held in Toronto.

In the initial seminar in Canada, 13 of the 33 members were from Canada. Larry Hale, the moderator, recommended that API return to

Canada "again and again and again." One seminar a year in Canada became a fixture.

In less than a decade, API had greatly expanded its flexibility, with the "western presence" seminars—usually two a year, the regional three-day workshops for reporters, copy editors and advertising salespersons, the Curtis seminars that addressed especially urgent problems in the newspaper industry, and the seminar in Canada.

Then in 1990, it added another dimension called the Issues Forum. The idea was to mount one-day programs on issues of the moment. The first forum examined press performance in election coverage, the second dealt with coverage of the war in the Persian Gulf. The latter convened a number of the print and broadcast journalists who had reported from the Gulf, together with discussion leaders including Pete Williams, the Pentagon spokesman. Lively, even heated, exchanges developed.

Since the inception of the Journalism Educators Seminar in 1980, API had encouraged participation by minority faculty members through a handful of scholarships. In the summer of 1991, after raising a corpus of $60,000 for the special purpose from newspapers and newspaper-related foundations, API held its first Minority Journalism Educators Fellowship Program.

Twelve fellows from 11 different colleges and universities attended a 10-day seminar at API, which was followed by one-month newsroom internships.

Also in 1991, API shortened all of its regular seminars to no more than six working days, with the majority being five days. That was in response to the desire of newspapers for lower training costs and shorter personnel absences from staffs that had in many cases been reduced in size, a reaction to lower profits.

Shortening the remaining 10-day seminars to six or five days forced difficult decisions on which topics to condense or eliminate, but API, like newspapers themselves, found it necessary to adjust to its market.

Then, as happened in the recession of 1982 and earlier economic slumps, API was buffeted by the 1991 recession. In fiscal 1989-90, as the economy began to sputter, API accommodated 1,084 members in 34 seminars and 213 members in six regional workshops. In 1990-91, attendance sagged to 760 in 32 seminars and 139 in five regional workshops.

After several years of relative budgetary comfort, API in 1991 again faced financial pressures and not just because of the recession. With the main building 17 years old and its wing at age 11, API invested nearly $400,000 in improved air-conditioning, added electronic projection equipment in the red conference room, new carpeting, a new roof and other refurbishing.

That outlay followed an expenditure of nearly $100,000 during the previous three years to computerize administrative functions.

As part of the move to new technology 45 manual typewriters, long used in the writing rooms by members, were donated to the World Press Freedom Committee, which shipped them to newspapers and schools in Africa and the Caribbean.

The capital expenditures and the vagaries of the stock market reduced the endowment portfolio, which had appreciated under professional management from a June 1989 high of $4.6 million to a September 1990 level of $3.8 million.

And of course the costs of producing seminars went only one way—up. Newspapers continued to respond generously in their sponsorship contributions. Over the decade starting in fiscal 1979-80, annual sponsorships soared from $275,606 to more than $620,000.

Reacting to budgetary problems, API raised seminar tuition periodically and reluctantly until it reached $725 plus room and board for a five-day Reston seminar in 1991. The Board of Directors established a committee to study financial options, and one option that had been turned down in the past, that of seeking support from non-newspaper-related foundations, was being given serious consideration.

In October 1990, API welcomed its 25,000th seminar member. He was Lawrence Aaron, city editor of the Westchester Rockland newspapers in White Plains, New York. Even as Aaron attended the institute, Winter and the associate directors were looking ahead to new directions for the institute.

On the drawing board were plans for satellite delivery of API training direct to newspaper sites; a new senior newsroom executives seminar focusing on new product development and the creative management of change; a new "summer school at API" series of two-day programs based on university campuses around the United States; and development of an intensive advanced management seminar focusing on key leadership issues.

In early 1991, where this narrative ends, the only certainty for API was continuing change. As Winter put it: "We're keeping the best of the past, but we're also working to change as we need to and lead the newspaper industry into the future."

With API's golden anniversary only five years away, it seemed appropriate to look back to 1946, when an experiment called the American Press Institute began, and to a sentiment that gained meaning with the years.

When API ended its first year, these were the words of W. S. Gilmore, editor of the Detroit News:

"This is the first time American newspapers as a group have done anything intelligent to improve the quality of newspapers, and it was about time they did it."

About the Authors

Don Carter was introduced to the American Press Institute in 1953 when he attended a City Editors Seminar from the Atlanta Journal. He was invited back as a discussion leader a year later for the first of 75 such appearances over the next 30 years.

His newspaper career took him from Atlanta to New York to become the first executive director of the Dow Jones Newspaper Fund; to Washington, where he was founding managing editor of the National Observer; to Bergen County, New Jersey, where he was executive editor of the Record; and to Knight-Ridder Newspapers, where he had successive assignments as executive editor of the Macon (Georgia) Telegraph and News, publisher of the Lexington (Kentucky) Herald-Leader, and as a corporate vice president/news in Miami.

For several years, he was a member of the American Press Institute's Board of Directors. His long association with Monty Curtis, Walter Everett, Mal Mallette and Frank Quine—all directors of API—led to his participation in the preparation of this book.

Retired now, Carter and wife Carolyn live at Sea Island on the coast of their native Georgia.

Mal Mallette studied journalism at Syracuse University, intent on a newspaper career. But it was delayed first by Air Force service during World War II and then by seven seasons as a lefthanded pitcher in professional baseball. He saw brief service with the Brooklyn Dodgers in 1950 but underwent shoulder surgery and left baseball two seasons later.

He newspapered for 15 years in North Carolina, on the Asheville Citizen and Times and the Winston-Salem Journal and Sentinel, where he became managing editor. He attended an American Press Institute Managing Editors Seminar in 1961. That led to a dozen appearances as an API discussion leader and then an invitation to join the API staff in 1966.

In 21 years with API, he conducted more than 80 seminars and served successively as associate director, managing director, director and director of development before retiring in 1987.

Mallette and his wife Eleanor live in Reston, Virginia. His retirement activities include serving as director of projects for the World Press Freedom Committee.

Appendix A

These were the 25 members of API's first seminar, Managing Editors and News Editors, September 30-October 18, 1946, at Columbia University in New York City:

Charles M. Egan, news editor, Evening Star, Washington, D.C.
John F. Day, managing editor, Dayton Daily News
Frank Dennis, assistant managing editor, Washington Post
Carl W. Erickson, news editor, Worcester (Mass.) Telegram
Fred Gaertner Jr., managing editor, Detroit News
J. Frank Gordy, assistant managing editor, Mobile (Ala.) Press Register
Harold F. Johnson, assistant managing editor, Daily Oklahoman, Oklahoma
    City
M. M. Kesterson, managing editor, Grand Rapids (Mich.) Press
Earl E. Keyser, managing editor, Intelligencer Journal, Lancaster, Pa.
Claude P. Kimball, managing editor, San Diego Daily Journal
William S. Kirkpatrick, managing editor, Atlanta Journal
Thomas S. Logan, assistant managing editor, San Francisco Chronicle
Theodore W. Long, news editor, Salt Lake Telegram
Neil MacNeil, assistant night managing editor, New York Times
Felix R. McKnight, assistant managing editor, Dallas Morning News
Hugh McMillen, news editor, Evening Bulletin, Philadelphia
Frederick H. Moore, managing editor, Sacramento Bee
Eugene J. Moriarty, city editor and assistant news editor, Boston Traveler
Newton A. Noyes, assistant managing editor, Buffalo Evening News
Michael J. Ogden, news editor, Providence Evening Bulletin
Russell H. Reeves, news editor, Cleveland Plain Dealer
Norman Shaw, managing editor, Cleveland Press
Howard Swain, managing editor, Brooklyn Eagle
Ernest Von Hartz, night managing editor, Chicago Sun
Nick B. Williams, news editor, Los Angeles Times

Appendix B

This Appendix lists, with their years of service, all members of the API Advisory Board, Board of Directors, chairmen of the Advisory Board and Board of Directors, Staff Directors or Executive Directors, and Associate Directors from the founding in 1946 through mid-1991:

ADVISORY BOARD CHAIRMEN

Grove Patterson, editor-in-chief, Toledo Blade, 1946-48
Sevellon Brown, editor and publisher, Providence Journal and Evening Bulletin, 1948-1956
Ben M. McKelway, editor, Evening Star and Sunday Star, Washington, D.C., 1956-58
Paul Miller, president, Gannett Newspapers, Rochester, N.Y., 1959-1963
Barry Bingham, editor and publisher, Courier-Journal and Louisville Times, 1963-68
James H. Ottaway Sr., chairman of the board, Ottaway Newspapers, Campbell Hall, N.Y., 1968-1974

ADVISORY BOARD MEMBERS

(Early Bulletins of the American Press Institute did not designate the job title of Advisory Board members other than the chairman. The Advisory Board was dissolved when API left Columbia University in 1974. Its members at the time became members of the Board of Directors of the American Press Institute, Inc., a non-stock company incorporated in Virginia.)

W. S. Gilmore, Detroit News, 1946-52
Lloyd Gregory, Houston Post, 1946-52
Grove Patterson, Toledo Blade, 1946-53
John Carter, Lancaster Newspapers, Pa., 1946-54
Alexander F. Jones, Washington Post, 1946-54
Sevellon Brown, Providence Journal and Evening Bulletin, 1946-56
A. H. Kirchhofer, Buffalo Evening News, 1946-57
M. H. Williams, Worcester Telegram and Evening Gazette, 1946-61
Turner Catledge, New York Times, 1946-1970
E. Z. Dimitman, Chicago Sun, 1947-48
Ben M. McKelway, Evening Star and Sunday Star, Washington, D.C., 1947-61
Louis B. Seltzer, Cleveland Press, 1947-66
Paul Smith, San Francisco Chronicle, 1948-54
Ben Reese, formerly St. Louis Post-Dispatch, 1951-71
Loyal D. Hotchkiss, Los Angeles Times, 1953-59
Felix McKnight, Dallas Morning News, 1953-59
Carl K. Stuart, Daily Oklahoman and Oklahoma City Times, 1953-59
Paul Miller, Gannett Newspapers, 1954-63
Barry Bingham, Courier-Journal and Louisville Times, 1954-72
Edward Lindsay, Lindsay-Schaub Newspapers, Decatur, Ill., 1954-1974

Joseph Pulitzer Jr., St. Louis Post-Dispatch, 1956-74
Sevellon Brown III, Providence Journal and Evening Bulletin, 1957-66
Russell McGrath, Seattle Times, 1959-60
John E. Motz, Kitchener-Waterloo Record, Ontario, 1959-74
James H. Ottaway, Ottaway Newspapers, Campbell Hall, N.Y., 1959-74
Nick B. Williams, Los Angeles Times, 1961-65
John P. Harris, John P. Harris Newspapers, Hutchinson, Kan., 1961-69
Jack B. Krueger, Dallas Morning News, 1961-74
Newbold Noyes, Evening and Sunday Star, Washington, D.C., 1961-74
Fred W. Stein, Binghamton (N.Y.) Press, 1963-70
Otis Chandler, Los Angeles Times, 1965-72
Frank R. Ahlgren, Memphis Commercial Appeal, 1966-69
Eugene S. Pulliam, Indianapolis Star and Indianapolis News, 1966-74
J. Montgomery Curtis, Knight-Ridder Newspapers, 1967-74
James E. Sauter, Booth Newspapers, Ann Arbor, Mich., 1967-74
John Troan, Pittsburgh Press, 1969-74
James Reston, New York Times, 1970-74
Allen H. Neuharth, Gannett Company, Rochester, N.Y., 1970-74
Frank Batten, Landmark Communications, Norfolk, Va., 1972-74
Howard H (Tim) Hays, Press and Enterprise, Riverside, Cal., 1972-74
William O. Taylor, Boston Globe, 1972-74

CHAIRMEN, BOARD OF DIRECTORS

James H. Ottaway, chairman, Ottaway Newspapers, Campbell Hall, N.Y., 1974-78
Howard H (Tim) Hays, editor and co-publisher, Press and Enterprise, Riverside, Cal., 1978-83
William O. Taylor, publisher, Boston Globe, 1983-89
Burl Osborne, editor and president, Dallas Morning News, 1989-

MEMBERS, BOARD OF DIRECTORS

Members of the Board of Directors sometimes held more than one newspaper position during their service on the API board. In most instances, only one of those positions is listed here. If a board member also served as chairman, the years as chairman are listed separately above.

Board members, with the exception of chairmen or past chairmen, were usually limited to three terms of three years each. However, to effect a staggering of terms not provided for in the original by-laws, the board, after a drawing of straws, authorized at one point an additional term of one or two years for several members.

John E. Motz, Michael Metcalf and C. K. McClatchy died during their terms of office.

Edward Lindsay, vice president of planning, Lindsay-Schaub Newspapers, Decatur, Ill., 1974-79
Joseph Pulitzer Jr., editor and publisher, St. Louis Post-Dispatch, 1974-84

John E. Motz, president and publisher, Kitchener-Waterloo Record, Ont., 1974-75
James H. Ottaway, chairman, Ottaway Newspapers, Campbell Hall, N.Y., 1974-84
Newbold Noyes, editor, Evening Star and News, Washington, D.C., 1974-75
Eugene S. Pulliam, publisher, Indianapolis Star and Indianapolis News, 1974-85
J. Montgomery Curtis, vice president/development, Knight Newspapers, Miami, 1974-80
James E. Sauter, executive vice president, Booth Newspapers, Ann Arbor, Mich. 1974-78
John Troan, editor, Pittsburgh Press, 1974-83
Allen H. Neuharth, president, Gannett Company, Rochester, N.Y., 1974-76
Frank Batten, chairman, Landmark Communications, Norfolk, Va., 1974-85
Howard H (Tim) Hays, editor and co-publisher, Press and Enterprise, Riverside, Cal., 1974-90
William O. Taylor, publisher, Boston Globe, 1974-89
Robert W. Chandler, editor and chairman, Bulletin, Bend, Ore., 1974-85
Katharine Graham, publisher, Washington Post, 1974-76
Rollan D. Melton, president, Speidel Newspapers, Reno, Nev., 1974-84
Walter Everett, executive director, American Press Institute, 1974
Malcolm F. Mallette, director, American Press Institute, 1975-79
Arthur O. Sulzberger, publisher, New York Times, 1975-86
J. Patrick O'Callaghan, publisher, Edmonton Journal and Calgary Herald, 1976-88
John A. Scott, president, Frank E. Gannett Newspaper Foundation, Rochester, N.Y., 1976-77
Donald E. Graham, publisher, Washington Post, 1976-87
Peter M. Macdonald, Harris Enterprises, Hutchinson, Kan., 1977-84
Charles E. Glover, president, Cox Enterprises, Atlanta, 1978-89
Michael G. Gartner, editor and president, Des Moines Register and Tribune, 1979-85
Clayton Kirkpatrick, president and chief executive officer, Chicago Tribune, 1980-81
Don E. Carter, vice president/news, Knight-Ridder Newspapers, Miami, 1980-84
Eugene C. Patterson, chairman, Times Publishing Company, St. Petersburg, Fla., 1983-88
Byron C. Campbell, publisher, Record, Hackensack, N.J., 1984, and 1986-
Larry D. Franklin, executive vice president, Harte-Hanks Communications, San Antonio, 1984-90
Madelyn P. Jennings, senior vice president/personnel, Gannett Company, Arlington, Va., 1984-
Larry Jinks, vice president/news, Knight-Ridder, Miami, 1984-
Wayne T. Patrick, president and publisher, Evening Herald, Rock Hill, S.C., 1981-
A. L. Alford Jr., president, editor and publisher, Lewiston (Idaho) Morning Tribune, 1986-
John S. Goodreds, president, Ottaway Newspapers, Campbell Hall, N.Y., 1986-
Robert G. McGruder, managing editor/news, Detroit Free Press, 1986-
Michael P. Metcalf, chairman, publisher and chief executive officer, Providence Journal Company, 1986-87
Burl Osborne, president and editor, Dallas Morning News, 1986-
Franklin D. Schurz Jr., president, Schurz Communications, South Bend, Ind., 1986-
C. K. McClatchy, chairman, McClatchy Newspapers, Sacramento, 1987-89
Henry H. Bradley, publisher, News-Press and Gazette, St. Joseph, Mo., 1988-

William R. Burleigh Sr., senior vice president, Scripps Howard, Cincinnati, 1989-
Joseph Cantrell, president and publisher, Daily Press/Times Herald, Newport News, Va., 1989-
Milton Coleman, assistant managing editor/metropolitan news, Washington Post, 1988-
Clark W. Davey, publisher, Ottawa (Ont.) Citizen, 1988-
David E. Easterly, president, Cox Newspapers, Atlanta, 1990-
Ruth S. Holmberg, publisher, Chattanooga (Tenn.) Times, 1990-
David Laventhol, president, Times Mirror Company; publisher, Los Angeles Times, 1988-
Benjamin B. Taylor, executive editor, Boston Globe, 1990-
Gary L. Watson, president, Gannett Community Newspaper Division, Arlington, Va., 1990-
Arthur O. Sulzberger Jr., deputy publisher, New York Times, 1990-

EXECUTIVE STAFF DIRECTORS

Floyd Taylor, 1946-51
J. Montgomery Curtis, 1951-67
  Associate Director, 1947-51
Walter Everett, 1967-75
  Associate Director, 1949-58
  Managing Director, 1958-67
Malcolm F. Mallette, 1975-79
  Associate Director, 1966-69
  Managing Director, 1969-75
  Director of Development, 1979-87
Frank Quine, 1979-87
  Associate Director, 1969-78
  Managing Director, 1978-79
William L. Winter, 1987-1990
  President/Executive Director, 1990-

ASSOCIATE DIRECTORS

Claude A. Jagger, 1946-47
William M. Stucky, 1955-60
Russell W. Schoch, 1961-76
William C. Sexton, 1963-66
Clarence Dean, 1965-68
Paul Swensson, 1971-75
Allen H. Swartzell, 1975-76
Arthur E. Mayhew, 1975-78
David A. Roe, 1977-79
  Managing Director, 1979-80
Laurence S. Hale, 1977-90
Janet C. Sanford, 1979-82
John G. Finneman, 1979-1985
  Senior Associate Director, 1985-
Elwood M. Wardlow, 1980-89
Donald E. Lippincott, 1980-91
Becky B. Smith, 1984-86
Carol Ann Riordan, 1986-
Jeffrey A. Cowart, 1987-88
Malcolm K. Hughes, 1988-
Robert L. Secundy, 1988-
Sherry Brown, 1989-
Terri Dickerson-Jones, 1989-

Index

Several persons are mentioned so frequently in this book that to list here each mention of them would greatly clutter the index. Instead, each of these persons is noted here together with the chapter (or chapters) devoted principally to him.

Douglas Southall Freeman, Chapter 2
Sevellon Brown, Chapter 3
Carl W. Ackerman, Chapter 5
Floyd Taylor, Chapter 6
Alfred H. Kirchhofer, Chapter 9
J. Montgomery Curtis, Chapters 10, ll
Walter Everett, Chapter 12
Ben Reese, Chapter 17
James H. Ottaway, Chapter 23

A

Aaron, Lawrence 316
Abel, Elie 42, 255, 296
Acheson, Dean 135
Achorn, Robert C. 126
Advertising Research Foundation 117
Advisory Board
    159, 217, 230, 231, 233, 243
Advisory Committee 32
Afro-American Newspapers 55
Ahlgren, Frank 128
Akron Beacon Journal 101, 126
Al Hayat 137
Albany Times-Union 87
Alexandria Daily Town Talk 265
Allentown Morning Call and Evening
    Chronicle 126
American Association of Schools and
    Departments of 65
American Association of Sunday and Feature
    Editors 123, 124
American Federation of Labor 19
American Newspaper Publishers Association
    8, 242, 258
American Society of Newspaper Editors
    8, 84, 125, 169, 257

Amos Press 257
Andersen, Harold W. 265
Anderson, Marie 186
Anderson, Ronald C. 184
ANPA Foundation 264
Ansonia Evening Sentinel 181
API Round Table 270
Arizona Highways 124
Arizona Republic 186
Arizona Star 272
Arkansas State University 308
Arnold, Edmund C. 189, 193
Asheville Citizen-Times 216
Associated Builders 279
Associated Press 12, 18, 139
Associated Press Managing Editors 125,
    257
Associated Publishers 133
Atlanta Journal 10, 34, 61

B

Bagdikian, Ben 113
Baker, Frank S. 34
Baker, Lisle 126
Baker, Richard T. 17, 46
Baldwin, Donald K. 207

Balfour, Sir John 70
Ballew, Maston (Matt) 255
Baltimore Sun 261
Barber, Edith 13
Barber, Red 188
Barnard College 52
Barrett, Edward W. 41, 42, 156, 157, 158
Barrett, Edward Ware 156
Barry, David S. 21
Barry, Elizabeth Bonney 21
Barry, Mike 286
Barzun, Jacques 183
Batten, Frank 262
Beauge, Quinton E. 120
Beaver County Times 275
Beck, William O. 89
Beebe, George 90, 126, 280, 281
Bellamy, Paul 34
Bennett, Charles L. 207, 242
Bennett, Edward L. 194
Bentel, Dwight 76
Bentley, Richard T. 302
Berger, Meyer 123, 215
Berkshire Eagle 249
Bermingham, Don 101
Bernstein, Ted 189, 286
Berra, Yogi 188
Bertelson, Arthur R. 163
Bethlehem Globe-Times 113
Biggers, George C. 34
Biggs, Gloria 183, 186, 202
Bingham, Barry 118, 177, 212, 231, 241, 262
Bingham Jr., Barry 246
Binghamton Press 242
Birmingham News 88
Birmingham News and Age-Herald 173
Black, Brady 207
Black, Creed 99, 207, 208
Blackman, Sam 214, 215, 218
Blagg, Timothy A. 225
Blanchard, Felix (Doc) 105
Blanton, Mary Jane 40
Block Jr., Paul 35
Bloomington Pantagraph 61, 203
Boardman, Thomas L. 126, 207
Boone, Buford 126
Booth, George F. 35, 123
Borg, Malcolm (Mac) 188
Boston Globe 205
Boston Herald 32, 35
Bovard, O.K. 79, 165

Boyd, Hugh N. 126
Brennan, Edna 201, 228
Breuer, Marcel 256
Bristol Herald Courier and Virginia-Tennessean 126
Brito, Manoel Francisco do Nascimento 139
Britzke, Ronald A. 225
Broeg, Bob 87, 163
Brooklyn Eagle and Citizen 11, 32, 35, 55
Brown, Barry 26, 113
Brown III, Sevellon (Jeff) 15, 26
Brown, James Wright 35
Brown, Judith W. 198
Brown, Robert N. 175, 194, 256, 265, 269
Brown, Robert U. 30, 63, 142
Brown, Sevellon Alden 21
Brown, Sherry 312, 313
Brown University 22
Browne, Millard C. 78
Brucker, Herbert 29
Brzezinski, Zbigniew 183
Bucheit, Phil A. 126
Buchwach, Bucky 140
Buckwalter, I. Z. 126
Buffalo Commercial 83
Buffalo Courier 83
Buffalo Demokrat 83
Buffalo Evening News 5, 32, 35, 77, 78, 83
Buffalo Times 83
Bulletin, Bend, Oregon 174
Burgess, James E. 272
Burgher, Fred W. 30
Burnham Jr., Harry G. 197
Butler, Edward H. 35
Butler, J. Oliver (Ollie) 96
Butler, Nicholas Murray 27, 43, 129
Buttons, Red 188
Buxton, Charles R. 126
Byrnes, Garrett D. 18, 121, 124

C

Cain, Steve 101
Cameron, Barney G. 120
Campanella, Roy 216
Caniff, Milton 124
Cannon, Ted 110
Cano, Luis Gabriel 137
Capp, Al 124
Carey, James B. 13

Carlson, Raymond 124
Carradine, William J. 273
Carter, Don E. 174, 176, 193, 211,
    217, 234, 272, 274, 277, 281
Carter, John H. 30
Castillo, Enrique Santos 137
Cathedral Church of St. John the Divine 52
Catledge, Turner 2, 8, 9, 30,
    116, 131, 146, 154, 178, 218,
    246, 286
Center for Foreign Journalists 299
Chandler, Norman 35, 146
Chandler, Otis 247
Chandler, R. B. 35
Chandler, Robert W.
    174, 233, 262, 272
Chapman Jr., Alvah H.
    120, 126, 176, 192, 281
Charleston Evening Post 272
Charlotte News 89
Charlotte Observer 86
Chester Times 64, 72
Chicago Sun 32, 35
Chicago Tribune 170, 192
Choate, Robert 35
Christian Science Monitor 12, 122
Clark, Robert P. 234
Cleveland Plain Dealer 34
Cleveland Press 10, 64, 118, 126
Columbia Journalism Review 152
Columbia Spectator 56
Columbia University 2, 7, 52, 143, 251
Columbus Ledger and Enquirer 120, 126
Colver, Bob 284
Commager, Henry Steele 183
Concord Monitor and New Hampshire
    Patriot 272
Congress of Industrial Organizations 13
Contra Costa Times 296
Cook, Stanton R. 192
Cordier, Andrew W. 238
Corning Leader 170
Council Bluffs Nonpareil 170
Council on Foreign Relations 133
Couey Jr., James H. 88, 189
Cowart, Jeffrey A. 305
Cowles Jr., W. H. 35
Cox Commission 223, 226
Cox, James M. 35
Cheek Jr., Mrs. Leslie 16
Crespo, Tony 202
"Crisis at Columbia" 223
Cunningham, Elmer 86

Curtis, Allan Walker 94
Curtis, Alma 171, 283
Curtis, Zelda Epstein 95

D

Daily News-Sun 35
Daily Oklahoman 32
Daily Oklahoman and Oklahoma City Times
    35, 64
Dalgin, Ben 121
Dallas Morning News 32, 35, 64, 245
Dallas Times Herald 302
Daniels, Derick 234
Danzig, Robert 87
Davis, Glenn 105
Dayton Daily News and Dayton Journal-
    Herald 35, 64, 182, 186
De Piante, Robert D. 190, 193
Dealey, Edward M. 35
Dean, Clarence
    130, 194, 199, 215, 218, 228, 286
Deck, Arthur C. 126
Delaware County Times 275
Delaware State News 225
Deming, Clarissa 55
Denver Post 64, 126, 174
Der Tagesspiegel 134
Deringer, H. Hurtt 303
Des Moines Register and Tribune 213
Deseret News 126
Detroit Free Press 106
Detroit News 10, 32, 35, 62, 126
Dickerson-Jones, Terri 312
Dickey, Fred 90
Dickinson Jr., William B. 225
Dilliard, Irving 166
Dimitman, E. Z. 30
Dominion-News 100
Dougherty, John L. 180, 194
Dow Jones & Company 35
Doyle, James J. 194, 195, 226
Drew, Edward 113
Drukker Jr., Dow H. 35
DuBois, Earle 203
Duluth Herald and News-Tribune 190
Dunning, John R. 183
Durein, Ted 207, 212
Dwight Jr., William 302

E

Editor & Publisher
    9, 32, 35, 70, 142, 165, 167
Edmonton Journal 65

"Effective Writing and Editing" 302
Eisenhower, Dwight D.   128, 150, 173
El Espectador 137
El Tiempo 137
Elm Grove, West Virginia 86, 94
Endicott Bulletin 232
Endowment for International Peace 51
Endowment Fund Committee 305
Epstein, George 96
Ethridge, Mark F.   208
Etzioni, Amitai 183
Everett, Beth 115
Everett, Laura Bentley 108
Everett, Russell M.   108
Everett, William G.   112
Ewing, James E.   299
Executive Committee 237, 239
Executive Development Program 301

F

Facilities and Finance Committee 233
Facilities and Finance Subcommittee 236
Fackenthal, Frank D.   27
Fairchild, E. W.   35
Fairchild Publications 35
Fanning, Larry 207
Farley, James A.   110
"Fashion in Newspapers." 121
Fassio, Virgil 192, 194
Fell, Charles A.   173
Fichter, Thomas C.   243
Field Jr., Marshall 35, 126
Finneman, John G.   300, 303, 314
Flesch, Rudolf 189, 271
Fogarty, Hugh A.   61
"Food in Newspapers" 121
Foote, William J.   207
Ford Foundation 51, 129, 130, 135, 146
Fort Smith Times 126
Frankenmuth, Michigan 190
Franklin, Larry D.   308
Fredericksburg Free Lance-Star 261
Freedom Forum Media Studies Center 239
Friedmann, Werner 135
Fuller, Frank 68
Furnald's Exchange 90

G

Gaertner Jr., Fred 62, 67
Gallagher, Wes 68, 81
Gallup, George 13
Gannett Center for Media Studies 239
Gannett Company 85, 113

Gannett, Guy P.   35
Gannett Publishing Company 32, 35
Gaylord, E. K.   35
Gaylord, Edward L.   126
Gentzler, W. Emerson 158
Georgia Press Institute 66
Getlein, Frank 246
Gibson, Dorothy C.   55
Gilmore, W. S.   30, 317
Gilstrap, Max K.   12
Globe and Mail 65
Goheen, Robert F.   241
Gold Rail 59
Goldblatt, Leonard 203
Graduate School of Journalism
    13, 76, 150
Graham, Donald E.   272, 277
Graham, Katharine 3, 262
Grand Forks Herald 282
Grand Junction Sentinel 212
Greenwich Time 112
Gregory, Lloyd 30
Grier, Roger 191
Grimes, W. H.   30
Gross, Rebecca 56
Gunning, Robert 13, 189, 271

H

Hale, Betty Louise 55
Hale, Laurence S.   275, 276, 300, 314
Halliday, Duncan McNab 65
Hamilton, Alexander 54
Hamilton, Charles H.   68, 92, 123
Hamilton, Douglas E.   193, 209
Hanrahan, Margaret 40
Harding, Warren G.   98
Harrison, Luther 184
Harron, Robert 92, 155, 171, 173
Harte-Hanks Communications 308
Hartford Courant 20
Hartford Times 80
Hauser, Charles McC.   303
Hawaiian Economic Foundation 38, 71
Hayden, Martin S.   126
Hays, Howard H (Tim) 47, 126, 164,
    193, 249, 262, 272, 279, 306,
Heathcote, Earl 112
Heidee, Alma 95
Henninger, Edward 182
Heyduck, Marj 186, 194
Hill, I. William (Bill) 75, 88, 194, 196,
    206
Hilleboe, Herman 183

Hills, Lee 89, 104, 171, 281
Hobart Chief 165
Hobby, W. P. 35
Hodges, Gil 216
Hoffman, Paul G. 13
Hogate, K. C. 35
Hohenberg, John
  87, 89, 92, 173, 185, 204, 211
Holt, Robert L. 198
Holyoke Transcript-Telegram 302
Home News Enterprises 175
Honolulu Advertiser 140
Hornaday, Hilton 100
Hornby, William H. 207
Houston Chronicle 198
Houston Post 32, 35, 87
Howard, Roy 50
Hoyt, Palmer (Ep) 174
Hughes, Malcolm K. (Mike) 312
Humphrey, Hubert H. 137
Hunter, Edwin D. 87
Hurley, Frances 78
Hurley III, James F. 196

I

Indianapolis Star 64
Inland Daily Press Association 191, 265,
  273
Inter American Press Association 131
Inter-State Circulation Managers Association
  257
Interchurch Center 52
Internal Revenue Service 247
International Circulation Managers
  Association 257
International News Service 18
International Newspaper Advertising
  Executives 257
International Press Institute 146
Investigative Reporters Association 125
Irish Press 138
Isaacs, Norman E. 88, 119,
  194, 207, 215, 253
Issues Forum 315

J

J. Montgomery Curtis Memorial Can 178
J. Montgomery Curtis Memorial Seminar
  294
Jackson, P. L. 35
Jacobs, Albert C. 153
Jagger, Claude A. 12, 37
James, Edwin L. 9, 30

James, Harry 165
Jardine, William T. 185
Jay, John 54
Jennings, Madelyn P. 308
Jewish Theological Seminary of America 52
John Ben Snow Memorial Trust 298
John Jay Hall 10, 55
Johnson, Charles R. (Chuck) 202
Johnson City Press-Chronicle 126
Johnson, Earl J. 92, 173, 207
Johnson Hall 55
Johnson, Kenneth E. 212, 302
Johnson, Lyndon B. 138
Jones, Alexander F. 30
Jones, Carl A. 126
Jones, Vincent S. 48, 117, 120,
  138, 194, 200
Joplin Globe 165
Jornal do Brasil 139
Journal-American 11
Journalism Quarterly 61, 65
Juilliard School of Music 52
Jurney, Dorothy 186

K

Kane, Joseph F. 225
Kayhan 176
Keene Sentinel 299
Kellogg West 297
Kelly, Kathryn E. 55
Kent County News 303
Kentucky Irish American 286
Kerby, William F. 233
Kerney, James E. 35, 119, 217
Kilgore, Bernard 123, 176
King, Charles A. 233
King's Crown Hotel 55, 56, 57,
  207, 229, 239
Kirchhofer, Mrs. A.H. 282
Kirk, Grayson
  115, 131, 143, 150, 154, 155, 157,
  173, 204, 238
Kirkpatrick, Clayton 273
Kirkpatrick, William S. 61
Kitchener-Waterloo Record 65
Klein, Herbert G. 207, 208
Knight Foundation 294
Knight, James L. 171, 242
Knight, John S. 91, 281
Knight Newspapers 132
Knight-Ridder Newspapers 91
Koon, Warren H. 302
Kreuger, Jack 245

Krimsky, George A. 299
Krushchev, Nikita 137

L

LaCour, Joseph 133
LaFollette, Amy Lee 99
Lagens, Annemarie 129
Lake, John B. 92
Lambert, Eugene 280
Lancaster Newspapers 32, 35, 126
Law, Dolly 100, 101, 103, 171, 176
Law, Louis 171
Law, Rosemarie 100, 101
Law Sr., Mr. and Mrs. Harry C. 100
Leard, John 17
Lebherz, Ed 101
Lee Enterprises 272
Lesher, Dean 296
Lever Brothers Company 113
Lewis, Wilmott (Bin) 186
Lindsay, Edward 146, 247, 262, 277
Lindsay-Schaub Newspapers 146, 172
Lindstrom, Carl E. 80
Lippincott, Donald E. 182, 217, 300, 304
Lister, Agnes 227, 252
Livingston, Robert R. 54
Lock Haven Express 56
Longmont Daily Times-Call 137
Longview Daily News 296
Los Angeles Times 10, 32, 35, 64, 170
Louisville Courier-Journal 60, 64, 178
Low, G. Prescott 126, 171, 206
Low Library 54
Lubell, Samuel 109, 112
Lundquest, William C. 252
Lundy, Walker 181
Lux, John 282
Lyons, Louis 212

M

MacArthur, Douglas 135
MacDonald, Stewart 265
MacNeil, Neil 67
Macon Telegraph and News 126
Mahoney, D. H. 35
Mallette, Bruce 255
Mallette, Eleanor 140
Mallette, Malcolm F. 118, 130,
    140, 154, 167, 178, 181,
    191, 193, 210, 214, 215, 219,
    220, 224, 252, 255, 265, 267, 271,
    272, 274, 276, 277, 279, 303, 307
Mannes, Marya 183

Mansfield, Jayne 140
Marcel Breuer and Associates 246
Maria Moors Cabot Award 108, 158
Markel, Lester 124
Masthead 71
Mayes, Herbert 183
Mayhew, Arthur E. 275
McCartin, Thomas R. 303
McCormack, Buren H. 266
McCrohon, Maxwell 303
McEvoy, Eileen 255
McGeehan, W. O. 49
McGill, William J. 238, 254
McGruder, Robert G. 308
McGuckin Jr., Eugene C. 190, 194
McKelway, Ben M. 231
McKim, Mead & White 54
McKnight, C. A. (Pete) 86, 180, 194, 207
McKnight, Felix R. 126
McLean, Robert 35
McMenamin, Edward B. 241
McMillan, John H. 181
McNab, Duncan 65
Meath, J. Allan 116
Meddoff, Jack 101
Medford Mail Tribune 273, 302
Melton, Rollan D. 85, 262, 298, 273
Memphis Commercial Appeal 128
Merced Sun-Star 302
Merritt, Davis (Buzz) 280
Mesbahzadeh, Mostafa 176
Metcalf, Stephen O. 22
Meyer, Eugene 30, 35, 242
Meyer-Dietrich, Helmut 134
Miami Daily News 35
Miami Herald 55, 64, 126
Michie, Charlie 82, 101
Mid-Atlantic Circulation Managers Association 257
Miller, Donald P. 126
Miller, Eugene R. 181
Miller, Paul 91, 164, 213, 231
Millis, Walter 46
Milwaukee Journal 21, 126
Minneapolis Star and Tribune 62, 185
Minot, George E. 30
Mirror 11
Missouri School of Journalism 76
Mobile Register 10, 35
Monroe, Marilyn 24
Monterey Peninsula Herald 207
Montgomery Advertiser 203
Mooney, Jean 186

Moore, Leslie 71, 123
Morgan, Perry 101, 273
Morningside Heights 52
Morningside Park 222
Morris, Edgar 35
Morris, Gouverneur 54
Mott, Frank Luther 76
Motz, John E. 65, 262
Mrowa, Kamel 137
Murmann, Trudi 89
Murphy, Patrick J. 183

N

Natchez Democrat 302
National Conference of Editorial Writers
    71, 123, 124, 257
National Newspaper Association 264
National Press Club 83
Natt, Ted 296
Neely, Paul 124
Neill, Rolfe 86, 175, 176, 218, 282
Neitzel, Hal B. 194
Neto, Julio de Mesquita 139
Neuharth, Allen H. 176, 192, 207, 208,
    233, 242, 262
Nevins, Alan 183
Newburgh Evening News 225
New Britain Herald 198
New Brunswick Daily Home News 126
New England Association of Circulation
    Managers 257
New York Daily News 11
New York Herald 21
New York Herald Tribune 4, 11, 35, 120
New York Journal of Commerce 20
New York Journal-American 69
New York Newspaper Women's Club 13
New York Post 11
New York Sun 11, 13, 21
New York Times 10, 11,
    32, 35, 64, 126
New York World-Telegram 11, 50
New Yorker Hotel 225, 226
Newark News 108
News of the World 140
Newsom, Douglas Ann 198
Newspaper Enterprises Association 186
Nicholas B. Ottaway Foundation 247
Nicholas Murray Butler Hall 57
Nizen, Donald A. 273
Norfolk Virginian-Pilot and Ledger-Star
    178
Noyes, Frank B. 35

Noyes Jr., Newbold 116, 207, 208, 240,
    262
Nye, Joe 239, 254

O

O Estado de Sao Paulo 139
O'Callaghan, J. Patrick 65
O'Dwyer, William 132
O'Farrill Jr., Romulo 141
Ogden, Michael J. 9, 21, 58, 207
O'Keefe, Jimmy 102
Oklahoma City Times 32
Omaha World-Herald 61, 265
Oregon Journal 32, 64
Oregon Statesman and Capital Journal 181
Osborne, Burl 309, 313
Ottaway, Elmer James 232
Ottaway, Ruth 232

P

Pacific Financial Research Company 305
Pacific Northwest International Circulation
    Managers Association 257
Pampa Daily News 275
Pape, William J. 35
Parker, Gordon 229
Pasadena Star-News 310
Passaic Herald-News 32, 35, 64, 177
Patrick, Wayne T. 303
Patterson, Belknap and Webb 240
Patterson, Eugene 3, 307
Patterson, Grove
    12, 30, 121, 142, 169, 230
Paxson, Marjorie B. 272
Pennsylvania Newspaper Publishers
    Association 66
Perrin, Dwight S. 30
Philadelphia Daily News 175
Philadelphia Evening Bulletin 10, 32, 35,
    64
Philadelphia Inquirer 99
Phillips, Warren H. 175
Pittsburg Chronicle Telegraph 99
Pittsburgh Courier 133
Pittsburgh Post-Gazette 64, 99
Pohlman, Helen Curtis 94, 95
Policy and Programs Committee 272
Poorman, Paul A. 284
Pope, James A. 60, 65
Port Huron Times-Herald 232
Potter, George W. 31, 70
Powers, Murray 126, 211
Poynter, Nelson 171, 176

Primm, Alex 163
Princeton University 241
Professional Training Survey Committee 272
Programs and Services Committee 233, 236
Providence Journal and Evening Bulletin 8, 15, 32, 35, 64, 111, 134, 178
Public Opinion 272
Publicacaciones Herrerias 141
Pulitzer, Joseph 7
Pulitzer Jr., Joseph 28, 35, 163, 207, 243, 262
Pulitzer, Michael E. 272
Pulitzer Prizes 15, 53, 152
Pulliam, Eugene S. 126, 207, 243, 249, 262

Q

Quincy Patriot Ledger 126
Quine, Frank 167, 178, 184, 191, 210, 219, 220, 228, 241, 252, 255, 264, 267, 276, 279, 295, 296, 303, 307
Quinn, John C. 113

R

Raglin, James H. (Rags) 197
Rathom, John R. 22
Record of Bergen County 179
Reese, Estelle 161
Reese Jr., Ben 161
Reese, PeeWee 216
Regional Advisory Boards 303
Reid, Ogden 35
Reston, James B. (Scotty) 240, 244, 262
Reston, Virginia 251
Reynolds, Donald M. 126
Rhind, Flora 129
Rhydwen, David A. 65
Richmond News Leader 4
Richmond Times-Dispatch 17
Ridder Publications 192
Righter, Katie 90
Riordan, Carol Ann 304, 313
Riordan, Thomas A. 304
Riverside Church 52
Riverside Daily Press and Daily Enterprise 47
Riverside Park 222
Robinson, Jackie 216
Rock Hill Herald 260
Rockefeller Foundation 72, 129, 130, 135, 136, 146

Rockefeller, Nelson A. 114
Roe, David A. 187, 275, 276
Rogers, Floyd D. 46
Rollow, Cooper 202
Roper, Elmo 13
Ross, Charles G. 166
Ruggles, William B. 30
Rumble, Cleve 229
Ryder, Stephen W. 273, 302, 303, 307

S

Salisbury Post 196
Salt Lake City Tribune 110
San Francisco Chronicle 32, 35, 64, 128
San Jose Mercury News 90
Sanders, William R. 302
Sanford, Janet C. 275, 276, 310
Sargent, Wayne 57
Saturday Evening Post 43
Saturday Review 173
Sauter, James E. 233, 262
Savino, Frank J. 182
Savoy, Maggie 186
Saxe, John Godfrey 153
Schaleben, Arville 126
Schaub, Fred W. 172
Schoch, Mary 229
Schoch, Russell W. 130, 139, 167, 199, 213, 220, 226, 228, 252, 267
Schroth, Frank D. 35
Schugardt, Emma M. 81
Schuyler, George S. 133
Scofield, James 228
Scott, Joyce 255
Scripps, W. E. 35
Scripps-Howard 186
Scripps-Howard Newspapers 32, 35
Search and Screen Committee 308
Seattle Post-Intelligencer 192
Secundy, Robert L. 312
Seltzer, Louis B. 30, 118
Sexton, William C. 130, 214
Seymour, Gideon 285
Shadid, Woodrow (Woody) 203
Sharpe and Hamaker 251
Sheraton Reston Inn 106, 251, 257, 260
Sidney Daily News 257
Simon, Robert E. 243
Smith, Allen W. 30
Smith, Becky B. 304
Smith, Everett M. 122
Smith, Gilbert P. 175

Smith, Hamilton
   246, 250, 256, 257, 277
Smith Jr., Joe D.   265
Smith, Paul C.   35, 128
Smith, Red   188
Snider, Duke   216
Society of Newspaper Design   125
Southam Press   11, 273
Southern Newspaper Publishers Association
   146, 273
Sovde, Roger   260, 302
Spartanburg Herald and Journal   126
Speidel, Merritt C.   35
Speidel Newspapers   35
Spezzano, Vince   307
Spilman, Charles H.   18
Spina, Tony   106
Spokane Spokesman-Review   35
Sproat, Robert A.   302
St. Louis Post-Dispatch   32, 35, 87, 161
St. Petersburg Evening Independent   219
St. Petersburg Times   92, 171
Starzel, Frank   131
State Department   131
Steele, Richard C.   249, 265
Stein, Fred W.   242
Steinman, J. Hale   35
Steven, William P.   62
Stiff, Robert M.   270
Stockton, J. Roy   163
Stoia, Alex   239
Stoneman, Christopher H.   240, 244,
   248
Storey, Karen   302
Strohmeyer, John   113, 194, 234, 260
Struby, Bert   126
Stucky, Bill   122, 137, 139, 141,
   144, 153, 213
Stucky, Robert   213
Stucky, Robyn   213
Stucky, William Jr.   213
Stucky, William M.   130, 136, 212
Students Afro-American Society   223
Students for a Democratic Society
   156, 223
Sulzberger, Arthur Hays
   29, 30, 35, 47, 134
Sulzberger, Arthur Ochs (Punch)   4, 167,
   255
Supreme Court   24
Swanson, Gloria   188
Swartzell, Allen H.   275
Swensson, Paul   219, 220, 252, 267

Syracuse University   182, 189
Szulc, Tad   139

T

Tacoma News Tribune   32, 34
Tallahassee Democrat   181
Tatarian, Roger   87
Tate, H. Clay   61
Taylor, Marion   46, 148
Taylor, William O.
   234, 249, 262, 272, 305, 306, 311
Teachers College   52
Texas Christian University   198
Thompson, Jack B.   11, 72
Tobin, Nancy   182
Toledo Blade   12, 32, 35
Tompkins, E. F.   69
Tong, Hollington K.   44
Trenton Times   32, 35, 119, 177, 217
Tribune-Democrat   302
Troan, John   262
Truman, David B.   224
Truman, Harry S   114, 166
Tuscaloosa News   126

U

U.S. Information Agency   131
U.S. Military Academy   105
Ungaro, Joseph M.   254
Union Theological Seminary   52
United Press   18, 21
University of Miami   242
University of Missouri   109
University of Nevada-Reno   297
University of West Virginia   91
USA Today   113, 261
Utica Observer-Dispatch   48, 175

V

Valley News-Dispatch   192
Van Anda, Carr   43, 79
Virginia Commonwealth University   189
Virginian-Pilot and Ledger-Star, Norfolk   273
Visalia Times-Delta   276
Vosburgh, William W.   30

W

Waddell, Harry Lee   189, 193
Walker, Jerry   120
Wall Street Journal   32
Walla Walla Union-Bulletin   170
Wallin, David R.   162
Walsh, Joseph F.   138

Walters, Basil L. (Stuffy) 132
Wardlow, Elwood M. (Woody) 80, 84, 304
Washington Evening Star 10, 32, 35, 64
Washington Post 3, 32, 35, 64, 261
Wasson, Don 203
Waterbury Republican and American 32, 35, 55, 64
Weber Jr., Hugo 281
West End 59
West Virginia Fourth Estatesman 99
West Virginia University 99
Westchester Rockland Newspapers 254
Wheeler, Warren G. (Spike) 265
Wheeling Daily & Sunday News 85, 97
Wheeler, John N. 79
White, Ronald A. 186, 193
Whited, Charles 87
Whitney, John Hay 104
Wichita Eagle Beacon 280
Wiggins, J. Russell 126
Williams, Barbara S. 272
Williams, M. H. 30
Williams, Nick B. 126, 195
Williams, Talcott 43
Williamsport Sun and Gazette 120
Wilmington News-Journal 192
Wilson, Edwin B. 30
Wilson, George W. 272
Wilson, Ruth A. 224
Winship, Thomas 299
Winston-Salem Journal 215
Winter, William L. 210, 308, 309, 310, 311, 313
Worcester Telegram and Evening Gazette 32, 35, 64, 126
Worcester, Willard C. 194
World Press Freedom Committee 316
Worrell, T. Eugene 126

Y

Ylvisaker, Paul N. 183
Young, Charles E. 81, 103, 182, 194

Z

Zavitz, Lance 101
Zeitung, Suddeutsche 135
Zluticky, Steve 281